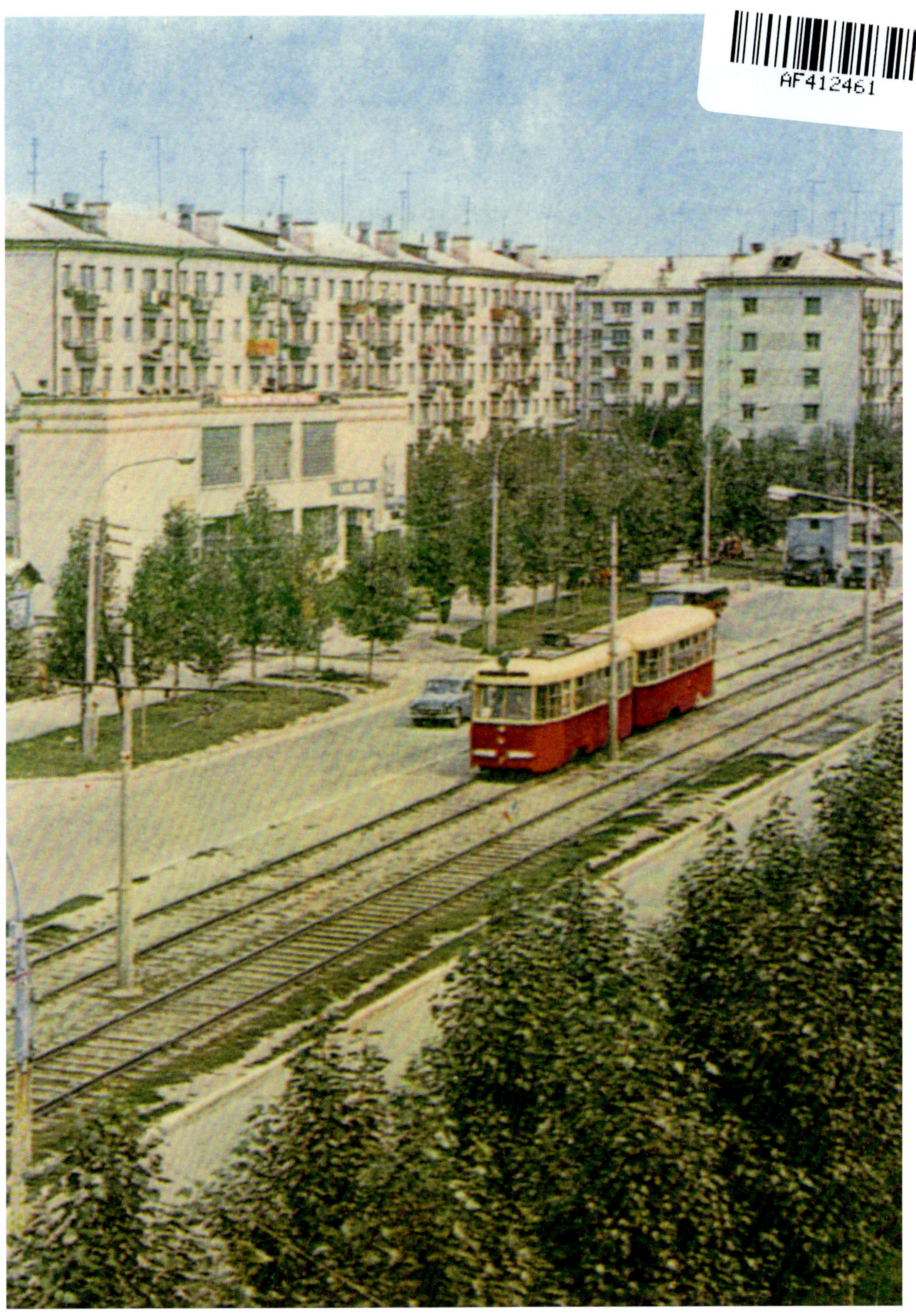

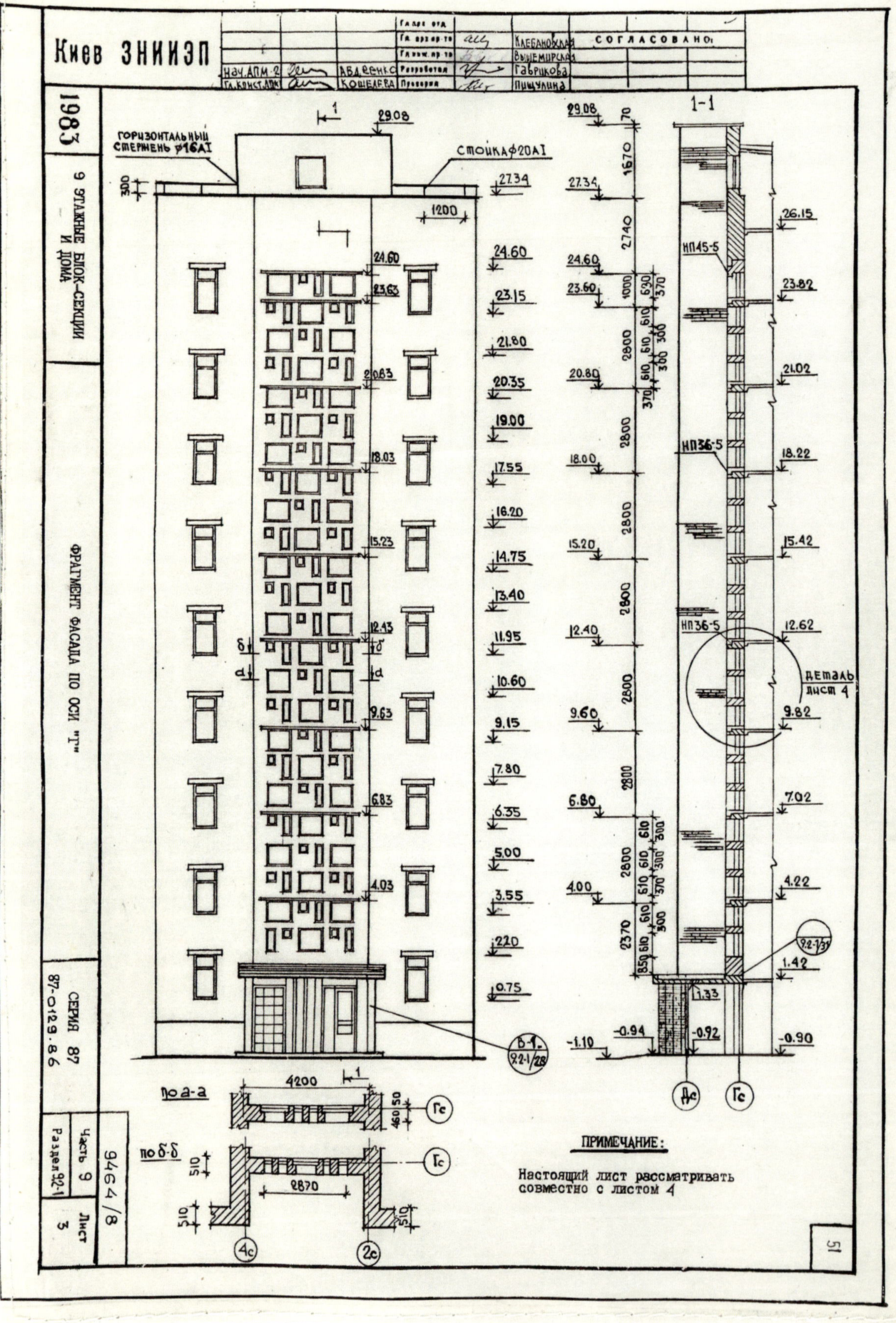

Киев ЗНИИЭП
1983
9 ЭТАЖНЫЕ БЛОК-СЕКЦИИ И ДОМА
ФРАГМЕНТ ФАСАДА ПО ОСИ "Т"
СЕРИЯ 87
87-0129.86
ГОРИЗОНТАЛЬНЫЙ СТЕРЖЕНЬ ⌀16АI
СТОЙКА ⌀20АI
1-1
деталь лист 4
ПРИМЕЧАНИЕ:
Настоящий лист рассматривать совместно с листом 4
по а-а
4200
по б-б
2870
НП45-5
НП36-5
НП36-5
Часть 9
Раздел 32-1
Лист 3
9464/8
51

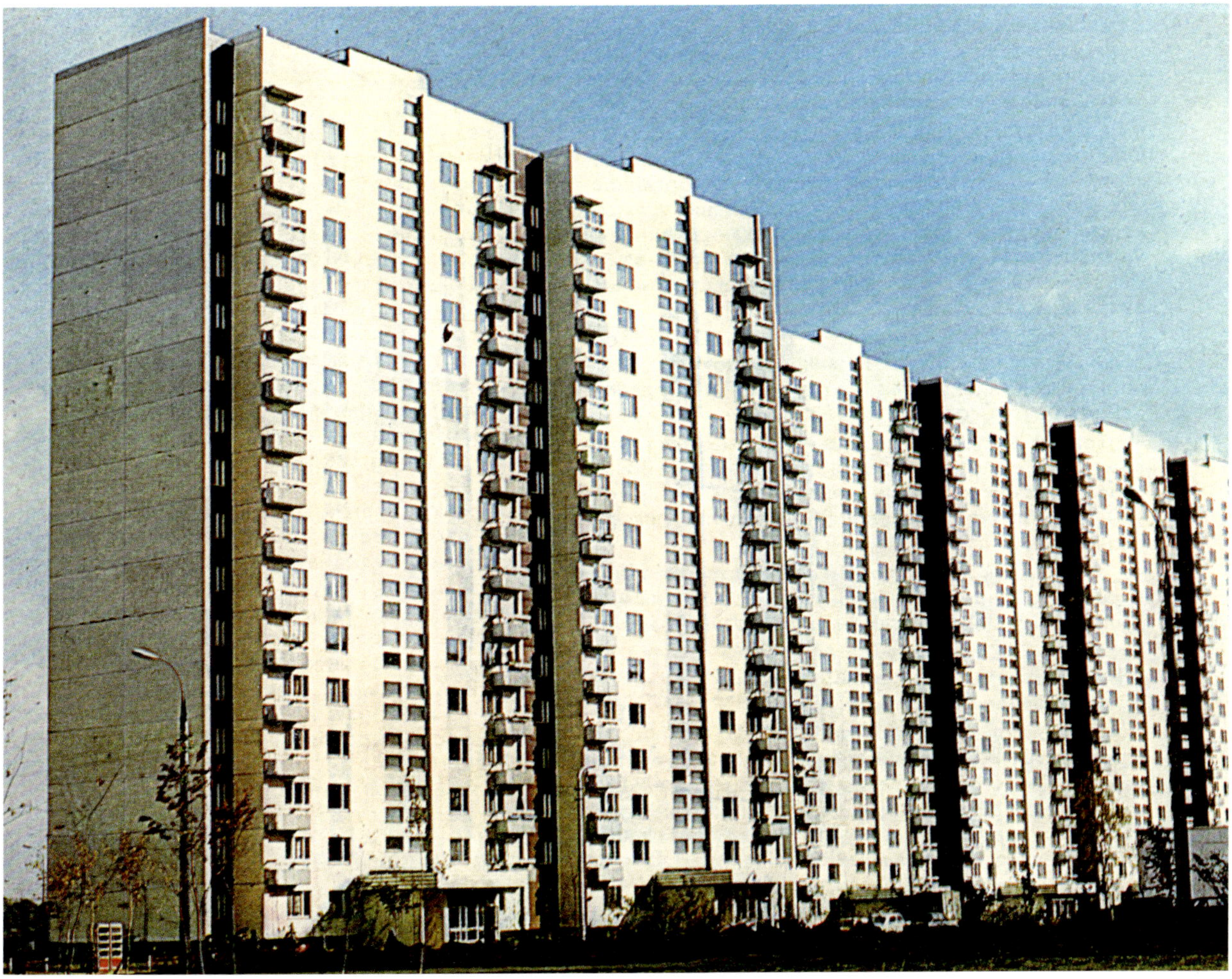

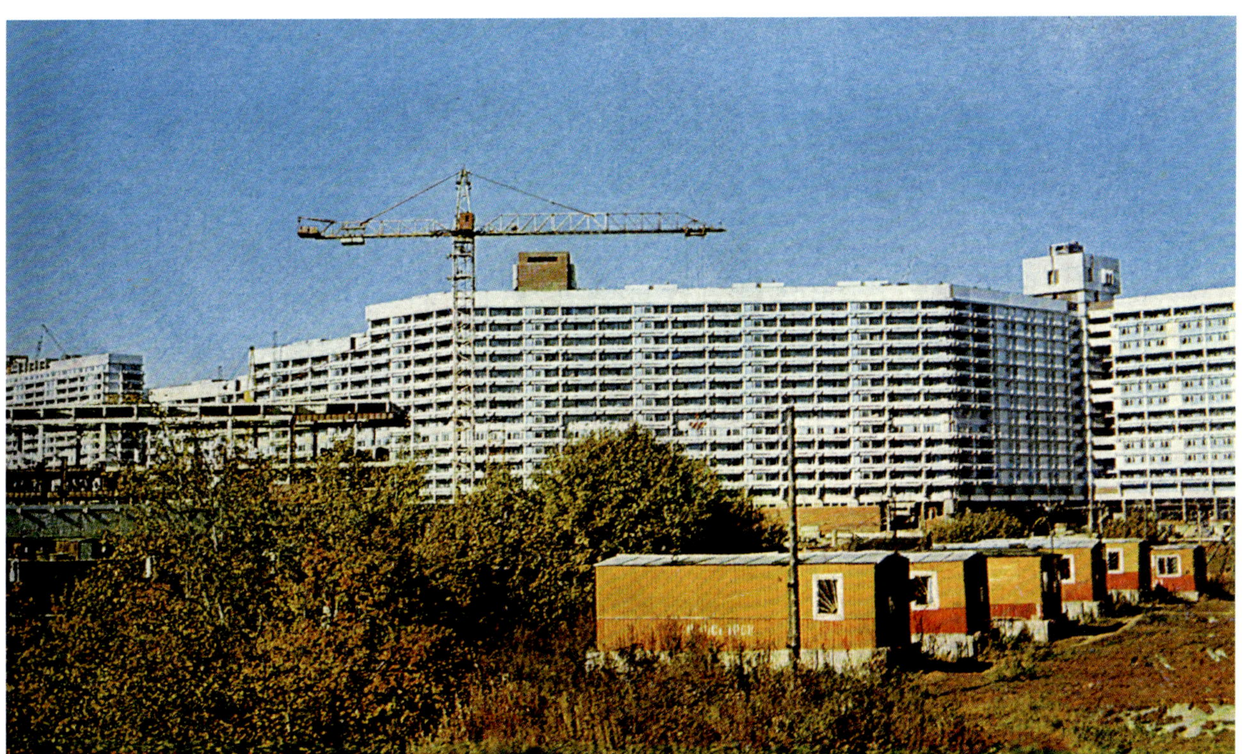

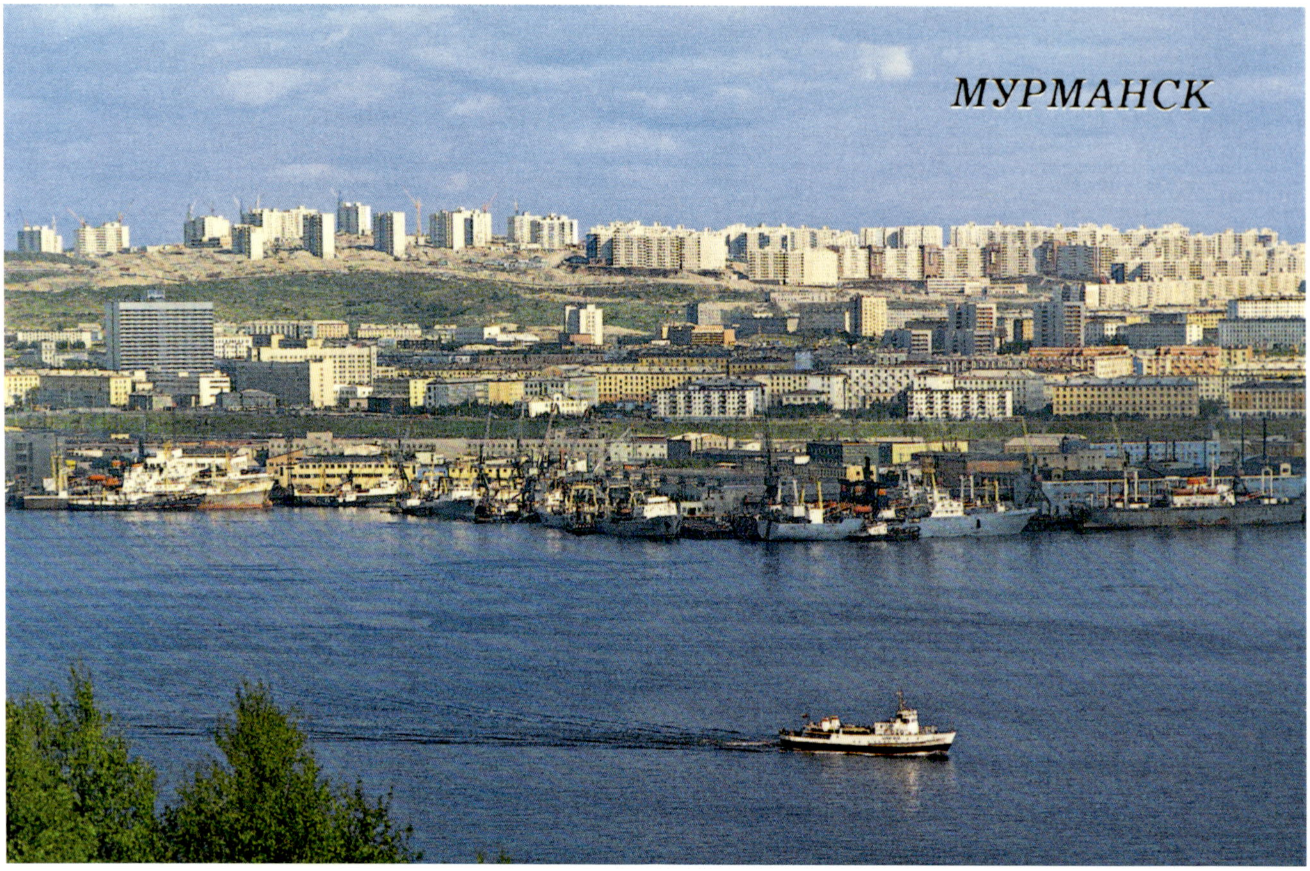

МУРМАНСК

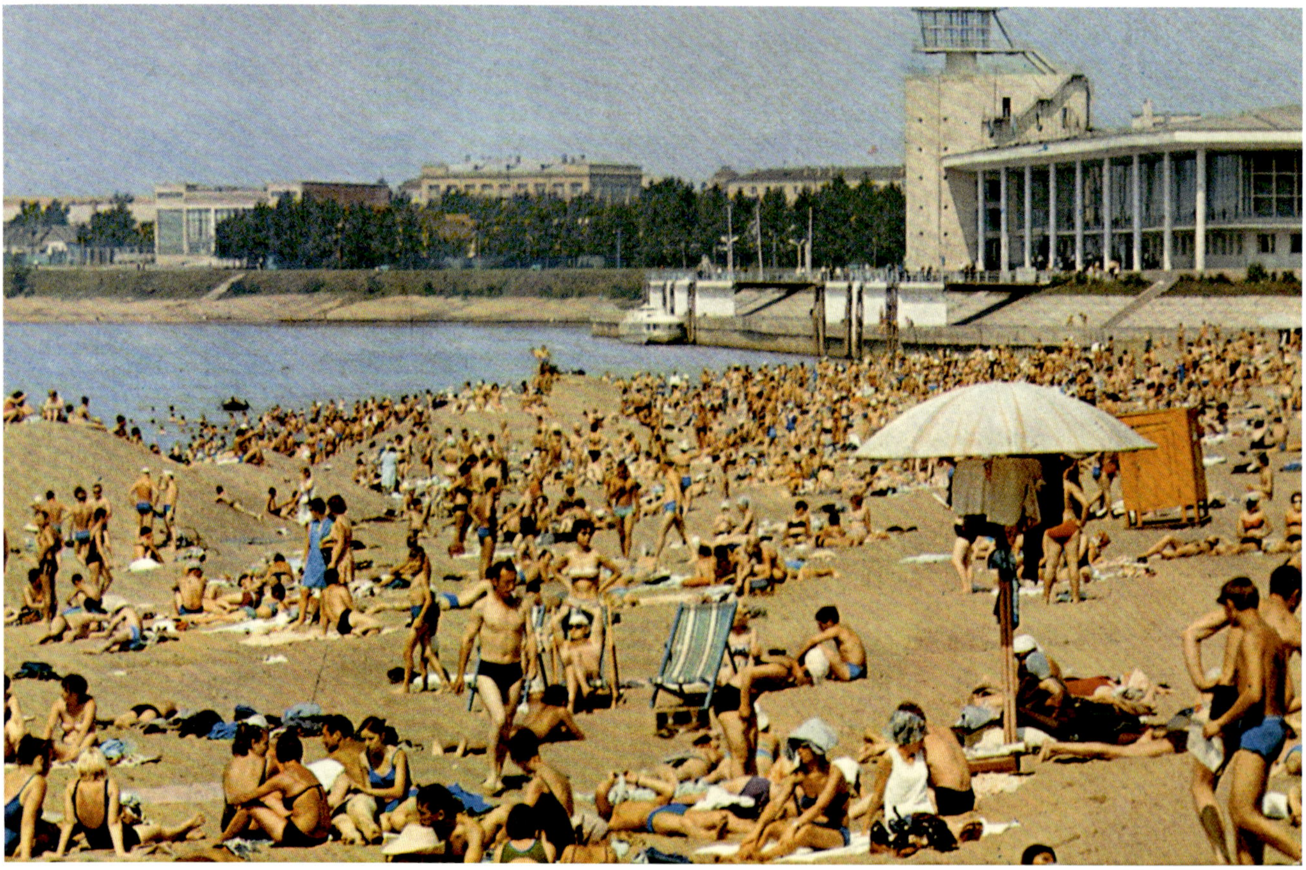

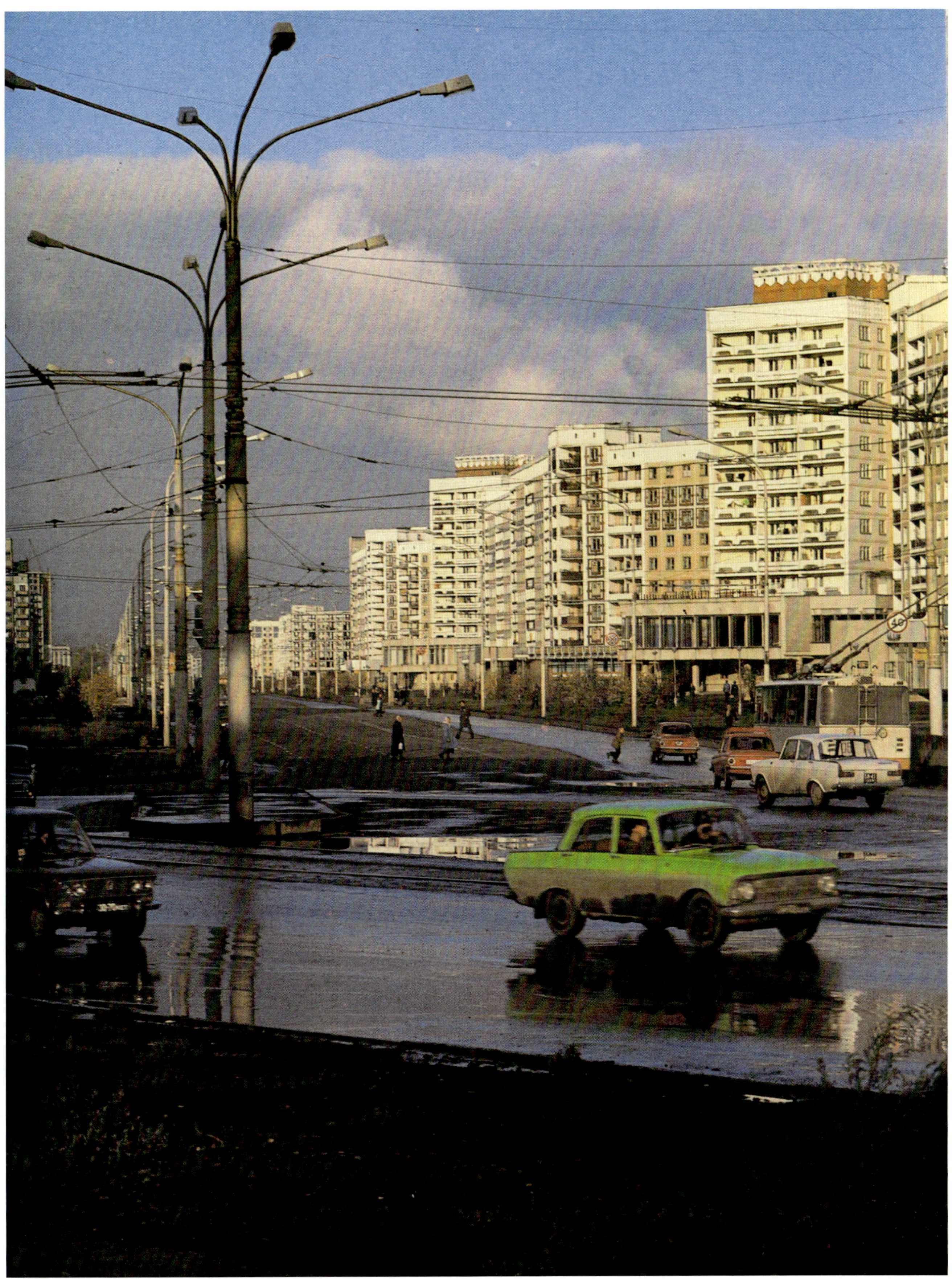

THE WAY OF ENTHUSIASTS

Marsilio

*Publishing project inspired
by the exhibition*
The Way of Enthusiasts

Conceived and edited by
Katerina Chuchalina
and Silvia Franceschini

*The exhibition and publication
are produced by*
V-A-C Foundation
Moscow 119021
Olsufievskiy per. 8 bld. 2
v-a-c.ru

The exhibition was held in
August 29 - November 25, 2012
Casa dei Tre Oci, Venice

*Within the collateral program
of the 13th International Architecture
Exhibition* Common Ground

Curated by
Katerina Chuchalina, Silvia Franceschini

With the architectural expertise of
Daria Paramonova, Kuba Snopek
assisted by Blazej Czuba

Assistant curator
Asya Klescheva

Organization
Civita Tre Venezie:
Silvia Carrer, Camilla Mozzato

Translations
Carleton Copeland
Christopher Doss
Jonathan Simon

Photography
Yuri Palmin

Graphic project and editing
Studio Polo 1116, Brugiolo Romanelli, Venezia

© 2013 Marsilio Editori® s.p.a. in Venezia

First edition May 2013
ISBN 978-88-317-1636

Reproduction, printing and binding
Grafiche Antiga, Crocetta del Montello (Treviso)
for Marsilio Editori® s.p.a. in Venice

C O N T E N T S

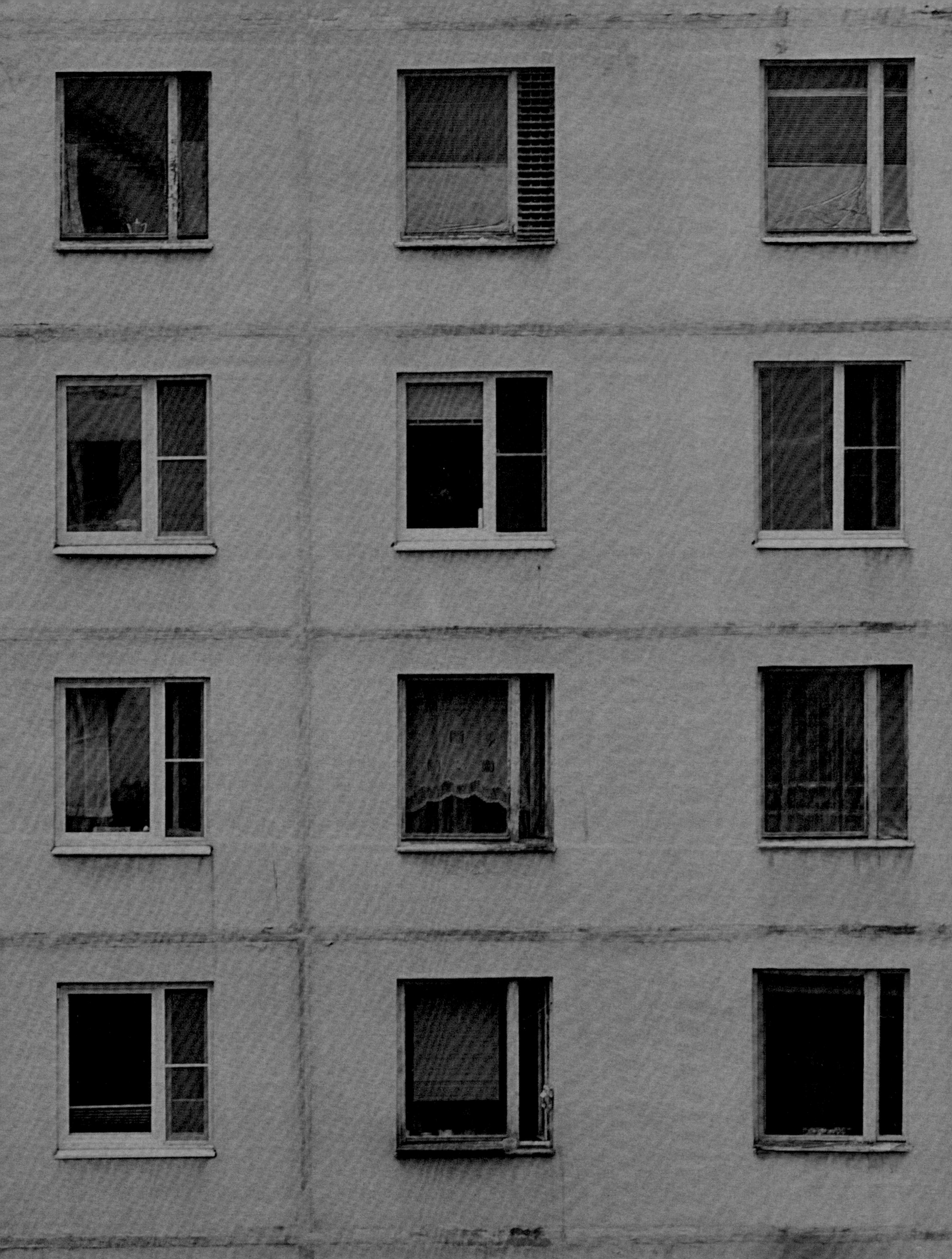

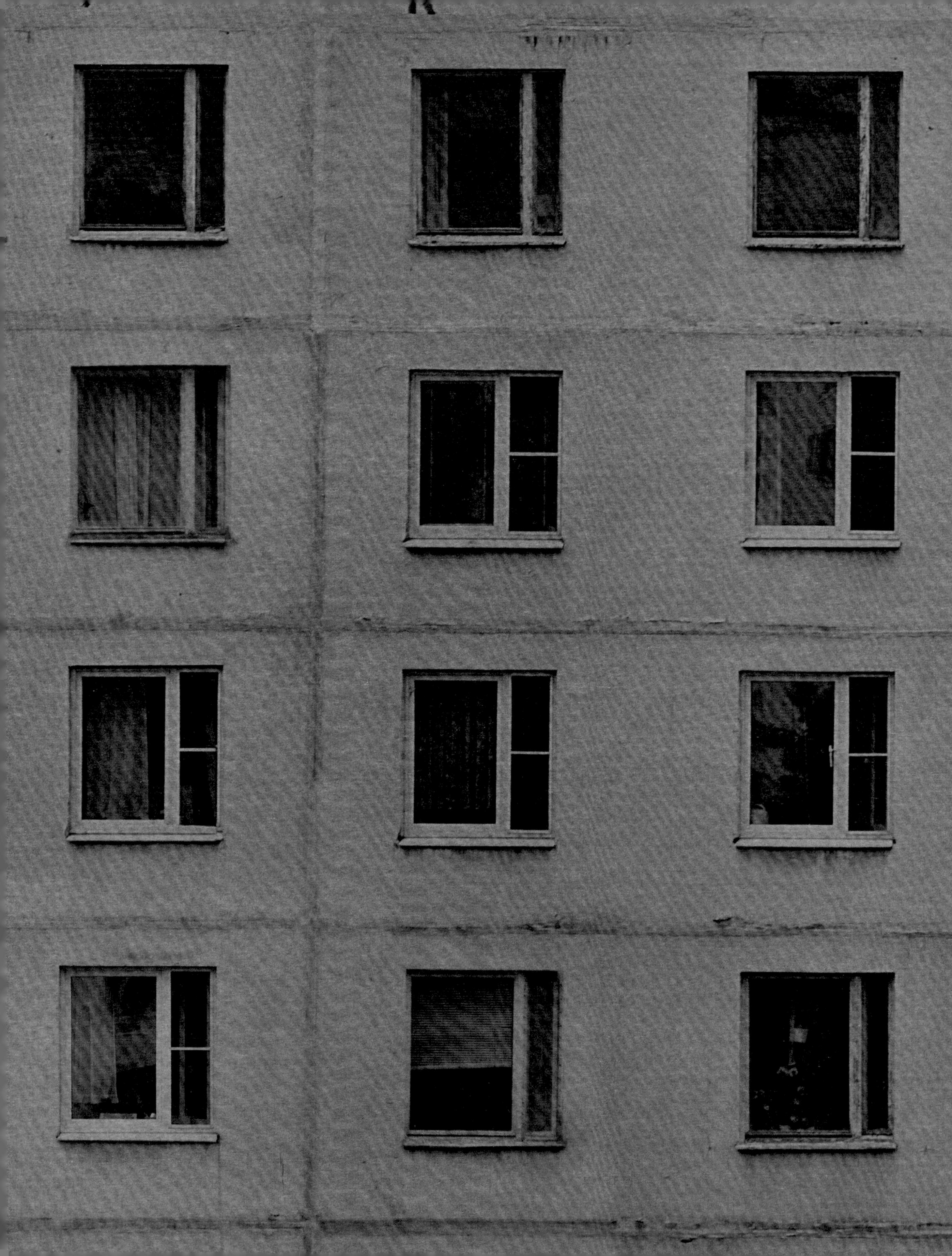

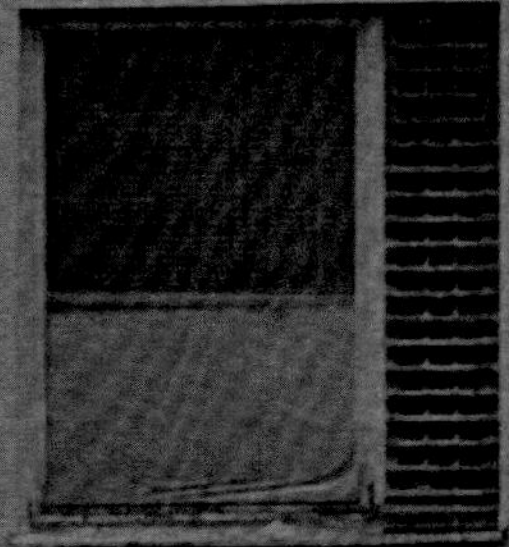
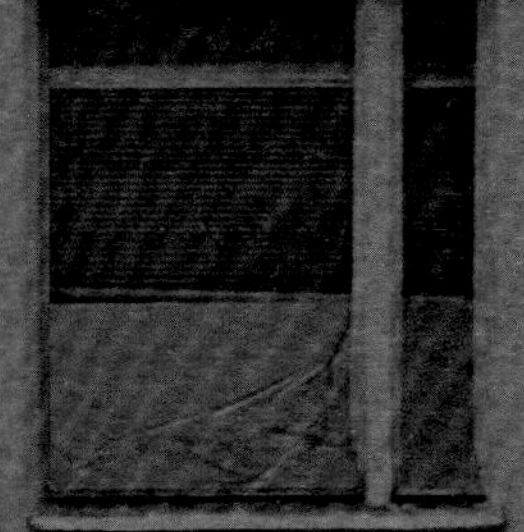

THE WAY OF ENTHUSIASTS

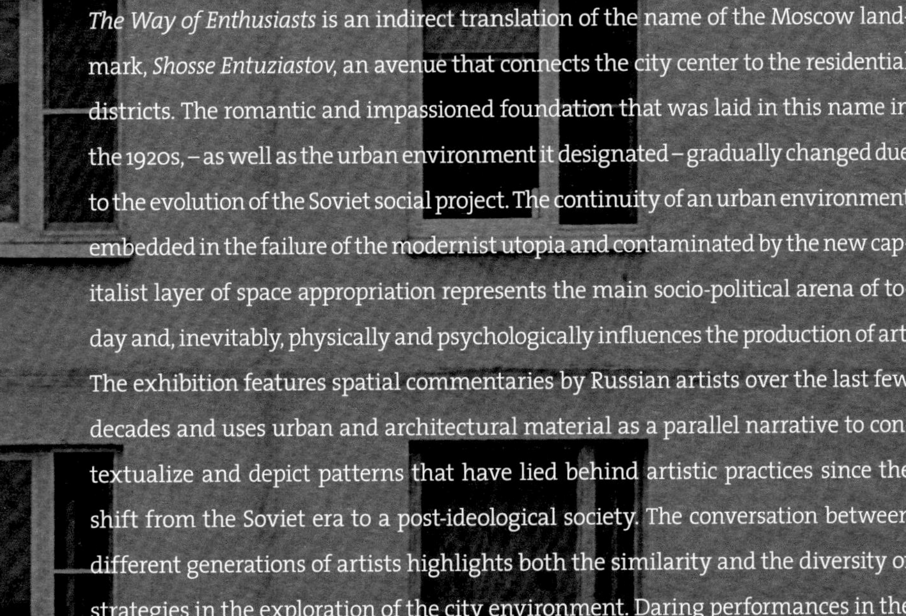

The Way of Enthusiasts is an indirect translation of the name of the Moscow landmark, *Shosse Entuziastov*, an avenue that connects the city center to the residential districts. The romantic and impassioned foundation that was laid in this name in the 1920s, – as well as the urban environment it designated – gradually changed due to the evolution of the Soviet social project. The continuity of an urban environment embedded in the failure of the modernist utopia and contaminated by the new capitalist layer of space appropriation represents the main socio-political arena of today and, inevitably, physically and psychologically influences the production of art. The exhibition features spatial commentaries by Russian artists over the last few decades and uses urban and architectural material as a parallel narrative to contextualize and depict patterns that have lied behind artistic practices since the shift from the Soviet era to a post-ideological society. The conversation between different generations of artists highlights both the similarity and the diversity of strategies in the exploration of the city environment. Daring performances in the urban field in the 1970s come into dialogue with the hermetic Collective Actions, the Moscow actionism of the 1990s and the youngest artists. In a society that has too rapidly been emancipated from its social, urban and artistic past there is thereof an urgent need to recognize the coherence or lack between these experiences.

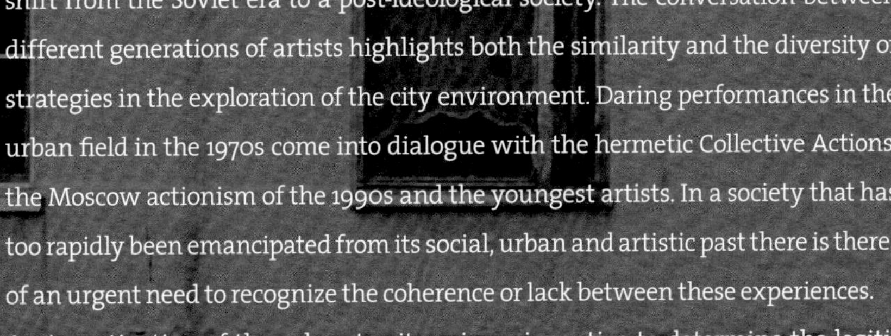

An investigation of the urban territory is an incentive to determine the legitimacy of art and the limits of its influence. Today the emerging civil society in Russia is starting to claim the city space for further activation. Can artistic expression preserve its critical potential and give a different impulse to build a new demiurgic paradigm?

The Way of Enthusiasts exhibition aims at outlining the area of interaction between artistic practices and urban spaces in Russia. The history of the transformation of urban environments here in the last decades encompasses several historical periods and therefore includes utopian, atopian and heterotopian narratives. Artists represented in the project describe, criticize, reformulate and re-invent the principles of organization of these spaces, which are experiencing a disintegration and re-stratification of forms, the aging and fading away of ideals and ideas in whose name they were constructed.

Chronologically the research encompasses the most recent three decades in Russian art, but viewers of the exhibition and reader of this book are invited to observe this landscape with backscattered x-rays rather than trying to build a temporally consistent story. None of the generations of artists lived in their cities in their original historical state, and many have not seen these cities before they were altered by Nikita Khrushchev's massive housing program. Declared and implemented in 1954 the program managed to centralize and consolidate Soviet construction to create a standardized set of building designs and then cheaply manufacture them. The fully standardized, optimized, and industrialized construction process allowed 90% of Soviet cities to be covered with the ready-made buildings composed in accordance with the authorized plans of *microrayons*. Shoddily built, they eroded so quickly that in the 1980s Russia had colossal anonymous fields of decaying urban projects that no longer displayed the near-mystical enthusiasm for increasing industrialization that was present in the 1960s. The fact that contemporary post-ideological urban reality still operates within this historical environment and exploits it as a habitat provokes many arguments reflecting upon the cultural processes in contemporary Russia as well as artistic practices in contemporary art.

The late Soviet stagnation of 1980s did not present any new mechanisms either in urban or in social relations. Although under these conditions of congealed time and rarefied space, numerous artistic groups; communities; independent artists; unofficial art schools and studios; apartment exhibitions; and poetic readings like those by the Mukhomor group, Gnezdo group, Dmitry Prigov, Collective Actions group, and SZ duo group all blossomed. Many of these artistic practices played with social and urban rituals. They revealed the rigid mechanisms of official public actions, street signs, and city graphics and turned them into carnivalesque events and theatrical gestures[1]. In 1978, members of the group Gnezdo marched down a Moscow street with a red banner normally used for mass demonstrations, replacing the usual slogan on it with a reproduction of an abstract composition by Franz Kline (*Demonstration. Art to the Masses*). A demonstration, "the embrace of the city and the citizen"[2] was one of the main urban rituals, a powerful collective action that underwent all the stages of solidification of sociocultural processes in the USSR. By the end of 1980s, the political pathos of revolutionary demonstration had become outdated; the ritual was transformed into an obligatory routine, all of its participants came to a silent consensus about the indistinguishability of meanings and formalized performance turned into a true urban feast. The Gnezdo group seized the form and performed it with simplicity, burlesque, and an elegant harlequinade. Some decades later Ivan Brazhkin in his video work *Clearing the Height* (2010), looking back at one of the rituals of Soviet space occupation, marked a tower of a boiler-house in the midst of a residential district with a red flag, which was observed by indifferent locals. Anastasia Ryabova assembled abstract compositions with empty flag holders (*Where is your flag, dude?*, 2011), urban rudiments deprived of content and historical meaning.

The artistic strategy of the Gnezdo group as well as of the Mukhomor group and some others was to a great extent nourished by Russian experimental poetry of 1920s. Seemingly spontaneous replacements of visual and textual elements and absurd defragmentation of solid concepts were similar to the efforts made by many poets like the OBERIU group (1928). "I doubt for instance that a house, a *dacha* and a tower are related to the notion of building. Perhaps a shoulder is closer to 4... I made sure of the falsity of the established relationships, but I cannot say what should be the new ones," wrote Alexander Vvedensky in his diaries.[3]

In Dmitry Prigov's visual poetry – *Poetrygrams* – letters, syllables, and words are stacked upon the surface of a piece of paper, forming columns and repetitions, piling on top of each other in layers. Graphemes form high-rise buildings and rows of residential buildings and construct areas of dizzyingly uniform constructions. However, these very graphemes also destroy them – their multilayered dances struggle to destroy the linearity of the poetic line, with the graphemes sputtering, falling apart, and tarnishing these areas. The typewriter is like a factory that enters a "mistake" into the construction of the poetic text; like a faulty panel, it breaks apart the integrity of the text, causing symmetrical rows of panels to fly apart into fragments.

Skersis and Zakharov in an SZ group collaboration (*Tags*, 1980) stenciled throughout Moscow the fragile and timid inscriptions – *Ouch! Oops! Here! How? Silly!* – and officially announced that "[...] the tags that have appeared in various corners of Moscow [...] are functioning normally." Instrumentalizing the dysfunctional vocabulary of the municipal bureaucracy they also brought the text into the cityscape in order to question the presence of the arts in public spaces and urban environments. In 2006 Alexandra Galkina was engaged in a similar dialogue with an anonymous housing and utilities employee responsible for street orderliness. She wrote one word "Zhopa" (Ass), an innocent, childish swearword, persistently for two years on one of the residential buildings in the north of Moscow, which was not less obstinately answered by the caretaker with an image. The artist operated with the word; the caretaker painted it over with disturbingly colored rectangles, creating ever-new abstract compositions. Galkina continues the investigation of art in the streets, but contextualizes it within partizan tactics and "pudding" methods of political resistance.[4]

In the 1990s and 2000s the melting away of Soviet realities took place simultaneously with an affirmation of new capitalist paradigms of technology and communication. Russian cities experienced the full phenomenon of post-ideological urbanism: the seizure of public space by private owners; the appearance of phantasmagoric architecture, an orgy of individual taste in the construction of public and private spaces; and the final technological collapse of residential areas. In the art community, the newborn commercial and state-funded institutions of contemporary art were creating an autonomous area and developing their own discourse practically in the absence of any audience whereas in the 2010s they began to actively engage in the production of their audience, and struggled for the legitimacy of art. This time brought to the city a rapid stratification of society, intense waves of migration from the republics of the former Soviet Union, huge problems with transport, terrorist attacks in public spaces; all this, against the backdrop of a hardening, authoritarian political governance and ultraconservative state rhetoric, led to the mass protest movement of 2012. Indeed the city dwellers' taking to the streets signified the return of the citizen to the city.

A collective of artists, sociologists, and mathematicians published the *Problem Book* in the same year. The artwork suggested solutions to rather sophisticated math problems on urban situations that encapsulated core political and social diseases. The book approaches mathematics as an "obscure point where a situation concentrates its law"[5] in the surroundings of the soothing language of school arithmetic in order to construct a disturbing and unsafe field between rational and ideal. Math language distorted to the point of absurdity is utilized as well as criticized by the authors who are aware of its emancipatory and manipulative potentials. The empty ruled pages in the middle of the book are the wasteland for concretion of the environment and the instrument for its description, the city and the text.[6]

This is probably one of the very few works of art in *The Way of Enthusiasts* project presenting real people: the schoolboy Petya, Businessman X, the dreaming political activist, and the mayor of Moscow. Russian art concerning the city has, in the last few decades, been noticeably deprived of human faces and stories. The city envisioned by artists is surprisingly dehumanized. People and their stories are reduced to a silhouette in a window, an imaginary participant in a game, a fight, labor, or a childhood experience as a symbiosis of early spatial sensations. Alexander Povzner (*Playground*, 2011) investigates the educative potential, the physics and mechanics of very simple urban spatial constructions. Playgrounds constructed in the 1970s, very quickly became ruined zones of freedom and anonymity for people's creativity. For several decades, they remained an autonomous space lacking any social message. The merry-go-round, sandbox, pull-up bar, and hoops originating from street circuses and fairs with miraculous machinery, now became exercise apparatus modules for preparing a future participant in urban battles. The artist disintegrated its form and function, tracing the history from the forced city collectivity to the city as a set of acquired functions.

A photographer and artist from the south of Russia, Sergey Sapozhnikov, is even more radical in installing de-constructist views. He "builds a house that peeks into your window and by this penetrates into the house you imagined"[7]. Unlike the famous "trips out of town" by Andrei Monastyrski and Collective Actions group, his adventures aim at finding the physical territory, or rather *a terrain vague*[8] between the known and the unfamiliar, where the city becomes a thicket, a home becomes a nest, and a person becomes a rag hanging from a tree. His objects are based on the immediate, living reactions of people in play or their being drawn into an unexpected narrative "knot." In Venice, he did this with an inflatable mattress – a wonderful children's amusement (*Failed Views*, 2012). After having vaulted over the fence of an enigmatic house on the island of Giudecca he constructed a site-specific installation that appears twice in the space of the exhibition – the first time as photographs radiating with color, and again as only a glimpse in the depths of a garden out of the palazzo window.

Border areas of different registers, empty zones, voids and wastelands are the subjects of intended interest of many artists. Vadim Zakharov and Niklas Nitschke's work testifies to the spatial potential of the Dead Zone, a territory on the German-Polish frontier, as a free space and a systemic alternative to the reference framework of contemporary art. Through the reflection of relations between various places, spheres, actions, a map of the territory becomes a machine, which in turn generates further possibilities of action (*Creation of a Time Unit for the Dead Zone*, 2012).

In constant search for a place for art Arseny Zhilyaev installs a laundromat for the residents of the island of Giudecca in Venice with a separate entrance in an exhibition space. With this gesture, he manifests a return to the utilitarian and didactic potential of art, to the experience of the first avant-garde, and a categorical disregard for the established consensus of politics and aesthetics. Laundromats were considered a unit of residential arrangement in the Soviet city as early as in the utopian projects of the urbanists of the 1920s, and oddly enough this continued through the economic and ideological censorship of Khrushchev's reforms, becoming part of the life of microrayons in the 1970s as one of the few public areas in the city, a place of circulating people, ideas, and water. "The city still cannot take its eyes off of us, which always makes its head spin" (Jean Genet). The relationship between a modern Russian city and Russian art metaphorically recreates the relation between society and artist; they will never achieve a common identity but can promote the development of a symbiosis between each other. The rapid pulse of historical Russian urbanization, a phenomenon of its environment, offers an insightful perspective on problems in global modernity. The city is always interesting to an artist, after all it is a place of transformations and conferment, an object of all possible interferences; at the same time it is both the mechansm and the mythical symbol of socioeconomic and political policy; both hero and chorus. A forward-looking and far-sighted view, abandoned by the craft, like a chemical reactant reveals our opaque past and unclear future.

[1] Mikhail Bakhtin's term "canivalesque" is associated with the body and the public exhibition of its more private functions. Essentially, the act of inverting society through communication, whether it be in the form of text, protest, or something else serves as a communicative form of carnival, according to Bakhtin. Mikhail Bakhtin, *Questions of Literature and Aesthetics*, Moscow, Progress, 1979.
[2] Vladimir Paperny, *Architecture in the Age of Stalin: Culture Two*, Cambridge, Cambridge University Press, 2011.
[3] Alexander Vvedensky, *The complete works in 2 vol.*, Moscow, Gileya, 1993.
[4] Ulrike Meinhof, *Napalm and pudding*, in *Konkret* magazine, 1967 # 5.
[5] Alain Badiou, *Number and Numbers*, 1990.
[6] Michel de Certeau. *The Practice of Everyday Life*. Translated by Steven Rendall. University of California Press, 1984.
[7] Lucy Lippard. *The Lure of the Local: Senses of Place in a Multicentered Society*, New York, New Press, 1998.
[8] Marc Shuilenburg, *The Right to Terroir. Place and Identity in Times of Immigration and Globalization*, in *Open* magazine 2011 # 21.

The relationships between artists and the city in Russia dates back to a key moment, when the avant-garde and the 1920s constructivist movement laid down the bases for an entirely new understanding of the logic of space, including the design of urban architecture in the overall attempt to plan every aspect of life, especially those of the new common spaces of the future Soviet cities. The various generations of artists featured in the exhibition – covering the last four decades of Russian art – developed starting from the underground art scene of the late 1960s and 1970s, with an autonomous position towards any kind of official socio-political discourse and came up with a different way of approaching the city. The spatial and social perception of these generations of artists was drastically influenced by the aftermath of the implementation of Khrushchev Manifesto (1954)[1], which ushered in prefabricated living units on an inhuman scale all over the country, as well as by the radical changes of the post-Soviet period. Far from being involved in any kind of "construction," artists started to perceive the city and its concrete elements as topographical landmarks embedded within the political discourse, and every artistic gesture – from artists' exposure in public spaces to the moving of artists throughout and beyond the city – became a way of creating a field of meaning and of editing and commenting the space.

Collective Actions were the first to systematise an entire corps of works on the discursive potential of the urban space and, more specifically, of the centre-periphery dialectic, in their literary masterpiece *Poezdki Za Gorod*,[2] which contains the documentation of more than 120 actions that unfolded in the most neutral space possible in the Soviet Union: the outskirts of Moscow, a space free from social and ideological determination, which – especially in winter time – presented a tabula rasa, a space without any signs which might be found in the city space. *The corridor of Collective Actions* systematises 34 years of development of the Collective's aesthetics in a multidimensional installation made up of maps, diagrams, video documentation and texts, trying to show their internal functioning by providing an index of the location of each of CA's actions. They indicate various locations in the Moscow region and in Moscow city where CA organized its actions, clearly showing their preference for the Kievogorodskoe Field near the village of Kievy Gorky, an empty green zone where artists organised most of their actions during the Soviet period.[3] In the late 1990s, this idyllic tabula rasa started to fall apart, for every outlying plot was sucked into the general context of civilisation becoming the area of territorial "development" of the upcoming megacity, and conditioning CA to move aside, trying to open up and develop new territories, adjacent to this field, or in a completely new place in the field or in the city.

The Monastyrski series of black & white photographs *Earthworks* – conceived as a visual commentary on the text of the same title[4] – is an attempt to capture the pressure exerted by the urban context surrounding the artist in his everyday life. Here the "earth" is not bound up in the notion of the natural territory (nature is excluded *a priori* from Monastyrski's discourse) as in the American tradition of Land Art, inaugurated by the homonymous series *Earthworks* by Robert Smithson, but within the context of the city centre, where road-building, the digging of canals and foundations and the erecting of buildings affect and influence the artist's subjectivity much more then the neutrality of the out-of-town abstract space. While the surface of Moscow was for Monastyrski the main "expositional field," the Moscow Metro was for the Mukhomor group an operational field in which the artists, riding the subway from opening to closing and staging meetings at various stations, were trying to transform it into an inhabitable place for everybody, thus de-consecrating the Stalinist city. In this "Metro" action, the group adopted the same conceptualist strategy of acting within a hermeneutic scheme of references, following a specific plot and behaving like spies to escape police regulation. In a city where the walking is made impossible by virtue of its size, the subway was probably the only form of continuity is which is possible to bring about the idea of non-stop travelling and unitary urbanism.

Between the city centre and the outskirts lies a limbo, a grey zone of autonomous residential districts, stretching as far as the city limits. *Microrayon* is a mass housing project developed by architects as a standardized project of which the infrastructure was designed to include all the facilities within a single district in order to allow people to spend their entire life there: life should thus circulate within a defined framework including repetitive everyday procedures and a list of typical places.[5] The new pattern of life of the Soviet district with its modernist rationality and repetitiveness seems to be embodied in the very structure of Dmitry Prigov's *Poetrygrams*, the typewritten word composition in which the Soviet propaganda turns into concrete poetry. In the short novel *Belyaevo 99 and forever*, the artist imagines establishing his duchy in the district of Belyaevo, where he lives: Belyaevo will become a kingdom and an independent state where everything is included, along with the vision of a faraway and unattainable world. This dream world appeared to be the main heterotopia of Rayon's apartments which – after the collapse of the Soviet infrastructure – became nothing more than huge dormitory districts. In the paintings by Alexandra Paperno, the vision of the cosmos appears enlarged on a canvas among the ground plans of the *khrushchevka* houses.[6]

The communal spaces of these living areas disappeared together with the *microrayon* infrastructure and now returns in the work of contemporary artists in a sort of archaeology of modernity. Post-Soviet capitalism has dramatically altered the relationship between public and private spaces, influencing artists who now identify the Soviet past with the abandonment of social principles.[7] Stanislav Shuripa revives the *KT-A*, telephone booths, an indispensable element and an infrastructure unit of the *microrayons* now banished from the urban landscape. These disfunctionalised objects could entail a more intimate form of communication, an intimacy lost in Soviet (and contemporary) public spaces. For artists born in the 1980s, who experienced the Soviet Union only in childhood, the exploration of Soviet ruins becomes necessary to understanding their origins and their present, inevitably influenced by this immediate past. Kirill Glushenko, under the name of the publishing house Gluschenkoizdat, travels to small towns of the former USSR trying to capture the essence of a vanishing country and document the remnants of Soviet reality, featured in a book conceived as a piece of art bordering on both reality and fiction. In her video *Vanishing Spaces*, Xenia Sorokina explores the archive of the artist Valeriy Sorokin (1952), who was the creator of numerous decorative projects for Soviet public spaces which after the fall of the Soviet Union lost their function as objects of public pride and the communication of an ideology.

In the 1990s, the collapse of the ideological infrastructure was manifested in the city as the liberation from the Soviet regime, organizing public spaces that started to become more accessible and open also thanks to the appearance of commercial shops and 24-hour services. Against this background, the actions of Anatoly Osmolovsky may be perceived as an attempt to intervene in situations of extreme visibility in order to contribute in the ongoing deconsecration of spaces and monuments made "holy" in the Soviet era. In 1993 the artist climbed up onto the shoulders of the over 10-metre high statue of the poet Vladimir Mayakovski, as if to restore the revolutionary impulse to this avant-garde hero, appropriated by official culture. The deconsecration of spaces was accompanied by the de-territorialisation of artistic practices in the political arena. In 1991, with the collapse of the Soviet Union and the introduction of various liberal "shock therapy"[8] reforms, life started to become harsher and the general population lost interest in creative activities. Artists started to refuse the white cube, and went in search of a stronger relation with reality and society, which they found mainly in the urban sphere. In the late 1990s, together with Radek Community and Avdei Ter-Oganyan, Anatoly Osmolovsky carried out a series of actions under the name of Non-Governmental Control Commission, testing art as an indirect medium of political struggle. In May 1998, the group organized the action known as "Barricade on Bolshaya Nikitskaya Street," in which an entire street was blocked by artists shouting the slogans of the French demonstrations of May 1968. While it may be objectively impossible to "reclaim the streets" in post-Soviet conditions, it was possible to create an inner space of political and critical potential in the very existence of the action: like Situationism, the "moment" and "situation" had the revolutionary potential to change the present. But while in Situationist practices the accent was on "continuity," here the accent was on dichotomy and extremes: between vertical and horizontal, inside and outside. These actions continued until the end of the 1990s when the wall of political pressure became stronger and a general disillusion with democratic develop-ment started to become widespread throughout society. Artists understood that the main role in the conquest of space was being played out not by the ordinary people, who went to demonstrations to express their views, but rather by the representatives of the class of the new owners of private capital who really did take hold of spaces: seizing parks and factories and privatising them.

The private sector fenced in these spaces and with the claim of creating new European-looking "public spaces," inserted aggressive cultural industries, mak-ing artists instead of a driving force of gentrification a mere parasite of the system. The Urban Fauna Lab, an interdisciplinary research-based workshop, tried to understand the position of these unneeded creatures in the evolution of the city through the metaphorical element of urban animals, such as feral cats, which have established symbiotic and at the same time parasitic relationships with the residents of the Elektrozavod industrial site. Some elements of this site were saved from dereliction (e.g. a big window, ground plans of the factory and lamps) and featured in the exhibition as part of an environmental installation. The coming-of-age of Putin's "stable" 2000s, an amnesiac period of resource-based strong economic growth, hid a backstage of governmental and social tur-bulence, tangible at the urban level. This unpredictable urban friction appeared in David Ter-Oganyan's work *Scale* (2008-2012), an ongoing series of small, hay-wire sketches of demonstrations and urban riots jotted down in an everyday notebook and then turned into large printed canvases. This colourful iconog-raphy of moving masses, borrowed from the leftist discourse and impressed in David's mind ever since his participation in Osmolovsky' sections, turns out to be the representation of possible acts of violence which might explode in the city at any moment. These dense sketches seems to embody what Brian Holmes define ecstasy and fear, anxiety and desire that structure the relationship be-tween the individual and the urban multitude.[9]

The renewed control of public life on behalf of the authorities is manifested physically at an urban level in the flagholders, the subject of a sculpture work by Anastasia Ryabova, *Where is your flag, dude?*, in which the artist displaces and deconstructs these leftovers of the great ideological machine in a new form. This technique of altering established ideological devices is mindful of the practices of Gnezdo in the work *Demonstration. Art to the Masses* (1978), in which the artist replaced the central text of the slogan of a Soviet banner with an abstract composition, and marched through the centre of Moscow with it, thus discrediting one of the most powerful Soviet public rituals: the celebratory march.

After 4th December 2011, in the wake of the presidential elections, the mass protests changed atmosphere giving the sense of something moving and growing. The difficulties the protesters faced in their attempts to make their discontent visible by gathering in central urban places led to a growth of interest and discussion on urban public spaces. Like secondary-school maths problems, a collective of artists, architects and sociologists examined the contradictions embodied in the urban fabric in the publication *Problem Book* (2012). By narrating such problems, apart from delivering unconventional, ironic and exaggerated observations, it also includes utopian visions of urban renewal under the pressure of competing political forces. The daily political agenda seems to become the main subject of the new generation of politically engaged artists like Arseniy Zhilyaev. Reviving a form of urban planning that dates back to constructivist communal houses, with the installation *Forthcoming Dawn* (2012), the artist offered a free laundry service to the population of the Giudecca Island. The major installation, deprived of any aesthetic meaning, represents a clear gesture to promote the inclusion of art in everyday life and the public sphere.

In Moscow, the Occupy movement that monopolised the Chistye Prudy Park in 2012 (with the participation of a lot of artists) represented a real-time window of hope and enthusiasm for the potential of self-organized democratic spaces. The arrests and trials of activists accused of participation in "non-approved" public events entailed an active discussion about citizens' right to use city spaces. Since last year, the renewed passion for open spaces has grown hand in hand with the repressive policies of the new government, silencing all spontaneous artistic gestures in the city and issuing various laws against the freedom of expression.

In conclusion, we might say that the last 40 years have witnessed a gradual transformation in the strategies of relating, deciphering, and acting in the urban context towards the re-territorialisation of artistic practices within the city. Nowadays, in a censored city where the only expressive potential of the collective eros lies in the libidinal capitalist economy[10] or within defined boundaries, it's necessary to think once more of autonomous spaces of expression. Hence we see the beginnings of a shift towards a different way of fitting into the folds of society, through systematic activism, tactical networks, mimesis, the viral spread of communication and indirect public participation. The deconstruction of the past seems to be an additional tool, yet one necessary in order to make a clean break with the current situation and carve out new spaces of imagination for the future.

[1] Khrushchev's Manifesto at the Resolution n. 1871 of the Central Committee of the Communist Party of the Soviet Union and the Council of Ministers from 4th November 1955 titled *On the elimination of extravagances in design and construction* was a reaction to the great demand for new housing, heralding the era of mass construction of standard housing in the USSR.

[2] Andrei Monastyrski, *Poezdizagorod. Kollektivniedestviya (Trips Out of Town. Collective Actions)*, 1983.

[3] Octavian Esanu, *Transition in Post-Soviet Art*, Central European University Press, 2013.

[4] Andrei Monastyrski, *Earthworks. The theme of the peacock and the condor on the expositional Sign Field, Andrei Monastyrski*, Moscow Museum of Modern Art, 2011.

[5] Kuba Snopek, *Belayevo Forever. The Intangible Heritage*, Moscow, Strelka Institute for Media Architecture and Design, 2011.

[6] *Khrushchevka* is a standard five-floor panel-and-brick building typical of the Khrushchev period.

[7] Ekaterina Degot, Elena Sorokina, *The Uninhabited Spaces of Democracy* in *(Im)possible Spaces,* Newspaper of the Platform Chto Delat/ What is to be done? Issue n. 12, March, 2006.

[8] In economics, "shock therapy" refers to the sudden release of price and currency controls, withdrawal of state subsidies, and immediate trade liberalisation within a country, usually also including large scale privatisation of previously public-owned assets, as happened in the USSR, the world's largest state-controlled economy, when it traumatically converted into a market-oriented economy.

[9] B. Holmes, *Ecstasy, Fear & Number: From the 'Man of the Crowd' to the Myths of the Self-Organizing Multitude*, Red Thread e-journal, Issue 1, 2009.

[10] Kety Chukhnov, *Soviet Material Culture and Socialist Ethics in Moscow Conceptualism*, in Boris Groys, *Moscow Symposium: Conceptualism Revisited*, e-flux Journal and Sternberg Press, 2012..

B I B L I O G R A P H Y

Dictionary of Moscow Conceptualism.
An adaptation of Andrei Monastyrski slovar'
terminov moskovskoi kontseptual'noi
shkoly. Translated, annotated and illustrated
by Octavian Esanu. ContImporary, 1999

Andrei Monastyrski, *Poezdki za gorod.
Kollektivnie dejstviya=Trips Out of Town.
Collective Actions*, vol. 1-11, Vologda,
Herman Titov Publishing House, 1983

Dmitry A. Prigov, *Citizens! Please mind
yourselves! Works on paper, installations,
books, readings, performance, and opera,
1940-2007.* Edited by Ekaterina Degot,
Moscow, Moscow Museum of Modern Art
Publishing Program, 2008

Octavian Esanu, *Transition in Post-Soviet Art*,
Central European University Press, 2013

Boris Groys, *History becomes Form. Moscow
Conceptualism*, Cambridge, The MIT Press,
2010

Boris Groys, ed., *Empty Zones: Andrei
Monastyrski and Collective Actions*, London,
Black Dog Publishing, 2011

Boris Groys, ed., *Moscow Symposium:
Conceptualism Revisited*, e-flux journal
and Sternberg Press, 2012

Nancy Holt, *The Writings of Robert Smithson*,
New York, New York University Press, 1979

Henri Lefebvre, *The production of space*,
Wiley-Blackwell, 1992

Simon Sadler, *The situationist city*,
Cambridge, The MIT Press, 1999

(Im)possible Spaces, Newspaper of the
Platform Chto Delat/ What is to be done?
Issue n. 12, March, 2006

Vadim Zakharov, Yuri Leiderman, Andrei
Monastyrski, *Kapiton* by Pastor Zond Edition,
Cologne / Vologda, The Library of Moscow
Conceptualism, edited and published by
German Titov, 2009

*Andrei Monastyrski. Objects and installations,
Earthworks* exhibition catalogue, Moscow,
Stella Art Gallery, 2005

Alexandra Obukhova, ed., *Mukhomor
(Toadstool)*, Vologda, The Library of Moscow
Conceptualism, German Titov Publishing
House, 2010

The Nest: Donskoy, Roshal, Skersis, Moscow,
National Centre for Contemporary Art, 2008

Andrei Monastyrski, *Esteticheskie
issledovaniya = Aesthetic researches*, Vologda,
The Library of Moscow Conceptualism,
German Titov Publishing House, 2009

The False Calculations Presidium, Exhibition
catalogue, Moscow, VAC Foundation, 2012

Edward Relph, *Place and Placelessness*,
London, Pion Ltd., 2008

Michel de Certeau, *The Practice of Everyday
Life*, Translated by Steven Rendall, University
of California Press, 1984

Kuba Snopek, *'Belyaevo Forever'. The
Intangible Heritage*, Moscow, Strelka
Institute for Media, Architecture and Design,
2011

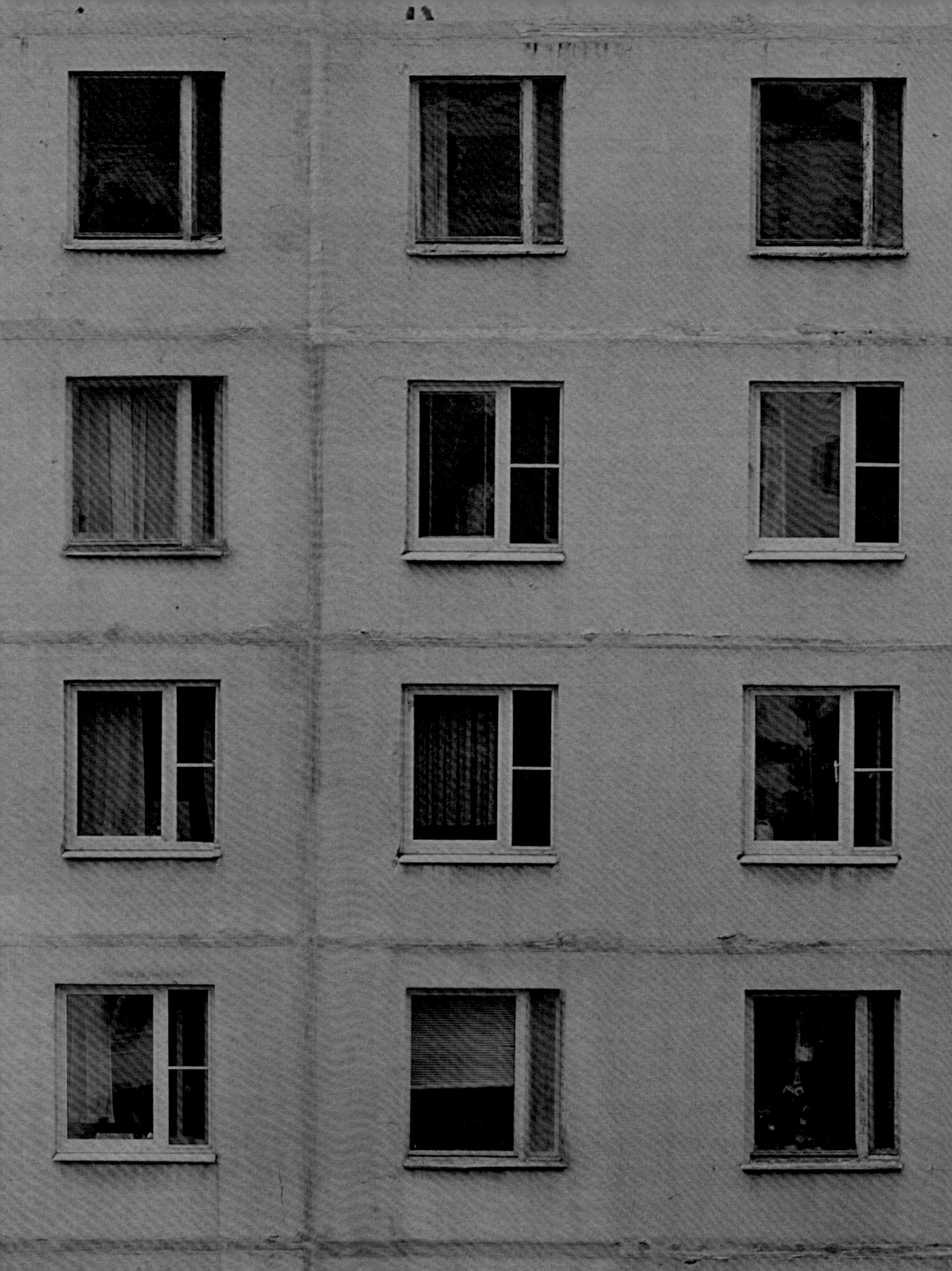

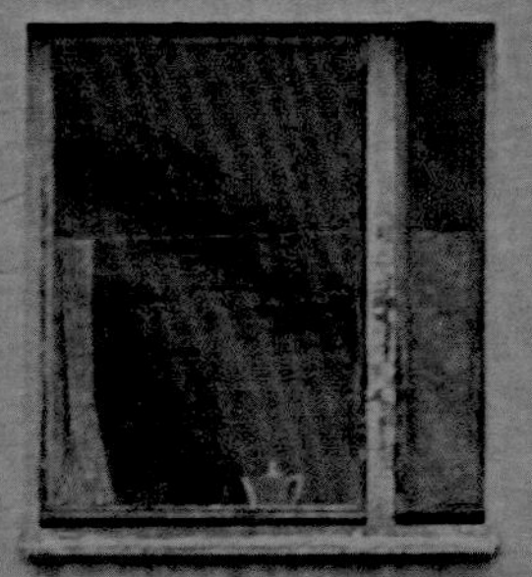
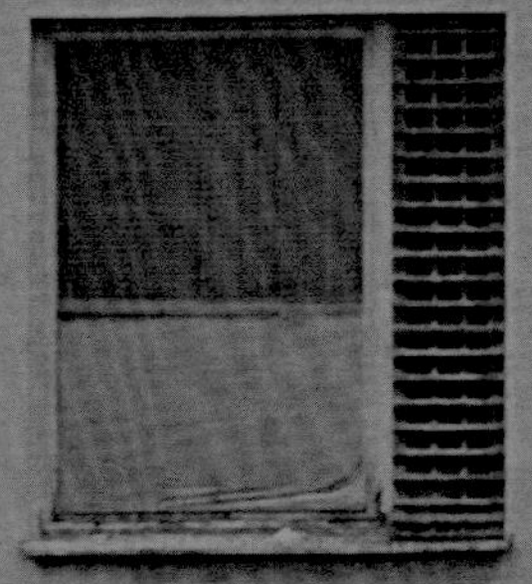
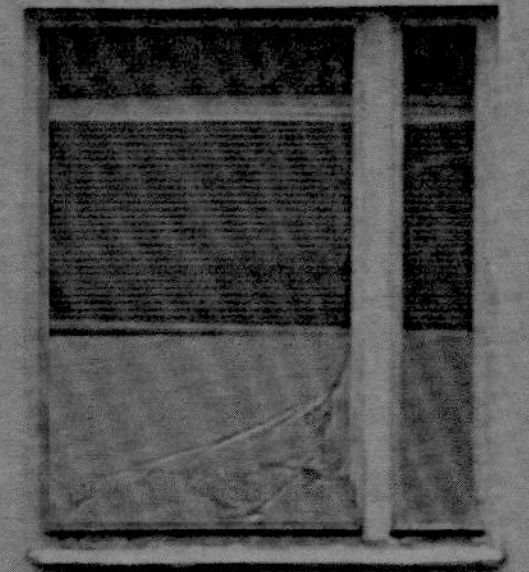

ARTISTS IN
THE EXHIBITION

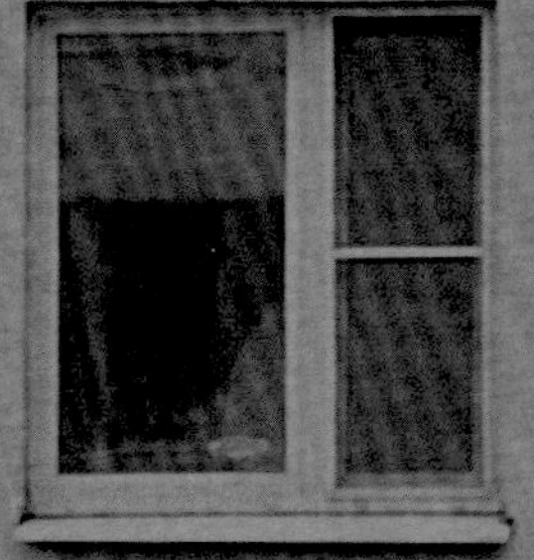
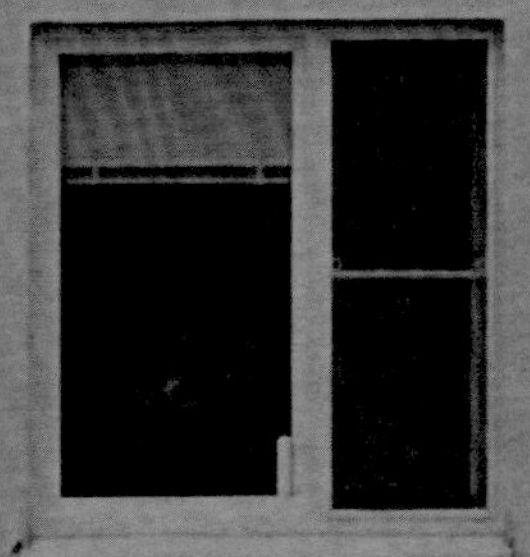
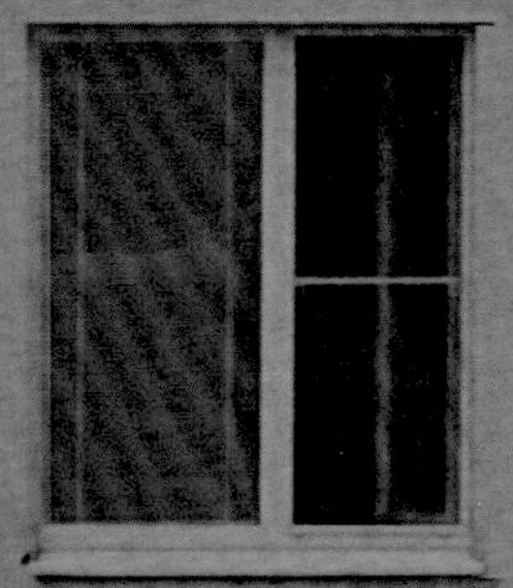
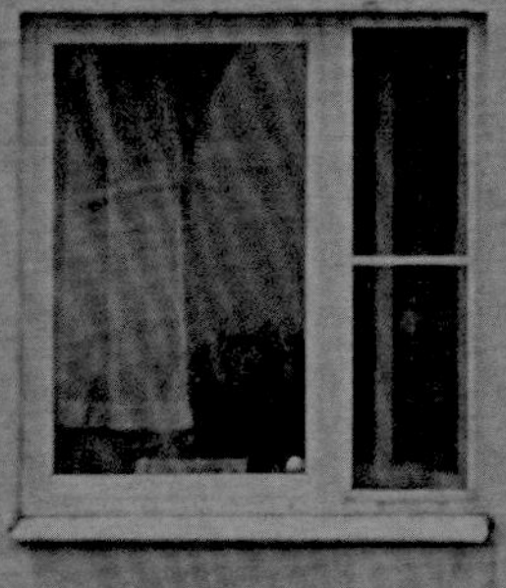
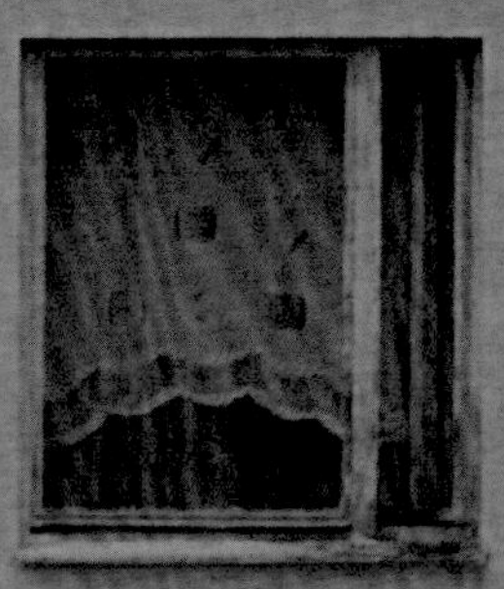
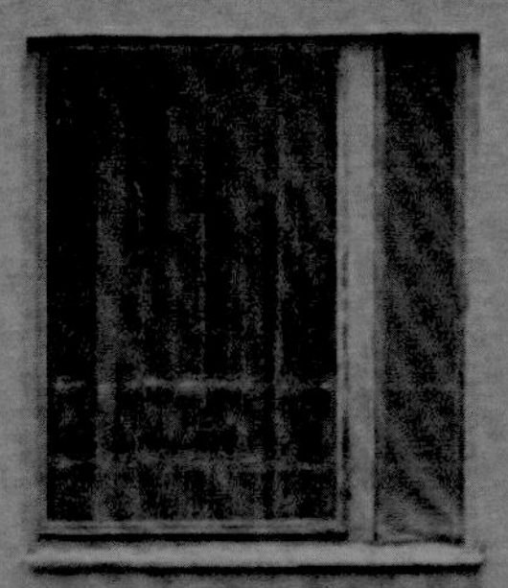

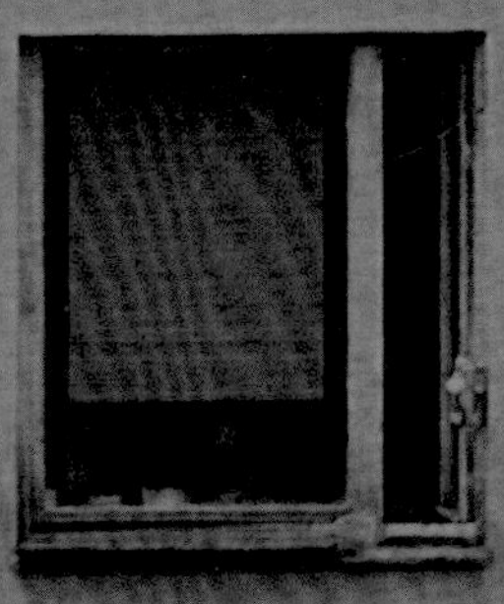

ARSENIY

FORTHCOMING DAWN 2012
COMMUNICATION PROJECT: PUBLIC LAUNDRY, WEBSITE NEWZARYA.ORG
COURTESY THE ARTIST

Public laundries were part of utopian urban planning that traces back to constructivist communal houses in which all aspects of private life had to be shared. This intention revealed itself in the architecture of the houses of the new type that were built starting from the late 1920s, where different private activities were supposed to be performed in public. Thus appeared the famous Soviet canteens or laundries that lasted in Russian cities until the fall of the Soviet Union, when the urban life became much more individualized and isolated.
The project of Arseniy Zhilyaev is an attempt to reenact this long-disappeared practice in a new and unusual context. This artwork suggests the creation of an authentic public space within the Giudecca Island: the system of laundries is supposed to offer a functioning service at the disposal of the local community. The main question is if art can reject its artificiality in favor of the real life production and if the exhibition space can blur its borders with the external environment. For Zhilyaev, artistic practice should be a gesture of shifting toward another territory where an open democratic project can become relevant for the local sociopolitical situation.
Forthcoming Dawn is an imaginary underground network of people reunited against the system of contemporary art that resembles a screenplay from Hollywood movies about the future of radical political groups.

ZHILYAEV

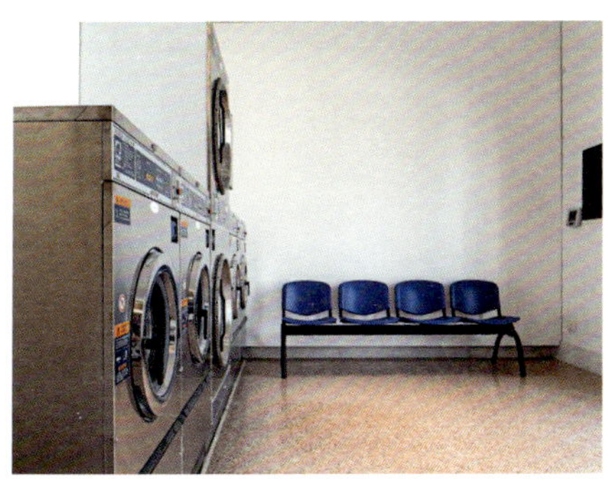
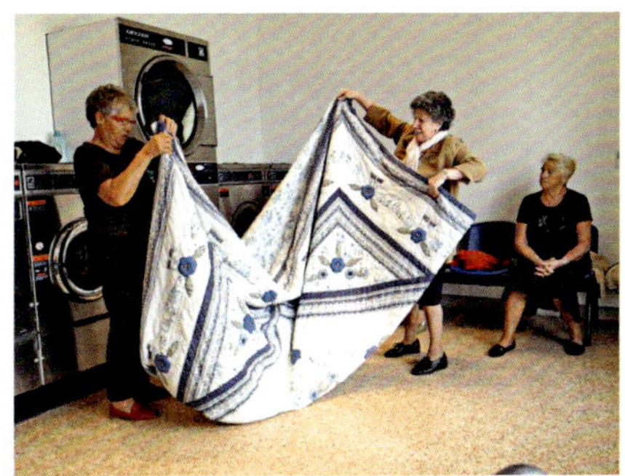
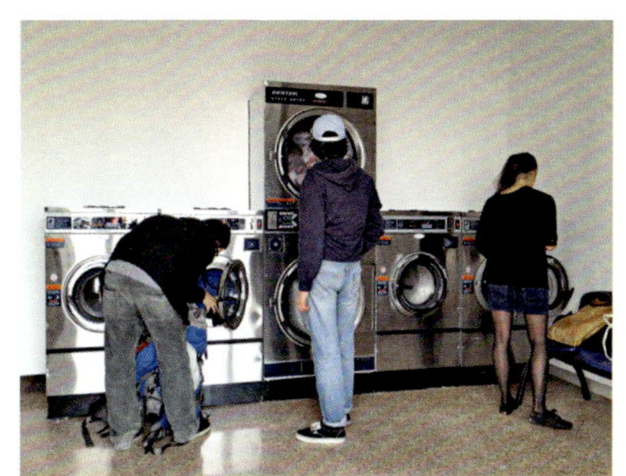
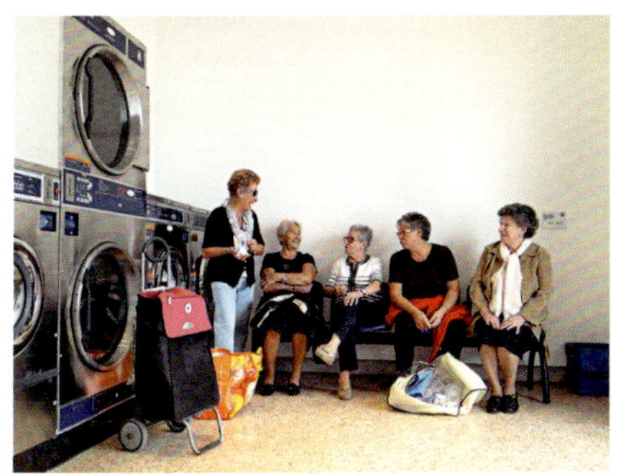
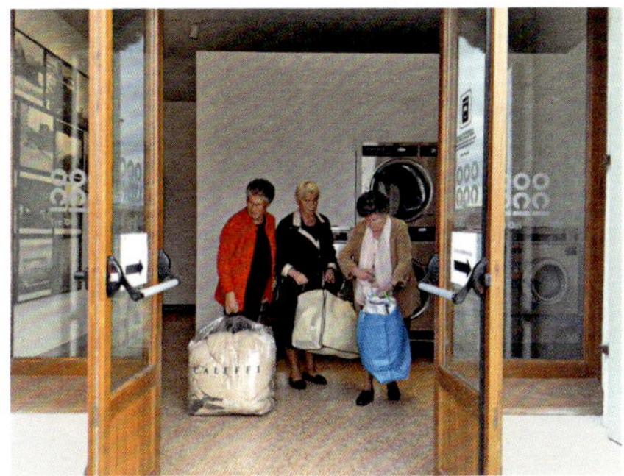
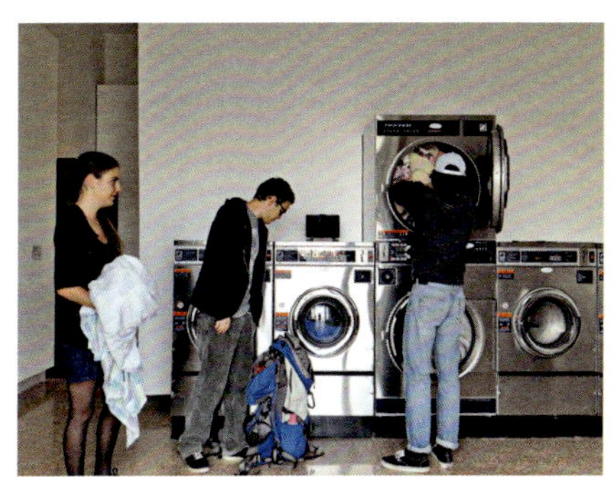
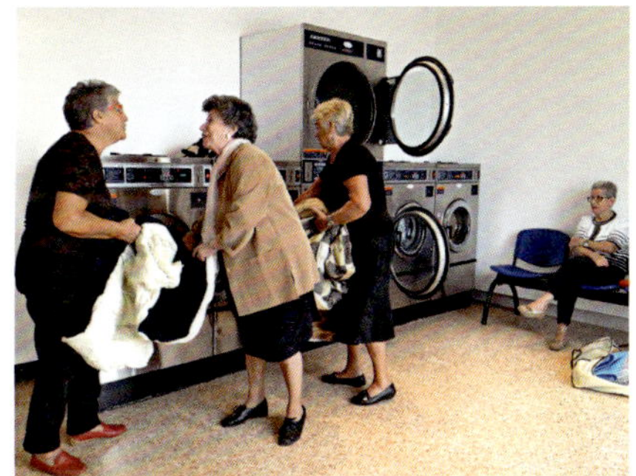
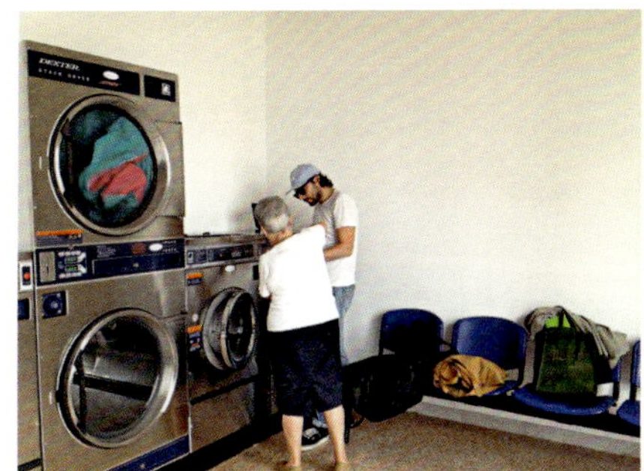
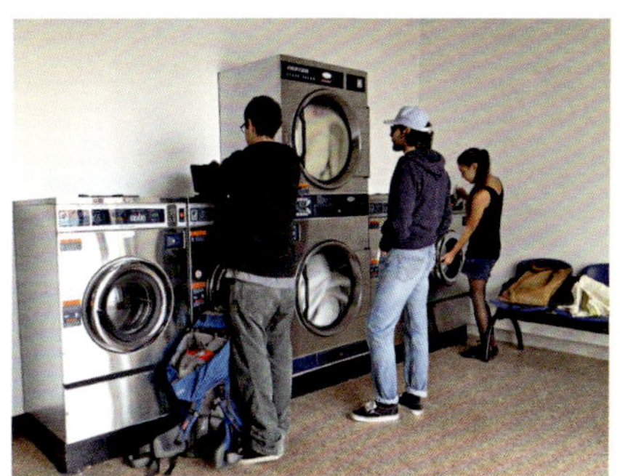
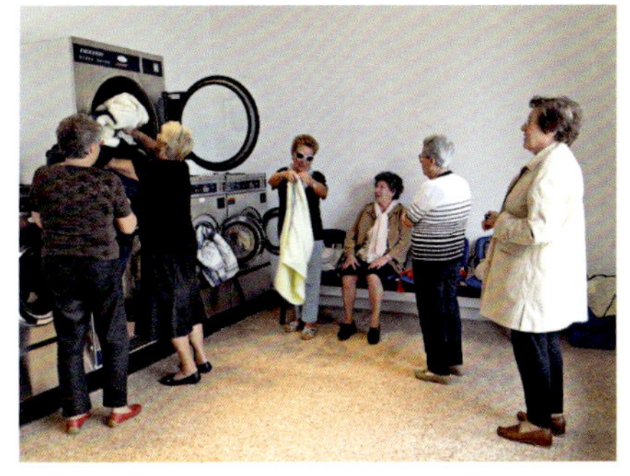
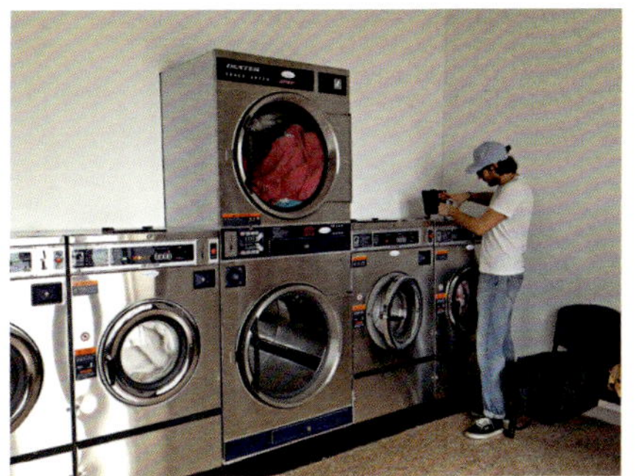
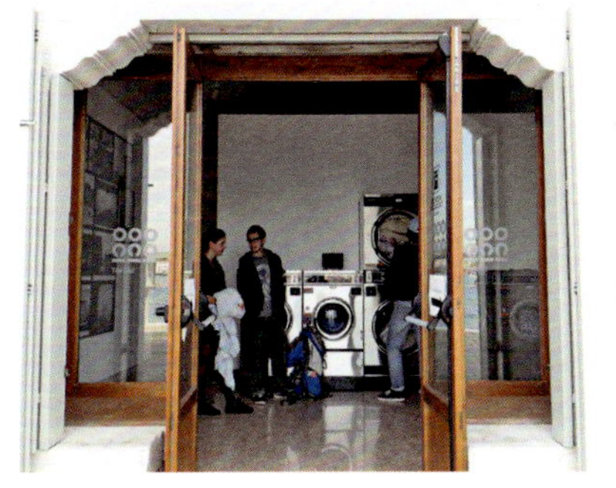

ANDREI M

EARTHWORKS 1987
SERIES OF 18 BLACK AND WHITE PHOTOGRAPHS
COURTESY GAZPROMBANK COLLECTION, MOSCOW

The series of pictures *Earthworks* was conceived as a part of the essay *Earthworks - The Theme of the Peacock and the Condor on the Expositional Sign Field of Moscow.* In this text, the root work of the artist's objectivity is defined in intricate detail. It is at once a specific text about a particular place (Soviet Moscow in the 1980s) and a text about the mode in which artists look at a place and use this specific reading in their work. It expresses also the notion of the Demonstrative Semiotic Field, a concept that stands for the dynamic center of the action, which is constituted by the totality of psychological (subjective) and empirical (objective) elements. As Monastyrski writes, "[...] the objectivity of these motivational contexts is not articulated through social, political, or any other kind of connections and relationships, but through concrete changes, through the building of roads, the digging of canals and foundations, the erection of buildings, the plowing of fields, etc."
Earthworks is an autonomous conceptual artwork in the form of a photographic excursion from the VDNKh exhibition complex to Turgenev Square that depicts various sacral inspirations that reveal what was influencing the practices of conceptual artists' practices in 1980s' Moscow. On the other hand, all of these underpasses, earthworks, above-ground sanitary constructions, trestles, can be simply considered as distinct points of interest around the neighborhood that Monastyrski loves to walk around and its sights.

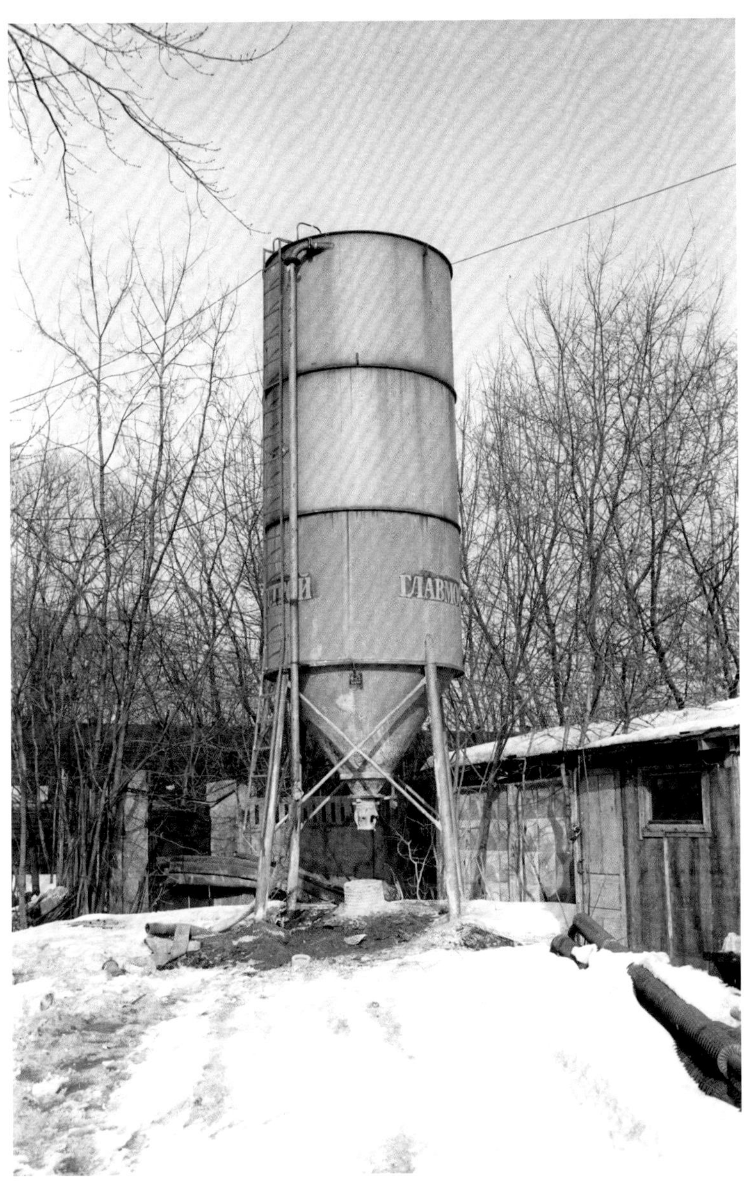

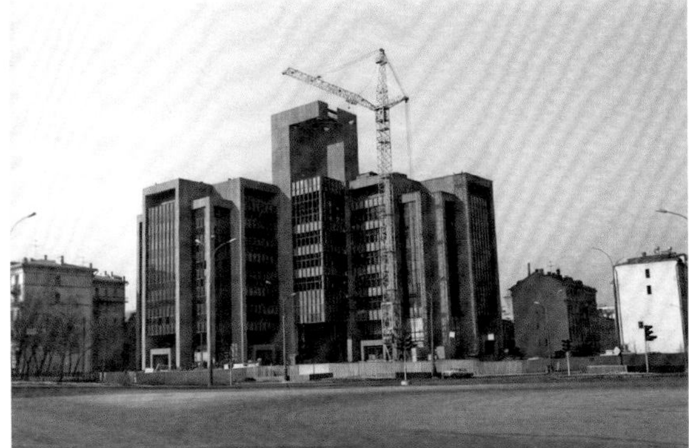

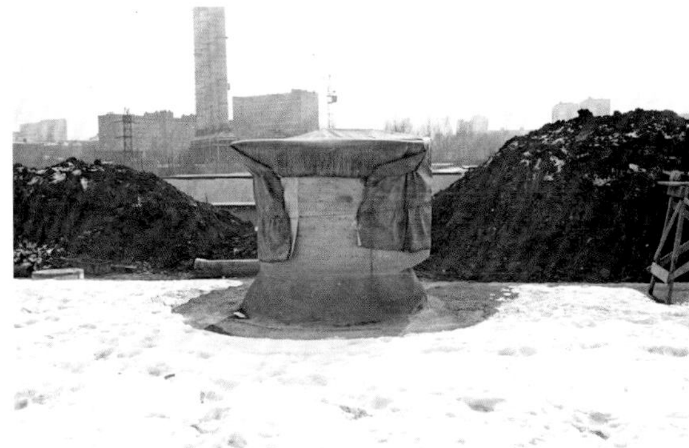

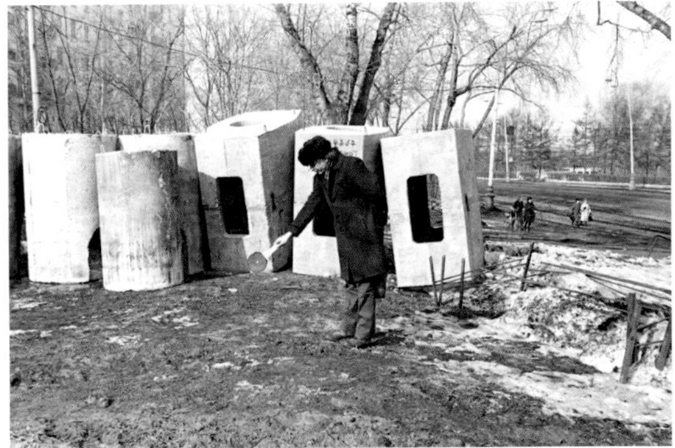

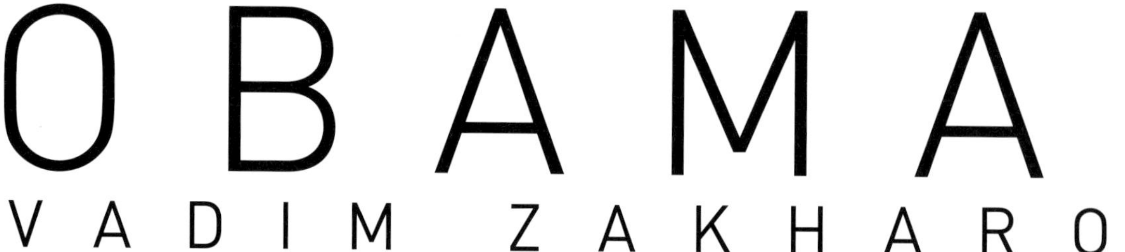

CREATION OF A TIME UNIT FOR DEAD ZONE 2012
PRE-ACTION INSTALLATION: 13 CUCKOO CLOCKS, SOIL,
UNDERGROUND CAMERA, MONITOR, MAP
COURTESY THE ARTIST

The action is to take place on a territory extended between Frankfurt (Oder)/ Slubice and Guben/ Gubin, both Germany and Poland, as depicted on the map in the corridor of the exhibition. On each of the circles centers a cuckoo clock will be buried. The clocks will work until the first set of batteries expires. In advance a single cuckoo clock was buried in the courtyard of the Casa dei Tre Oci, which is the first one set in motion and the only one set for Universal Co-ordinated Time. The other clocks are delayed by the time it took the authors to set them in motion one after the other, twelve times re-starting to count and this way creating a duration of delay which will be applied to dead zone as a time unit.

This is not an alternative or a local model, but a model built on other principles of description and understanding. The artists work on the border between architectural forms and their perception through the lens of culture. Small and detailed architecture, cuckoo clocks have been integrated into the Russian cultural code and are perceived as a Russian artifact, but in fact are adopted elements from Bavarian crafts.

NBERLIN

NIKLAS NITSCHKE

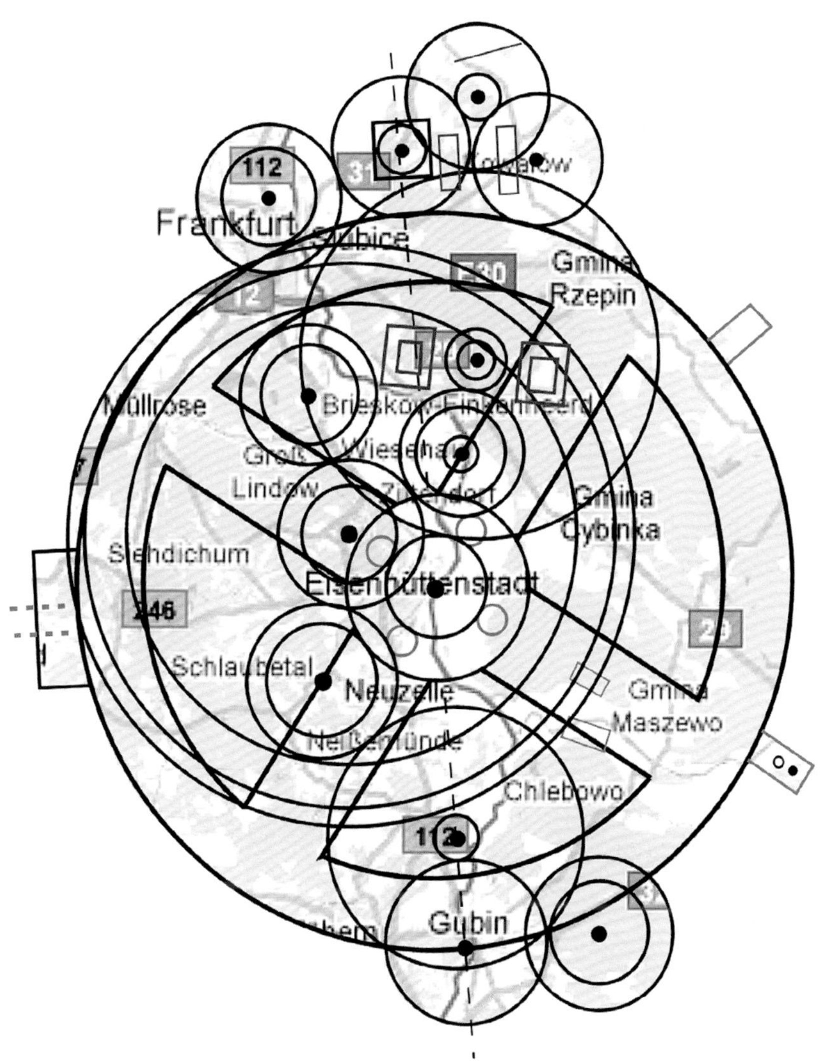

DMITRY

POETRYGRAMS 1970-1980S
TYPESCRIPT ON PAPER
COURTESY THE ARTIST

The series of *Poetrygrams*, like much of Prigov's works, were born from the Soviet climate of censor-ship surrounding cultural production. Particularly inspired by *samizdat* publishing, in which forbidden texts were copied using typewriters and distributed by hand, Prigov began creating these typewritten works on paper that turned propagandistic language into concrete poetry. As reminders of the primacy of language in Soviet mass culture, these works suggest a reflection on the meaning of the words themselves – what they can communicate or obscure.

In these examples of visual poetry, where the text is organized not only internally, but also spatially, the words became endlessly repeatable units suggesting different compositions. The conceptual and formal repetitiveness of the elements invite the viewer to compare the fragile architecture of these works with the plans of Soviet social architecture (in which the artist was also living), based on the repetition of prefabricated modules and conceived in the same period of time.

P R I G O V

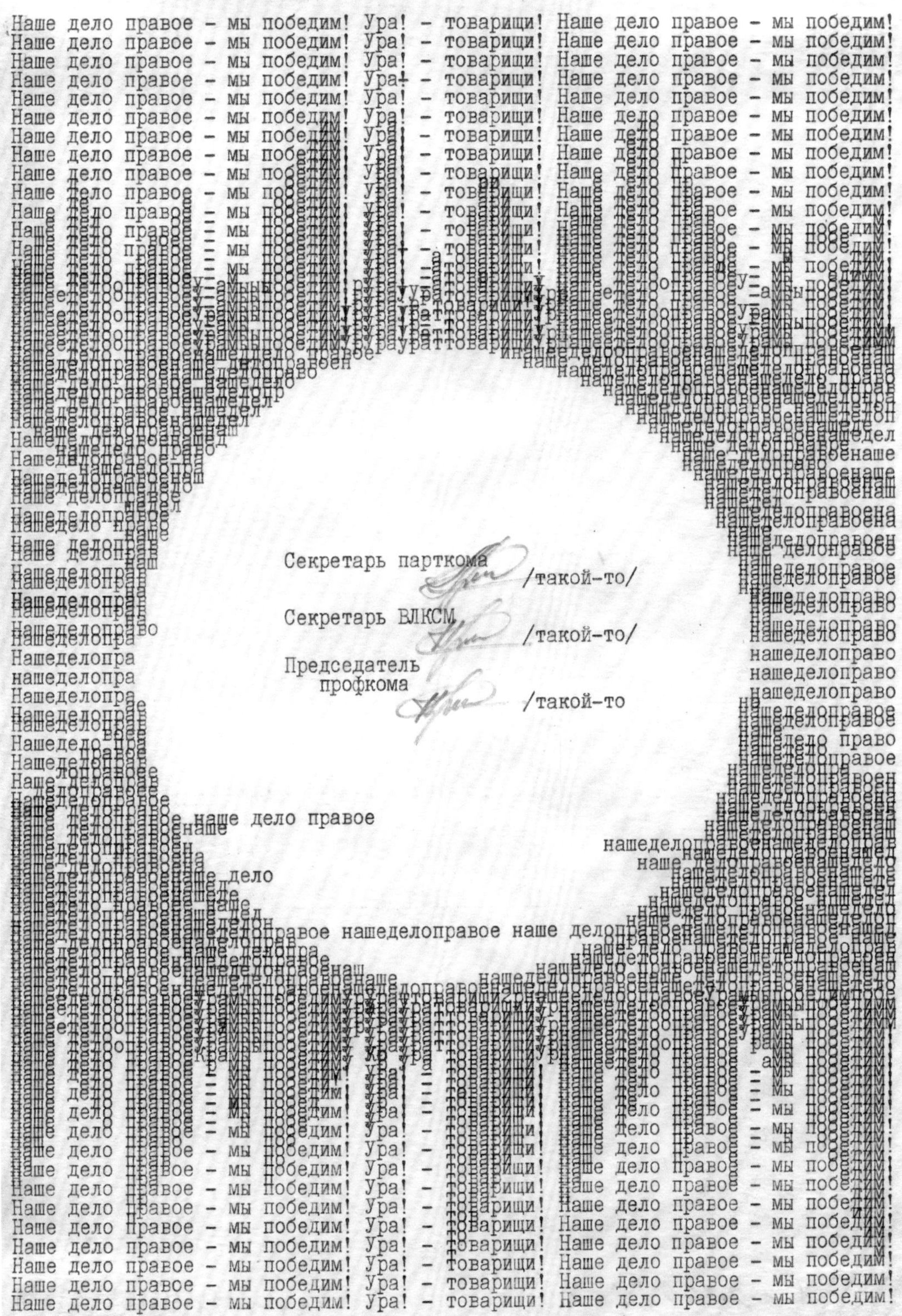

Наше дело правое – мы победим! Ура! – товарищи! Наше дело правое – мы победим!
Секретарь парткома /такой-то/
Секретарь ВЛКСМ /такой-то/
Председатель профкома /такой-то
наше дело правое
наше дело
наше дело правое нашеделоправое наше делоправое
Наше дело правое – мы победим! Ура! – товарищи! Наше дело правое – мы победим!

PROJECTS OF RESIDENTI[A] FOR MICROR[AYONS]

ORIGINAL BLUEPRINT, INK ON TRACING PAPER
COURTESY PRIVATE COLLECTIONS, MOSCOW

In 1954, Nikita Khrushchev started a revolutionary housing program. In a speech that he had directed to construction workers, he laid out very clear guidelines for the whole construction sector.

The ideas in the speech had appeared before in various texts and manifestos of modern architecture: simple and cheap prefabricated buildings, scales and distances deriving from human dimensions, replacement of pretentious details with honest simplicity. What was new in Khrushchev's approach was a very clear vision of how to introduce these ideas on a massive scale. He used all the power of the centralized Soviet state to consolidate construction enterprises and prepare a handful of models that could be cheaply manufactured anywhere. He managed to fully standardize, optimize, and industrialize the construction process.

A *microrayon* – a housing unit for around 100.000 people – was an almost perfect product of the machine era; the architect's role was limited to composing an abstract plan from ready-made buildings according to a set of strict parameters. From the point of view of the housing industry, it was the most optimal, rational, and efficient solution, probably the final stage of development of architecture based on rational, modernist thinking. The scale of this housing program was huge. It is enough to say that the new *microrayon* landscape of vast empty spaces filled with abstract repetitive objects covered around 90% of the area of Moscow.

KUBA SNOPEK

PREFABRICATED
L BUILDINGS
AYON 1981-1986

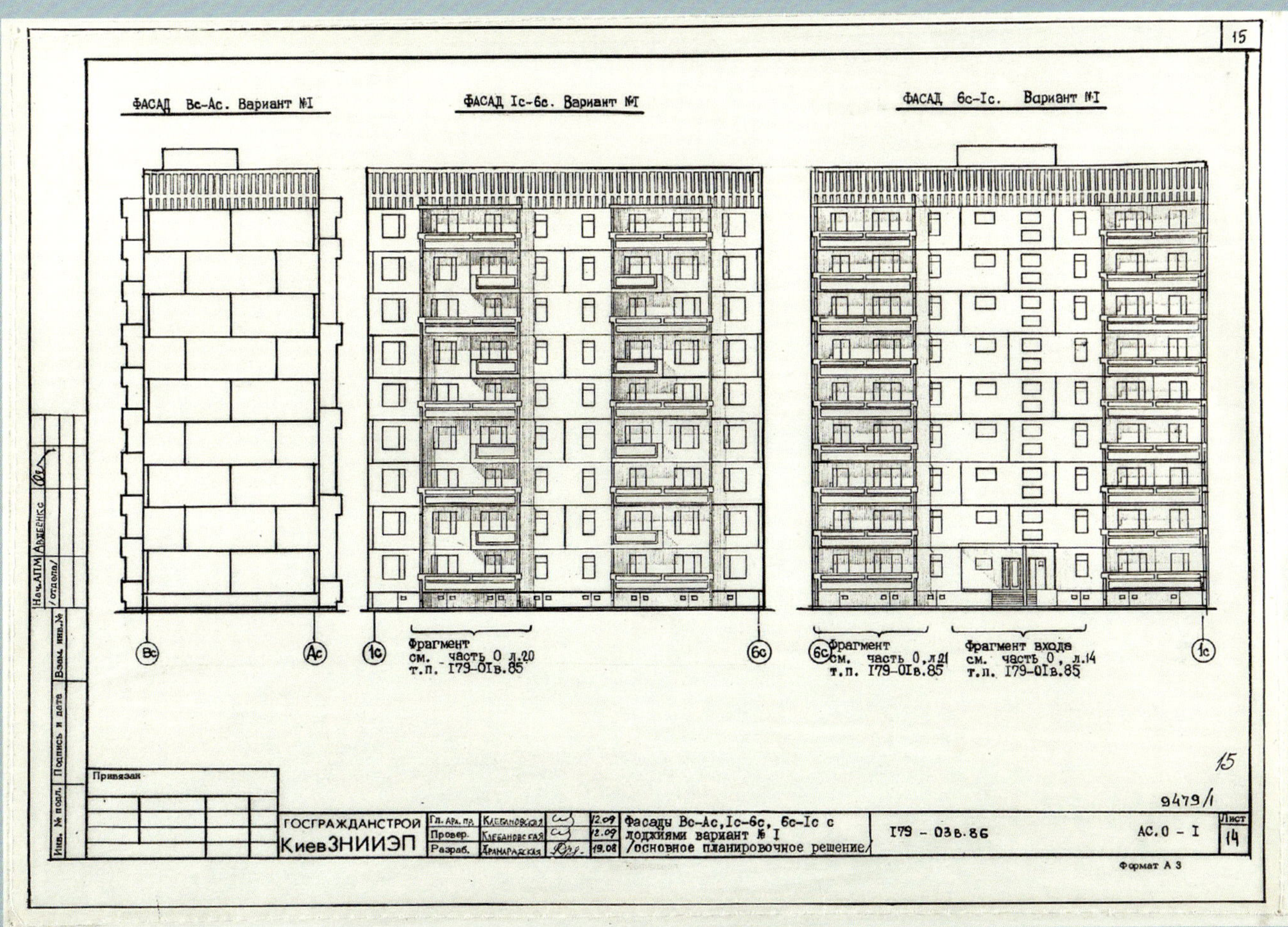

PROJECTS
CITY (L

CITY MASTER PLAN, CITY SQUARE, MONUMENT
ARCHITECT: STANISLAV BELOV 1970-1980S

ARCHIVAL MATERIALS
COURTESY PRIVATE COLLECTIONS, MOSCOW

Baikonur, a now Kazakh city and a site of the world's largest cosmodrome, was one of the dozens of closed cities of the Soviet Union that were built from scratch around secret research or manufacturing centres. Built in vast steppes according to a master plan by S.I. Belov, the city can stand as an example of the Soviet version of modernism with its strict spatial and functional hierarchy. Originally planned for a population of 100.000 but never fully realised, the city was split into four districts with each of them farther divided into a *microrayon* to achieve what was believed to be an ideal neighborhood size with all the daily services provided. The rationalist urban dogma of the time strictly defined every distance or size requirement within the neighborhood and outside of it and thus division can easily be read in the master plan with each of the functional zones clearly established in an axial monumentality of the design. Although the city centre by Belov has stayed on paper, the Korolev Square and Avenue presented in the exhibition stand as an example of what the finished design aimed for.
BLAZEJ CZUBA

OR BAIKONUR
ENINSK)

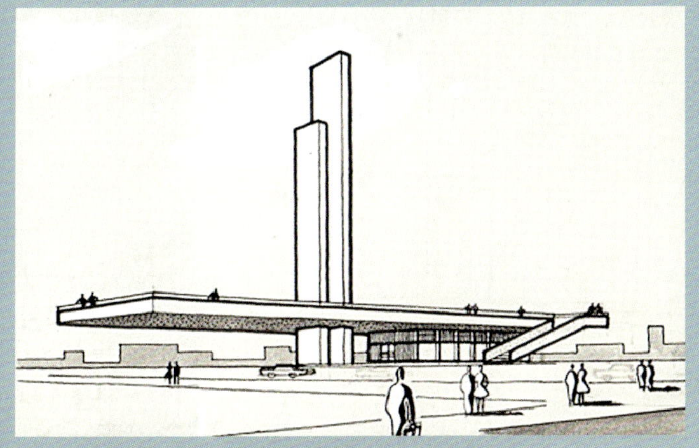

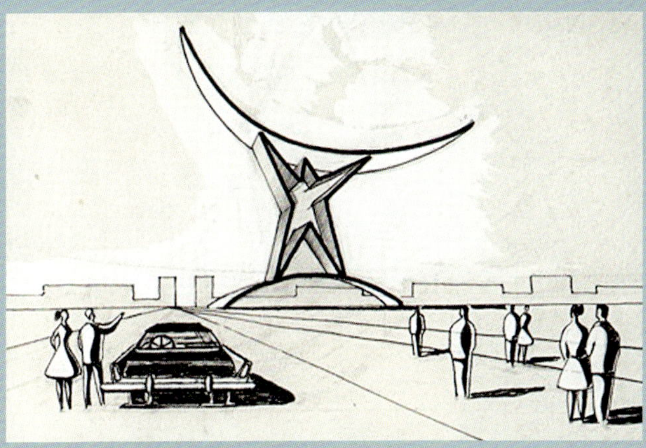

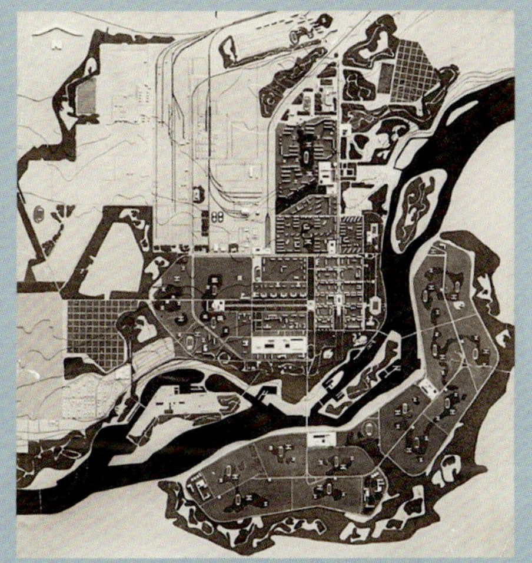

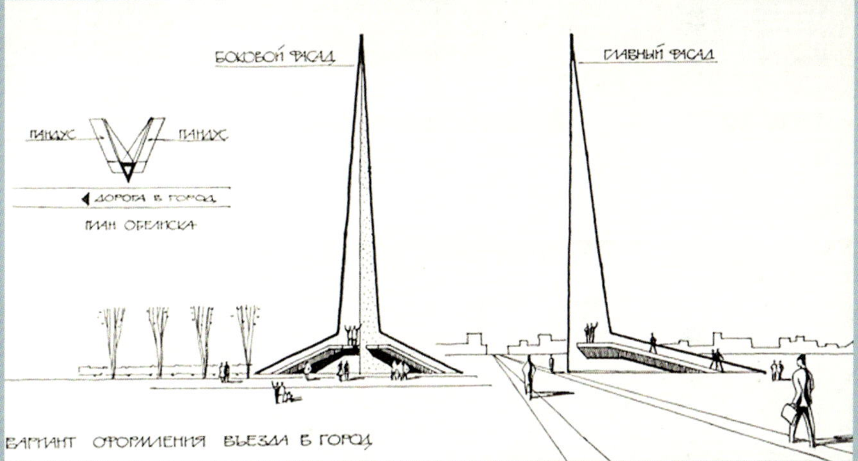

Y U R I

FROM THE SERIES **NORTH CHERTANOVO** 2001
6 PHOTOGRAPHS, PIGMENT PRINT
COURTESY THE ARTIST

North Chertanovo, depicted in Yuri Palmin's photos, is a very special residential neighborhood, a geometric utopia of Soviet planners, built in the 1970s with the latest technology then available. With its centralized program of housing, Chertanovo was a visionary experiment, proposing a series of improvements, both inside the apartments and in the spaces between buildings.

The buildings and objects in Palmin's photographs stand lonely in a deserted space, surrounded by ruins and objects that have lost their functionality. Huge residential buildings standing between empty staircases and ramps resemble the ruins of an ancient, long-gone civilization: despite Chertanovo's young age, it has already died spiritually due to the disappearance of the state, society and political system that created it.

Palmin's photographs show a certain shift in the perception of a *microrayons*, a change in its reputation. After decades of public criticism of this architecture, its Spartan aesthetics and dwellings, Palmin reveals its minimalist, timeless beauty. In these photographs, there is no focus on social problems or the *microrayons*'s being cold and inhumane; instead, Chertanovo is looked at with a dose of objectivity and curiosity and is portrayed in a neutral, almost scientific, way.

PALMIN

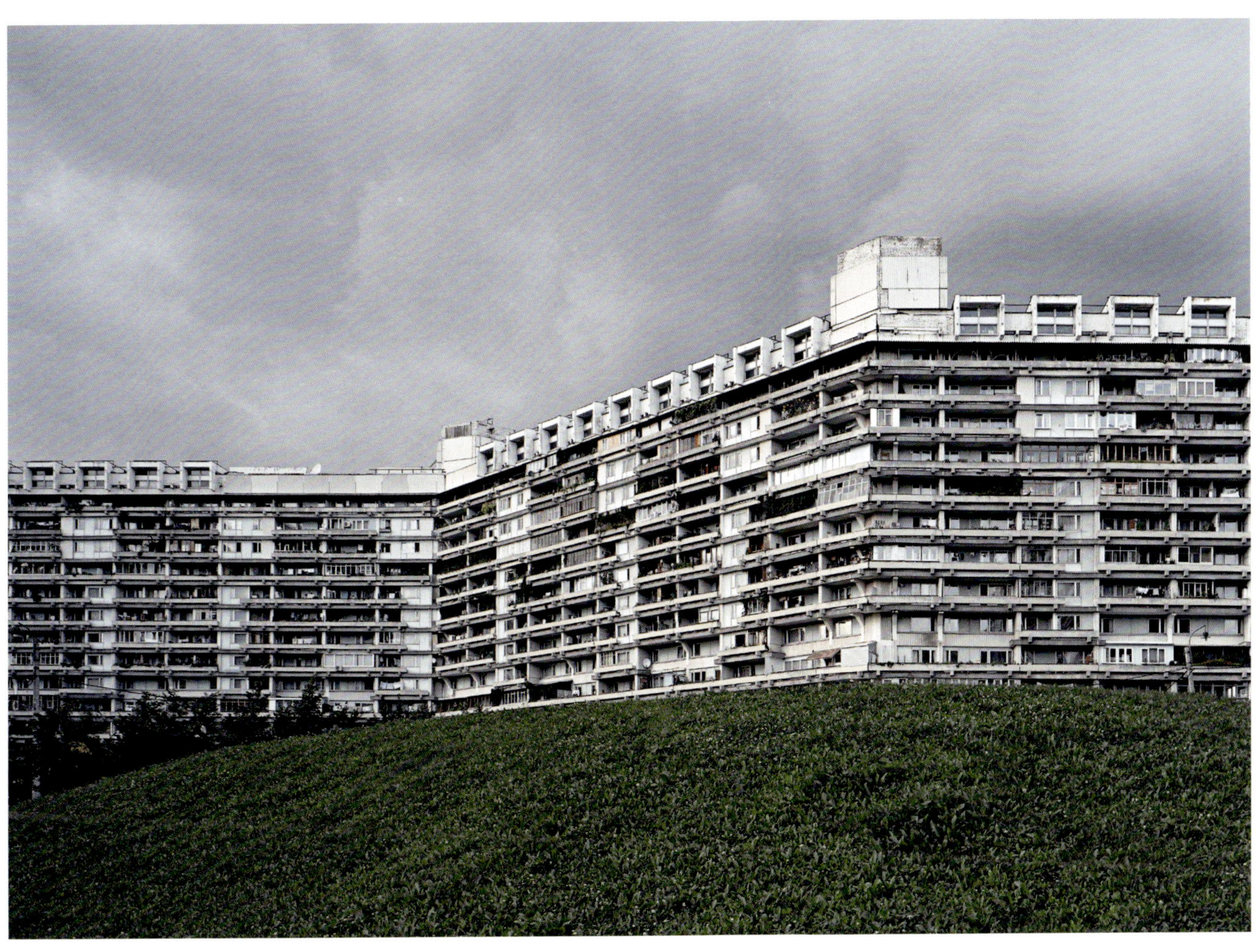

STANISLA

KT-A (PAYPHONE) 2012
OUTDOORS INSTALLATION, METAL
COURTESY THE ARTIST

KT-A series telephone booths are an indispensable element and an infrastructure unit of the *microrayons*, the residential district of the Soviet city. Twenty years after the fall of the Soviet Union, they have vanished from the urban landscape. The new project by Stanislav Shuripa is a life-sized reconstruction of these old telephone booths. The artist intends to recall how the public space was once organized in a time in which not every family had a phone or had to share one with neighbors; a booth could be regarded as the only place for a private telephone conversation, even though it was outside the home in a public space. At the same time, the territory around the chains of these cabins became a true, and perhaps the most intense, public space, where pivotal moments in life took place, as well as a notebook, as ever-more-important phone numbers were scratched into the booths. These numbers stayed on the surface even longer than the memory could retain the faces of the people to whom they belonged.

The main detail that defines the function of the booth – the telephone itself – is absent. People that stand inside two different booths can see each other and talk. If they look at the row of booths from the outside, they will see a tunnel of light. The work bears the traits of locality and autobiography, but concerns things and attitudes relevant to many people who were living in a Soviet city. Shuripa, artist, curator and writer, often deals with the idea of organization of urban and public space.

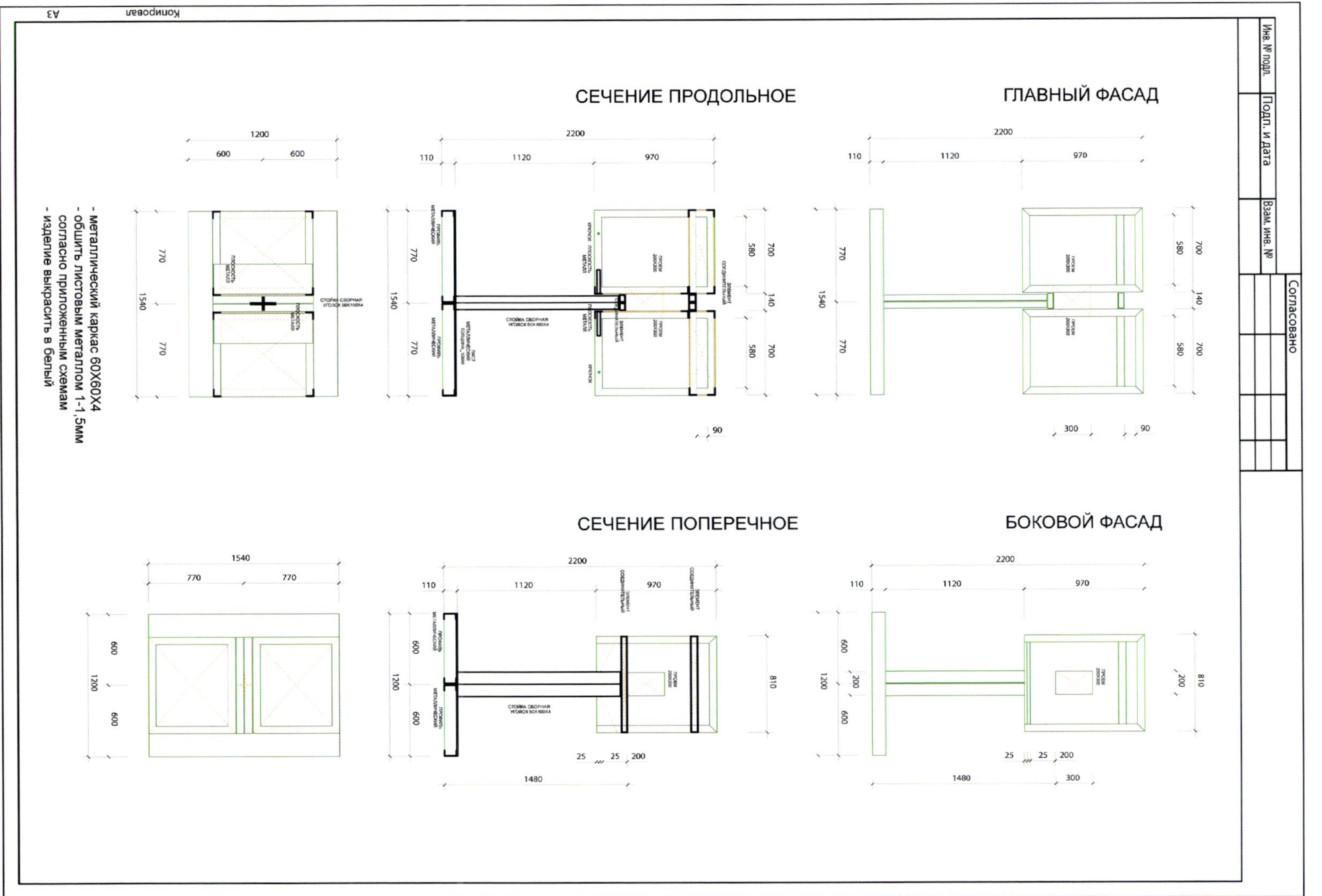

СЕЧЕНИЕ ПРОДОЛЬНОЕ
ГЛАВНЫЙ ФАСАД
СЕЧЕНИЕ ПОПЕРЕЧНОЕ
БОКОВОЙ ФАСАД
ПРОЕМ 200X300
ЭЛЕМЕНТ СОЕДИНИТЕЛЬНЫЙ
КРЮЧОК
ПЛОСКОСТЬ МЕТАЛЛ
СТОЙКА СБОРНАЯ УГОЛОК 50X50X4
ЛИСТ МЕТАЛЛИЧЕСКИЙ ТОЛЩИНА 10ММ
ПРОФИЛЬ МЕТАЛЛИЧЕСКИЙ
1200
600 600
770 770
1540
2200
110 1120 970
770 770
1540
700 580 140 580 700
90
2200
110 1120 970
770 770
1540
700 580 140 580 700
300 90
1540
770 770
600 1200 600
2200
110 1120 970
600 600
810
25 25 200
1480
2200
110 1120 970
600 600
200 810
25 25 200
1480 300
- металлический каркас 60X60X4
- обшить листовым металлом 1-1,5мм
  согласно приложенным схемам
- изделие выкрасить в белый
Инв. № подл.
Подп. и дата
Взам. инв. №
Согласовано
Копировал
A3

ALEXANDF

ON THE SLEEPING ARRANGEMENTS IN THE SIXTH FIVE-YEAR PLAN 2010-2012
INSTALLATION:
UNTITLED, 2012, DYPTICH, ACRYLIC ON CANVAS. 190 × 150 CM EACH
NORMS, 2012, SERIES OF 9 ELEMENTS, ACRYLIC AND RICE PAPER ON
CANVAS. 65 × 102 CM, 70 × 88 CM, 56 × 70 CM, 39 × 42 CM (3 ELEMENTS),
33 × 42 CM (3 ELEMENTS)
THERE WERE PICTURES HANGING HERE, 2010, FROM WALLS SERIES,
ACRYLIC AND RICE PAPER ON CANVAS. 130 × 110 CM
COURTESY GAZPROMBANK COLLECTION, MOSCOW

The installation consists of paintings of various sizes depicting plans of apartments in social housing projects, a wall, and a World Map.
In 1955, the Communist Party adopted the resolution *On the Elimination of Excess in Design and Construction.* The task set for architects was development of standardized projects and standardized designs, dramatically reducing the cost of housing and making it accessible to the working class. The goal of the project was that in 1980 every Soviet family would greet Communism in a separate apartment. Thus started the Sixth Five-Year Plan (1956-1960), marking the beginning of mass construction of block *khrushchevka* houses.
The map of the world soars up under the unforgiving ratio of living conditions that have been planned down to the centimeter. If the sleeping arrangement has been devised correctly, the Soviet schoolchild, upon falling asleep in any of the ten time zones of the wide country, sees this map on the wall before him. It hangs in the bedroom as a reminder of the great conquests of the socialist motherland and of victories yet to come on Earth and in space. Sleep and the painting gradually blur the registers of time and space. Plans, maps and other symbols – conventional images devoid of meaning – take on an entirely new tonality when brought to the canvas by the brush. The painting process instills new life into dead signs. It is an attempt to overcome the closed parochialism of artistic, social or scientific systems, an attempt to return to the subjective whole of practical experience. Among the external objects of contemplation is a bare wall showing only the shadows of things, or geometrically composed pictures of walls that look so much like floor plans. All these rhyming rectangles of the imagined past/future serve as a pretext for a very painterly metaphysics – a metaphysics of the single present, manifesting as a continuum of plastic modulations and constituting the central theme of this work devoted entirely to vision. It lives in the attention of the artist's eyes and congeals in words and interpretations.

PAPERNO

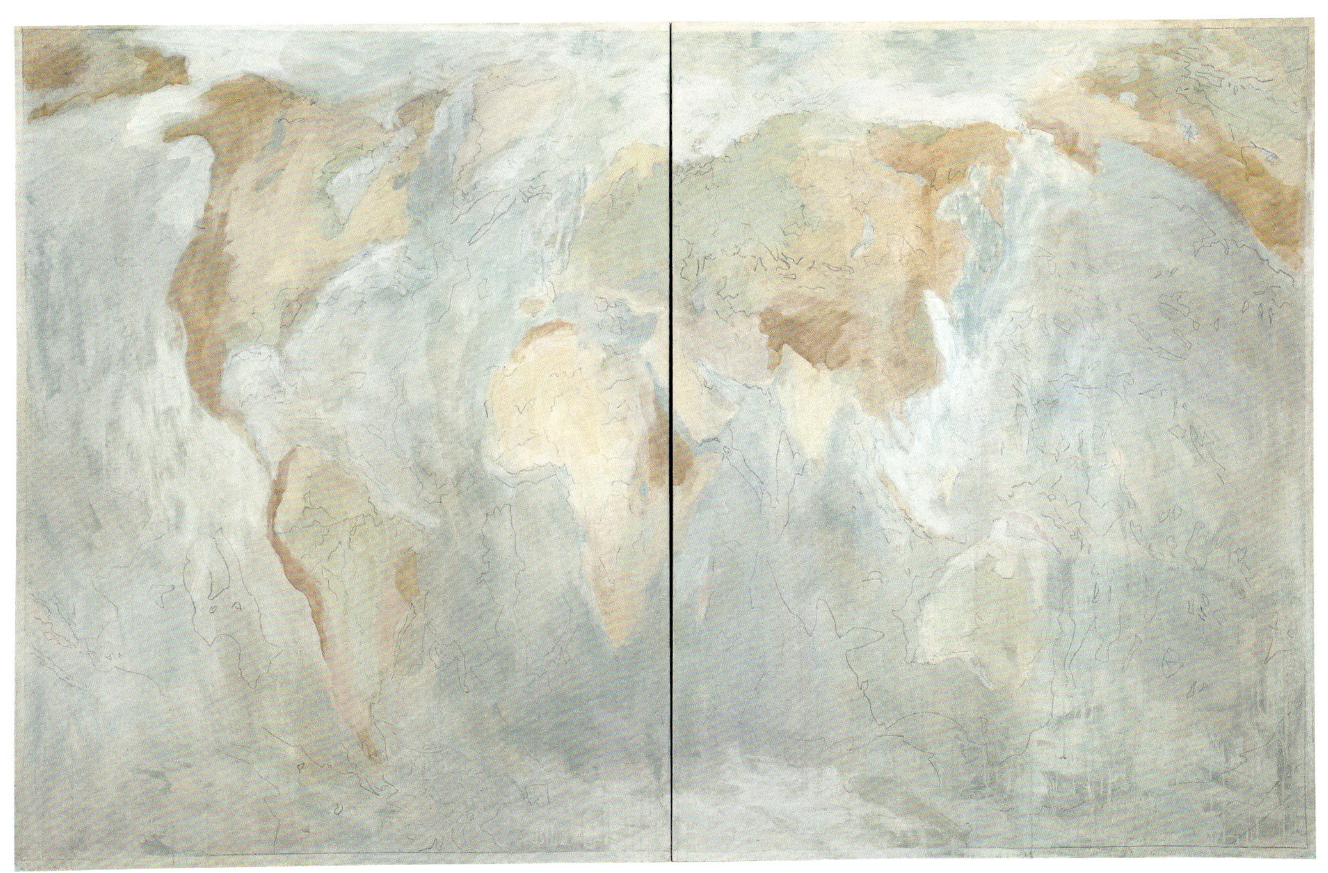

ALEXEY

EQUALITY 2012
WOOD, ACRYLIC
21 × 44 × 32 CM
COURTESY THE ARTIST

Dushkin's object *Equality* presents a deceptively ordinary piece of everyday furniture – a bed. In the set of classification of items of furniture, a bed is a rather intimate object. Subtly violating its configuration, Dushkin contorts the bed, bringing a quiet object to a nightmare scream. Purging the bed of all the rules of design, Dushkin constructs it as if it were a piece of furniture, but in reality moves it into the realm of the experiments of the Constructivists with their desire to rationally arrange daily life, into the forms of Soviet futurological design against the background of the violent discipline of Soviet daily life.
The First Five-Year Plan of Soviet Russia, which seemed an economic miracle to the world, inspired a great many architectural programs for arranging the new man's daily life, a mass-scale implementation of which could only take place in the Sixth Five-Year Plan with the creation of generic residential buildings and apartments. The organization of the spatial living environment was exposed by architects to a rigid division according to function, in which sleep was of very little interest, as it demands passivity and isolation from a person. It was, however, impossible to completely exclude it from consideration, because the number of people who were to sleep in one bed together determined the meters that were to be allotted.
The endlessly heightened idealistic eternal struggle of humanity to equality, to an egalitarian society had, as it were, become petrified in a deadlock in an irresolvable struggle between the private and the common, the individual and the collective. In the drowsing consciousness of the creator of a new world – a macabre form of equality – the dream is of equal, but different, builders of our present. The object *Equality* belongs to the series of works *The Limits of Reason*, which also investigates the currently important problem of total equality in conditions of multiculturalism and globalizaton. In the search for a balance between justice and equality, the socialist experiment gives a great deal of material for answer the question of which is more just – equality of opportunities, or equality of results?

DUSHKIN

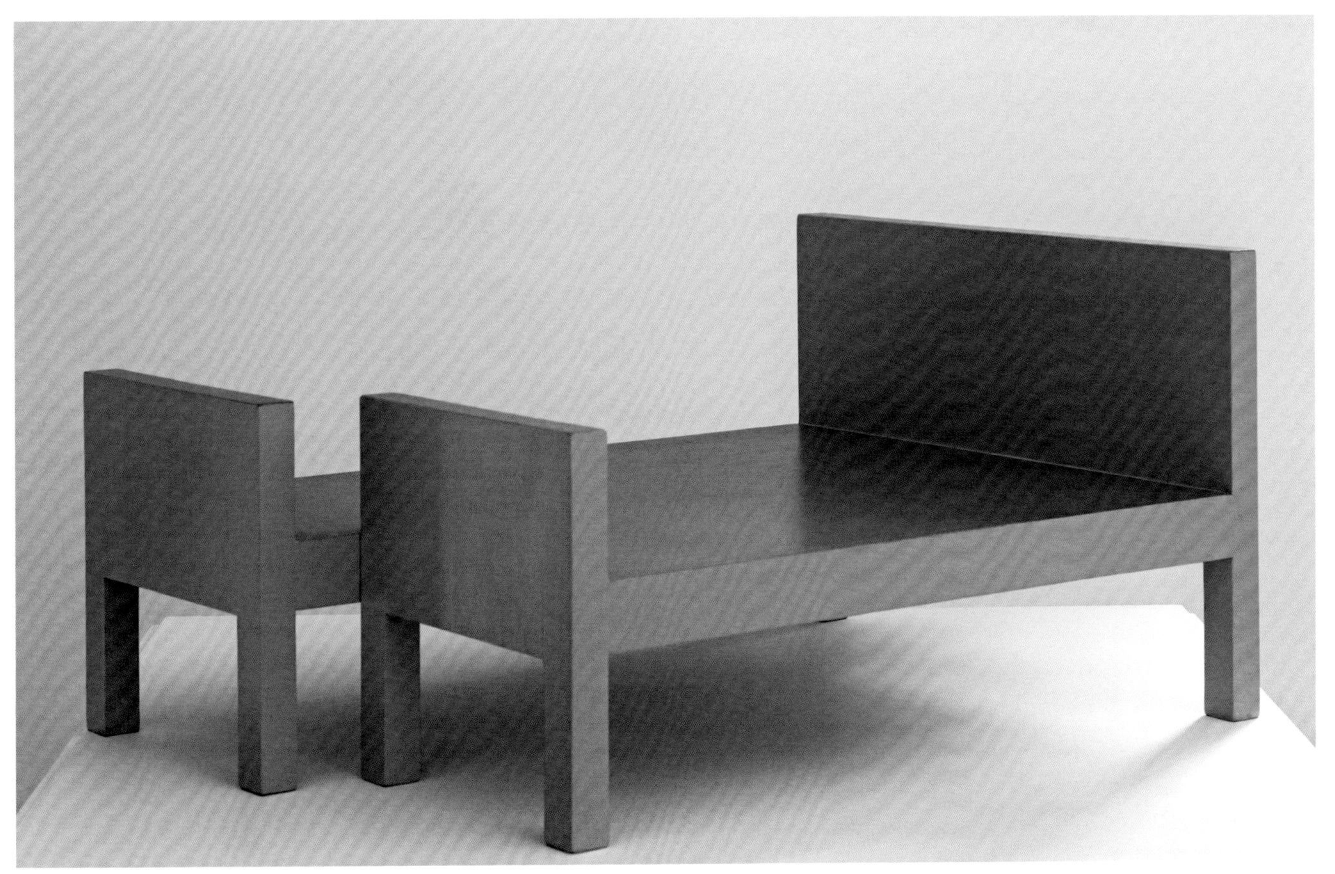

ALEXANDE

PLAYGROUND 2011-2012
OUTDOOR INSTALLATION, METAL
COURTESY THE ARTIST

Alexander Povzner's project *Playground* is a reconstruction of a small public space designed for children's play or physical exercise. This kind of playground was a common object in every Soviet courtyard, surrounded by typical apartment blocks.

The *Playground* in the exhibition is filled with dangerous objects that only recollect the real constructions of a playground. All of them are made from pieces of iron fittings, crude chains, and car tires and testify to the industrial nature of the city. At the same time, they lack functionality: the carousel never turns, the ladder never reaches the top and the sandbox is empty. They are disfigured, and some seem to exist in different dimensions.

The playground, another indispensable part of the city district, is a unit in reporting of municipal improvements. The configuration and the architecture stayed the same for many years, and is still the subject of standardized arrangements. The artist treats the playgrounds as the place of initial spatial education, the moment of physical contact between a child and a city. The standard set of behavioral patterns of citizens can be in fact decoded by the alphabet of the objects of the playground, which are usually esthetically and morally neglected by the municipal authorities.

Working in the ready-made tradition Povzner deforms the context of use of the objects and places them in the unusual situations. At the same time, he slightly distorts the ready-made nature of things with which he works, rather using urban space itself as a ready-made.

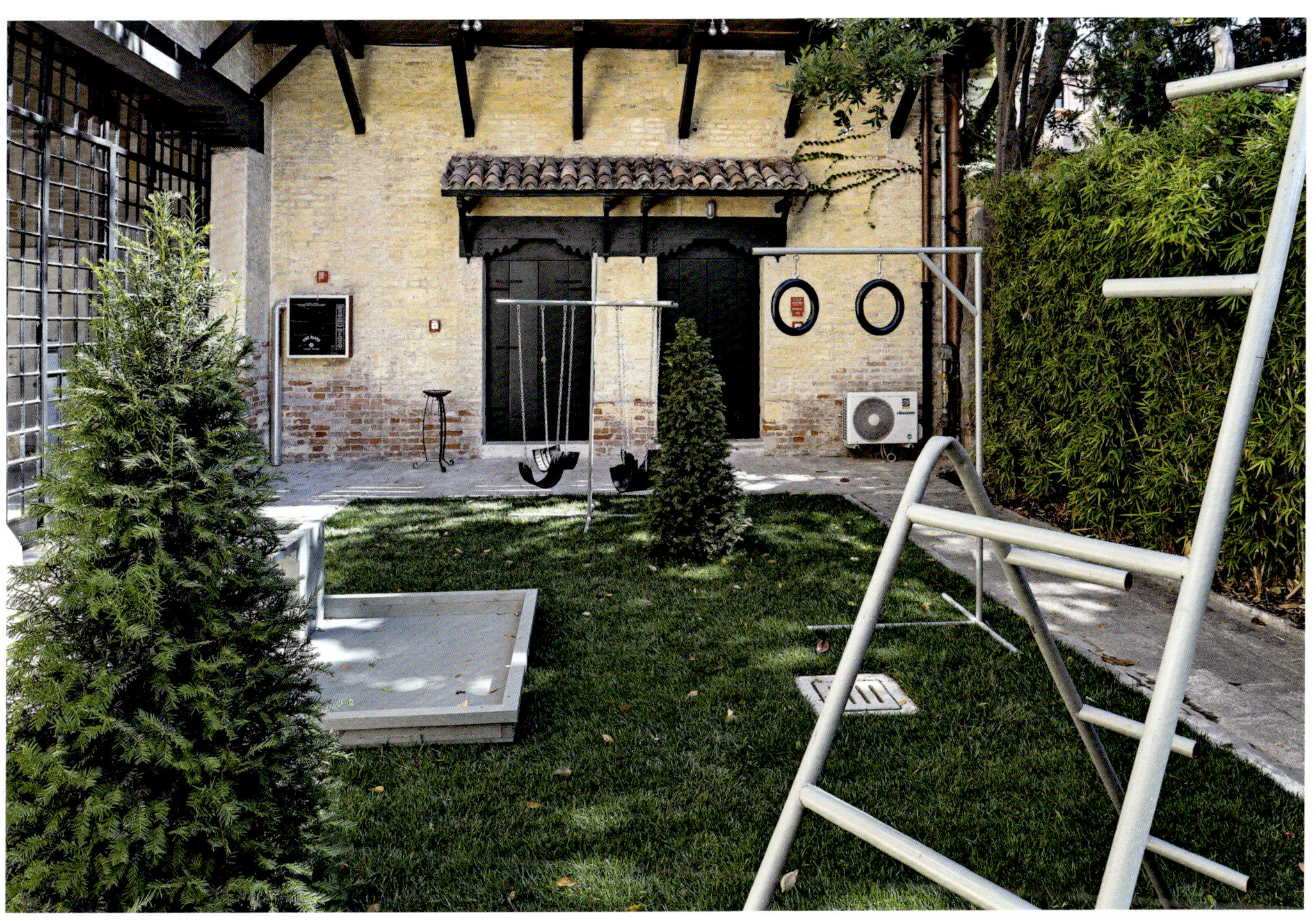

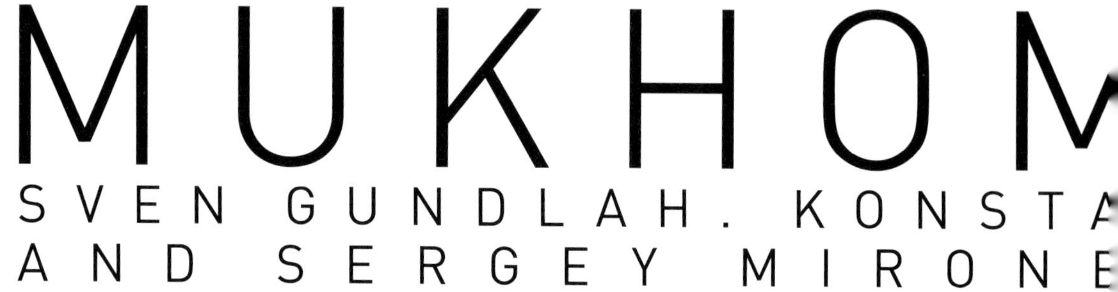

METRO 1979
ACTION DOCUMENTATION: FOLDED ALBUM, FELT PEN ON PAPER, BLACK
AND WHITE PHOTOGRAPHS, TYPESCRIPT ON PAPER
COURTESY THE ARTIST

On October 28, 1979, the members of the group Mukhomor went into the Moscow metro at the opening time of 6 o'clock in the morning and moved in every direction around the metro stations until 1 am in the night. Different pathways were coordinated according to a predetermined schedule that included the finding of other people at certain stations. The meetings with invited friends and accidentally encountered people were systematically noted on a checklist. During the action, the group members recorded an account of events and took photos.

One of the goals of this action was to master the metro as a space for living and, at the same time, to master it as a mythological space – after all, the Soviet metro, the most beautiful in the world, was created as a promise of a new, heavenly world. On the other hand, the Mukhomor group was always involved in a hidden polemic with Moscow's conceptual milieu, for which the zone of life always lays beyond the limits of social space.

The actions performed by the artists with a hermeneutic system of references seemed meaningless to the casual observer, who hardly could separate the performance from the surrounding background. The riding on the subway from opening to the closing, the mapping of the trajectories, the assigning of meetings at various stations, and the obsessive practice of "following" recall today's ritual of flash mobs in public spaces.

OR GROUP

N ZVEZDOCHETOV. VLADIMIR
KO. ALEKSEY KAMENSKY

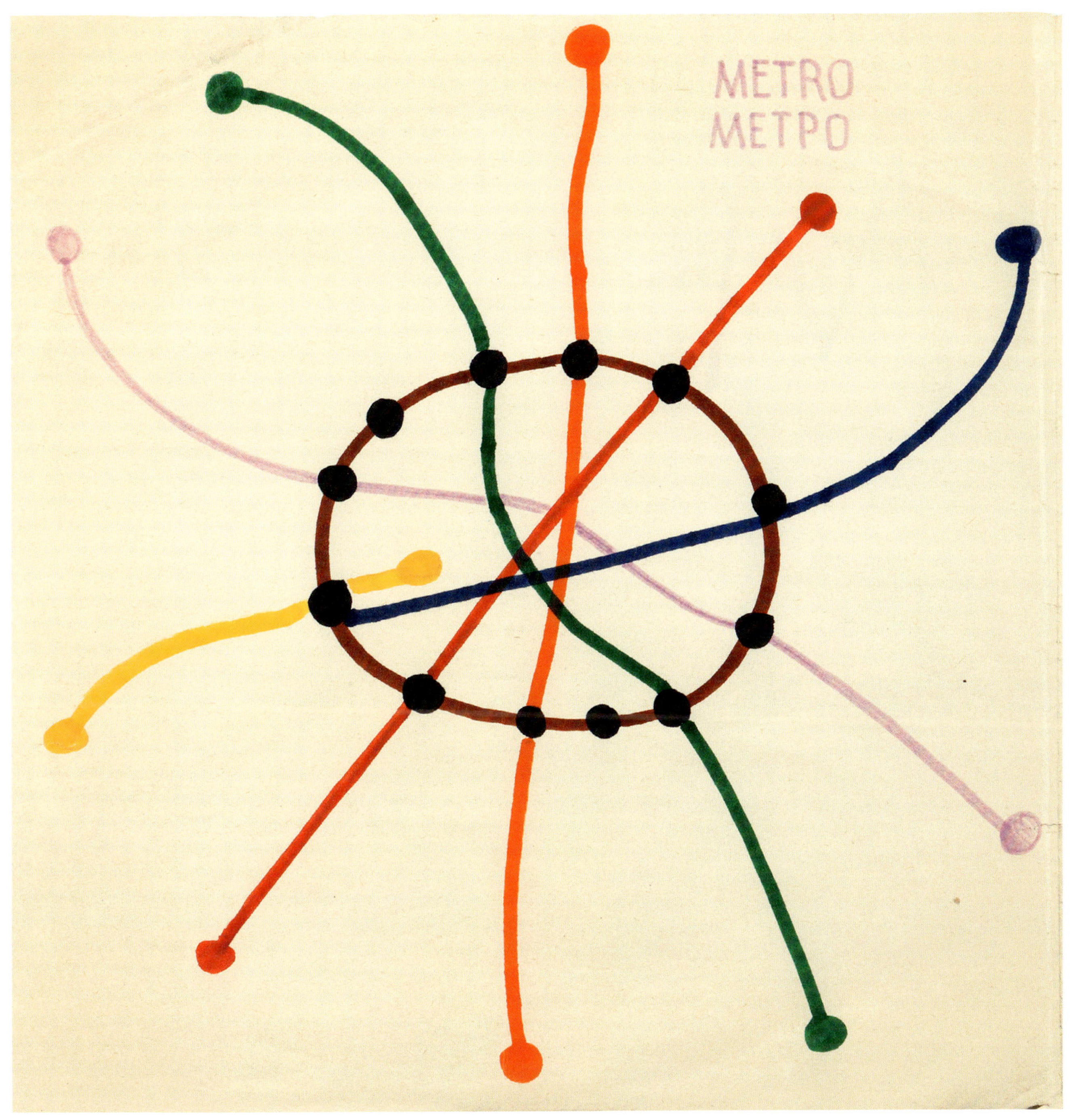

DOCUM F
OF ICI

PRODUCED BY CENTRAL STUDIO OF DOCUMENTARY FILMS

HIGH-RISE BUILDINGS BY GLAVMOSSTROI (CENTRAL MOSCOW CONSTRUCTION INSTITUTE), 1983
DIRECTOR VLADIMIR KISSELEV PART 1-3. 25'32"

NEW MICRORAYON OF MOSCOW (TROPAREVO, STROGINO, MARINO), 1981
DIRECTOR ANNA SOLOVIEVA 09'03"

MOSCOW STEPS AHEAD TO THE FUTURE. MOSCOW NEWSREEL, ISSUE #9. 1973
DIRECTOR VLADIMIR KHODYAKOV 09'32"

Propaganda movies are another abundant source of information about the previous epoch, showing us its idealized version, an image of the country Soviet leaders were aiming to create.

Architecture in these short movies is an excuse to talk about politics: to indoctrinate about the leading role of the Party or show the excellent state of affairs in the economy, which was beating the capitalist states. This is where the curious language comes from – as if architecture was another branch of industry. Buildings, and the city in general, are viewed mostly from the perspective of growing numbers – the best way to illustrate constant development and the superiority of the socialist state. These short films would rather speak about the scale, speed, and quantity than about composition, aesthetics, and facade materials. While the camera shows a vast construction site, voice of the speaker speaks of about the huge number of newly erected buildings. When the camera shows an enormous apartment-building plant filled with panel blocks, the background voice states that the conveyer belts never stop and building material is being provided 24 hours a day. This special atmosphere is directly linked to Khrushchev's speech from 1954, which had started the massive housing program, and the way he saw the role of architects. In the speech, Khrushchev demanded to see construction fully industrialized: rational, efficient, and very modern. His dream had been introduced and affected thinking about architecture. The consequences could be seen even in short propaganda movies.
KUBA SNOPEK

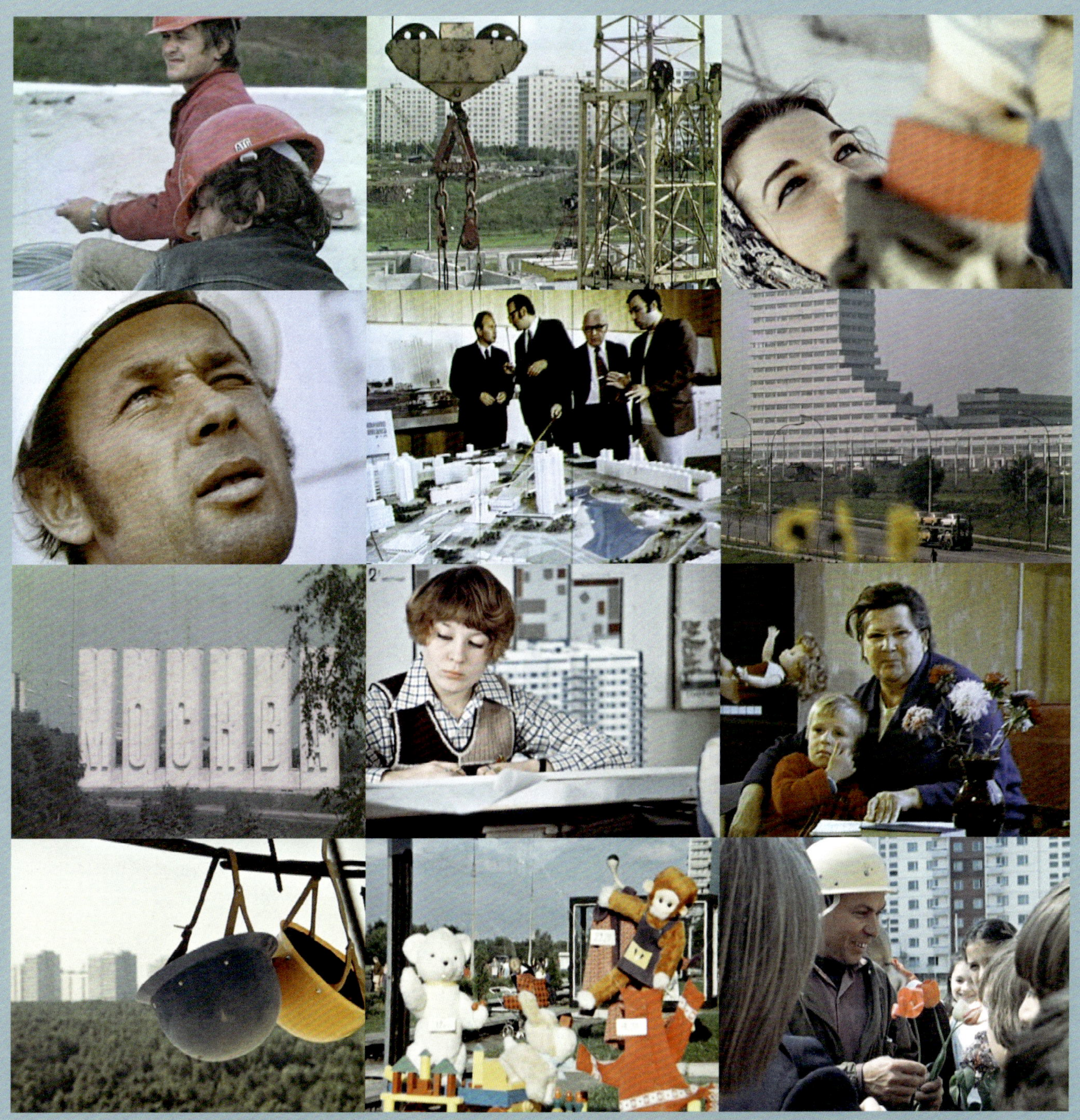
MOCKBA

WHERE IS YOUR FLAG, DUDE? 2010
INSTALLATION: METAL FLAGHOLDERS
COURTESY PRIVATE COLLECTION, MOSCOW

Flagholders are an object in urban architecture that serves as part of the language of state power in the city. Like the names of the streets, the flagpoles are places where political power is legitimated in the eyes of the masses.
In a postideological society, these objects lose their sense: deprived of content and historical meaning, their pervasive presence in the city becomes evidence of inertia that opposes real changes of the current political situation.
The wall installation consists of metal flagpoles assembled in different combinations. The artist isolates these signs from their context and tries to rebuild them in a new deconstructed form that aims at the loss of a preconceived structure.
Where is your flag, dude? is a provocative question and an invitation to spectators and to citizens to invent their own sign of power over the city and to play an active role in the formulation of a future that probably will not need to represent itself in concrete symbols or physical reminders.

A RYABOVA

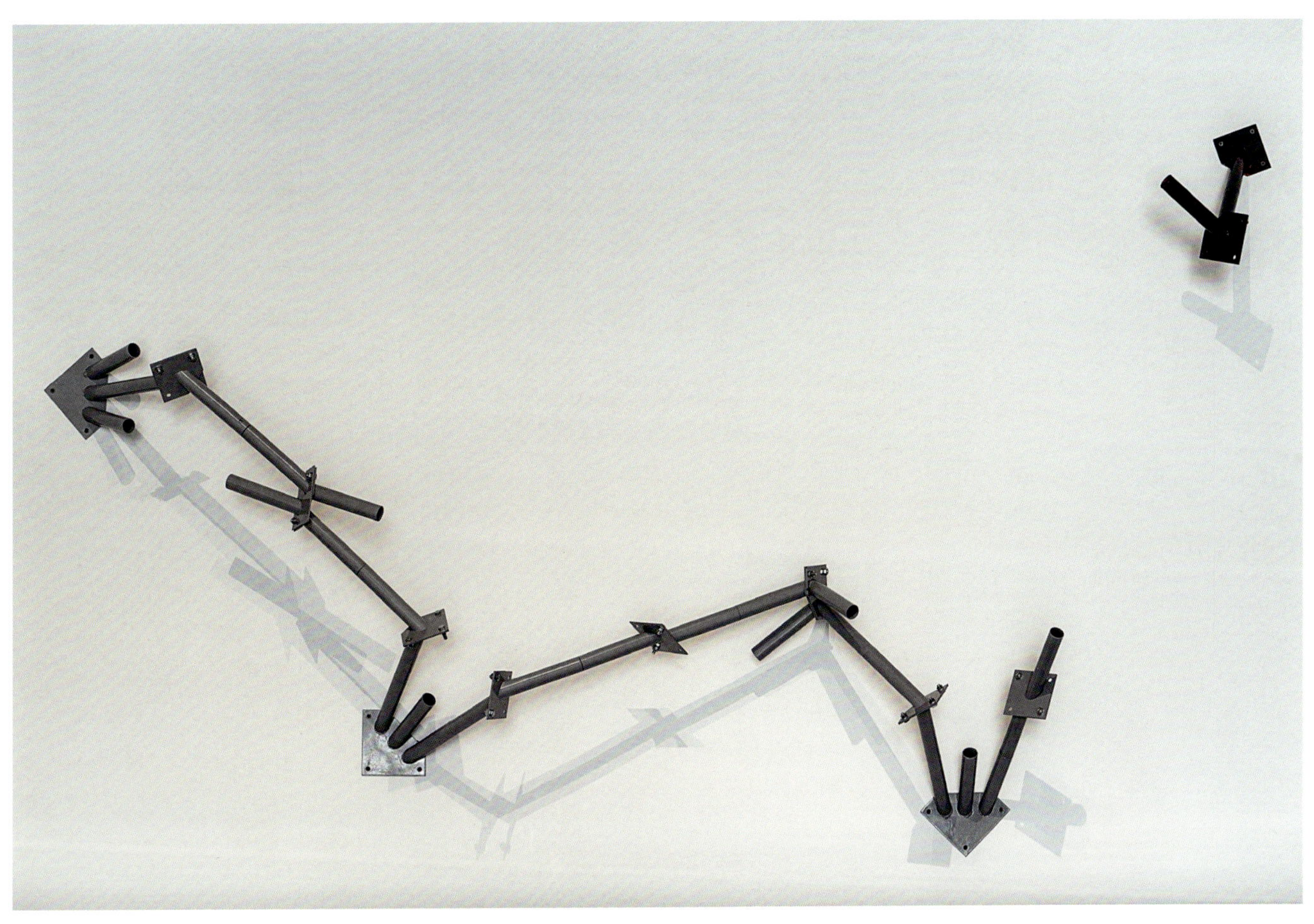

DAVID TE

FROM THE SERIES SCALE 2008-2012
DRAWINGS PRINTED ON CANVAS
COURTESY PRIVATE COLLECTION, GAZPROMBANK COLLECTION, MOSCOW
AND THE ARTIST

Since his first experiences with the Radek Community David Ter-Oganyan engaged in rebellion and interference in areas dominated by power. The three canvases here presented by the author are part of the on-going series of works called *Scale*. Small and quickly done drawings of public manifestations and urban riots sketched in an everyday notebook become large printed canvases.
The complex scenes of fights represented on canvas appear on closer examination to resemble notes made in a notebook. The tiny sketches of genre scenes, reproduced in a magnified scale, become a heavy, oppressive image of violence. The notebook's grid remains visible and plays the role of a line of division, an abstract indicator of scale. The transformation in scale is the artistic touch necessary for the image to become stamped with authenticity.
The artist tries to delimitate and measure the space of control (or non-control) of freedom. The discontinuity between scales, times, the original and the copy seems to embody the logic of the speed of history and the politics of contemporary society.
The artist embodies the paranoia that determines the general consciousness of the public before such things as an invisible enemy, terrorism, war, antiglobalism and the critique of capitalism. These subjects have been returned to for years obsessively in Ter-Oganyan's works in many different ways as a constant syndrome of our times.

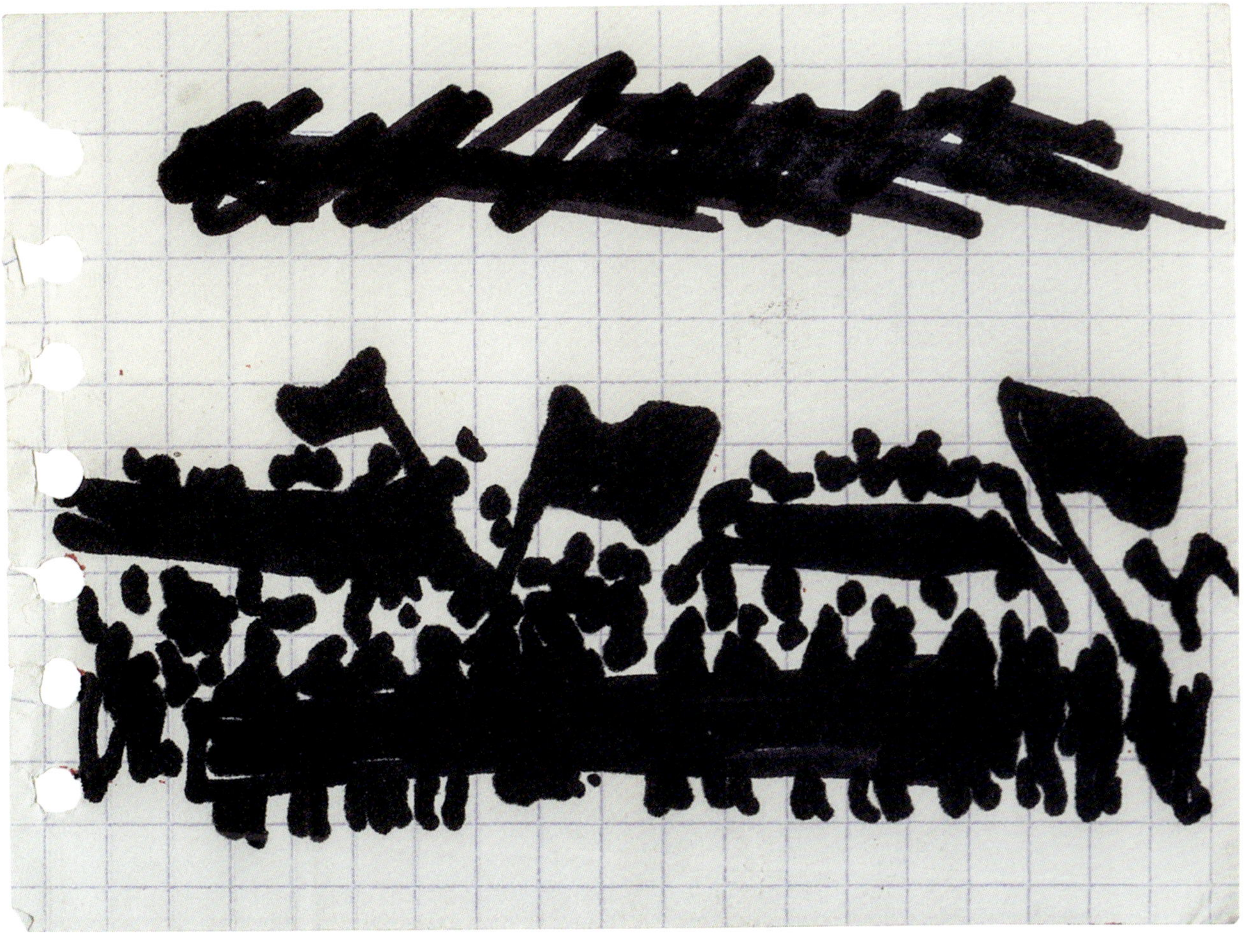

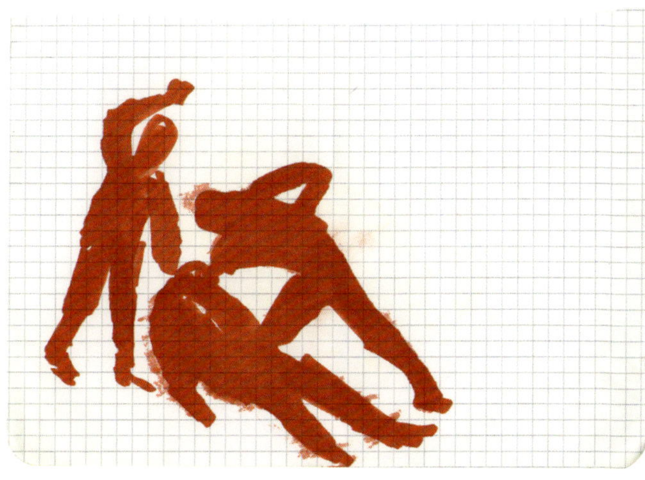

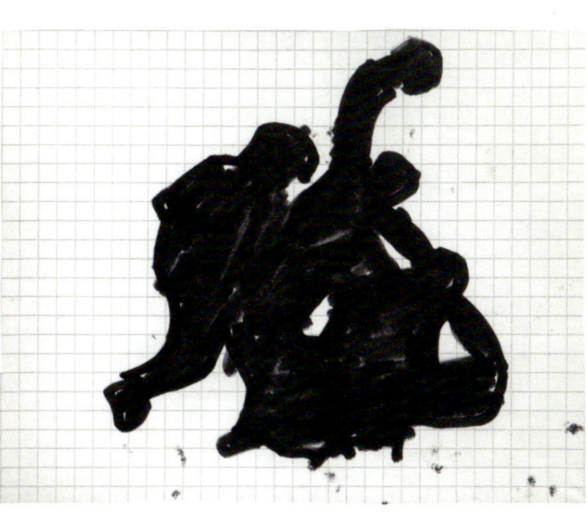

IVAN BRAZHKIN. ALEX RYABOVA. VLADISL SPIVAKOV. TZUCHIE

PROBLEM BOOK 2012
PUBLICATION CONCEIVED BY THE ARTISTS, PUBLISHED IN VENICE, ITALY,
AUGUST 2012

Problem Book is a booklet with mathematical exercises concerning current political events and the general political situation in Russian cities made by a group of artists, architects, and sociologists. The simple form of a secondary-school mathematical problem becomes a tool for the investigation of a range of contradictions faced by the residents of a certain territory, city, area, street, etc. These clashes and conflicts become aggravated in a situation of open confrontation between the government and citizens: the city turns into a territory of struggle, where the authorities have the advantage of force. The exercises try to scientifically prove the absurdity of the circumstances of the socio-political situation and ask for active involvement of the spectator by stimulating his practice of thinking. If mathematics has often been used for the managerial functions of the state and capital, this work proposes the use of mathematics as a tool of emancipation. This exercise booklet is also intended to be the basis for elaboration of experimental classes in social studies with middle-school students.
After a period of total individualization in art, a new generation of collectives is starting to appear on the Russian art scene. As in the tradition of collectives, the borders of this heterogeneous workgroup are undefined and continuously change, testing the limits and the potential of interdisciplinary collaboration.

IDR BURLAKA. ANASTASIA
SHAPOVALOV. MAXIM
THO. DMITRY VOROBYEV

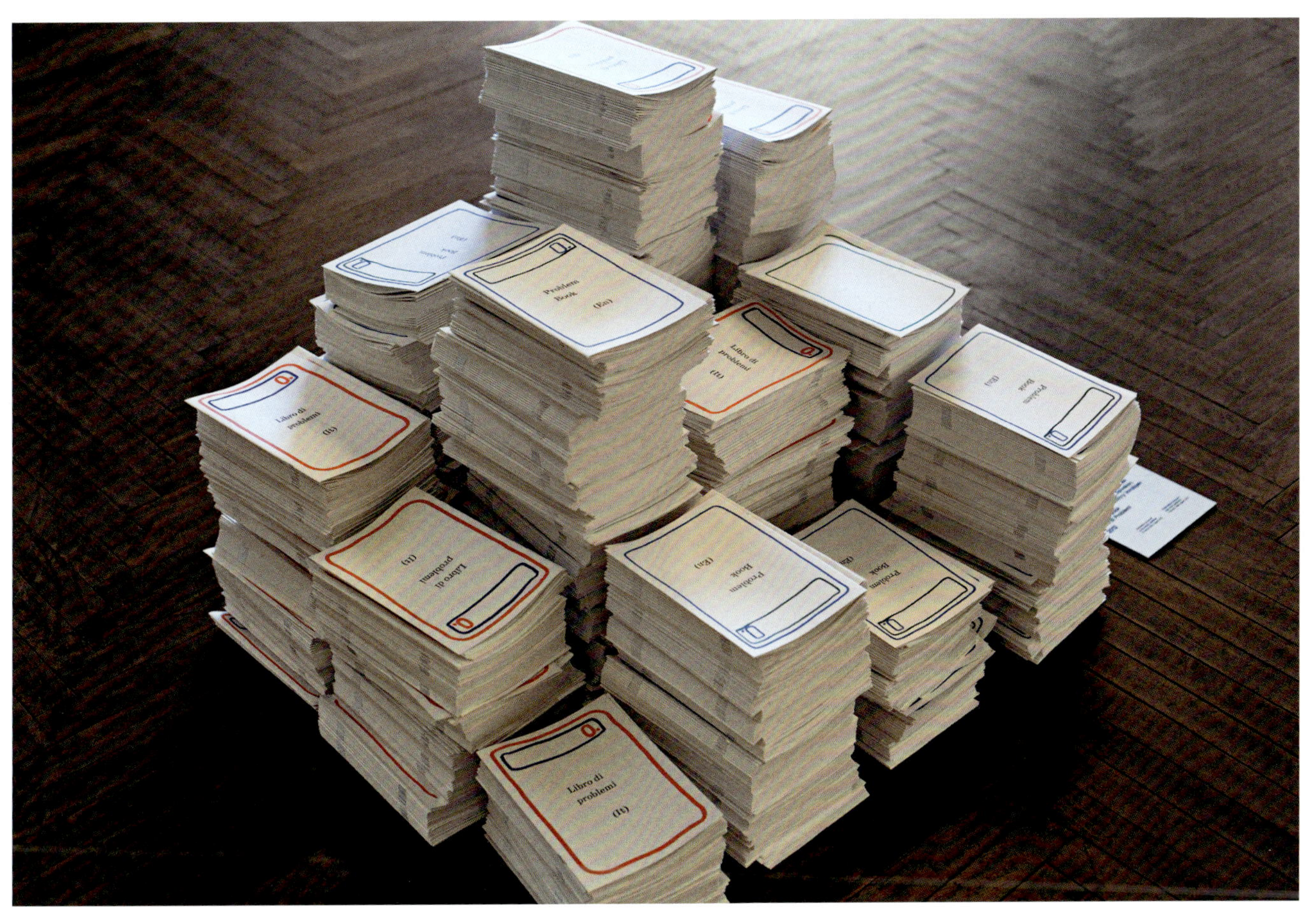

VLADIMI

UNTITLED 2012
HD VIDEO
COURTESY REGINA GALLERY, LONDON AND MOSCOW

Vladimir Logutov's new work is a set of videos focused on the urban space where different signs of boundaries, refractions of the optics of vision, and alteration of the visual field over a distorted image of the nature of a post-Soviet city. The combination of natural footage with computer montage and three shots from a fixed camera conveys a contemplative sense of the large open spaces of Samara, the artist's native city. A variety of different cityscapes – the central square, the outskirts, and the natural empty zones of the city – coexist in a non-narrative that emphasizes the absurd monotony of everyday life. As is typical of Logutov's work, there is no single narrative binding the videos; rather, they work together as a complex system of perceptions. Logutov is primarily known for his video works, where he often combines film and computer editing to highlight the concepts of accidental and spontaneity amidst the routine.

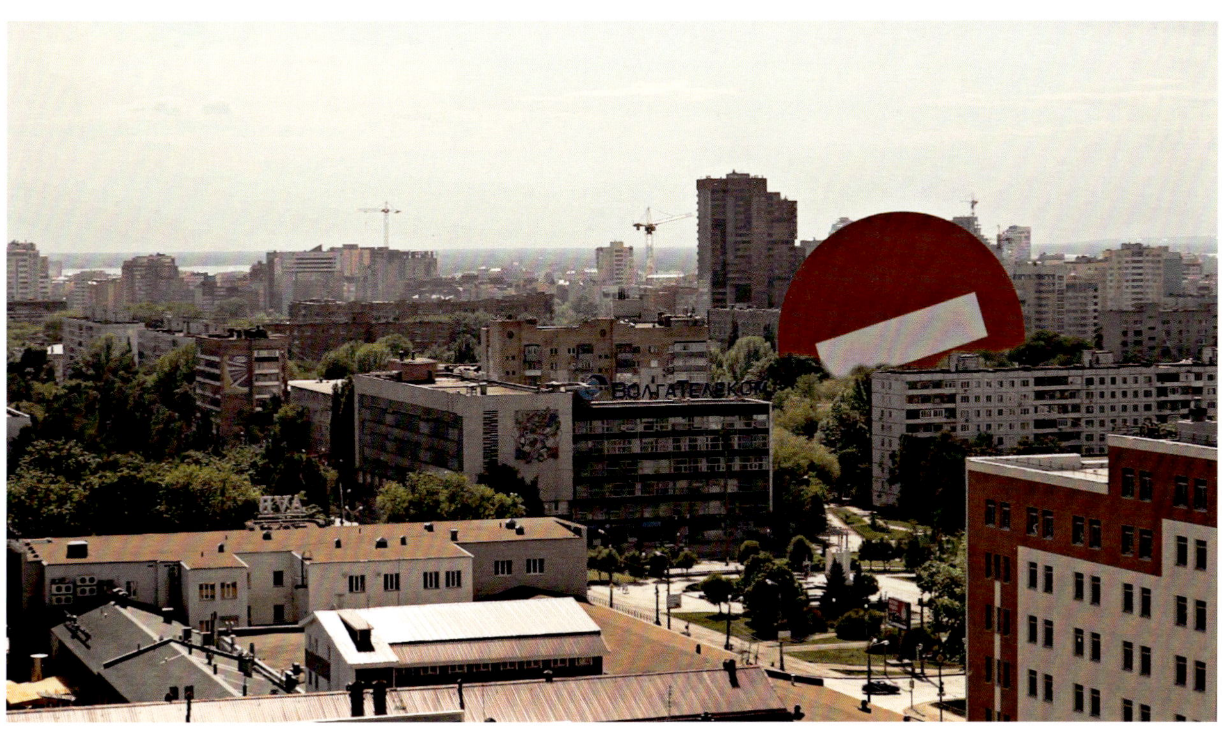

EXPANSIVE SPECIES OF MELZ 2012
INSTALLATION: ORIGINAL WINDOW FROM ERNST THALMANN LACE
FACTORY IN MOSCOW, DRAWINGS ON PAPER, DRAWINGS ON TILES,
DOCUMENTATION, WEBSITE JOURNALURBANFAUNAIAB.ORG,
FOUND MATERIALS FROM ELECTROZAVOD LAMP FACTORY IN MOSCOW
COURTESY THE ARTISTS

The gentrification of large industrial areas of Moscow started several years ago. Urban animals have become one of the subjects of this gentrification. This installation of the Urban Fauna Lab is dedicated to the explosion of feral cats in Moscow's MELZ electric plant, a factory built in 1907 and particularly important for the rise of Soviet industry. In 1990s, most factories ceased functioning and vast territories were abandoned. Today, people have started to return, and finding them inhabited by urban animals. They occupy vacant areas of factories and live there together with artists, architects and entrepreneurs.

The particular display in the exhibition is a representation of the parasitic culture of feral cats and is an attempt to predict the utopian development of this culture in the future. Like the explorers of the Enlightenment, the artists investigate the traces of the partly lost feline civilization, document their behavioral patterns and activities, collect their artifacts, and record the activities of the species in watercolor, drawings on fabric tiles and technical tracing paper found during their trips to the factory. At the same time, they extrapolate the mythological representation of cats as symbols of plague, cruelty, and sexuality.

The multidisciplinary laboratory combines science, architecture and art in a work in progress dedicated to wild animals that live in the city as if it were their natural habitat, like pigeons, cats and rats. They are a part of nature and of the urban landscape, although they have no positive function and turn into parasites that attack the urban system. A parallelism with parasitism in the artistic context is easy to trace: art can preserve its autonomy in today's unfavorable conditions only by being a parasite. Parasitism is regarded as a behavioral strategy that has a special cultural meaning: the existence of parasites indicates the cultural complexity of the host system.

AUNA LAB

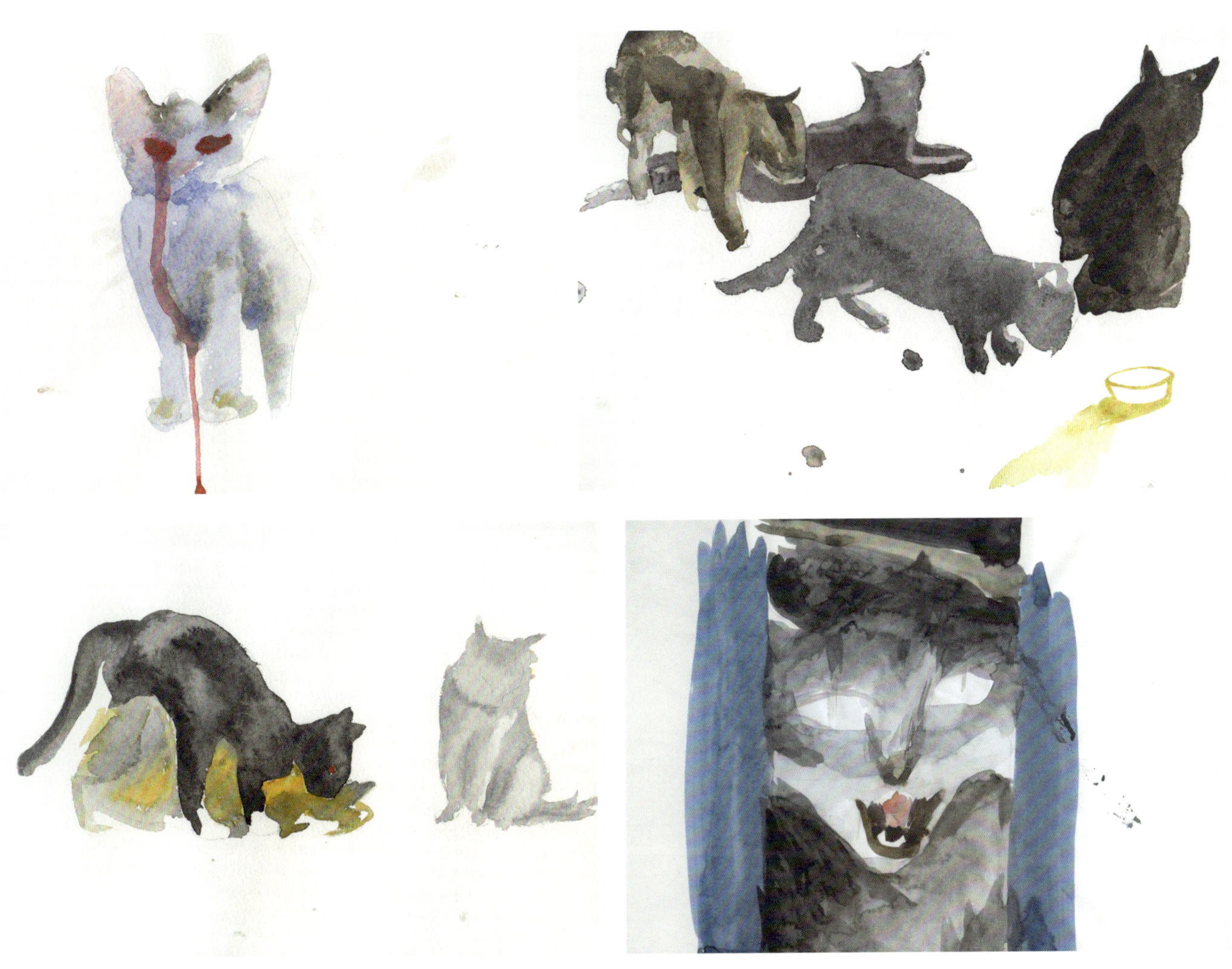

ANATOLY O

BARRICADE ON NIKITSKAYA STREET 1998
ACTION DOCUMENTATION: VIDEO
COURTESY THE ARTIST

This action is one of a series of the actions and happenings that were conducted in Moscow by the artist and theoretician Anatoly Osmolovsky together with Radek Community and Avdei Ter-Oganyan under the name of Non Governmental Control Commission.

It took place in the center of Moscow. The participants constructed a barricade that featured the slogans of the May 1968 in France: "It is forbidden to forbid!," "Imagination takes power!," "Take your desires for reality!" They put forward several demands, among which were legalization of marijuana, free travel to foreign countries, and a monthly salary. The two hundred policemen came to the barricade, their commanders being completely befuddled by this extraordinary street phenomenon.

The action was the first experience of using art as an indirect instrument of political struggle after the collapse of the Soviet system. The society that was born in the storm of barricades, strikes, and street fights of the Revolutionary years forgot its originally direct function, something that the Moscow actionism of the 1990s was to return to, as it inherited the great political tradition of Russian avant-garde.

The participants intended to announce their lack of trust in the government of the emerging democracy and the priority of the citizen's voice over the objective and realistic necessities of the state.

SMOLOVSKY

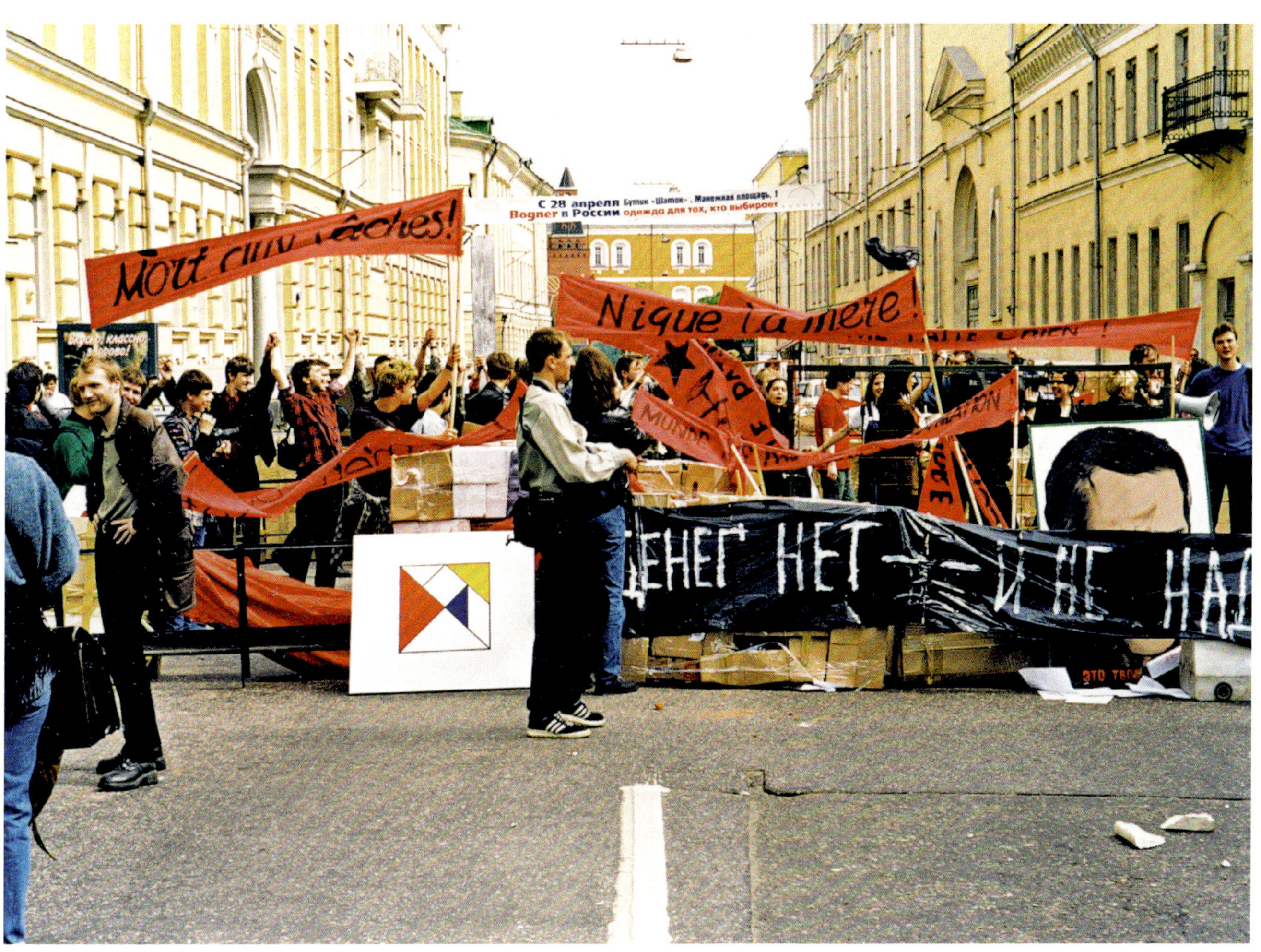

Mort aux vaches!
Nique ta mère!
FAITE CHIEN !
С 28 апреля Бутик «Шатон» · Манежная площадь, !
Bogner в России одежда для тех, кто выбирает
ДЕНЕГ НЕТ И НЕ НА
ЭТО ТВОЁ

ANATOLY O

**A VOYAGE OF NETSEZUDIK TO BROBDINGNAG
(MAYAKOVSKY-OSMOLOVSKY)** 1993
PERFORMANCE DOCUMENTATION: GELATIN SILVER PRINT
COURTESY VICTORIA ART FOUNDATION COLLECTION, MOSCOW

This photo depicts Anatoly Osmolovsky sitting on the shoulders of the monument of Vladimir Mayakovsky – a symbolic figure of the Russian avant-garde of the 1910-20s. It is part of the documentation of a performance held in 1993, when the young artist, without notifying the authorities, climbed up onto the over 10-meter-tall statue of the poet and sat on it for several minutes. Mayakovsky was one of the few revolutionary intellectuals recognized by the Soviet government that erected this monument in 1958 in the homonymous square in the center of Moscow. By becoming part of the Soviet pantheon, the figure of the poet lost his original place in history. The artist strives to return the revolutionary impulse to this degraded space of memory, crowning the statue of Mayakovsky with a radical gesture and underlining the avant-gardist sense of destroying the very fabric of historical discourse imposed by the authorities. This action is one of several attempts of the generation of artists just after the collapse of the USSR to use the main public spaces of the city both as sites and as places for political commentary. The performance is called *A Voyage to Brobdingnag*, an homage to the legendary giants in Swift's novel *Gulliver's Travels*.

SMOLOVSKY

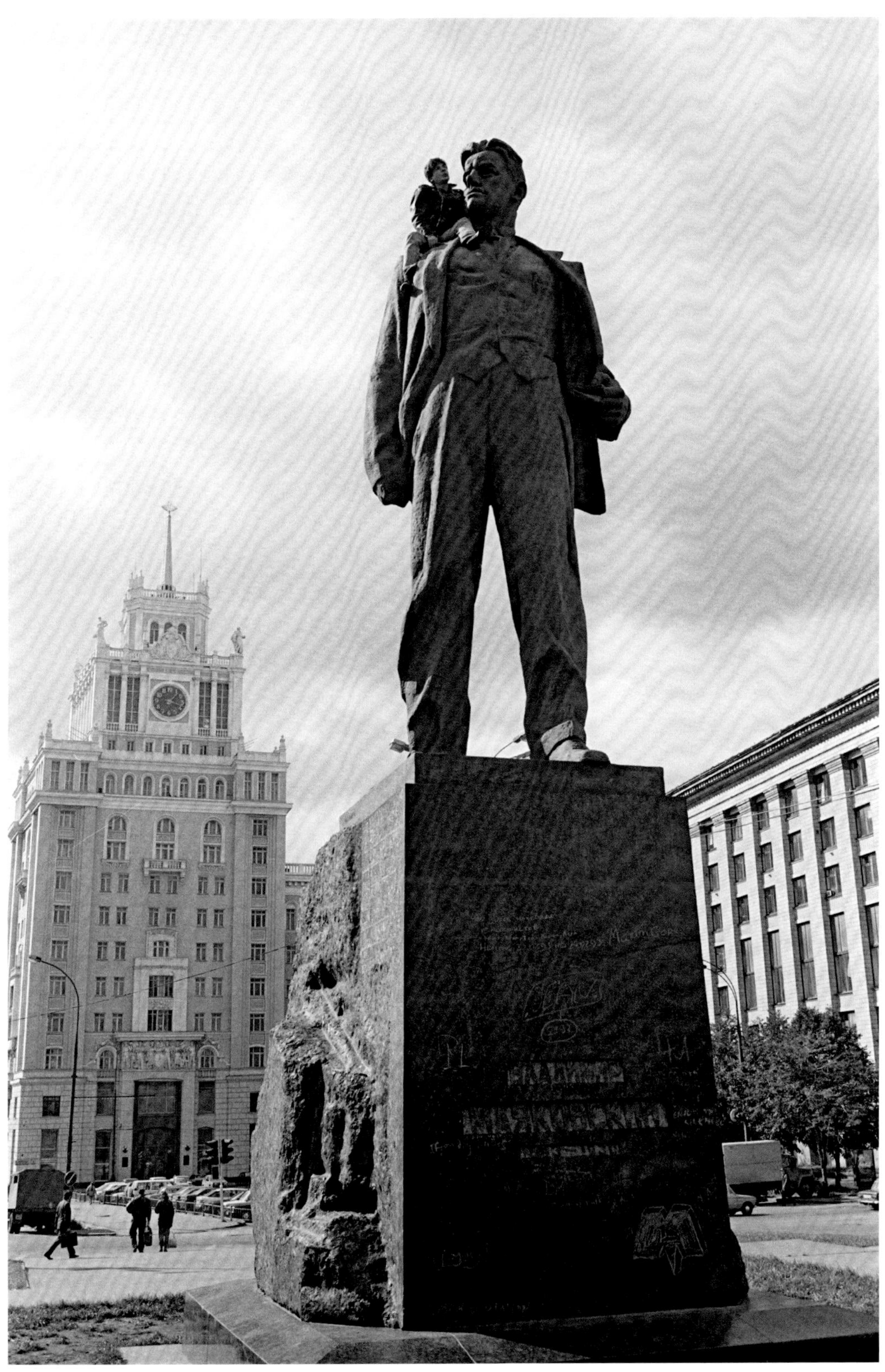

ALEXAND

ZHOPA 2007-2008
SERIES OF 16 COLOR PHOTOGRAPHS
COURTESY PRIVATE COLLECTION, MOSCOW

The work is a photochronicle of the act of writing the word "zhopa" on the wall
of an apartment building located on Vatutina street, Moscow. The municipal
authorities paint over graffiti and political slogans, but the color and shape
of painted figures have almost never blended with the color of the wall itself.
Having provoked the authorities many times into repeatedly painting over her
obscene graffiti, Galkina has photographed the resulting square from the same
point for two years (2006-2007).

The word "zhopa" is close in meaning to "ass" in English. Being common in graffiti, it loses its connotation of rudeness due to appearing everywhere in the city.
The unique linguistic flavor of "zhopa" in the context of the Russian language is
why the title is untranslated. This is a sort of graphic dialogue between an unknown creator from the municipal authorities and the artist. Galkina always
writes the same word, and the painter always chooses a new color and a new
configuration, creating an abstract painting on the city wall.

Galkina continues the traditions of the avant-garde, working with geometric
forms and abstract art, trying to find and show their useful nature and role in
the construction process of the current conditions of existence.

RA GALKINA

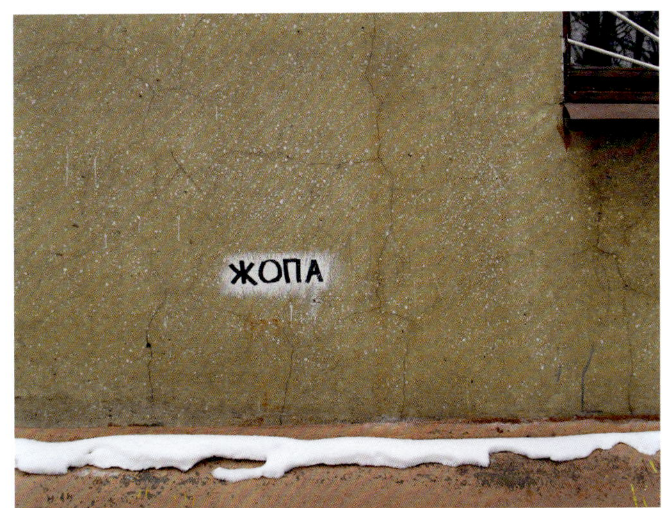

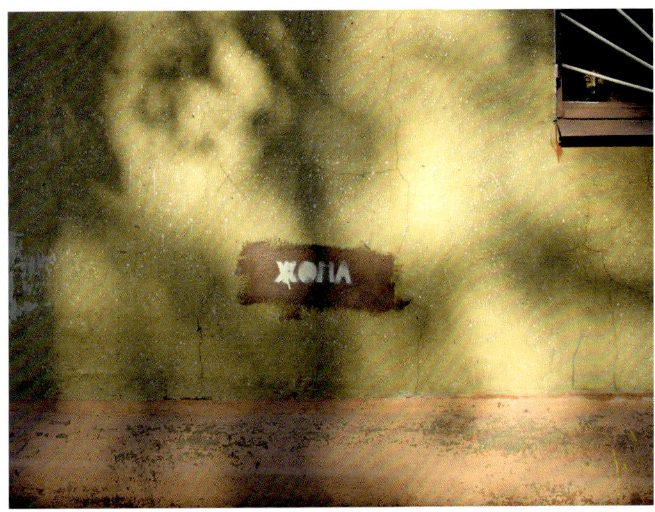

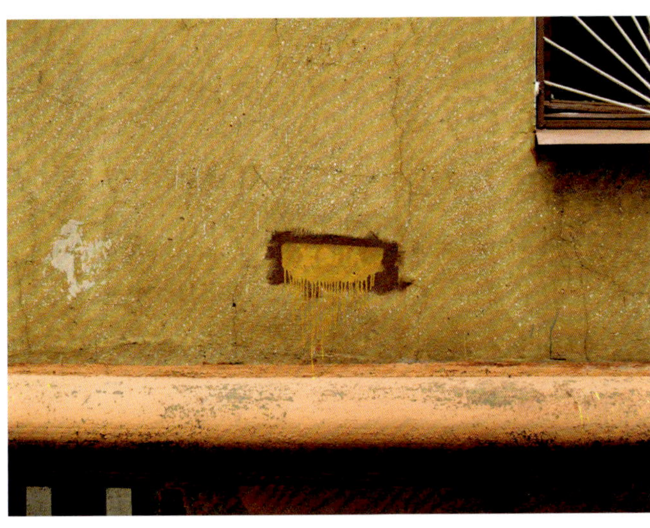

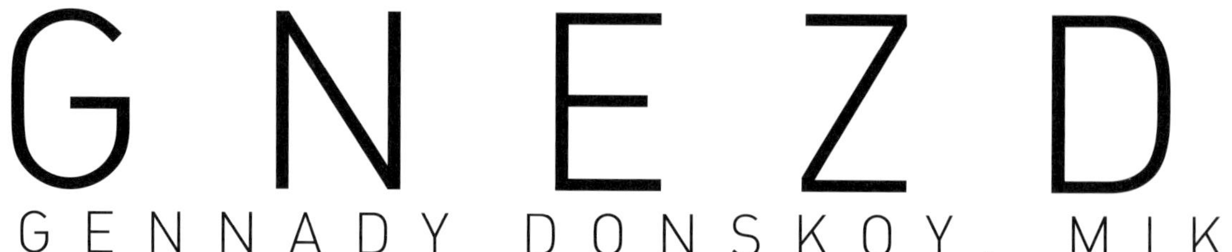

DEMONSTRATION. ART TO THE MASSES 1978
ACTION DOCUMENTATION: TEXTILE BANNER, PHOTOGRAPH
COURTESY THE ARTIST

The members of Gnezdo group made a typical Soviet banner, replaced the central text of the slogan with a reproduction of Franz Kline's abstract composition *Accent Grove* rotated at 90 degrees, and marched in the centre of Moscow with it. After a few minutes, the action was stopped by the police, the banner was destroyed, and the artists were arrested.

This playful gesture uses the celebratory march, one of the most powerful Soviet public rituals, which had been diluted and discredited by long use. It becomes a weapon in the struggle of the two irreconcilable ideologies – socialist ideals and the abstract art denounced by the authorities – transferred into the space of linguistic dialogues and poignant textual conflicts. Thus, the Gnezdo artists used postmodern instruments: "we would use a figure of speech in its literal meaning, like the popular Soviet slogan of bringing art to the masses."

Gnezdo organically falls into the general practice of the late 1960s and early 1970s, which aimed at expanding the borders of art and penetrating into life (and vice versa) and destroying the barrier between the gestures of the artist and nonartist in an absurdist, profane manner.

GROUP

IL ROSHAL. VICTOR SKERSIS

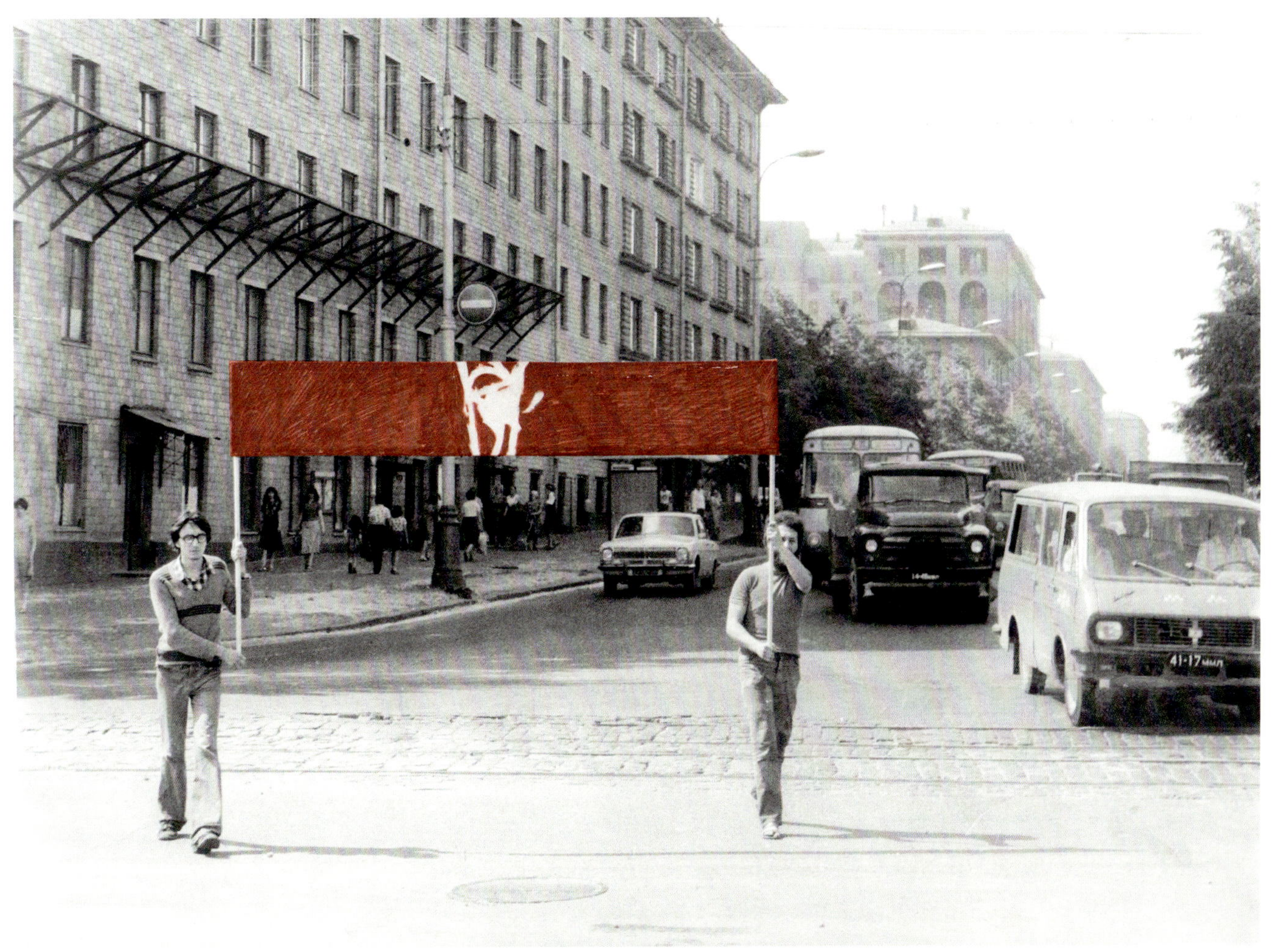

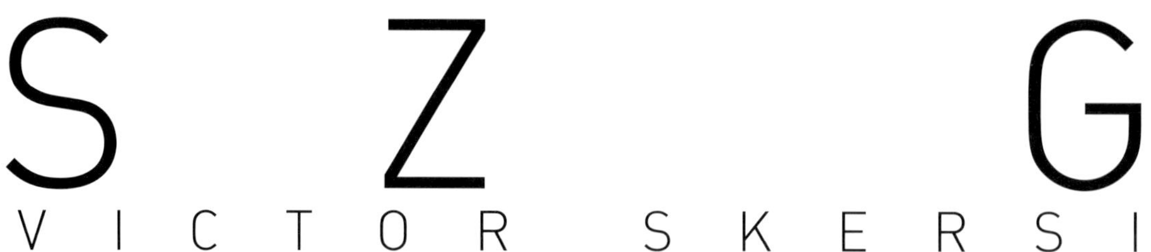

TAGS 1980
ACTION DOCUMENTATION: BLACK AND WHITE PHOTOGRAPHS
COURTESY THE ARTIST

The action took place in December 1980 in Moscow. The members of the group stenciled the tags "Ouch!," "Oops!," "Here!," and "Silly!" throughout the city. The work addresses the presence of the arts in public spaces and an urban environment and the ways in which they function within strict regulations of public life. The city of the 1980s was frozen by the official, decaying vocabulary and tools of the municipal bureaucracy that made the city-scape into a minefield. This regulation primarily acts through rules, in other words, through restrictions of thought. Some of them physically obstruct one from moving around by creating Kafkaesque situations, whereas others take the form of meaningful linguistic attractors that bring thought into conformity with the few approved ideas propagated by the state.

The artists found the regulatory restrictions to be abusive and oppressive: the only possibility to formulate new ideas and approaches to art is to create meaningful changes in routine thought processes. To create these distortions, which seemed to be the most suitable, since they do not refer to a particular object or action. They imply, without stating, and they were emotionally charged, but not directed toward anyone. They were stenciled throughout Moscow as hopeful seeds of a new beginning. In a statement dated December 18, 1980, the SZ group announced "with a feeling of great satisfaction that the inscriptions that have appeared in various corners of Moscow – Ouch! Oops! Here! How? Silly! and others – are functioning normally."

R O U P

VADIM ZAKHAROV

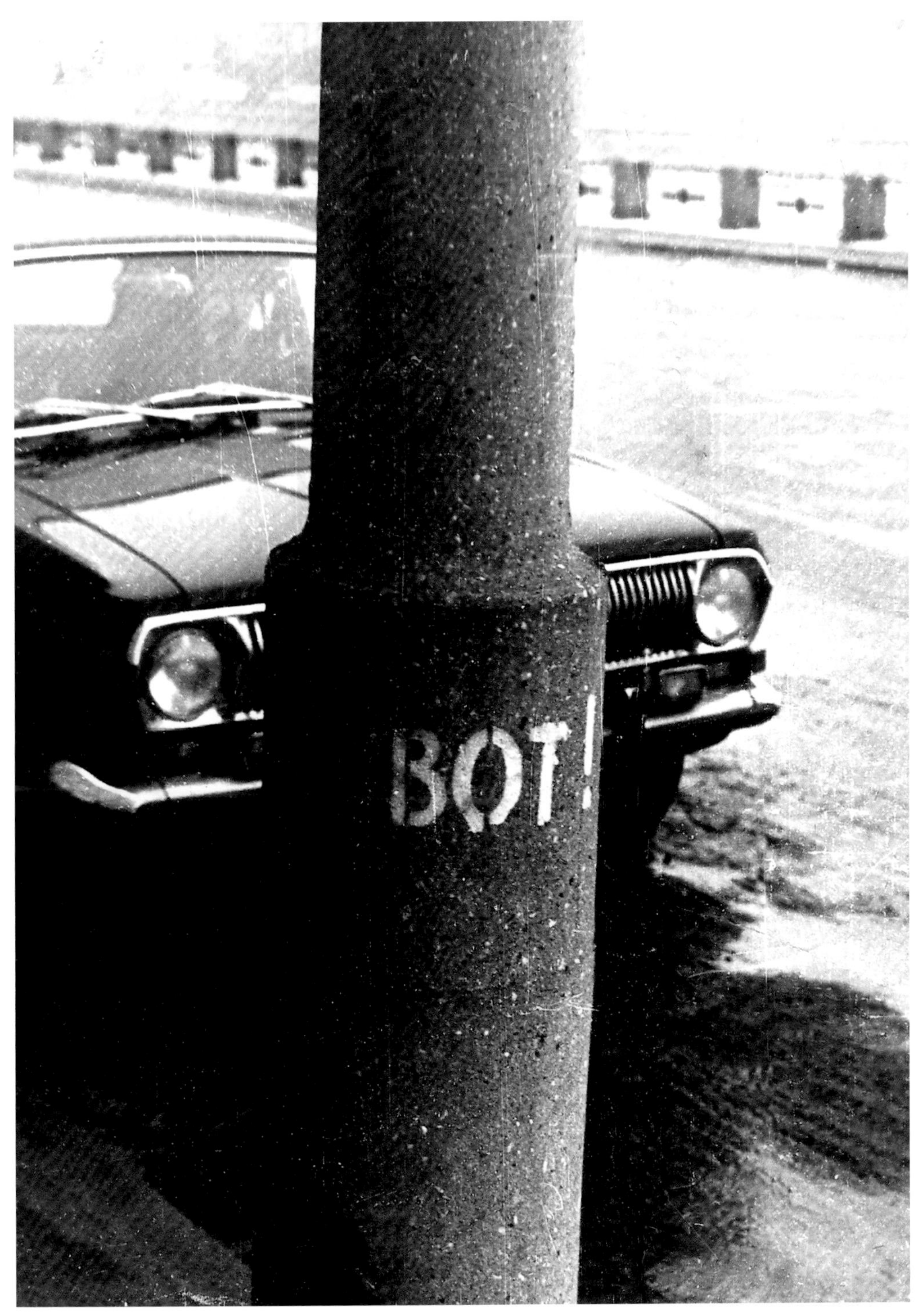

IVAN B

CLEARING THE HEIGHT 2010
ACTION DOCUMENTATION: VIDEO 4'13"
COURTESY THE ARTIST

The video is based on the artist's attempt to realize a symbolical occupation of the city space. Iconographically, it refers to the famous photograph of the *Victory Banner over the Reichstag* (1945), which depicts two Soviet soldiers raising a red flag over the building of the German Parliament. But, while that memorable photograph symbolizes the victory over fascism, *Clearing the Height* refers to another occurrence in Soviet history, namely, partisan resistance. When guerilla warriors recovered ground, they raised red flags on high areas of land to mark the space as theirs and show that the people living there were free. The video is a sort of metaphor for a victorious taking of an enemy building on a lost territory. Brazhkin occupies a space in today's rearward area, and he marks with his red flag a boiler-house tower in the midst of a residential district where nothing culturally significant ever happens. A residential district is a place that no one claims, it bears no marks of power, so any performative gesture seems lonely but still expressive, like crying out in the desert. The work is a figurative echo of the past: Brazhkin raises the flag, takes the territory and sends the district's residents the message that they are free.

RAZHKIN

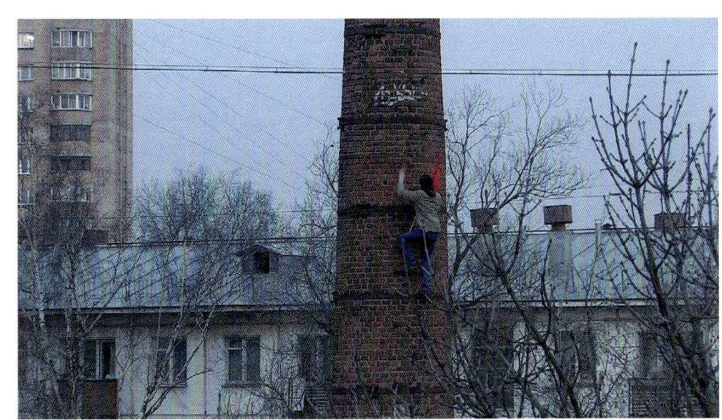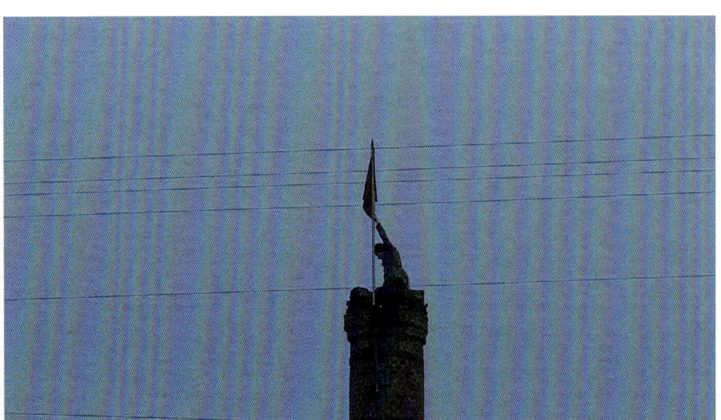

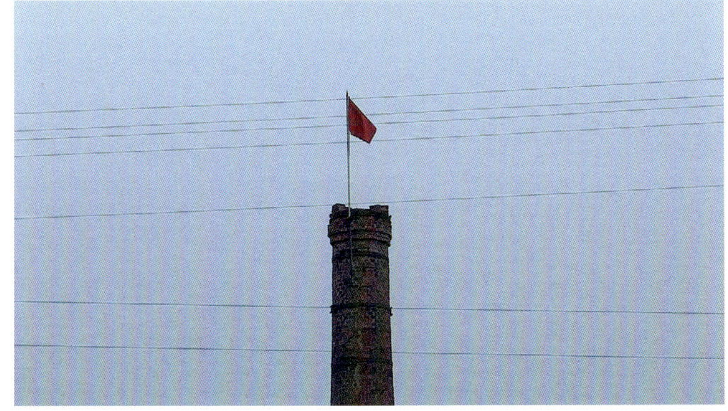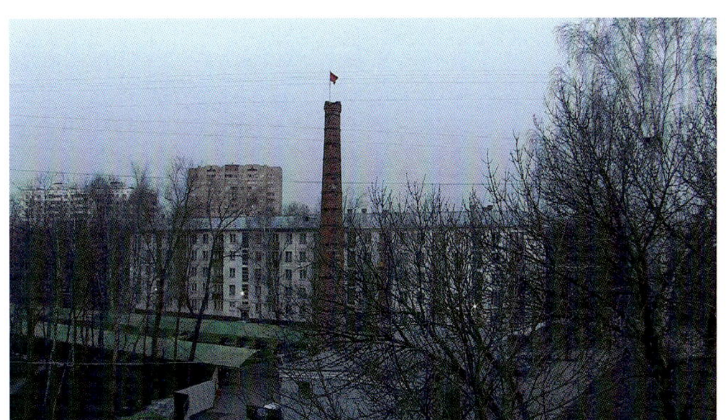

XENIA S
MARIA K

VANISHING SPACES 2012
ANIMATION VIDEO, 3'43"
COURTESY THE ARTIST

This project investigates the historical changes of monumental art in the USSR and post-USSR from the 1970s up to today, in which the practices of creating and decorating public spaces have almost been lost. It examines the influence of space on the individual living in it. This animated video represents art in the process of vanishing, displaced by complete European-style renovation and redevelopment, questioning the purpose of monumental art and decoration of public space.

The video features elements familiar to anyone who has been inside a typical Soviet public building like a House of Culture or hospital. Although today these spaces are not used in the way they were used before – those created in Soviet times are abandoned and no longer functional – they become spaces filled with plants and odd objects that are not relevant to the here and now. The video recreates this subtle space that does not appear real, but rather recollects disappearing frescoes, stained glass and graffiti – quickly dissolving, changing, temporarily existing.

The film features sketches by Valeriy Sorokin (1952), an artist who graduated from the Vera Mukhina Higher School of Art and Design in Moscow and was the creator of numerous decorative projects for Soviet public spaces such as cinemas, registries, airports, and hospitals. The music in the video is the *Adagio of Spartacus* of the famous Soviet composer Aram Khachaturian.

OROKINA.
APRANOVA

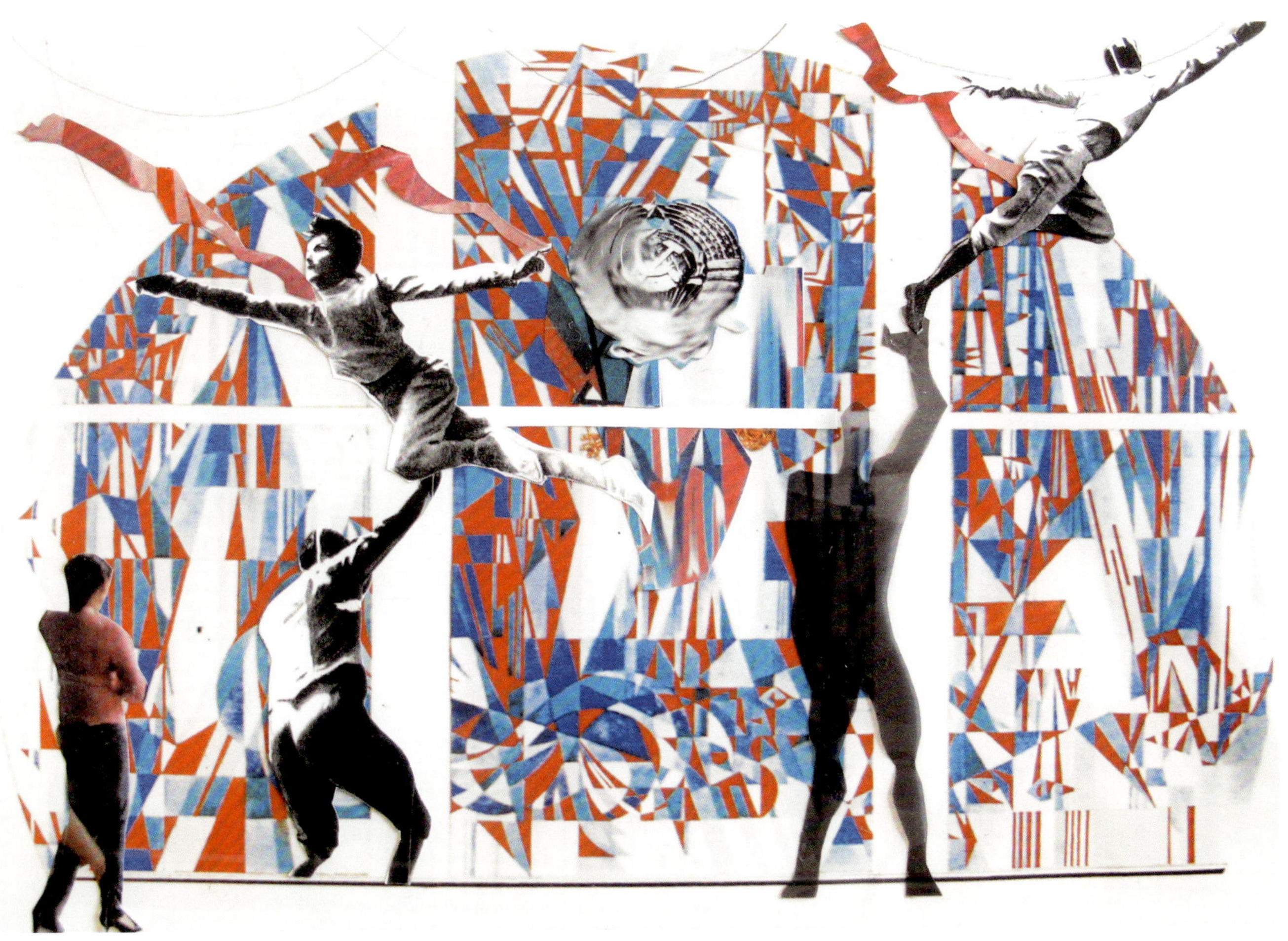

POSSIBILITI
ARRANGEMEN
PREFABRICATE

ALBUMS AND ARCHITECTURAL MODEL
COURTESY PRIVATE COLLECTION, MOSCOW

With the collapse of the Soviet Union the egalitarian homogeneity of its cities had to face with the society's rush to individualization. If the change was less apparent on an urban scale of *microrayon*, it was private apartments where the new freedom was best exercised.
The model represents a typical apartment in Moscow of a building series KOPE; it could be in one of the thousands of identical buildings of identical flats scattered around the whole city. The 1990s saw a radical notion to rub out any sign of thus standardization; households hurtled to put an end to their homes' uniformity and make them their castles; and more than once literally and figuratively castles. A scan through the work of the newly emergent interior designers of the time would show an offer ranging from Louis XVI palaces squeezed into 50 sq m two-bed apartments to full-mirrored, neon-lit caricature of a brothel-made-a-family-home. Attached to the model are three hypothetical catalogues of such projects showing both the kitsch and creativity of the time.
BLAZEJ CZUBA

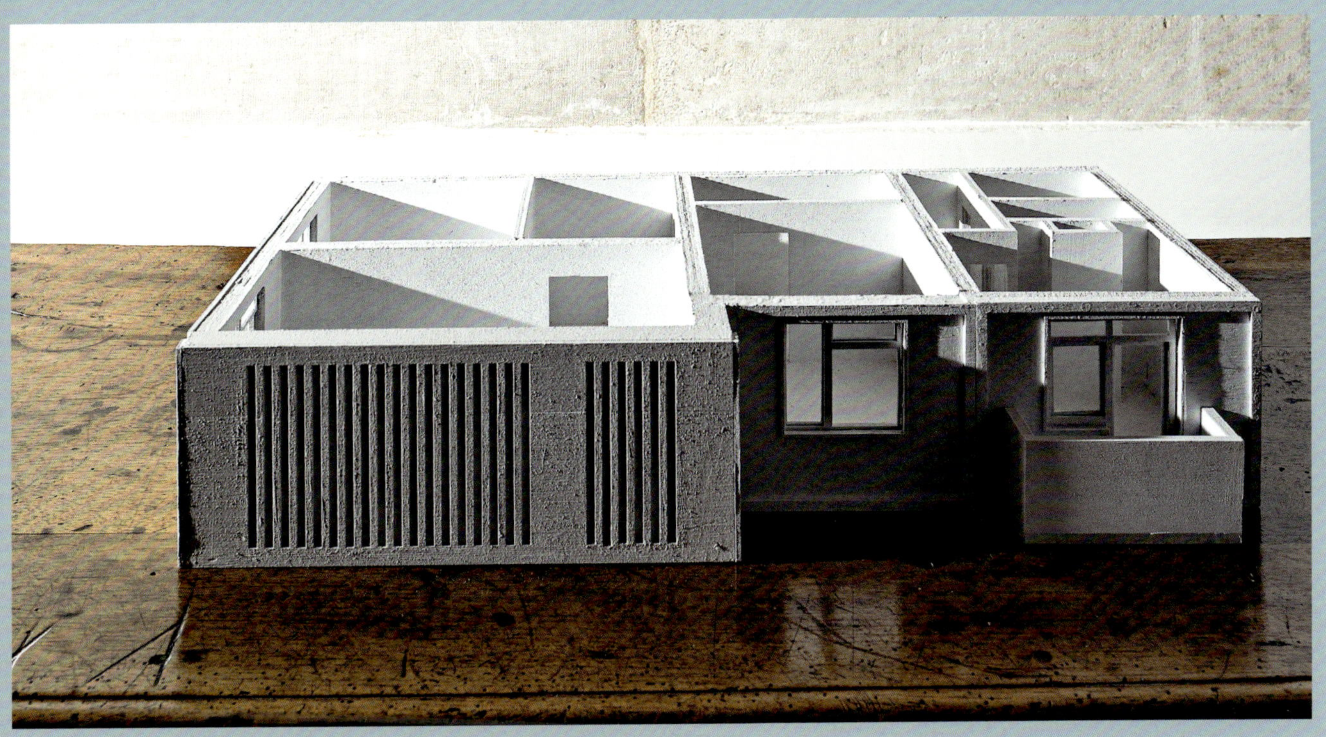

CLASSIFICATION O
OF THE LUZHKO

COLLECTION OF WEB-IMAGES

The architecture of the last two decades seems to be chaotic, but if we take a closer look, we can extract certain patterns, which in turn tell us a lot about certain facts, events and phenomena. It is even possible to carry out a classification of it.

The first group of buildings – *unique* – falls under the main idea of asserting a building's uniqueness. It is a reaction to the previous years of the Soviet architectural approach, as well as an attempt to become a distinctive product in the new-born world of a market economy. This direction was an explicit search for identity and an abrupt break with the previous paradigm of anonymity.

Massive is a category containing huge prefab residential districts. After the fall of the USSR, they continued to be built in capitalist Russia. Having become commercial and having lost the last remains of modernist ideology, they mutated, adjusting themselves to the new market economy. The existing manufacturing infrastructure – huge Soviet apartment-building factories – was set to work full-throttle, producing extremely tall and densely packed neighborhoods, forgetting about the initial microregional ideas of provide green space, sunlight and fresh air.

Generic is another category of buildings that try to fulfill the desire of obtaining a certain identity. At the same time, they are massive and therefore accessible to the emerging middle class. These could produce a certain strong image – starting from being modern or European, and ending up becoming another Stalinist skyscraper, while still being nothing more than generic residential blocks architecturally speaking. The category phoenix was begun with the idea of religious repentance, as an attempt to correct the mistakes of the Soviet era. In the beginning, a few religious buildings that had been demolished in the Stalin era were reconstructed. Later the idea mutated: buildings were demolished and immediately resurrected for political and economic reasons.

DARIA PARAMONOVA

THE ARCHITECTURES PERIOD 1992-2010

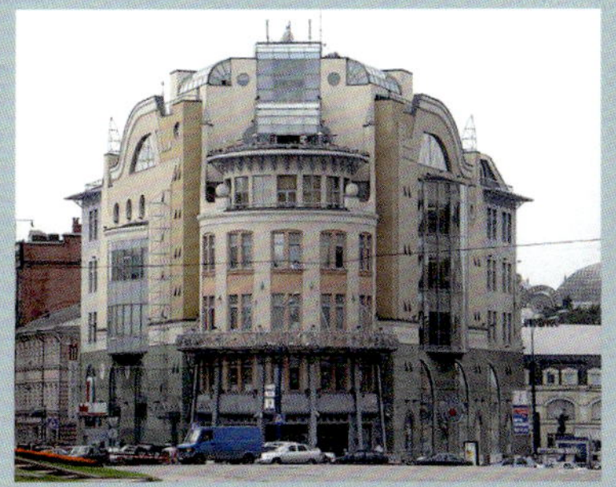
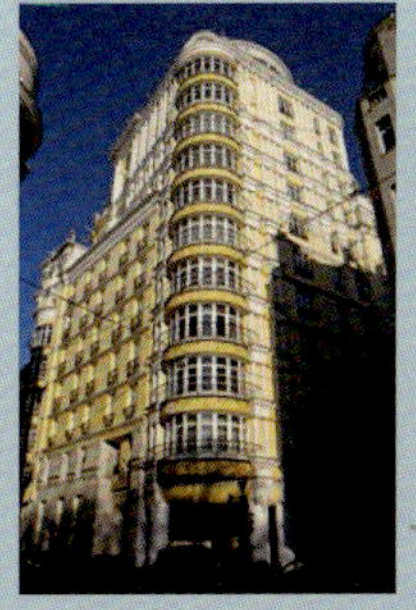
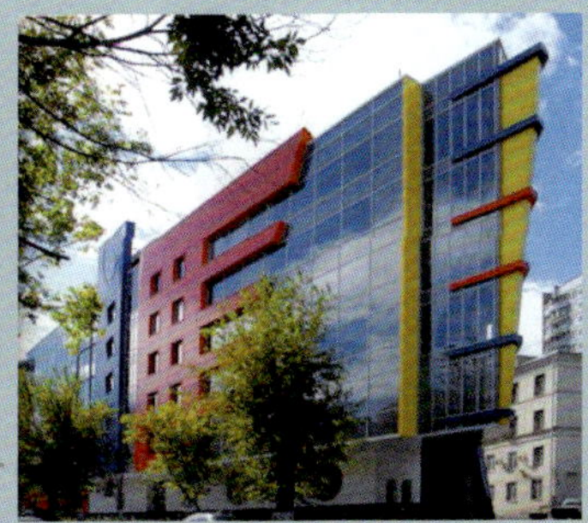
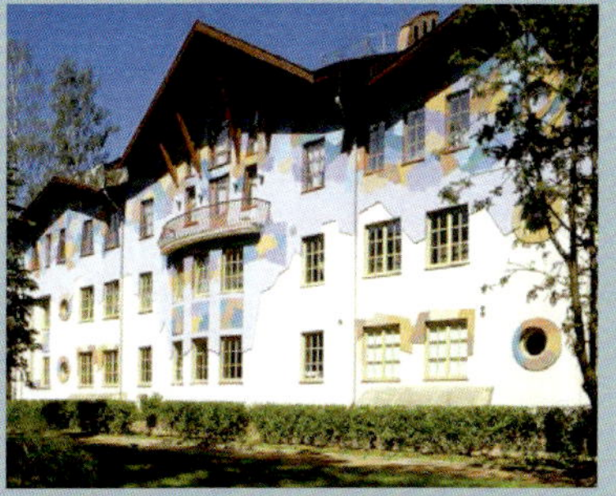
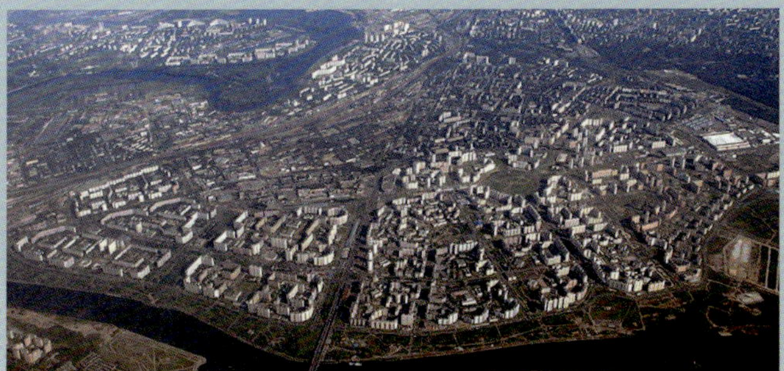
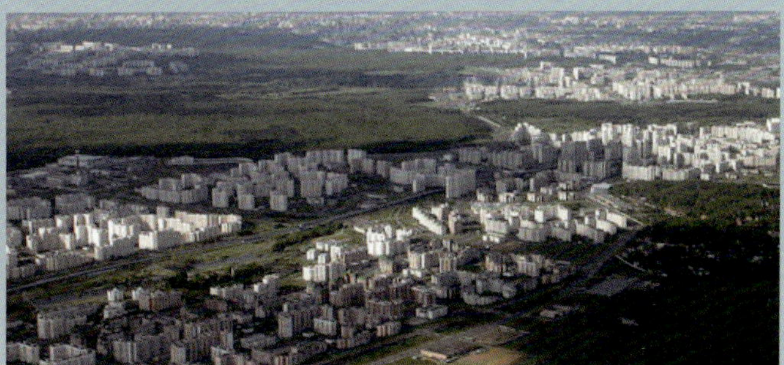
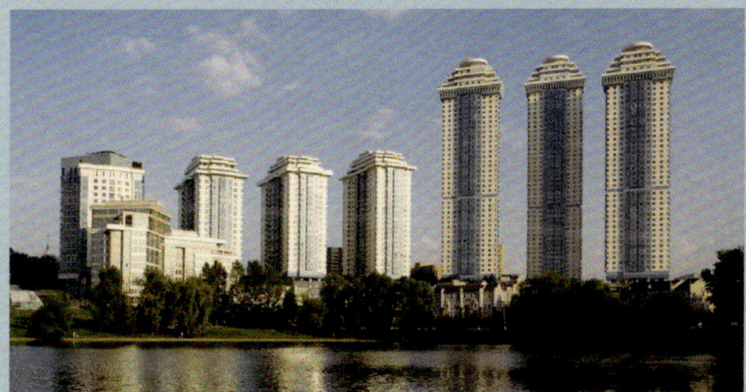
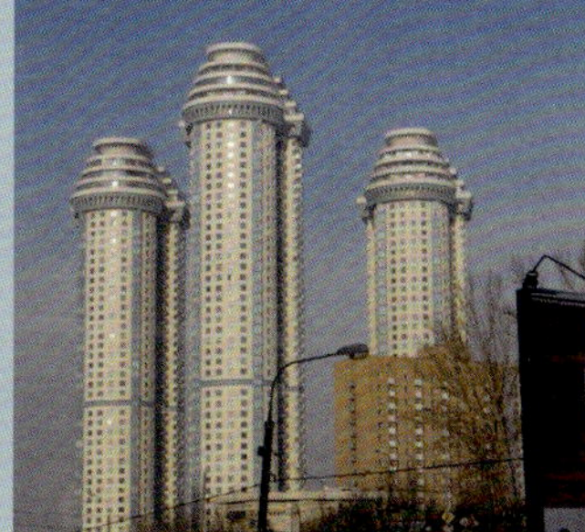
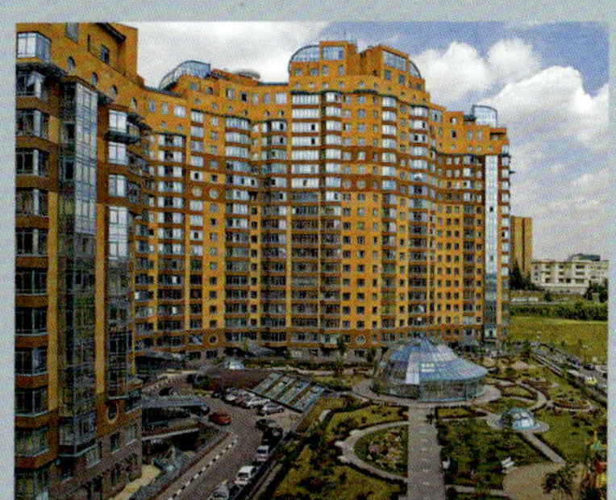
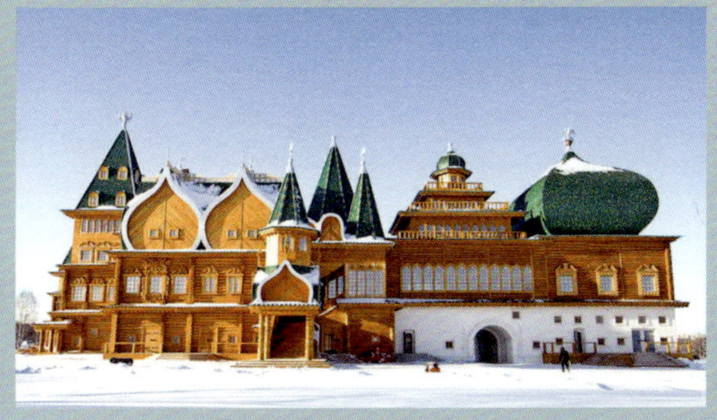
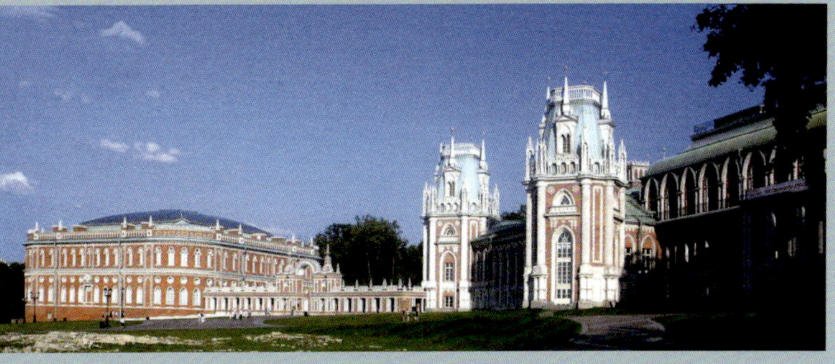

CATEGORIES OF
APPROPRIAT

COLLECTION OF WEB-IMAGES

The enormous sweeps of streets and boulevards, oversized squares, and vast chunks of land between residential blocks in the Soviet era all used to be realms of the totalitarian state, accenting its monolithic nature with pure order. Once freed from the grasp of the state, they rapidly started filling up with new buildings, new people and new uses. This appropriation of space is probably one of the most striking phenomena of the new Moscow.

The appearance of commercial activity leads to a phenomenon that can be termed commercial functionalism. Each piece of space could be a potential source of profit. Countless commercial objects of various sizes – kiosks, advertisements, banners, smaller and larger "commercial centers" and "shopping galleries," started covering more and more of the city's emptiness. The patterns of their appearance were strikingly similar to behaviors that can be found in nature. Analogically to mushrooms, "fungus" elastically adapted to the available space, independently of its shape and size.

Due to an increase in material well-being, a car became a symbol of prosperity. Rapid motorization not only brought hundreds of thousands of cars onto the streets, it also meant more roads, more highways, and more asphalt, less greenery and less public space. It meant more parking spaces, with cars parked virtually everywhere, on lawns and sidewalks, in yards and on former green areas. Throughout the last two decades, cars have become omnipresent, traffic dominating the urban space.

The emerging civil society started claiming city space for more and more political activity. Moscow, designed more for military parades than for democratic movement, is now experiencing an eruption of political meetings and demonstrations. The most interesting phenomenon is a lack of spatial stability – political protests pop up in random places, trying to find their niche in the city's public space.

DARIA PARAMONOVA

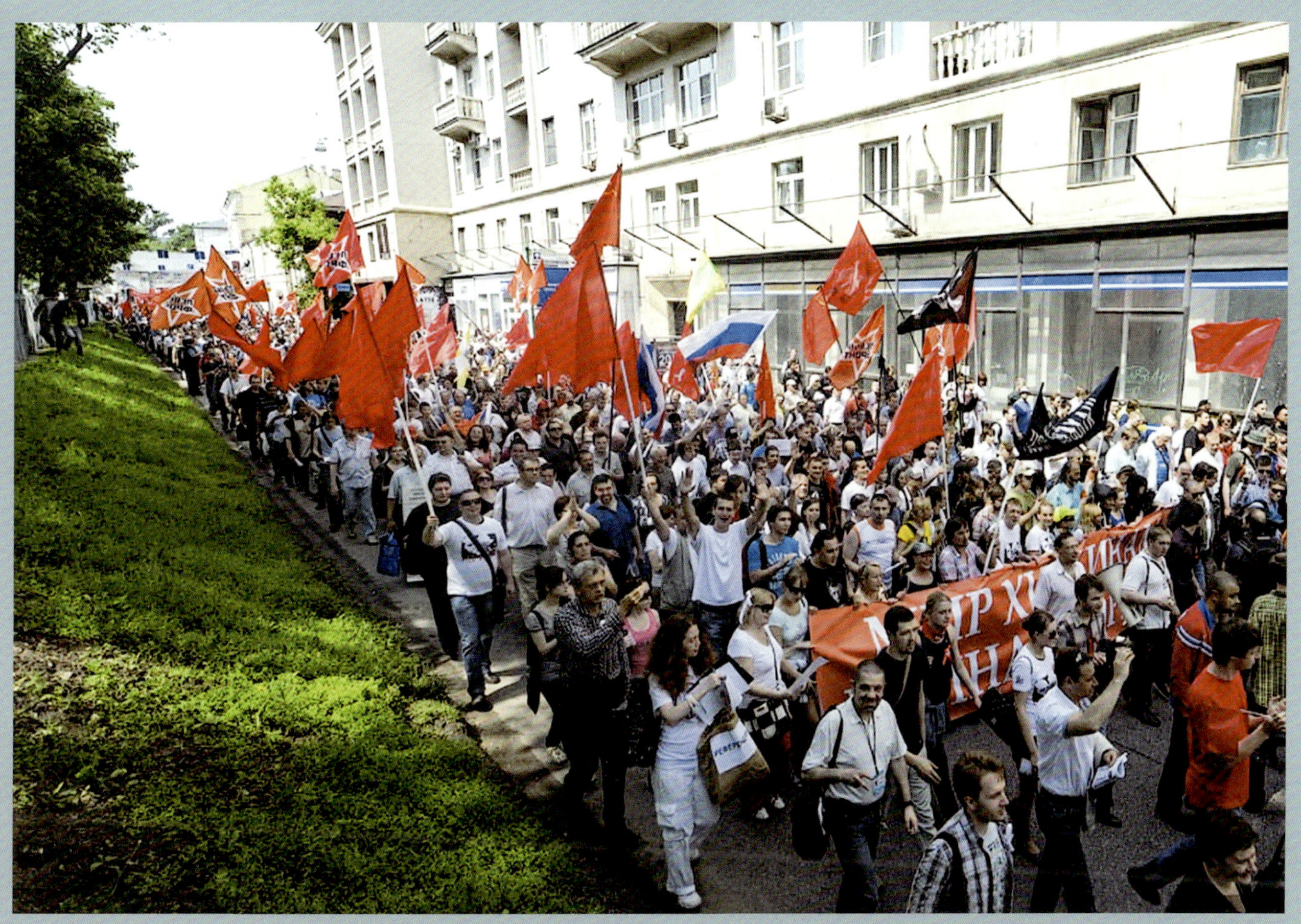

SERGEY S

FAILED VIEWS 2012
TRIPTYCH OF HAND-PRINTED PHOTOGRAPHS, SERIES OF POLAROIDS
COURTESY THE ARTIST

Sergey Sapozhnikov is a photographer who has worked a great deal, experimenting with filming artificial structures integrated into the half-natural, half-urban environment of the city outskirts. The chaos of his installations is a reference to the potential of liberation from the structure of organized space and codified behavior.

Venice gave him the idea of floating architecture, a house on the water with colorful inflatable mattresses. Sapozhnikov has selected the trees and bushes of the Venetian Hotel to build a new installation that better shows the possibilities of inflated mattresses and represents them extensionally and three-dimensionally. The artist has used such objects for a year, experimenting with their plastic and constructive capability.

Leaves and tops of trees supported by props recollect a drowned city. In a fictional construction site under the water, Sapozhnikov depicts all the attempts and mistakes involved in building a perfect stable structure. The artist inverts the physical elements of the world and builds an air-supported structure.

The installation was conceived as temporary architecture to be seen for a limited period of time from the balcony of Casa dei Tre Oci, and at the same time, as the subject of the several photographs that are now shown in the exhibition. The distance between different views creates a spectrum of interpretations of the act of looking and of his representation via different media.

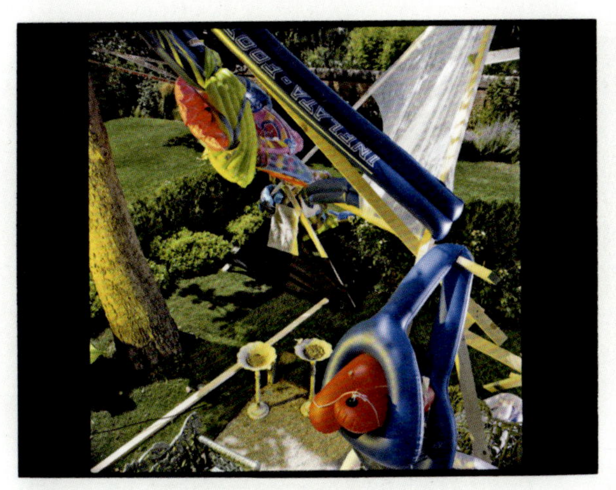
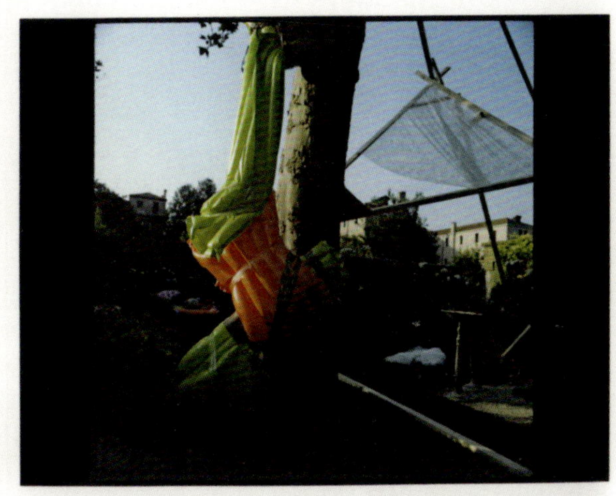
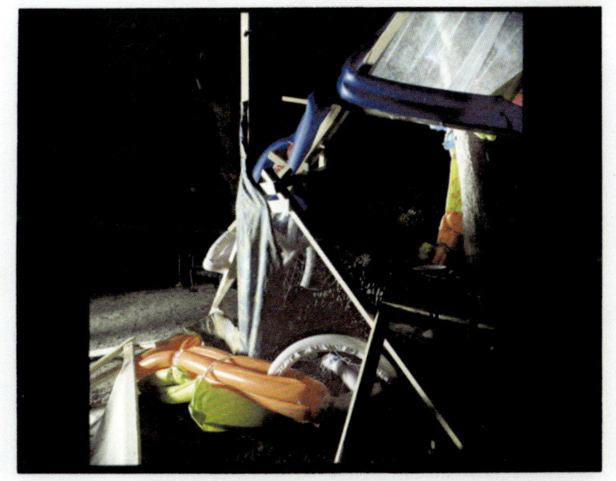
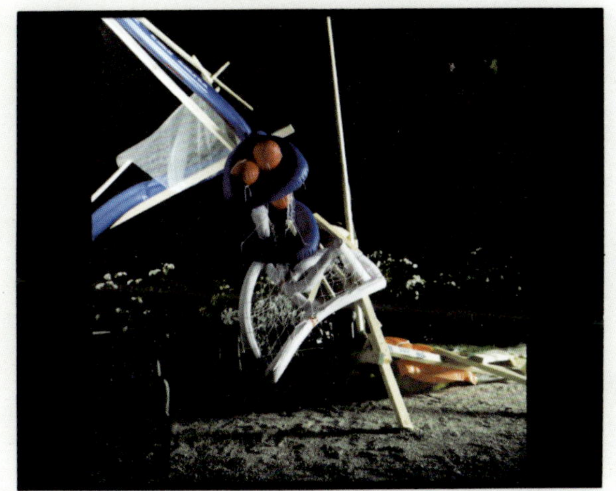

OLGA CH

WINDOWS 2007
16-CHANNEL VIDEO INSTALLATION
COURTESY FOXY PRODUCTION GALLERY, VOLKER DIEHL GALLERY

In her work *Windows*, Olga Chernysheva is engaged in surveillance, an activity beloved by artists, but she is not motivated by the curiosity of an artist who is merely reporting or an informer. Chernysheva records a chronicle of banality, a chronicle of the continuum that awaits for something solemn and meaningful to happen but in fact never does.

Life is fixed by a movie camera as a priceless, aimless movement, situated in the frame of the easily recognized silhouette of a window of a five-story Soviet panel building.

The time of day of these video shots is early evening, twilight, a time that is very important for the cities of central Russia, where for most of the year daylight begins late and ends early. Life begins in the twilight of the working day, precisely when what is really important happens.

Chernysheva is an artist that is very independent and consistent in her artistic method, which was formulated in the 1990s. Carefully investigating the examples and traditions of Russian cinematography and literature, she gathers that stardust that settles in people's hearts after the Big Bang of a social system.

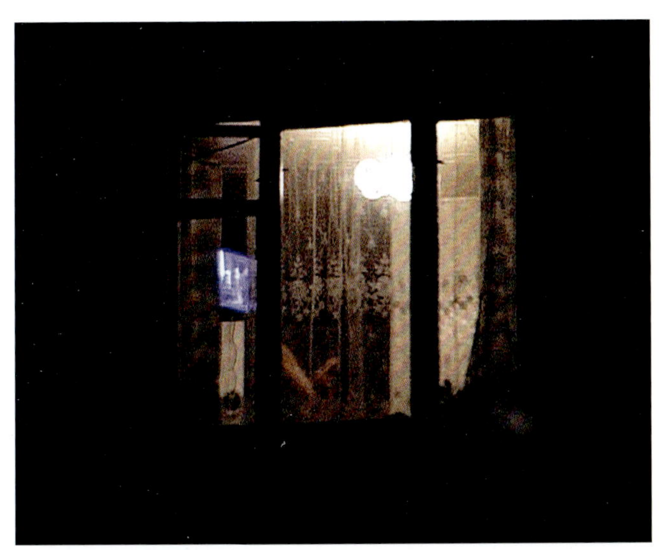
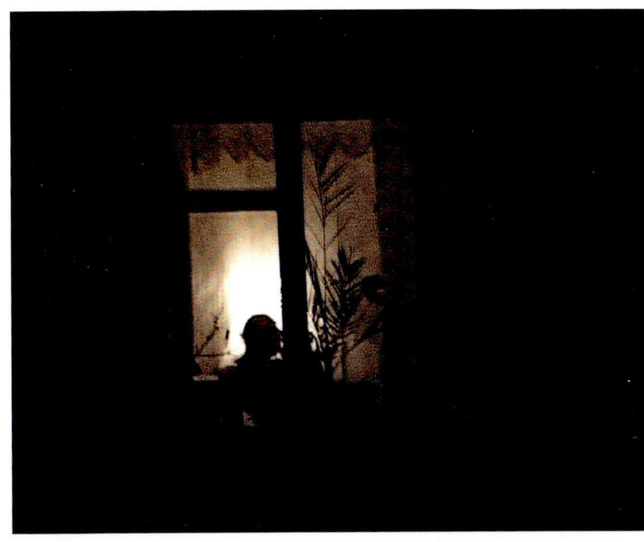
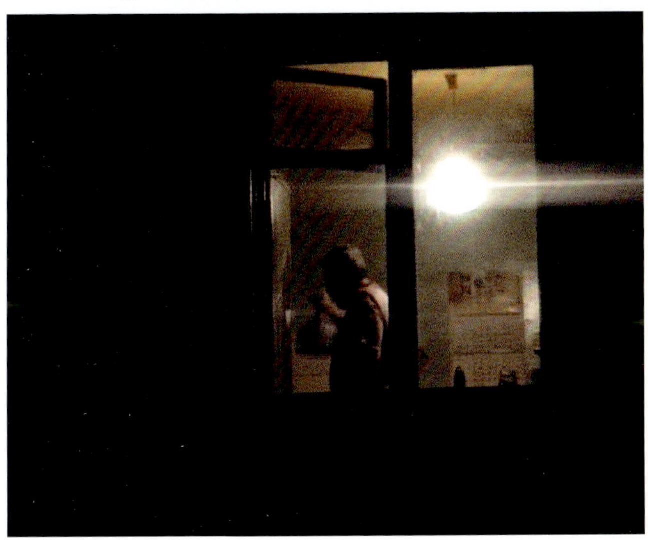
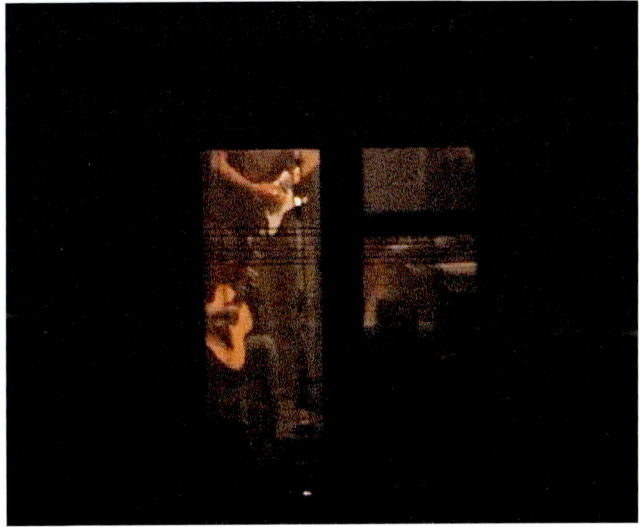

USTAL (I AM TIRED) 2008
PERFORMANCE DOCUMENTATION: COLOR PHOTOGRAPHS, PAPER
COURTESY OPEN GALLERY, MOSCOW

This early work of Andrey Kuzkin inaugurates a series of performances of the artist in the urban environment.
Kuzkin printed 4000 leaflets in A4 format with the word *Ustal* (I Am Tired) and made a small banner displaying the same word. He then stepped out of his house and sticked the leaflets on the doors and walls of nearby buildings, stores, etc. Next, he shook all the leaflets out of his bag and combined them into one pile. As a strong wind started to blow the leaflets away, the artist unfolded the banner and stood there, holding it with both hands, for an hour. The action continued until a police car appeared on the horizon. The performance took place in one of the so called bedroom districts of Moscow, on a weekday close to evening, not far from a footpath used by hundreds of people daily to get to the nearest metro station and back home.
With its extreme simplicity, this action informs us about a feeling that unites all the different people living in such districts: the everyday feeling of fatigue. This sensation is even amplified by the monotony of the architectural environment and its repetitive pattern.
Using his own body to establish direct contact with people and the public, Kuzkin tests its own limits, resisting the elements for several hours in the open air. For the artist, the first experience and the accompanying physical challenge are often the only true way to explore the surrounding reality.

KUZKIN

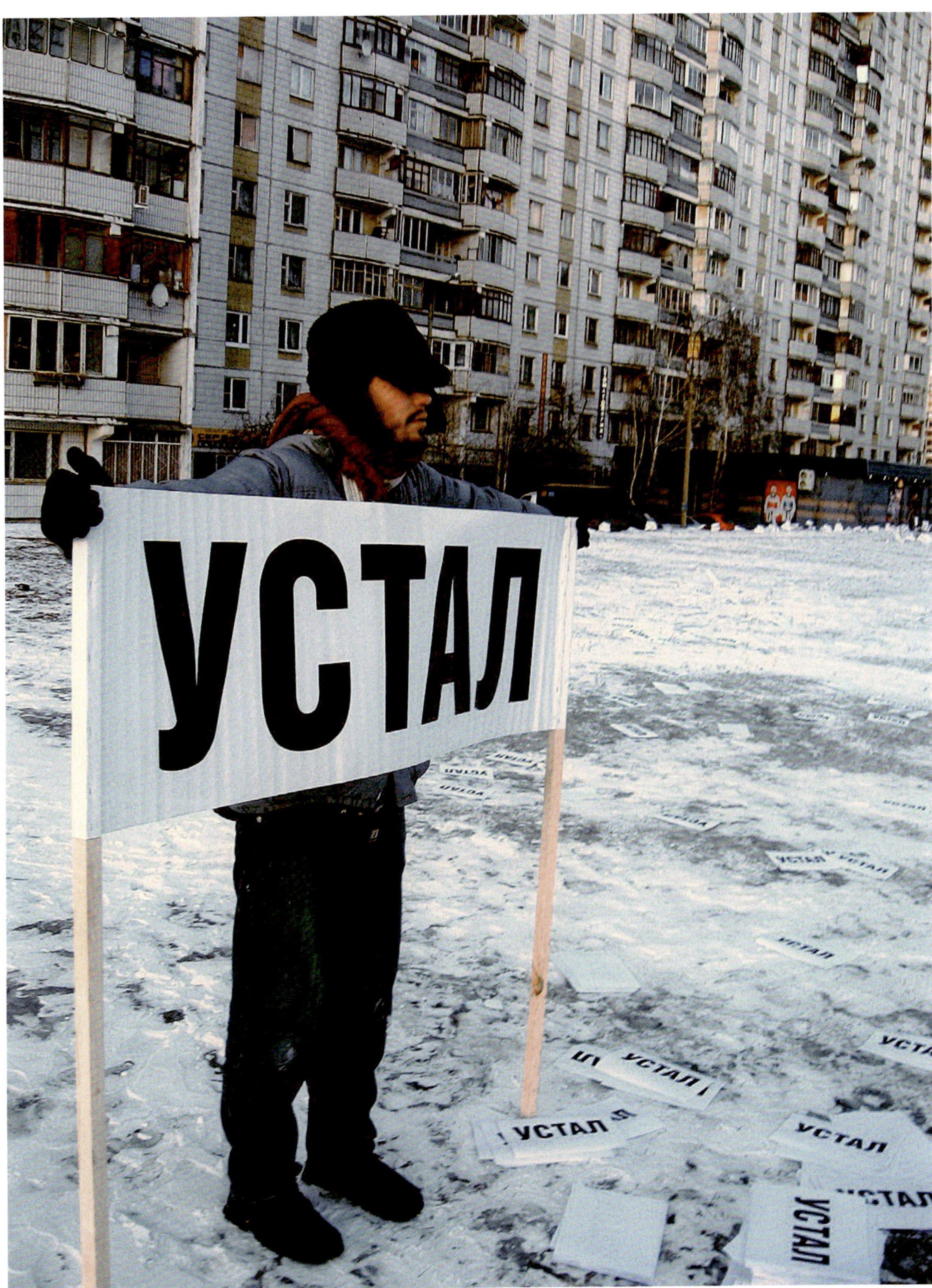

ANDREV

AND CHUBAIS 2012
EXHIBITION/ACTION DOCUMENTATION: VIDEO 10'52"
COURTESY THE ARTIST

One of the latest performances of Kuzkin summarizes his experience as an artist for a certain period of his career. The artist takes a critical look at his proper role within the system of the artist and spectator. The exhibition brings us back to his one year of experience in displaying enormous bread sculptures, the *Levitation Heroes* series, in Venice to the usual Biennale public. The uncomfortable environment makes him question if a work of art requires a certain audience to become more consistent, and what additional connotations it may acquire as part of an attraction for tourists. The performative exhibition was titled *And Chubais*, after the well-known Russian businessman, who visited the Venice exhibition and had a photograph of himself taken against the background of Kuzkin' immense and expressive people. Six months later, in winter, the artist goes to sell smaller copies of the bread sculptures in an underground passageway in Moscow for 5 rubles each. He spends much time looking for the audience and the right context for these works. The figurines were made of soaked bread mixed with salt, a traditional material for modeling used by prisoners. With this alternative market, the artist tries to find his place in the world of art and address a new public in the urban space outside the context of contemporary art. The exhibition/action took place in the underpass of Kashirskoe Avenue on March 11, 2012, lasted for 2.5 hours and was stopped by police.

KUZKIN

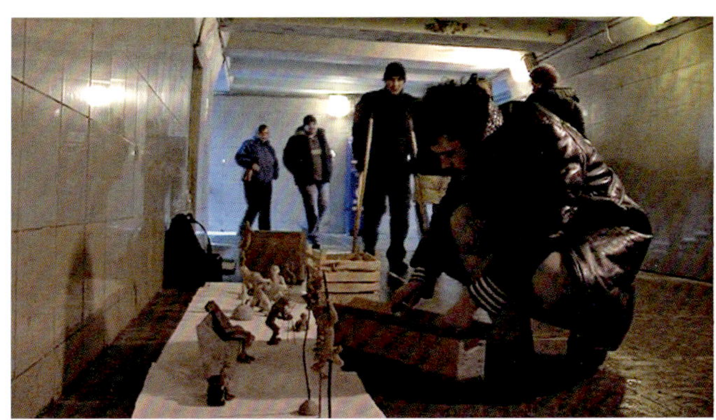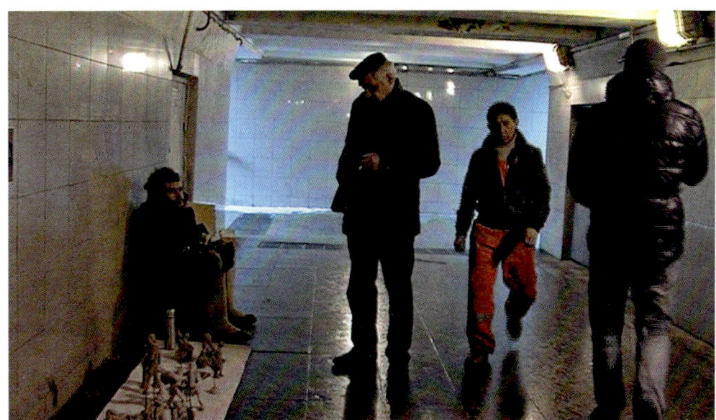

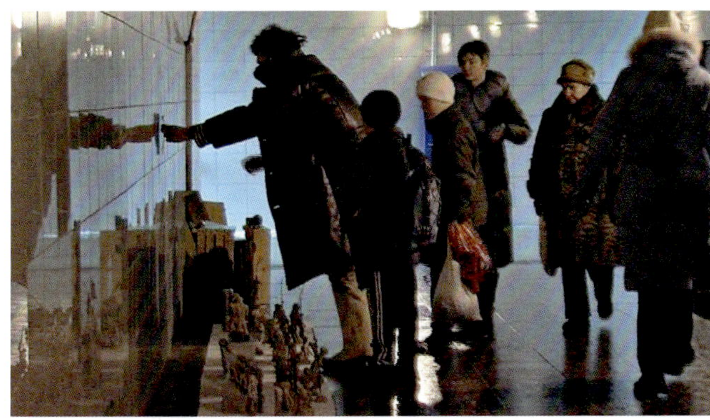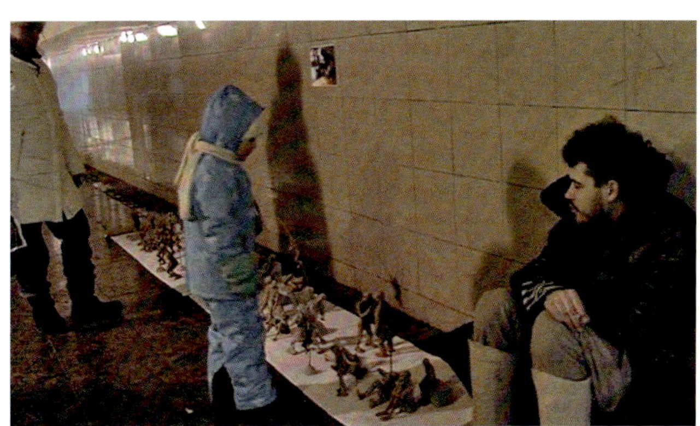

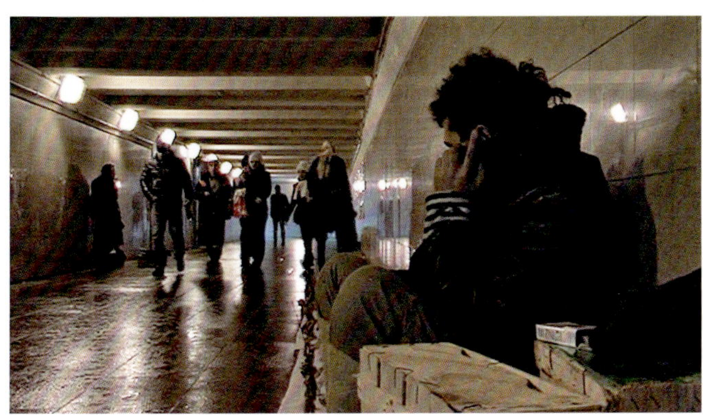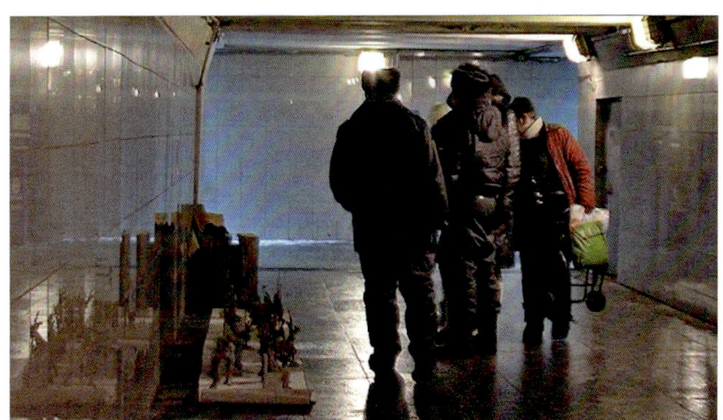

CORRIDOR OF COLLECTIVE ACTIONS 2011
INSTALLATION, VIDEO, SOUND, TEXTS

COLLECTIVE ACTIONS MAPS 2007
SERIES OF 11 ELEMENTS. C-PRINT

COURTESY THE ARTIST

The *Corridor of Collective Actions* (CA) is a corridor installation that includes maps, videos and texts to show some of the 120 actions conducted by the Collective Actions group since 1976 and during their *Trips out of Town*. It is not a straight documentation of the group's performances, but a work of art conceived by Andrei Monastyrski that uses different kinds of documentation to re-elaborate the artistic experience.

The first part consists of 11 Google maps that show the spots in the empty zones of Moscow and surroundings where the group's actions were taking place. The main installation part consists of 18 monitors, each one playing different Collective Actions performances. The soundtracks from all of the videos are directed into a separate room, where they mix together, creating a new humming sound, a metaphysical melody of the actions accomplished. Videos and sound are divided to mark the limits of perception of the essence of the actions, the communicational margins. The congested compressed sound accentuates the extreme silence that surrounded the artists in the place of an action, as well as the evident muteness of the Moscow audience.

The key for understanding lies in the third part of the CA corridor that consists of the texts: Monastyrski affirms that the text is the only thing that is left, and the only possible way to realize the ideas of the CA performances. The textological metalevel of the actions is a reflection upon the borderline between town and nontown (out-of-town) and, in more general terms, between art and life. The duality of gorod-zagorod (town and nontown) can be explained in simple terms of urbanization or enclosure and elaborated in a complex plot of multiple events and simultaneous narrations. The zagorodness becomes a destination: a vague and uncertain concept and, as such, psychologically erogenous.

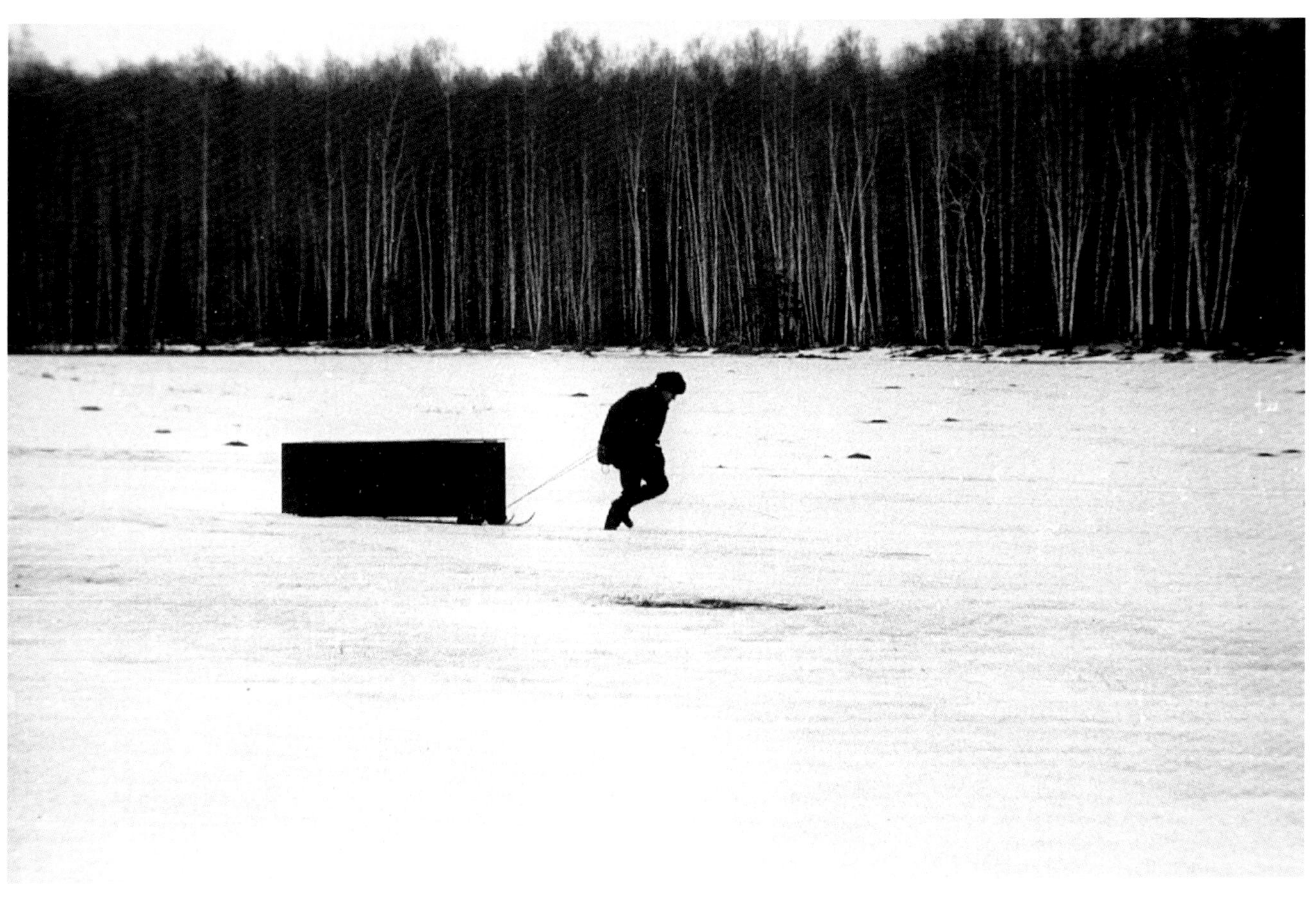

ALEXANDRA

MRAKOBAMBRA 2009-2012
PAPER, WATERCOLOR, FOUND OBJECT
COURTESY THE ARTIST

This small series of paper masks is a collection of fragile sculptures that give form to the artist's perception of time. The artist recollects her intricate biographical experiences influenced by different environments and represents them by indirect portraits. These empty masks, like boxes for memory, are a way to preserve information and shape it in space. As architectures of the mind, they act as reminders of people and sites of meanings. The absence behind them paradoxically produces presence, and the category of the unspeakable becomes an important dimension in the work. One of the masks contains an old art-nouveau door: it is for the artist a sort of spring, where the mask is a guarantee for the door, something that helps to hold it in place.
Folded paper was a common material for the presentation of design projects in Soviet Russia, and folded cardboard was always the most reliable medium for building architectural models for the coming urban environment. However, the pattern of the watercolored masks reminds us of the easily recognizable furniture surface of the standardized Soviet interiors.
The title *Mrakobambra* is a neologism invented by the author. In Russian, it phonetically recollects night and obscurity (deriving from "мрак") and, at the same time, has an elastic rumble.

SUKHAREVA

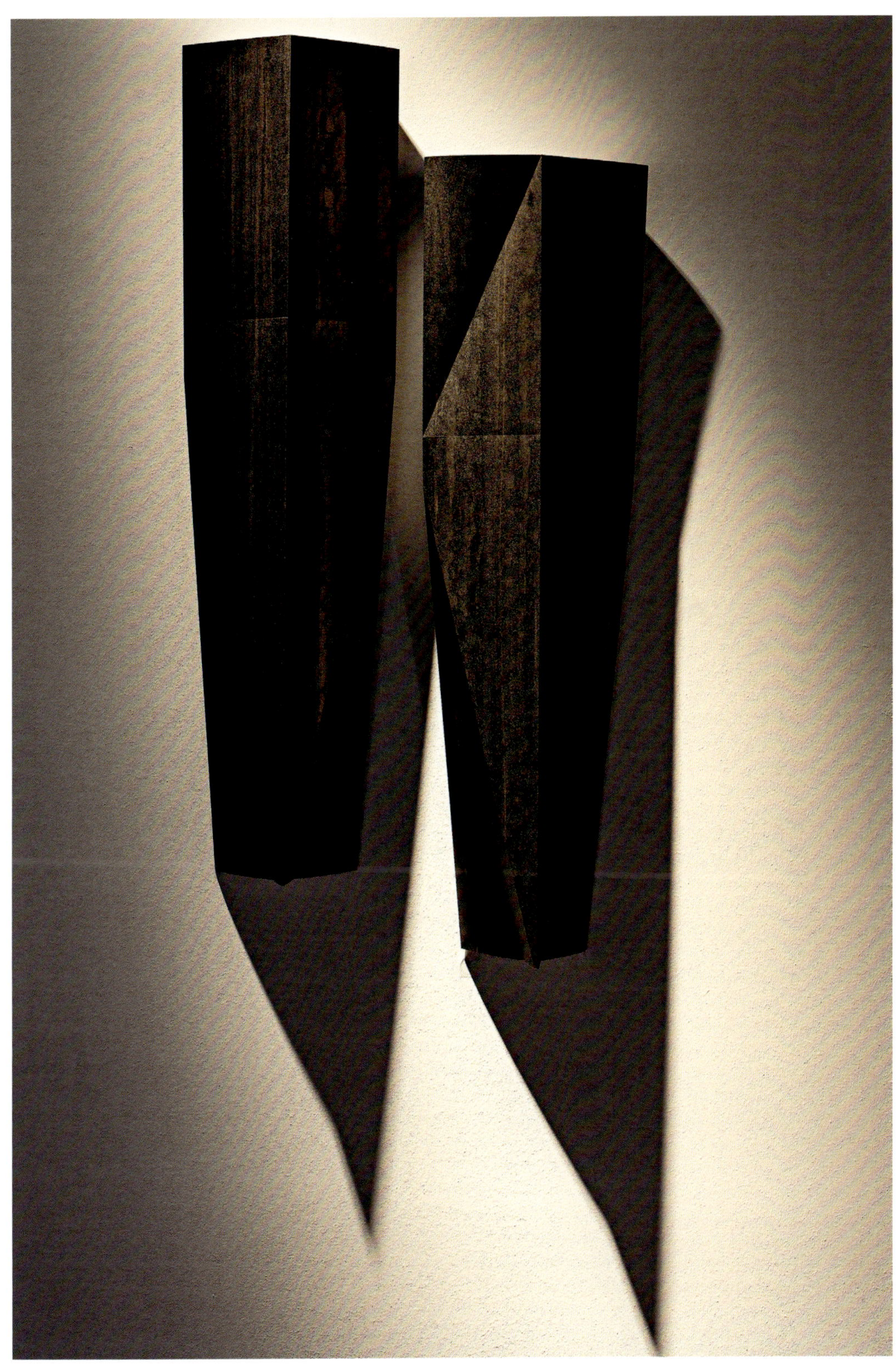

PSKOV 2010
BOOK BY GLUSCHENKOIZDAT (GLUSCHENKO PUBLISHING HOUSE)
COURTESY THE ARTIST

Gluschenkoizdat is a publishing art project by Kirill Gluschenko, a young artist who travels to small towns of the former USSR trying to make a mould of a vanished country. He documents and researches the remnants of Soviet reality – makes photographs, looks through old Soviet architectural magazines, and finds diaries of people who lived in the Soviet era and uses every possible mean to reconstruct the lost reality. The purpose is to regain the true image of the last years of the Soviet era. Those years have become a sort of a myth, especially for people who were still very young in the 1980s. This historical and artistic reconstruction of time and space should help the artist to understand his own generation.

The result is always a book conceived as a piece of art. This medium is crucial for the artist, because the recreated world he constructs on the border between reality and fiction. The real objects and places become a surreal continuity that an artist envisages as a Kafkaesque world.

Every book published by Gluschenkoizdat, the artist's imaginary publishing house, places a viewer in a situation in which he stops understanding where the boundaries are between the two worlds – the surrounding present one and the one recreated in the book. This book is a report of Gluschenko's three trips to Pskov, a town in northern Russia that he used to visit in his childhood.

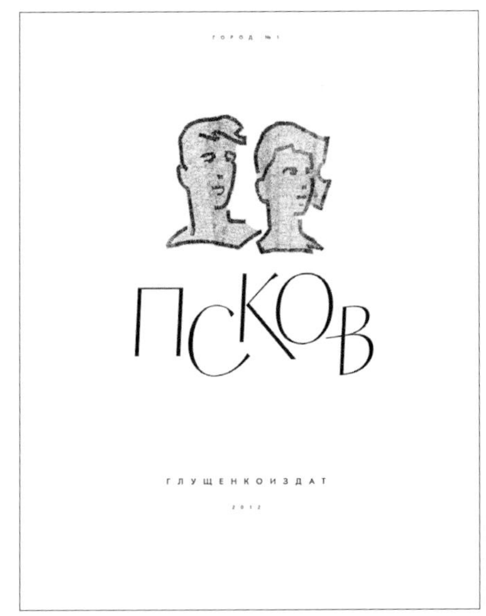

ГОРОД №1
ПСКОВ
ГЛУЩЕНКОИЗДАТ
2012

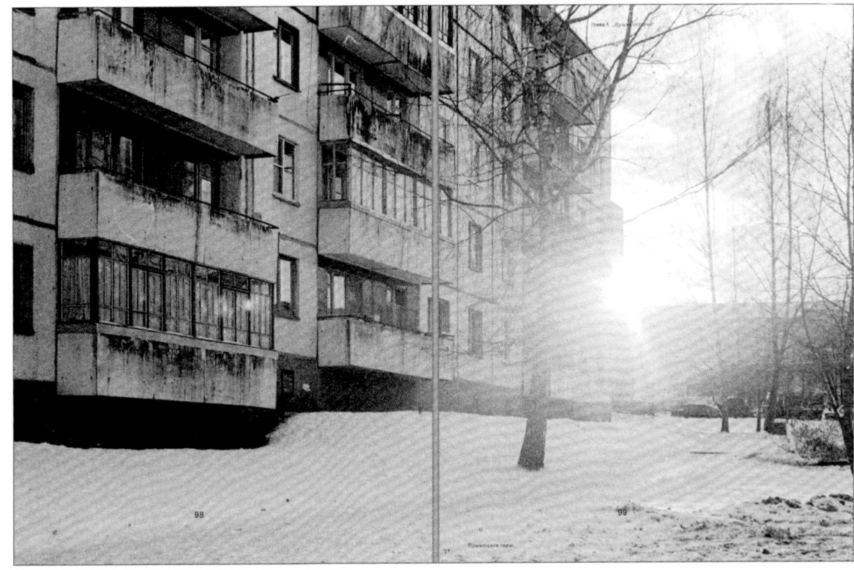

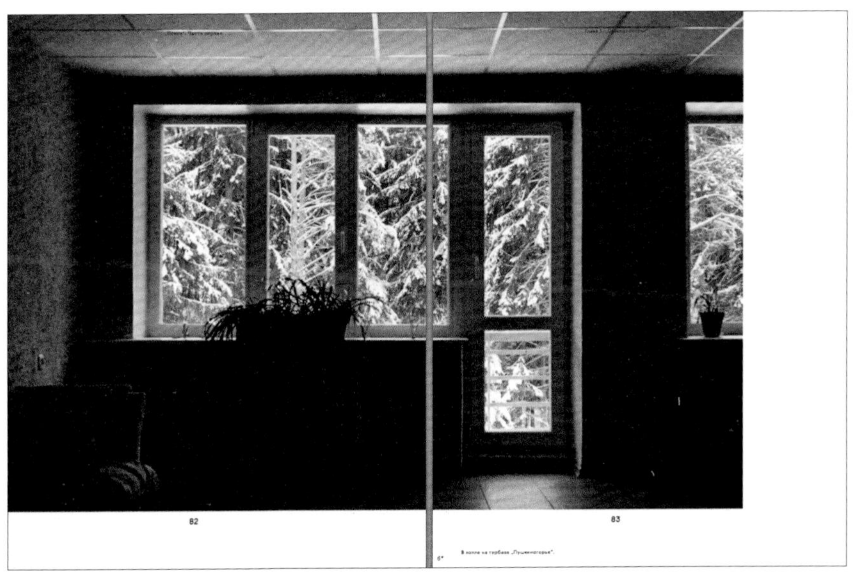

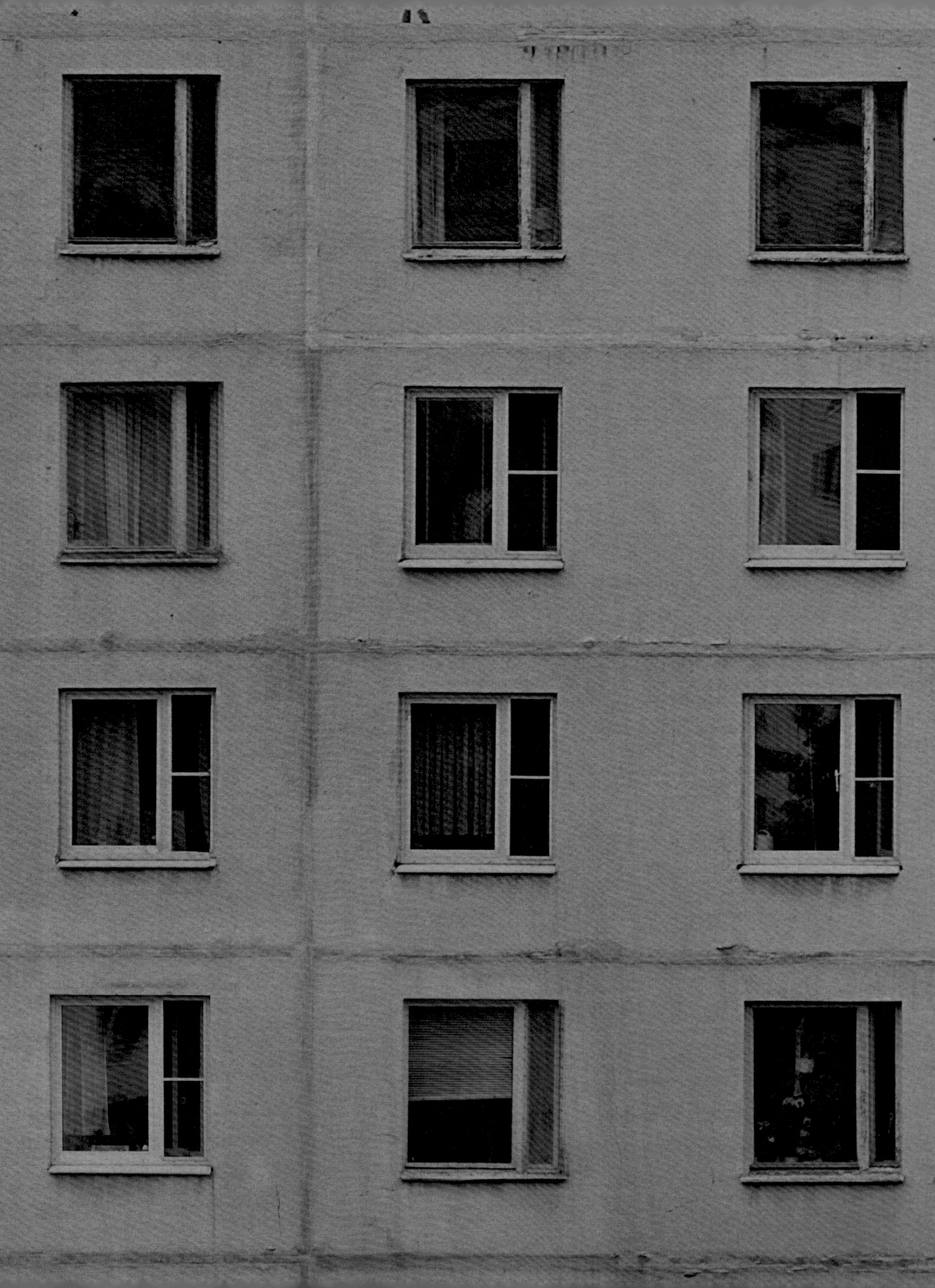

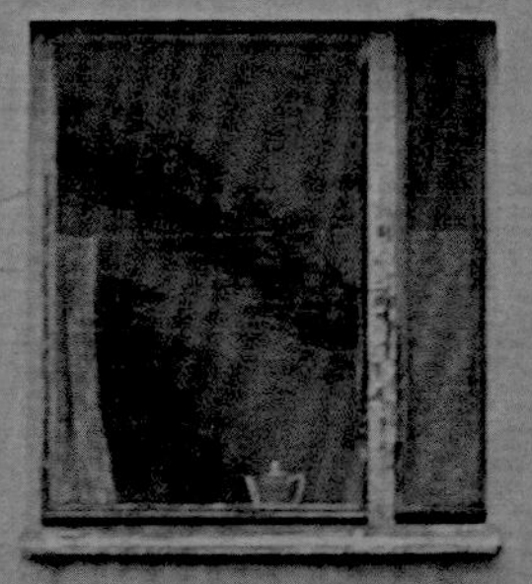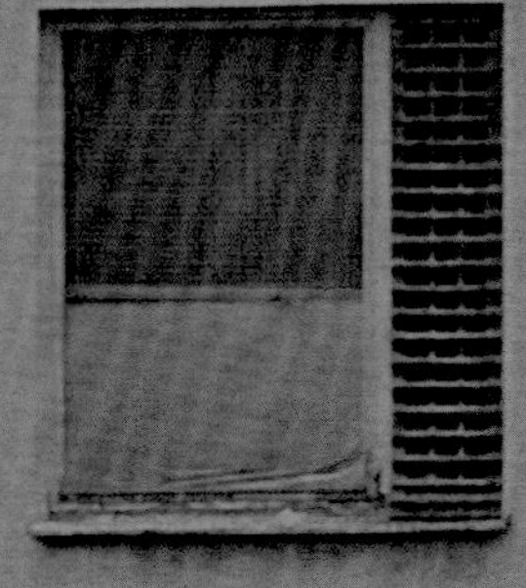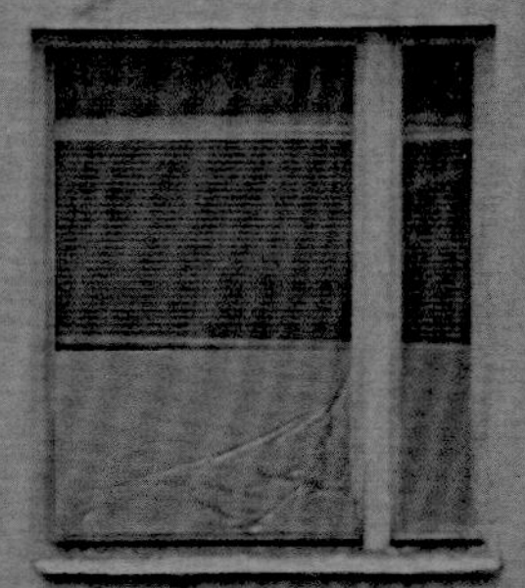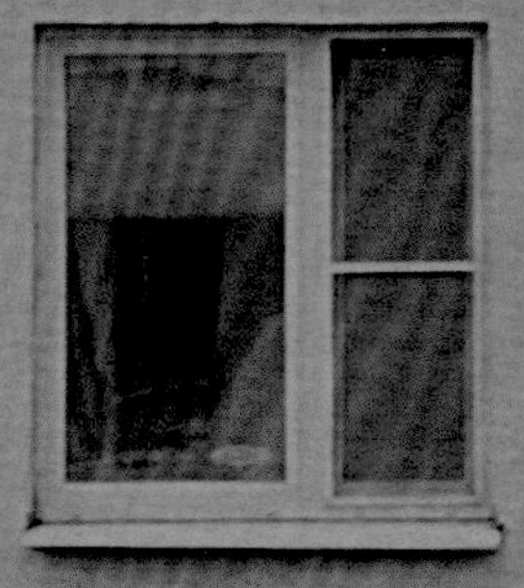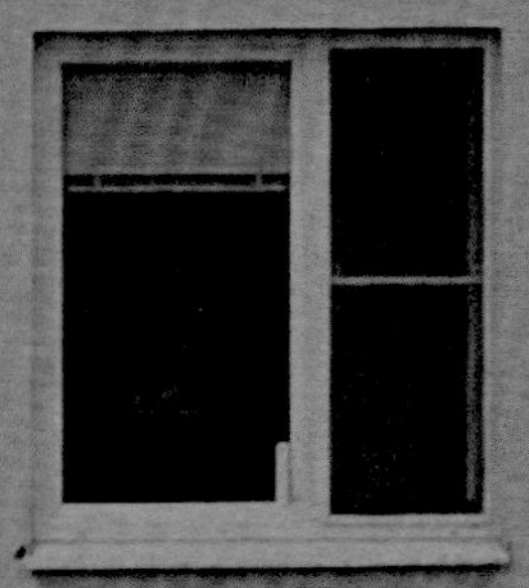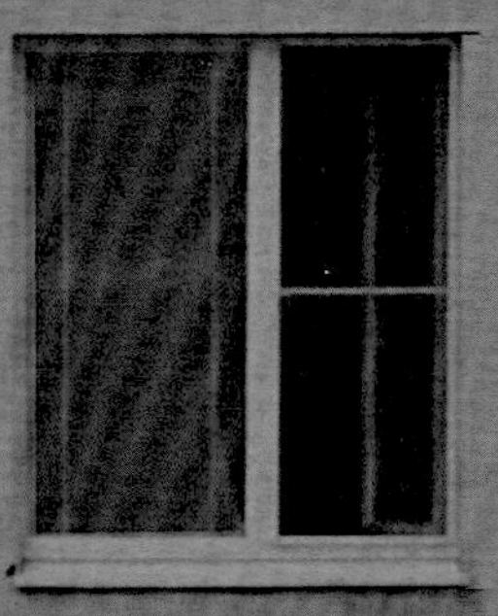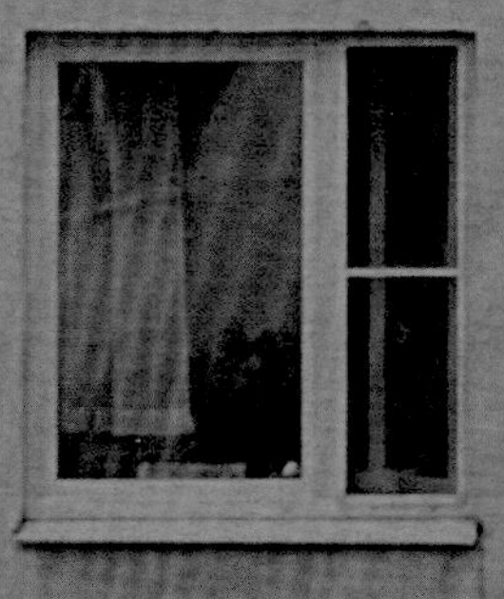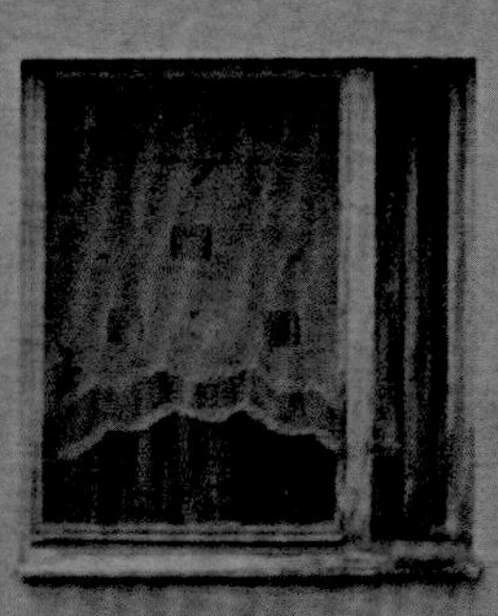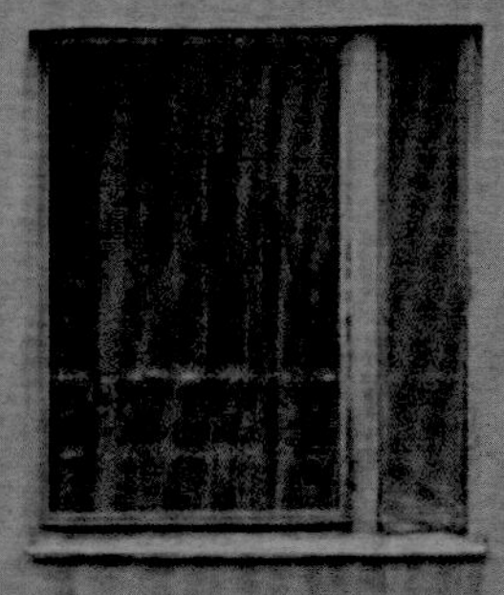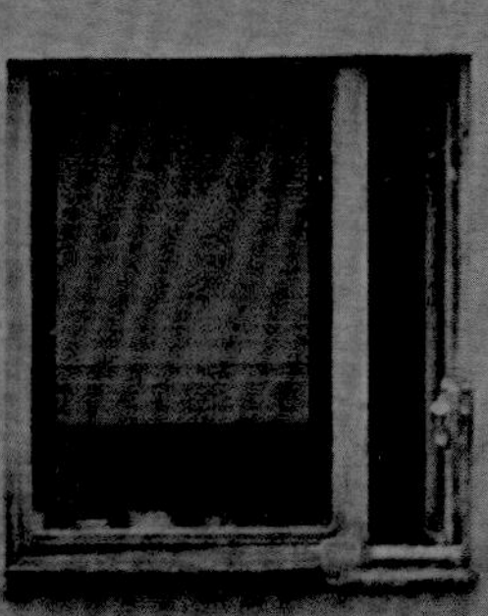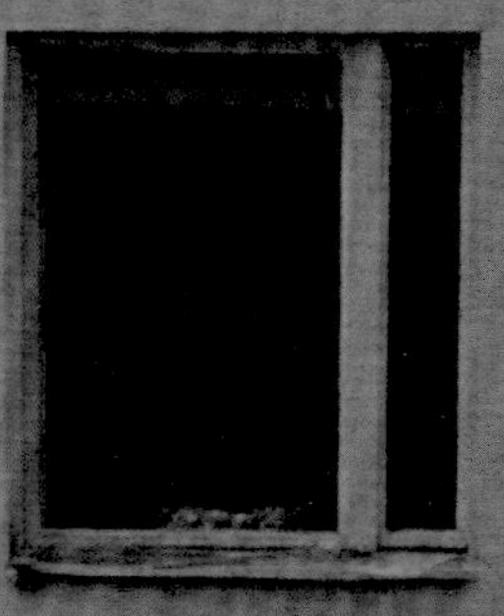

THE EXHIBITION

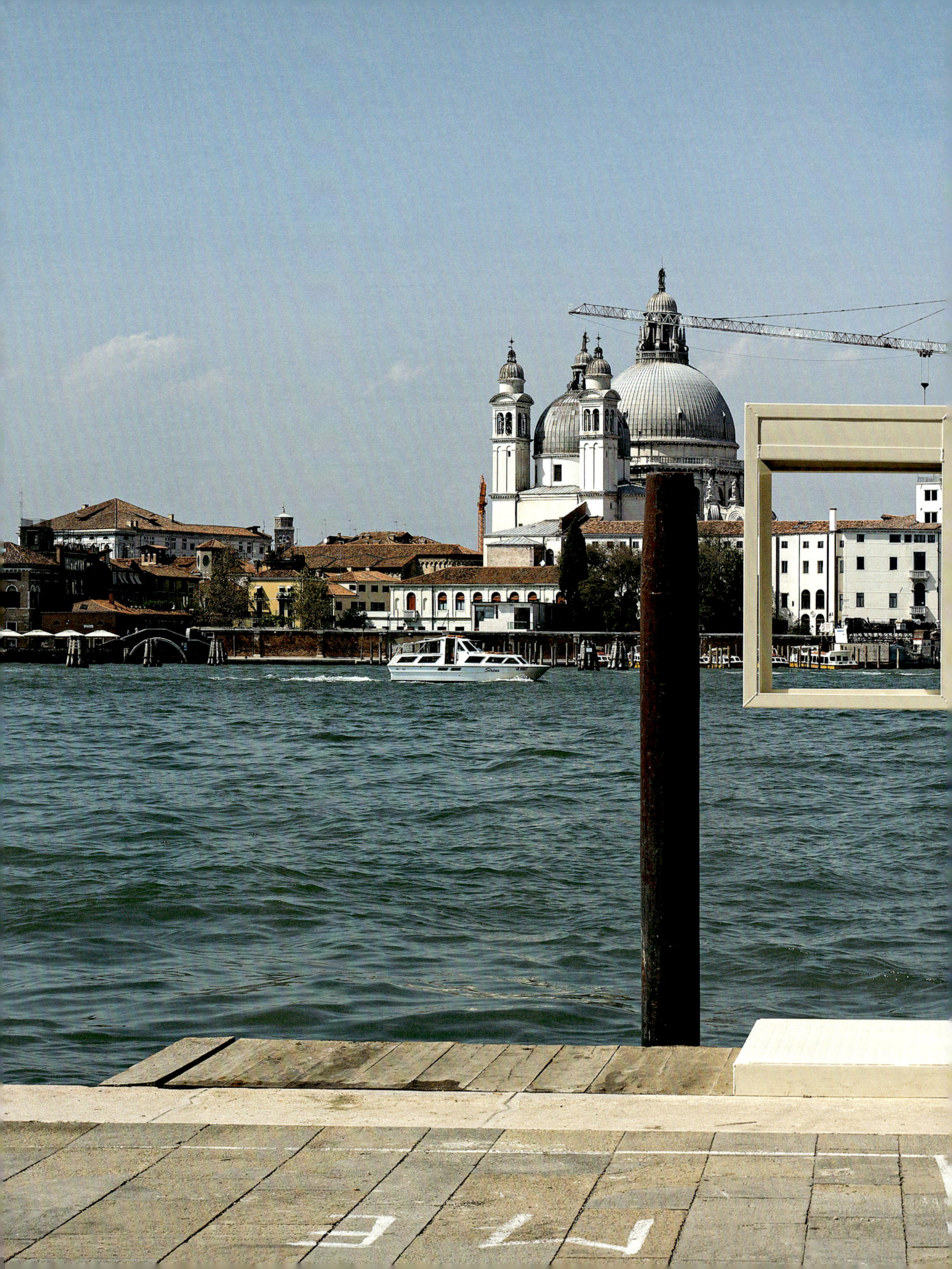

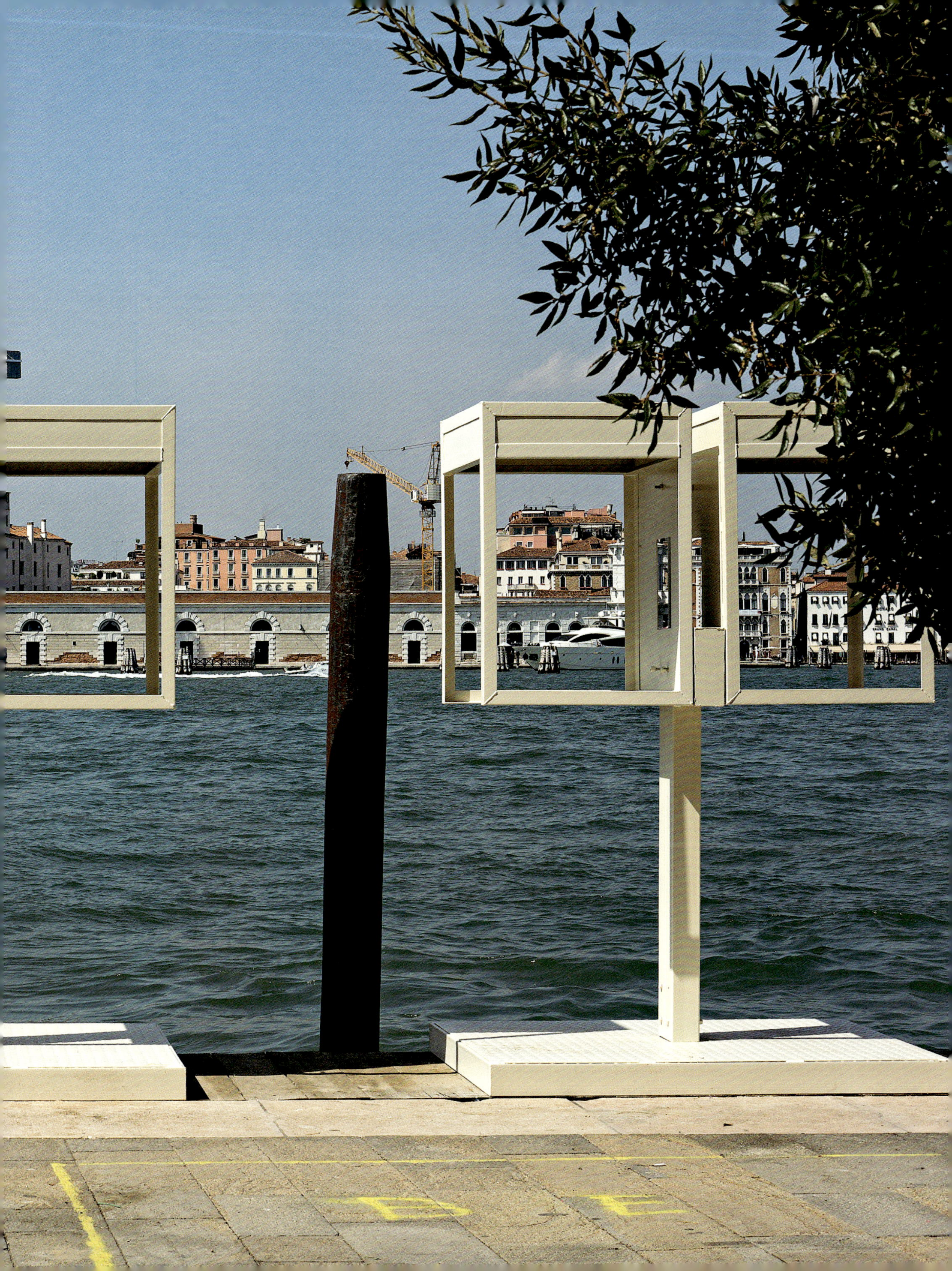

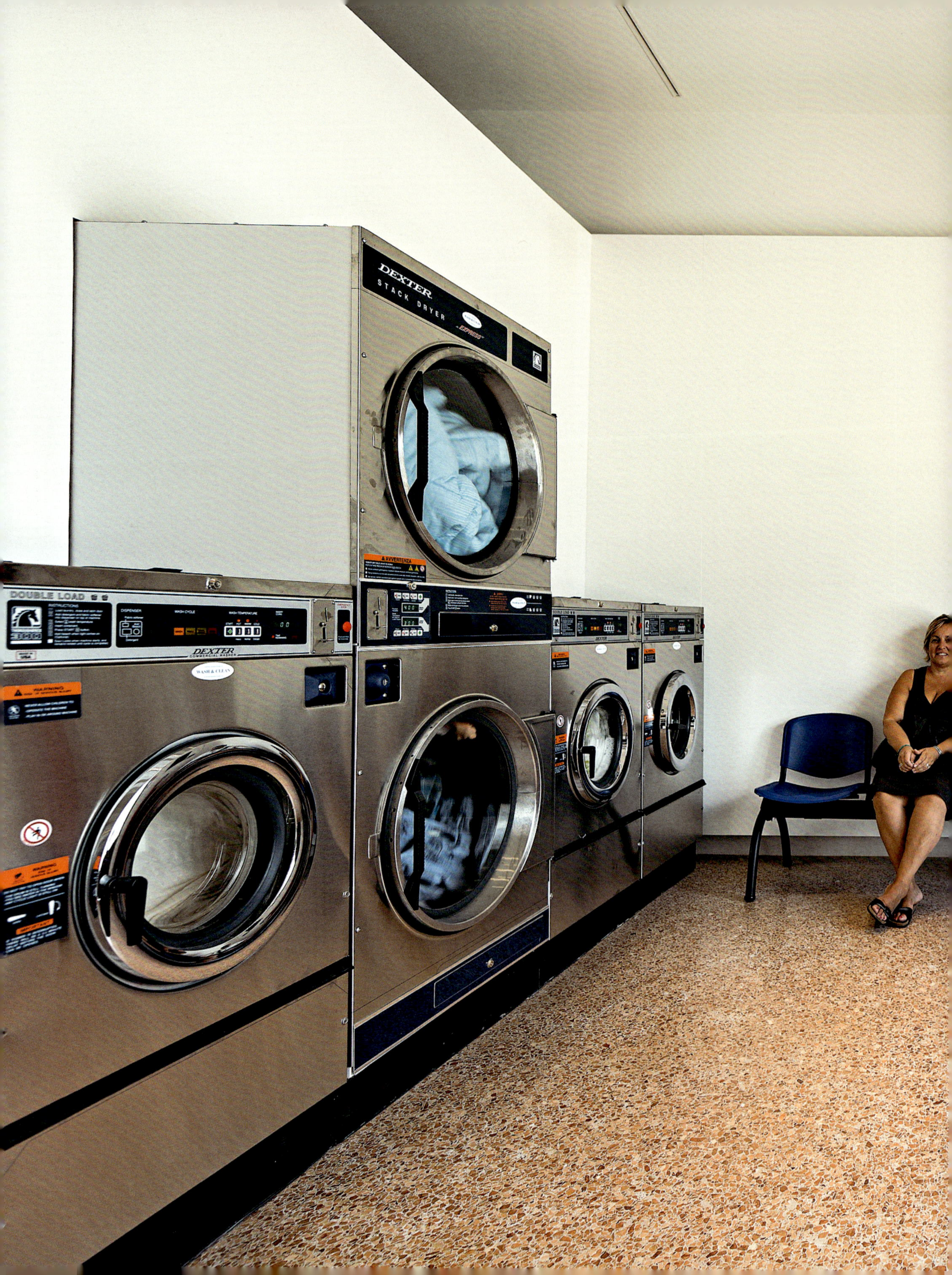

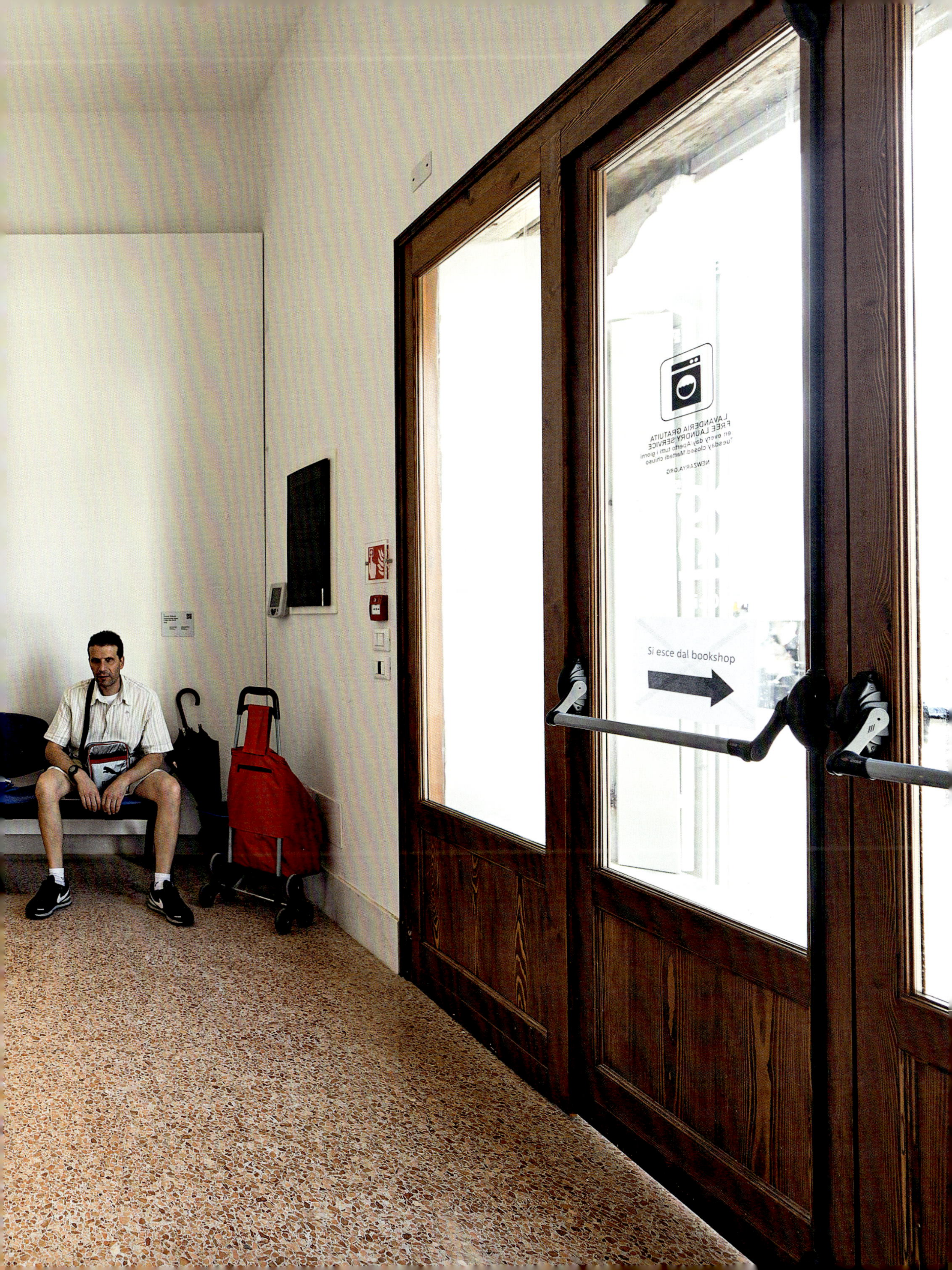
Si esce dal bookshop

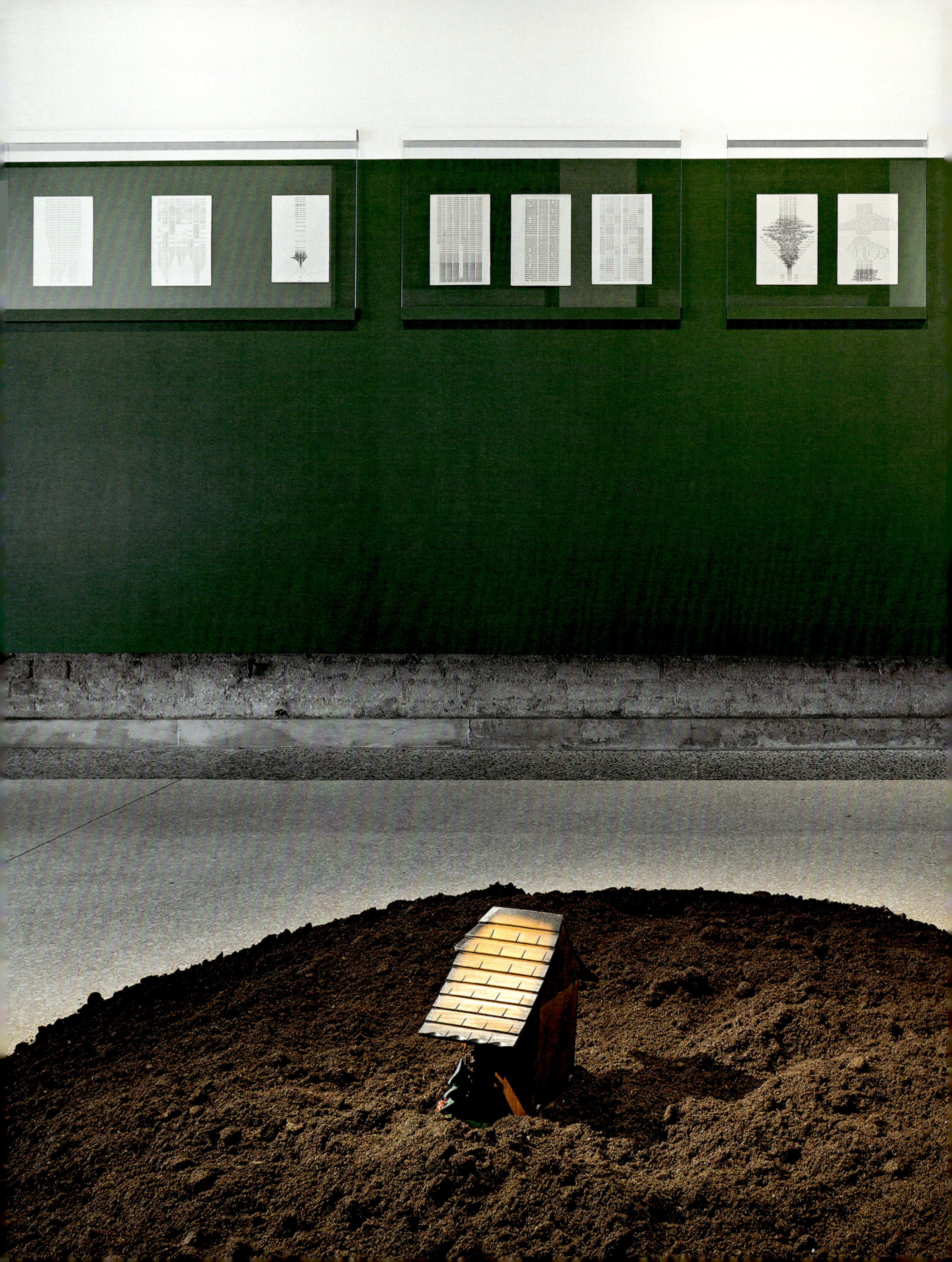

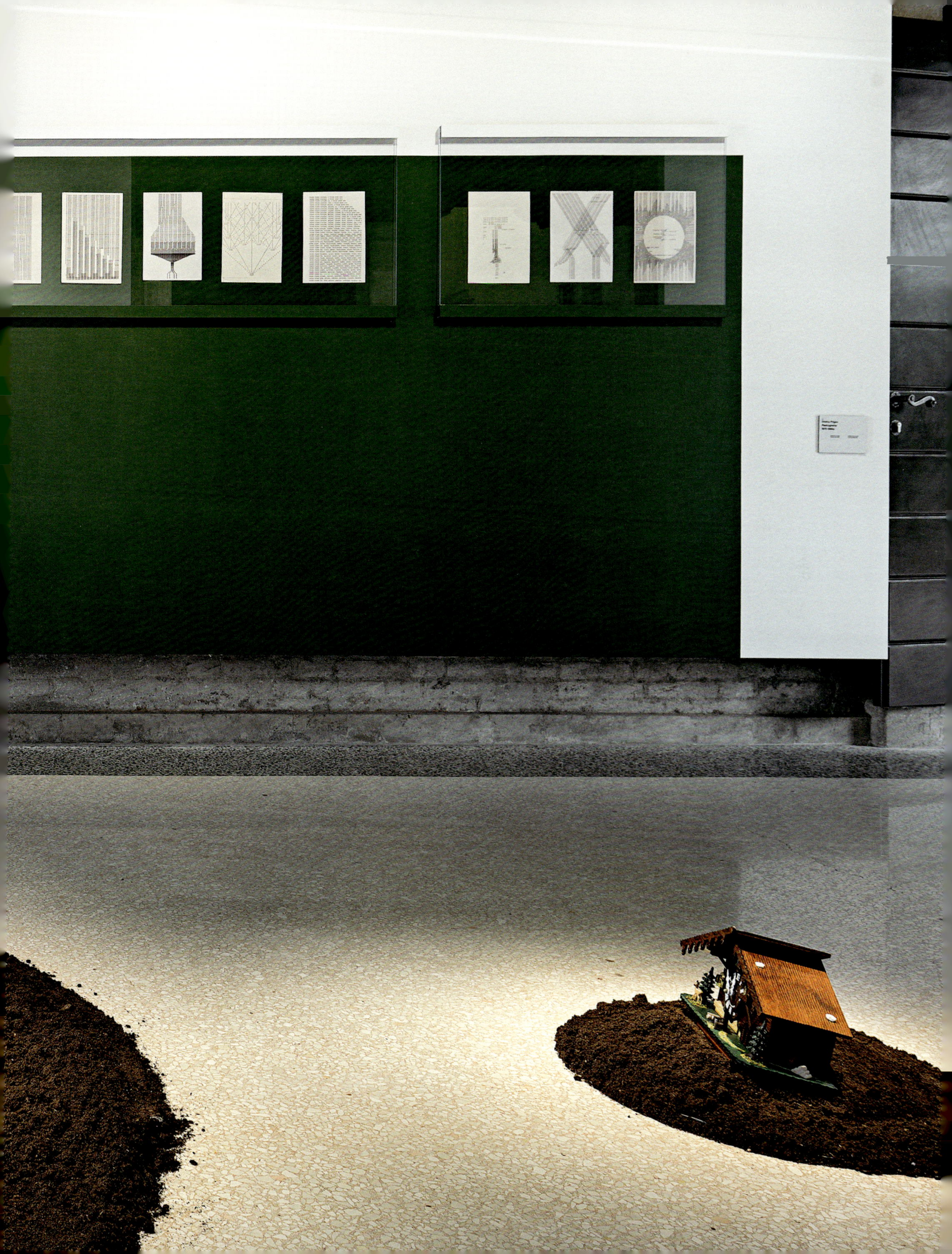

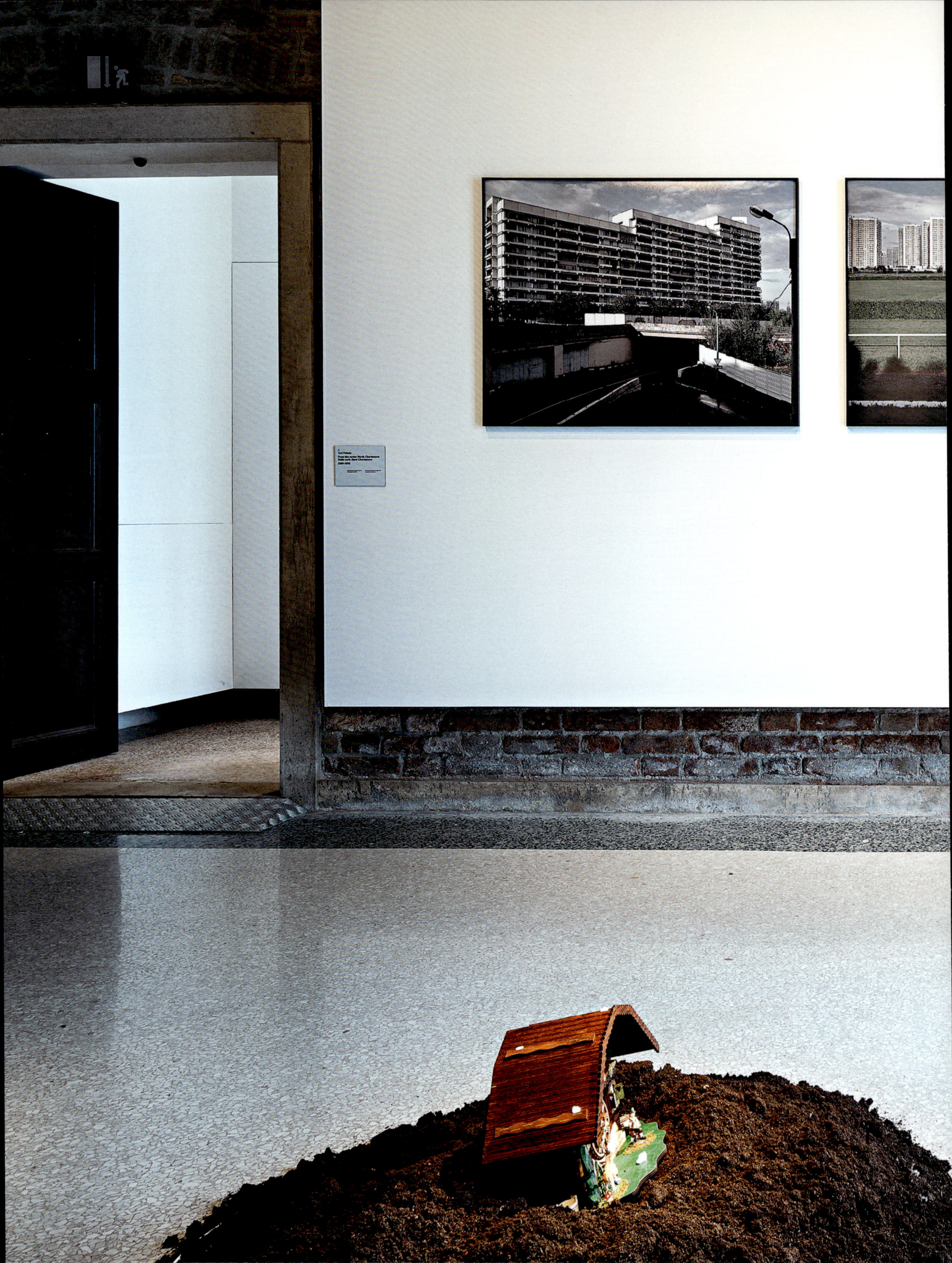

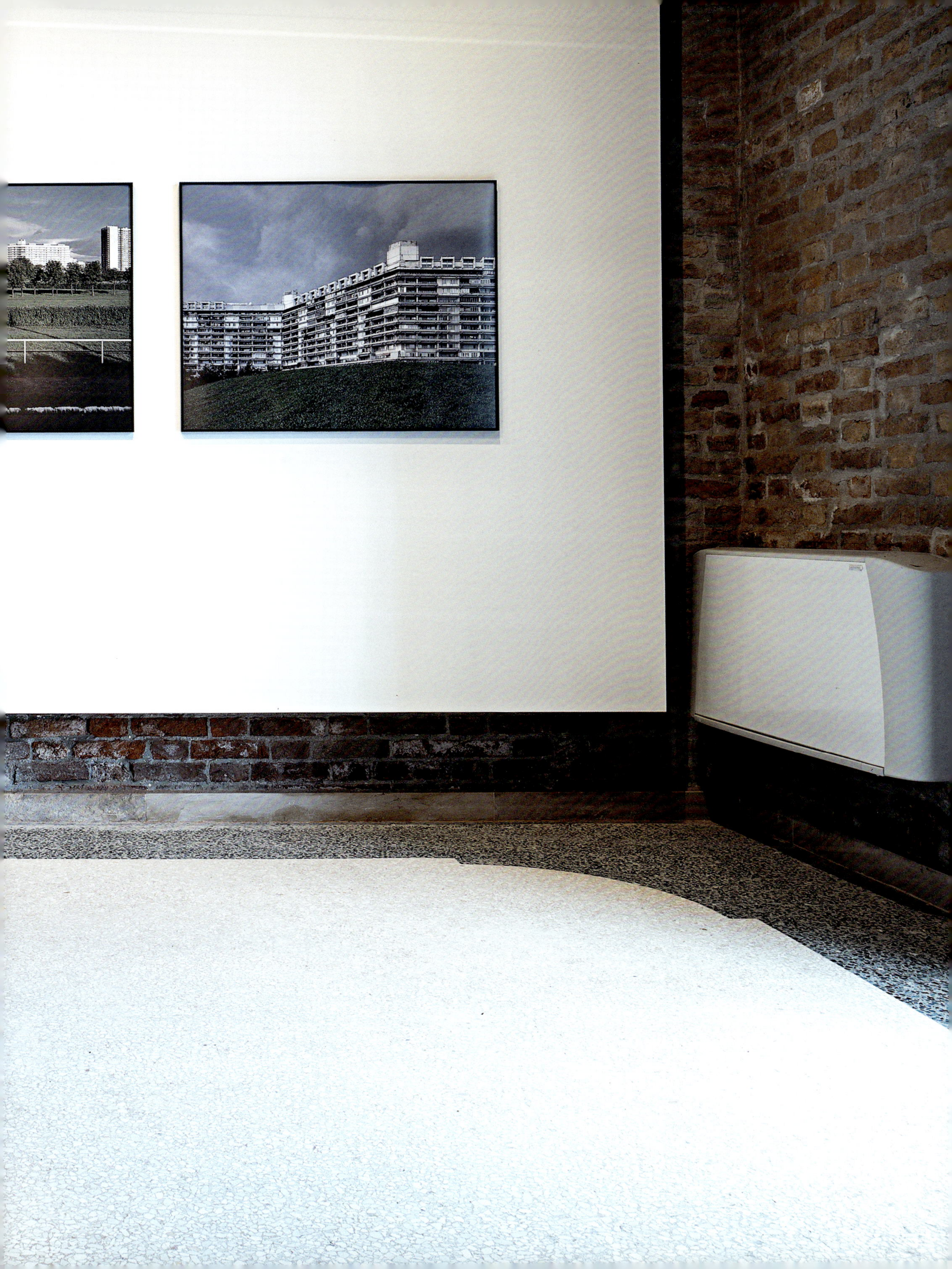

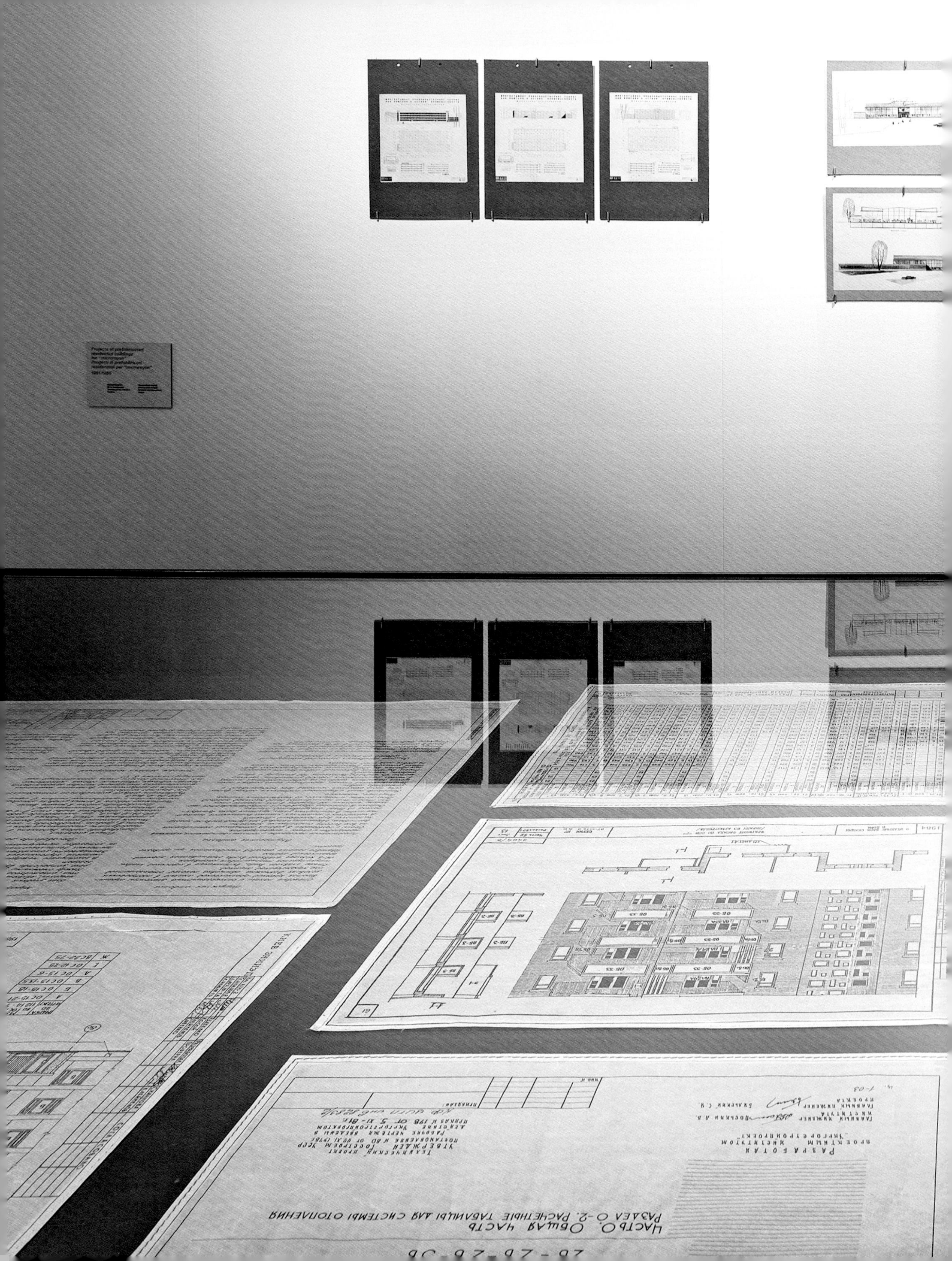

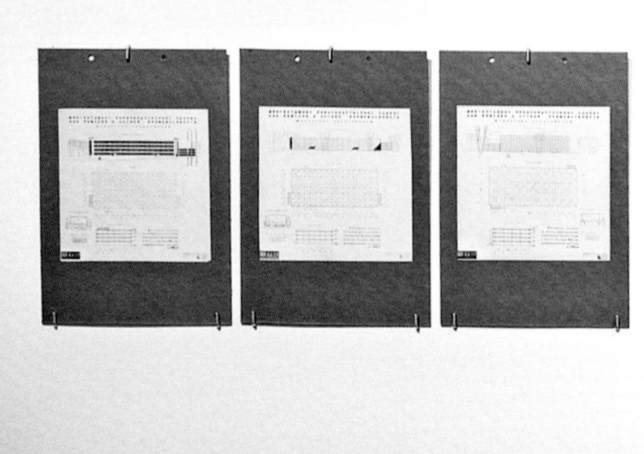
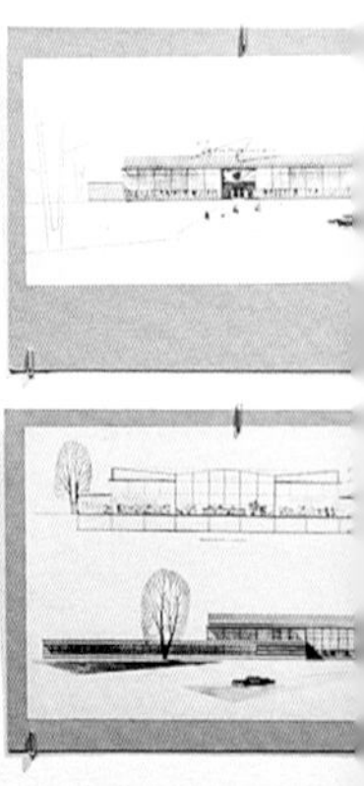
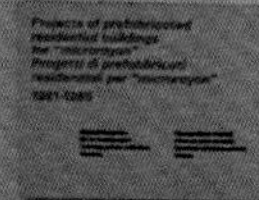

Projects of prefabricated
residential buildings
for "microrayon"
Progetti di prefabbricati
residenziali per "microrayon"
1961-1965

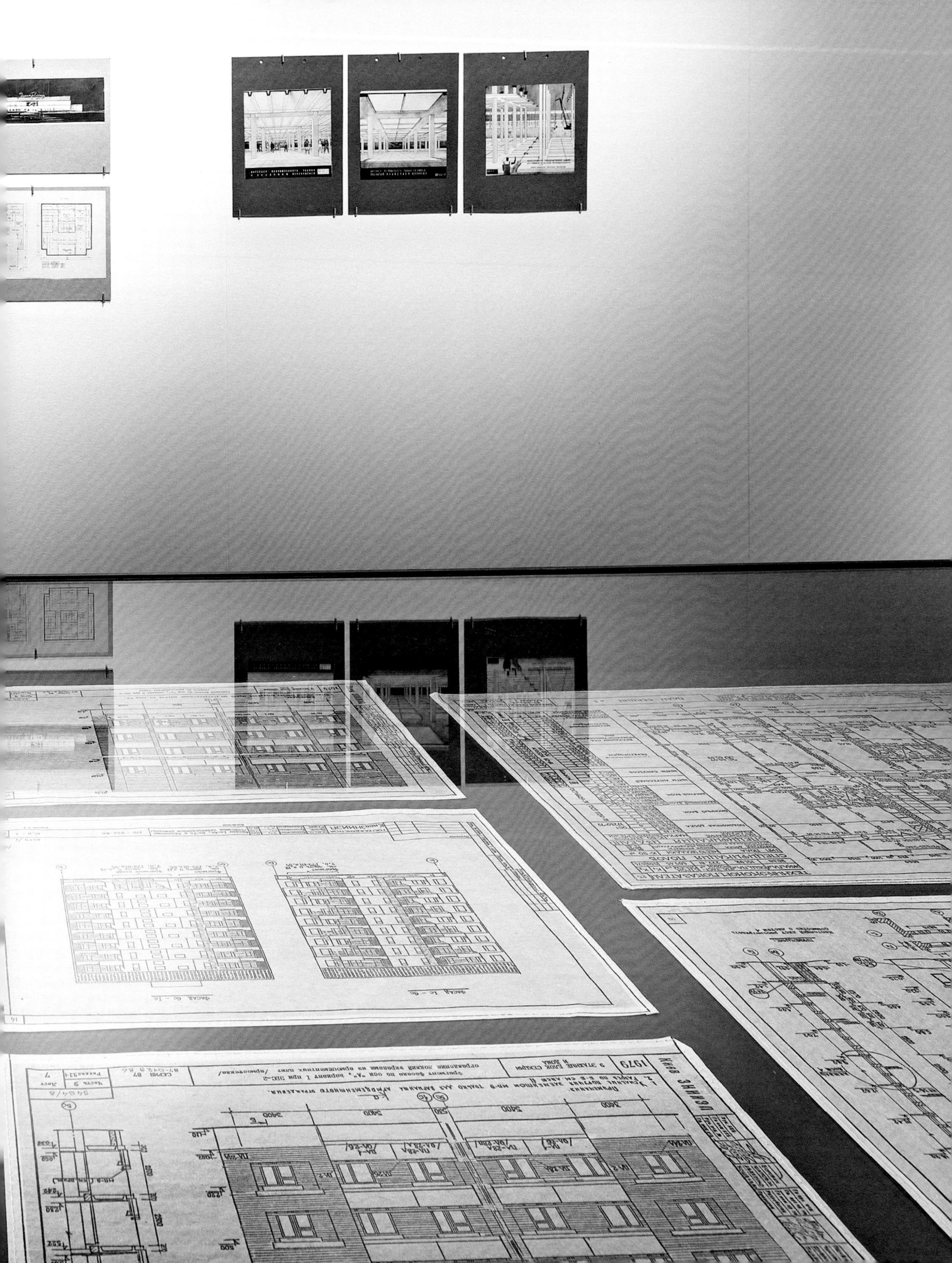

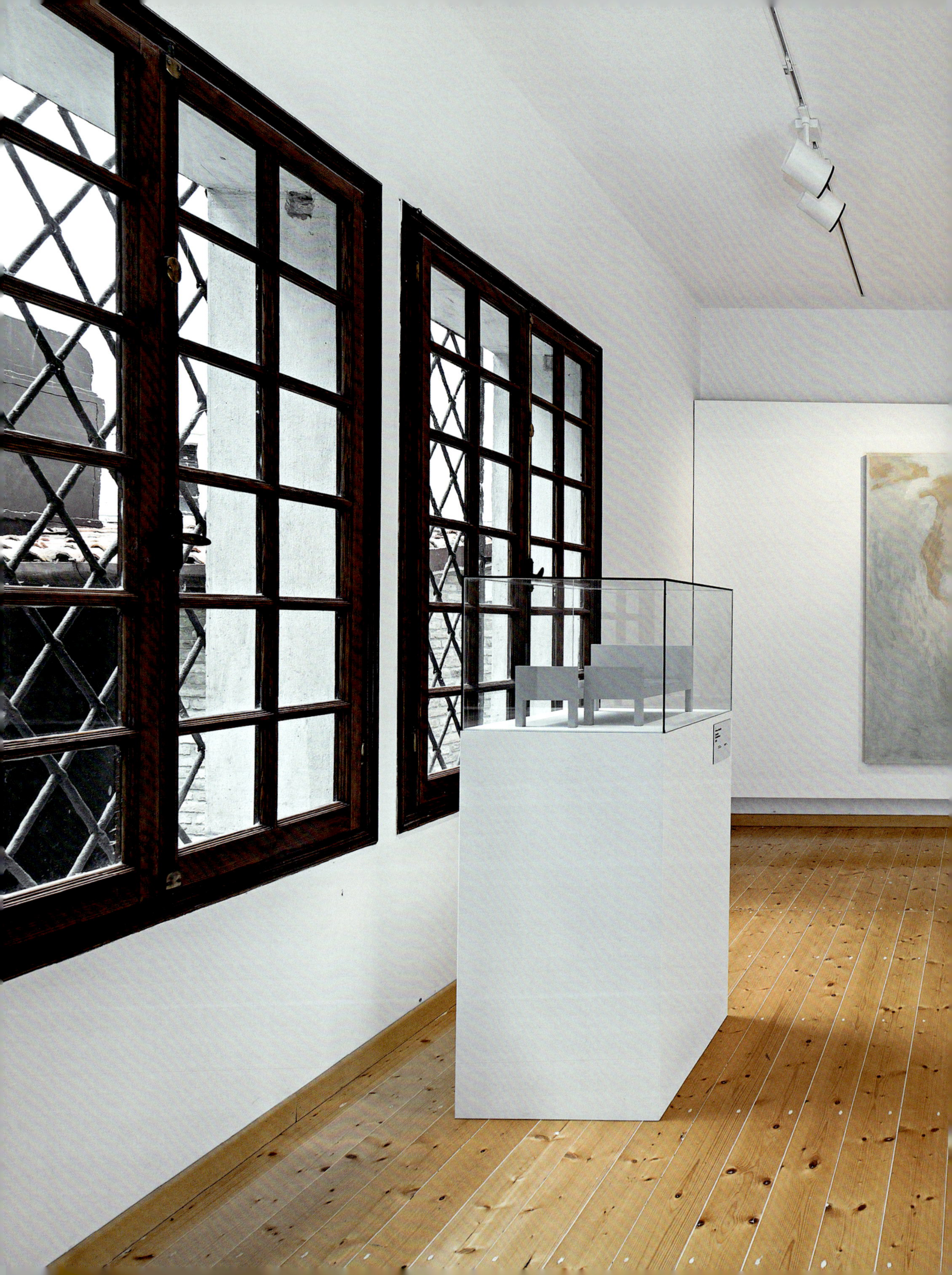

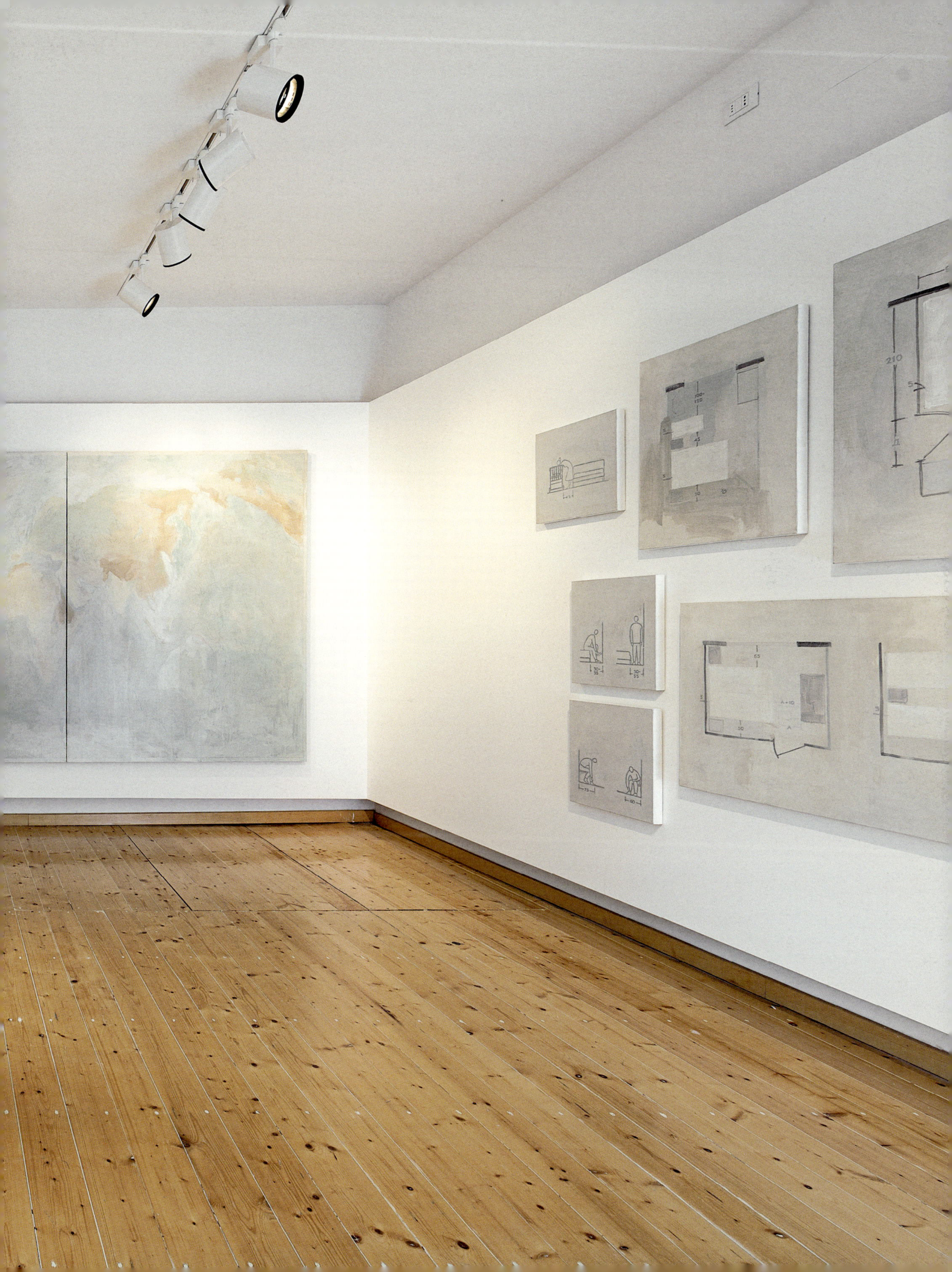

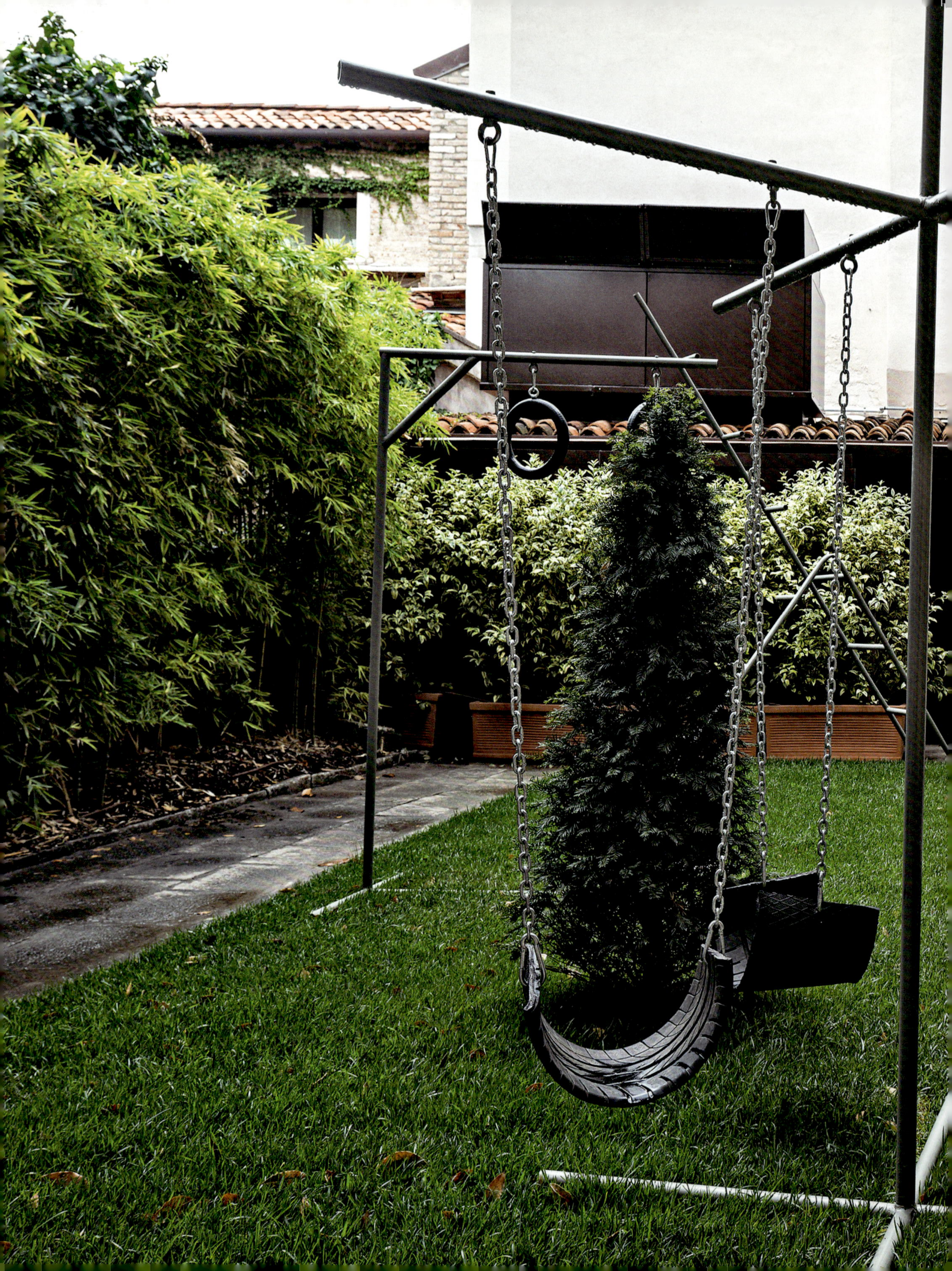

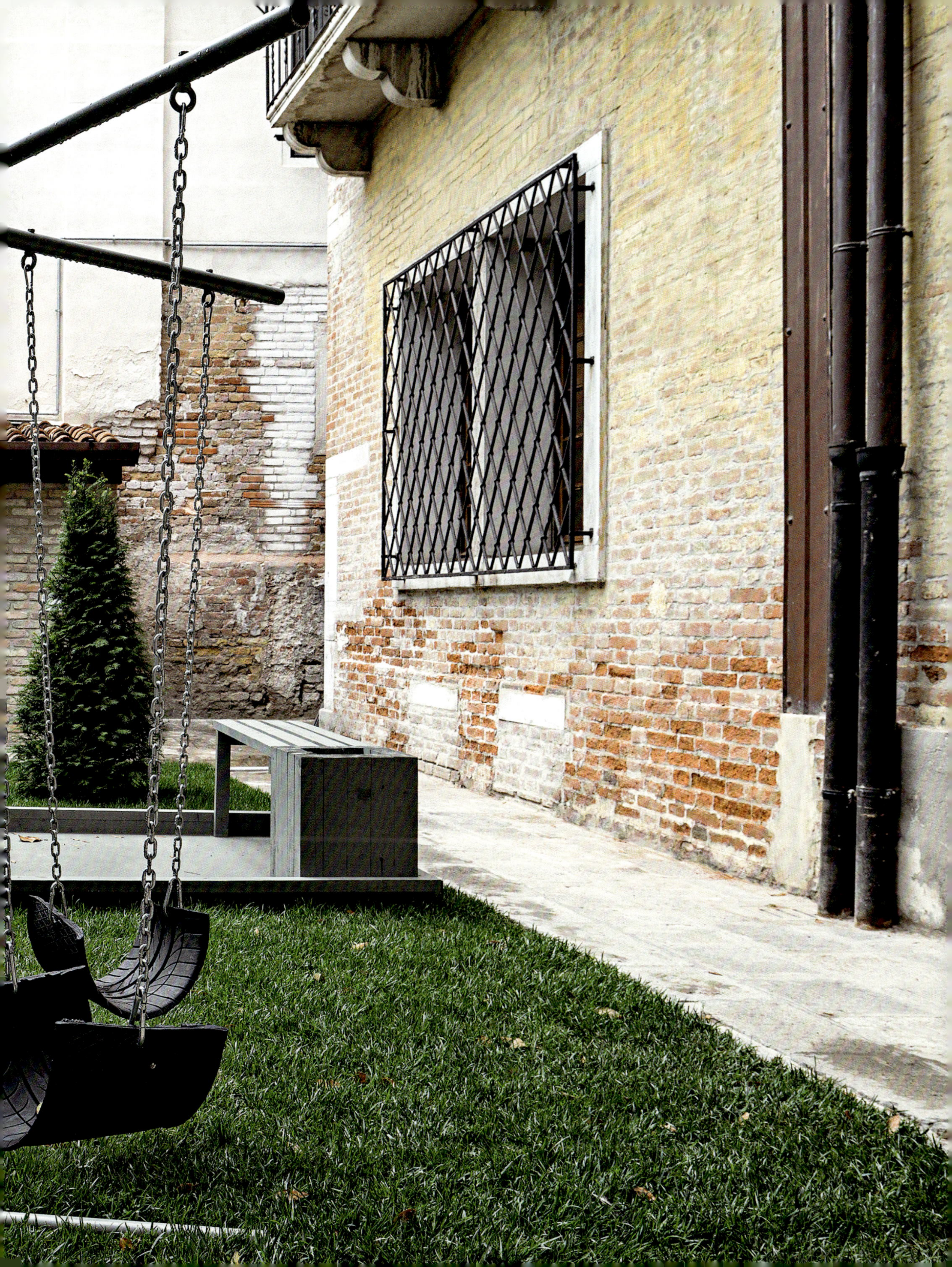

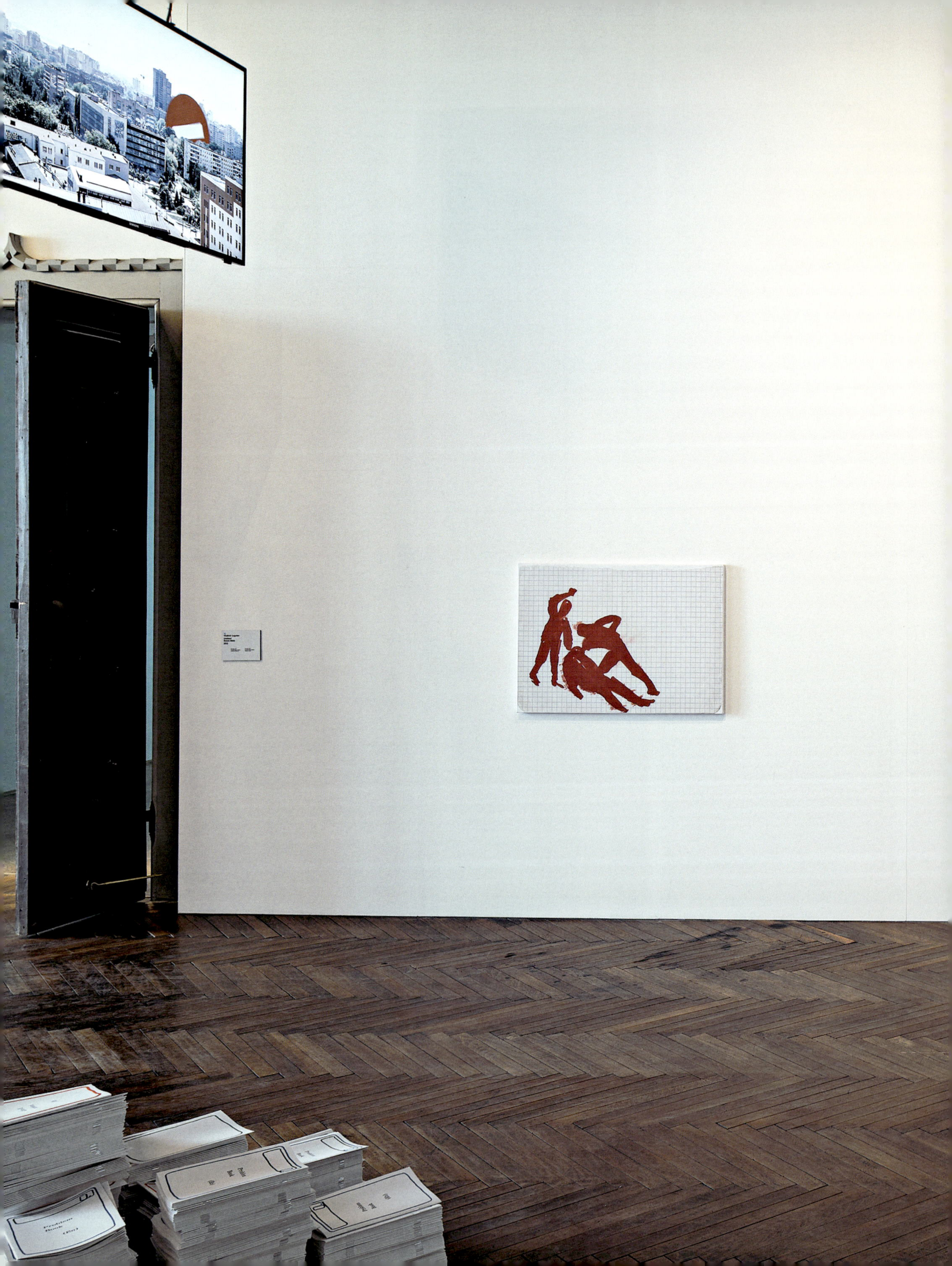

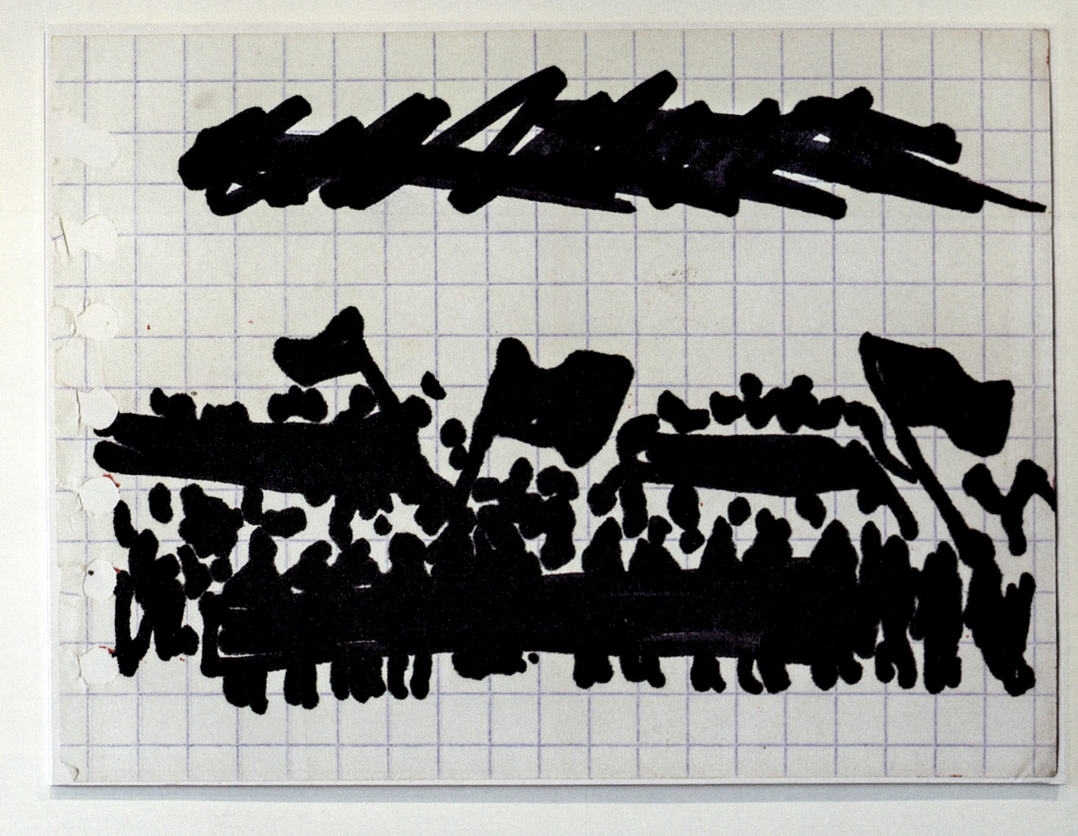
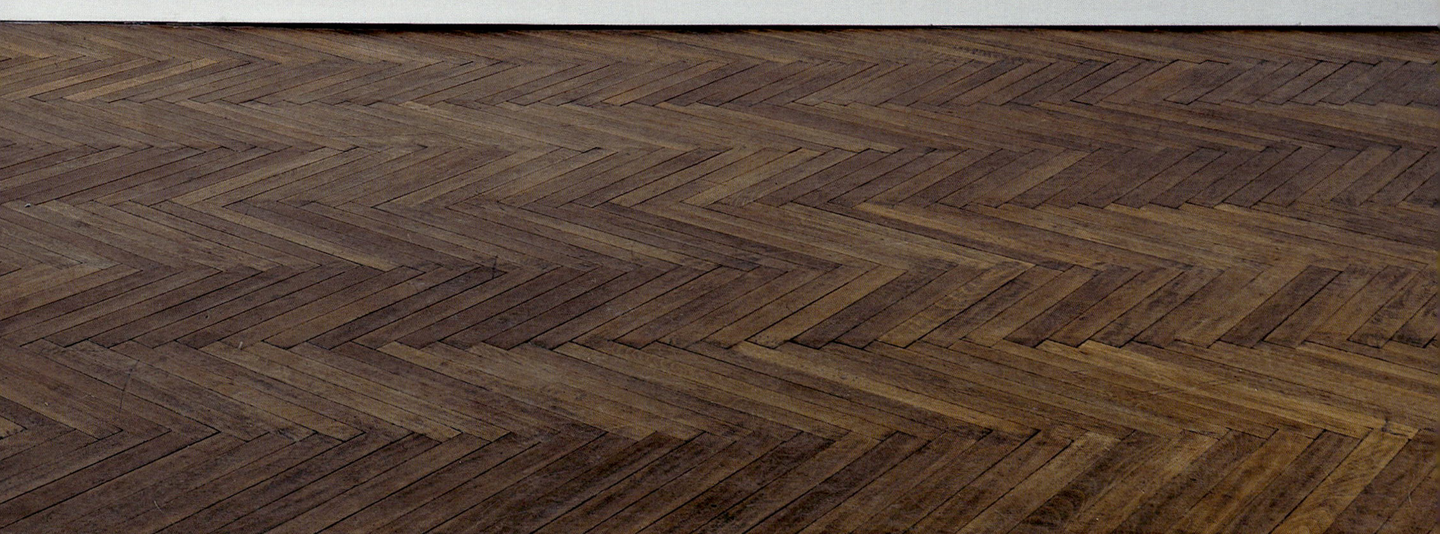

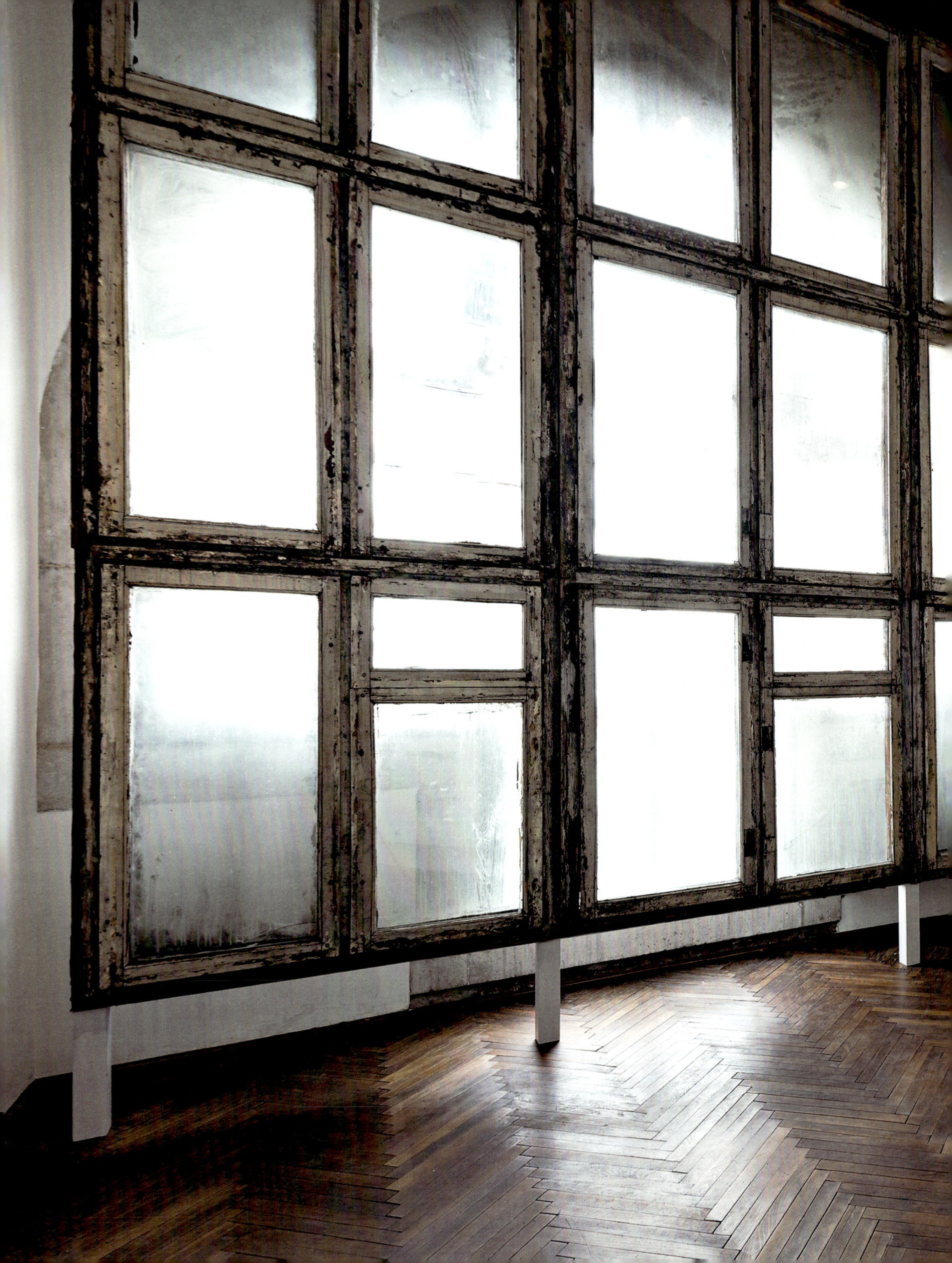

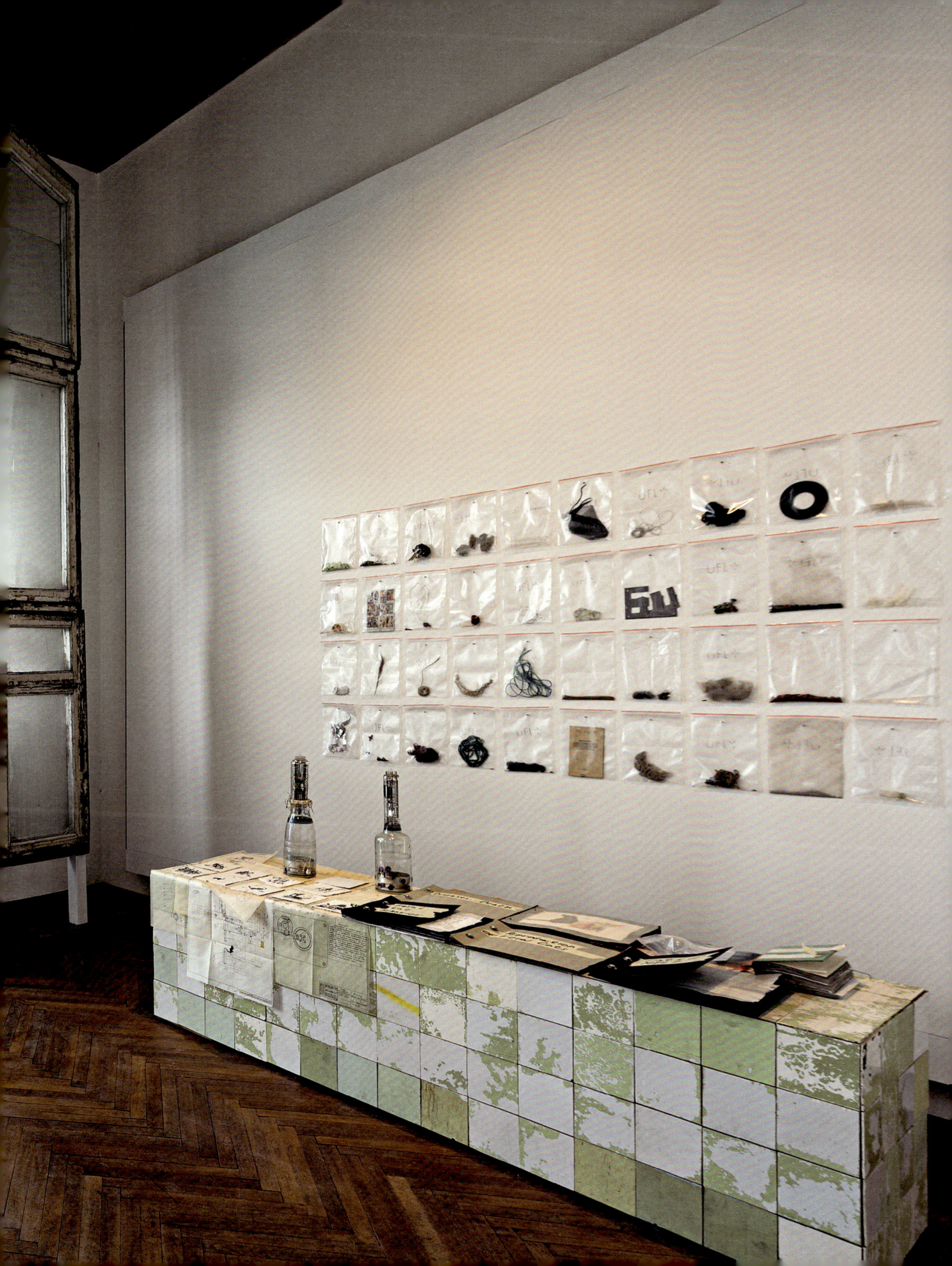

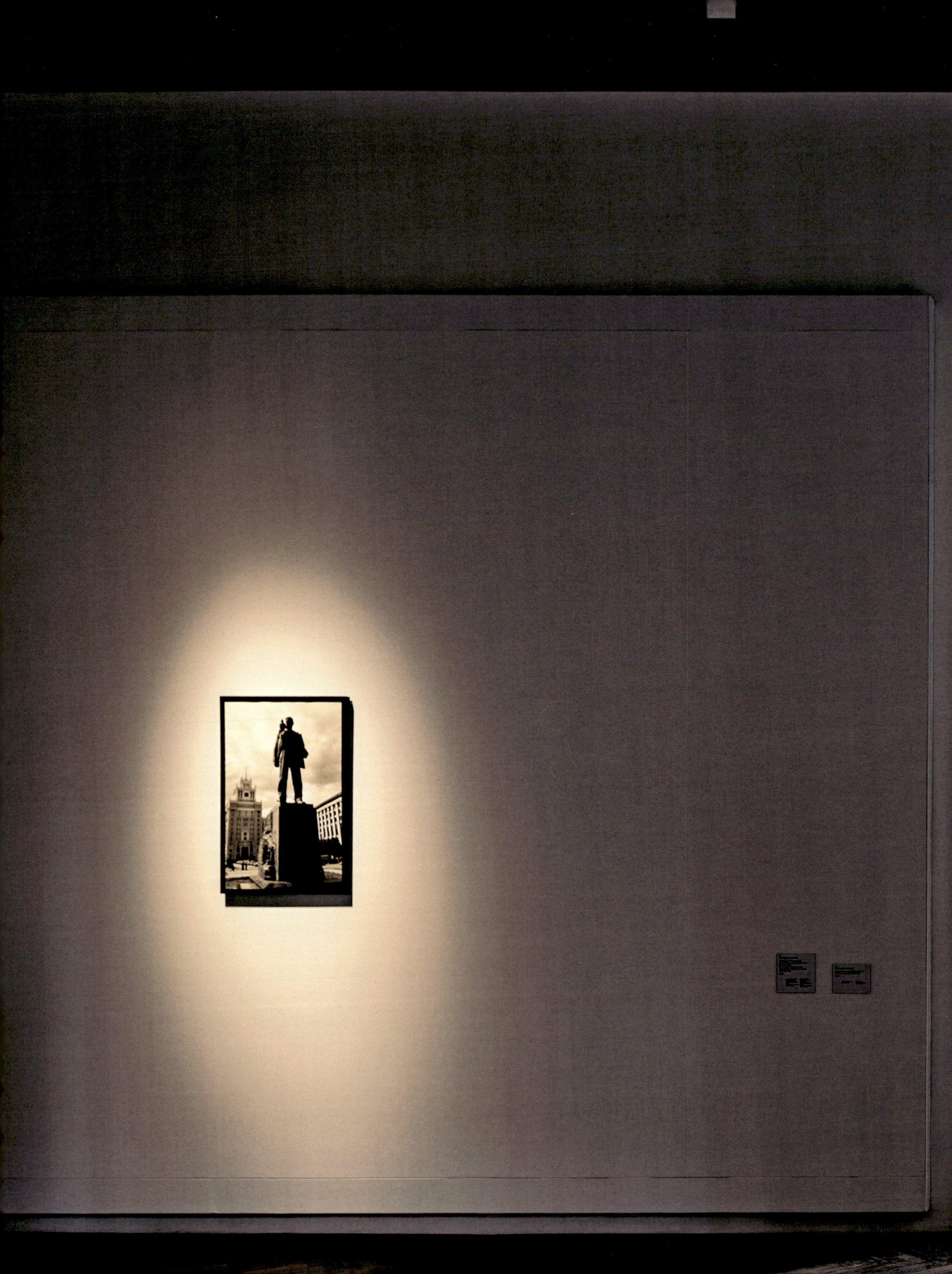

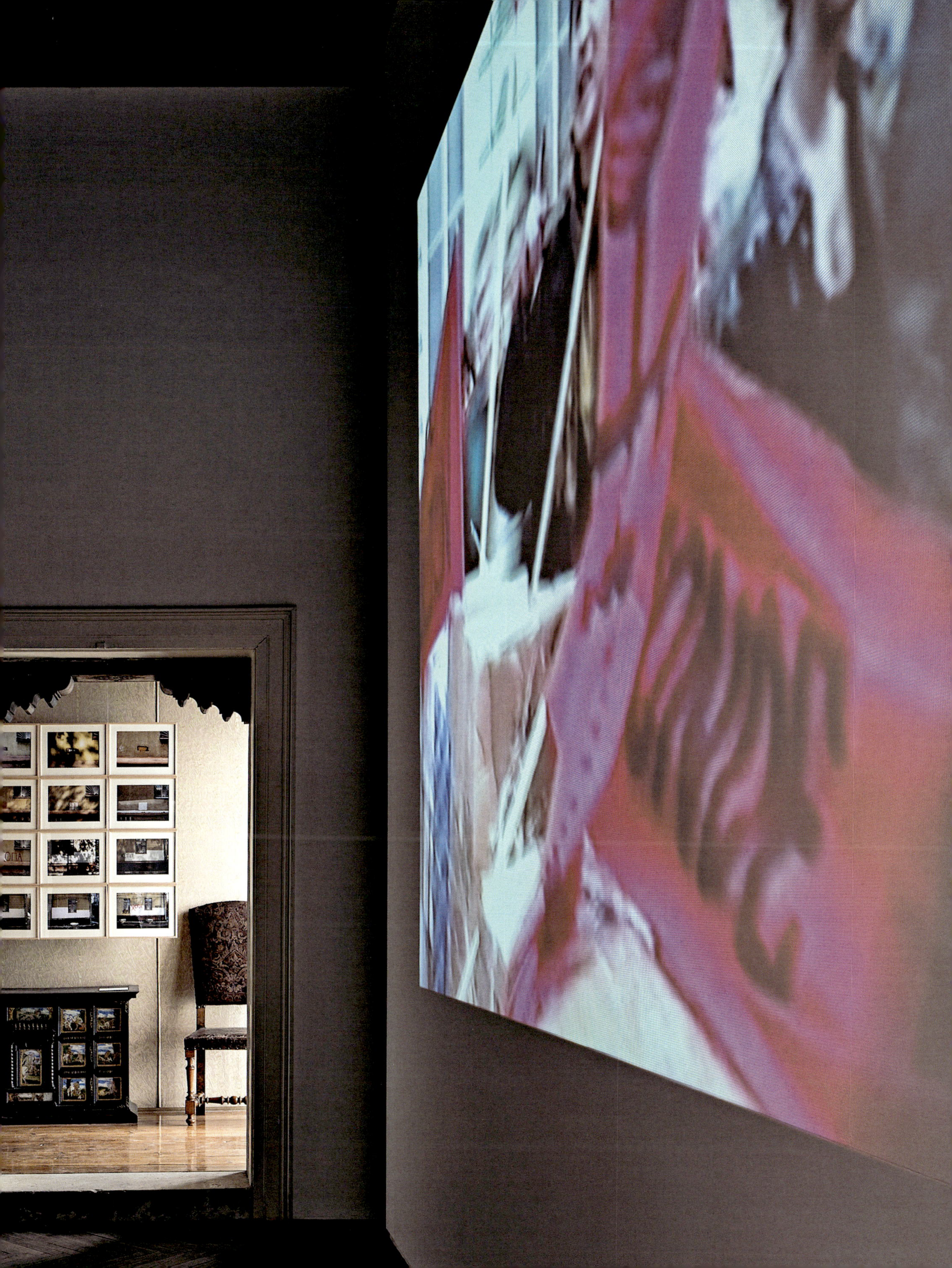

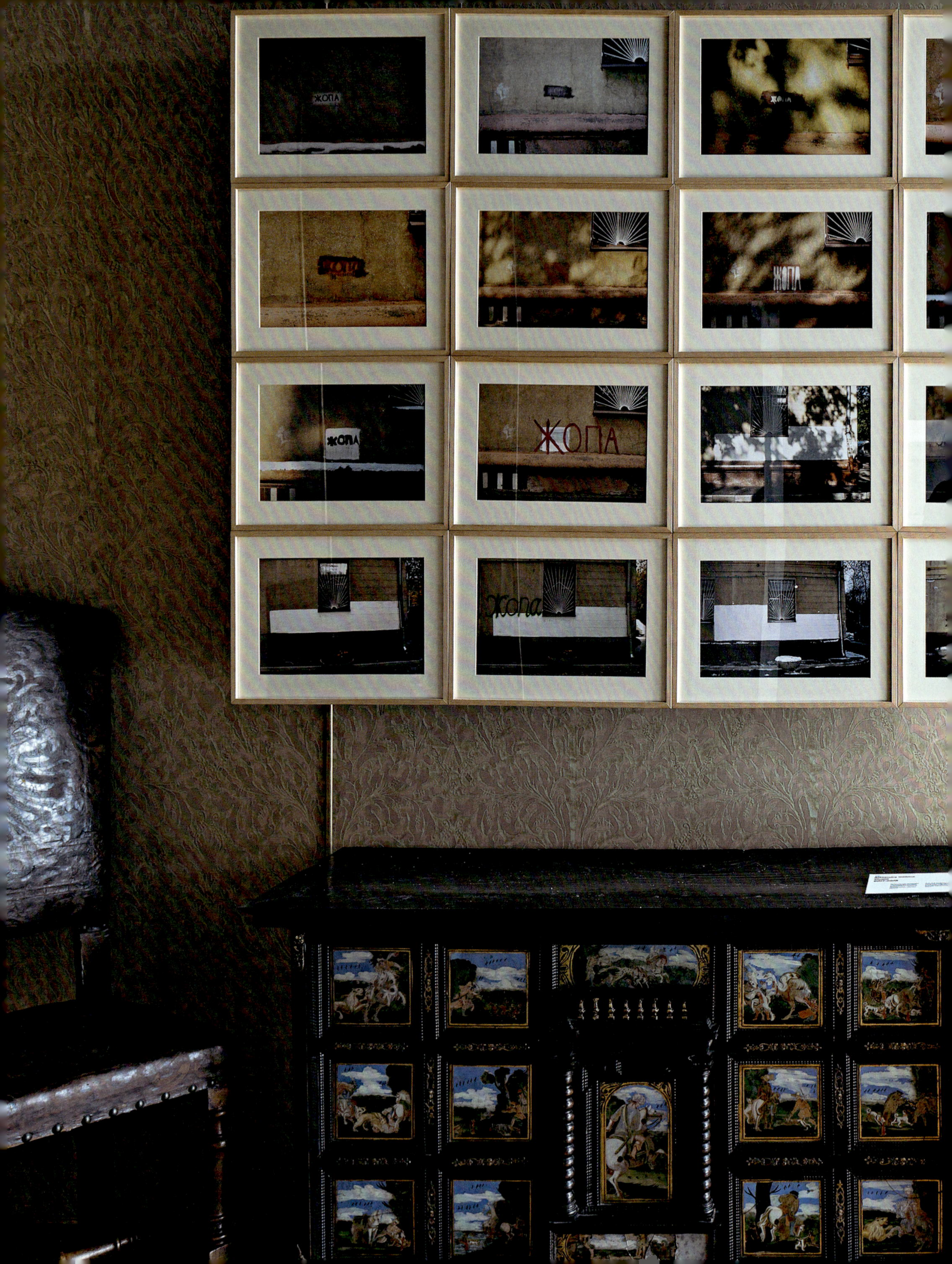

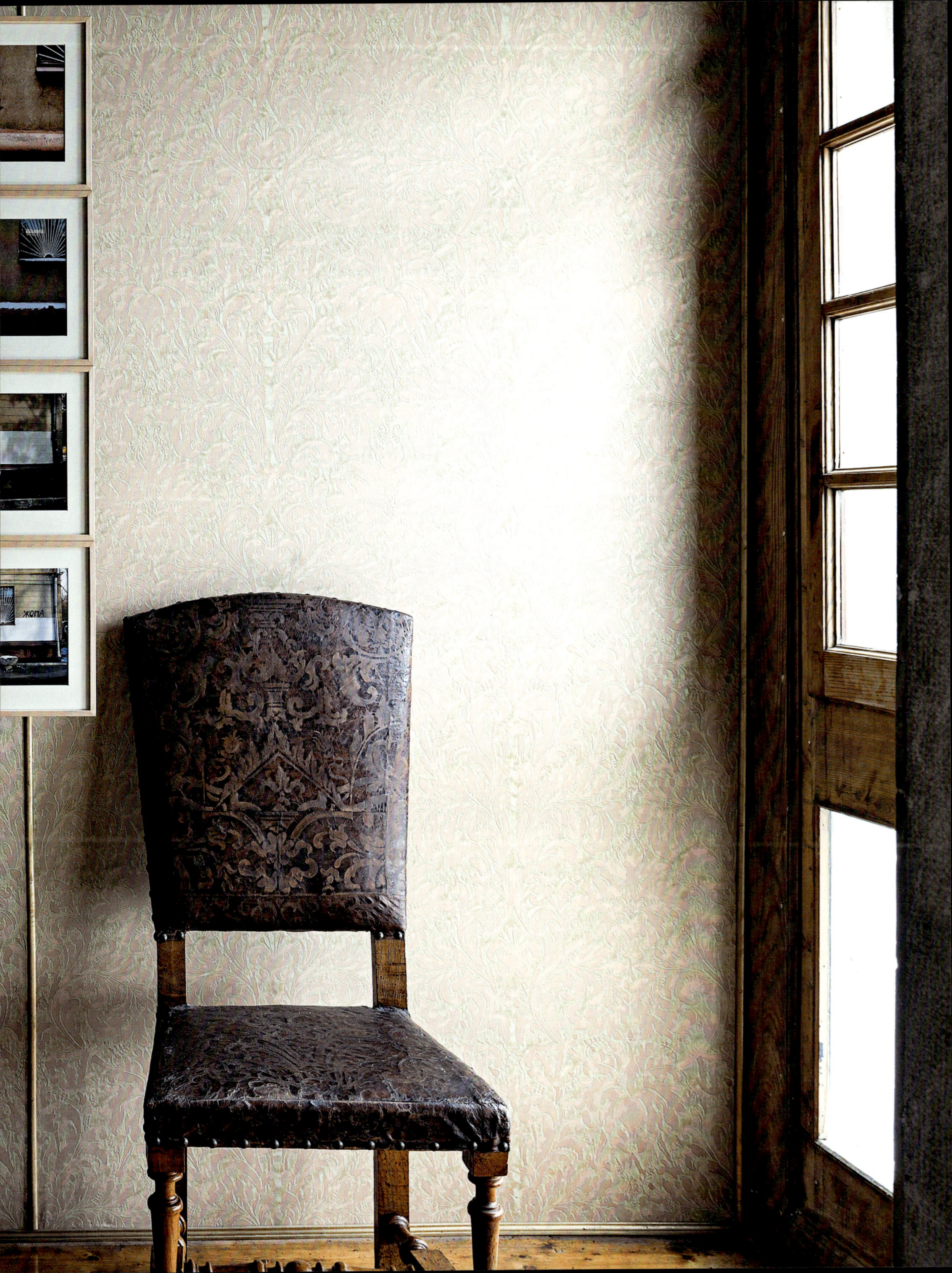

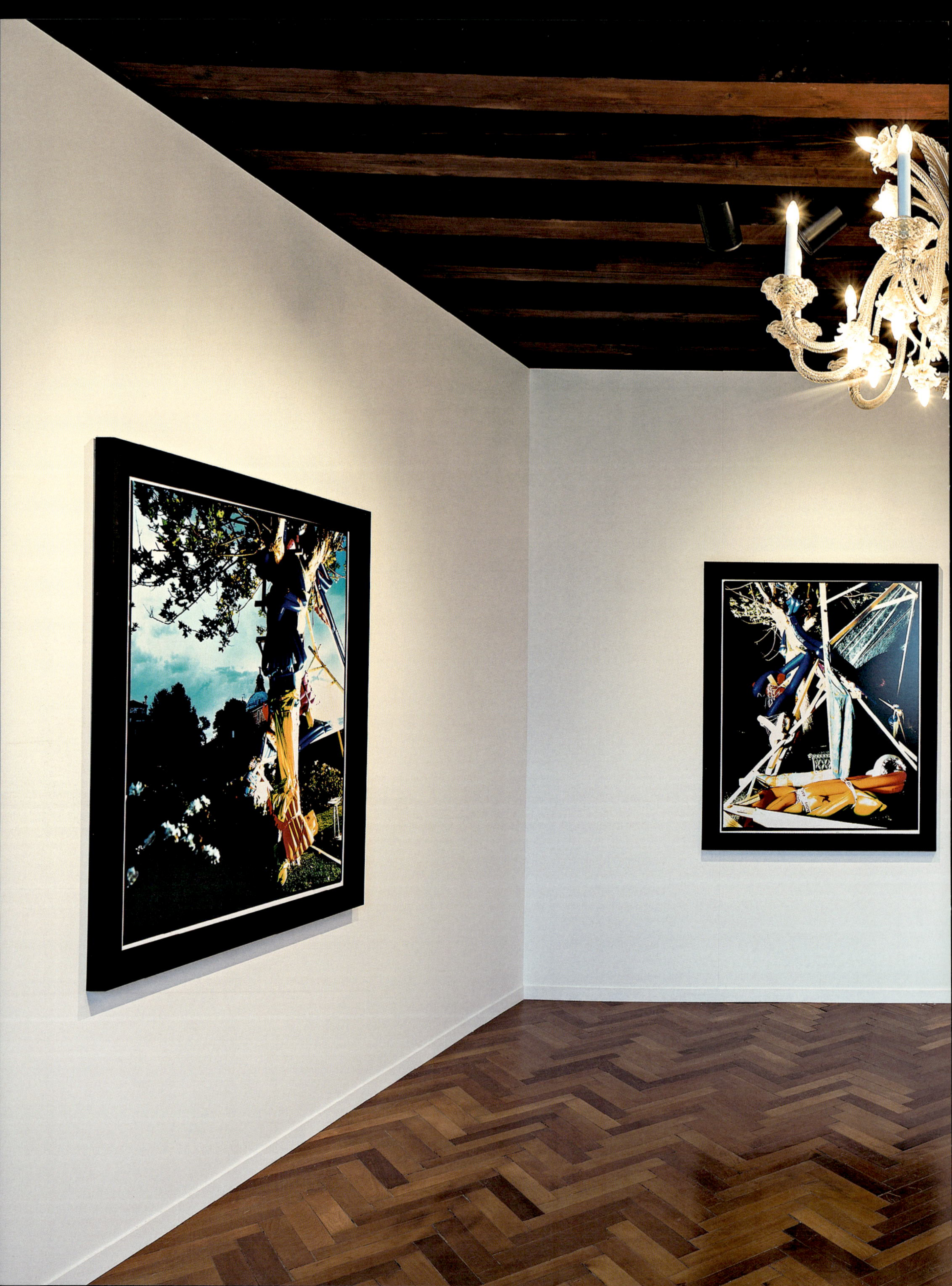

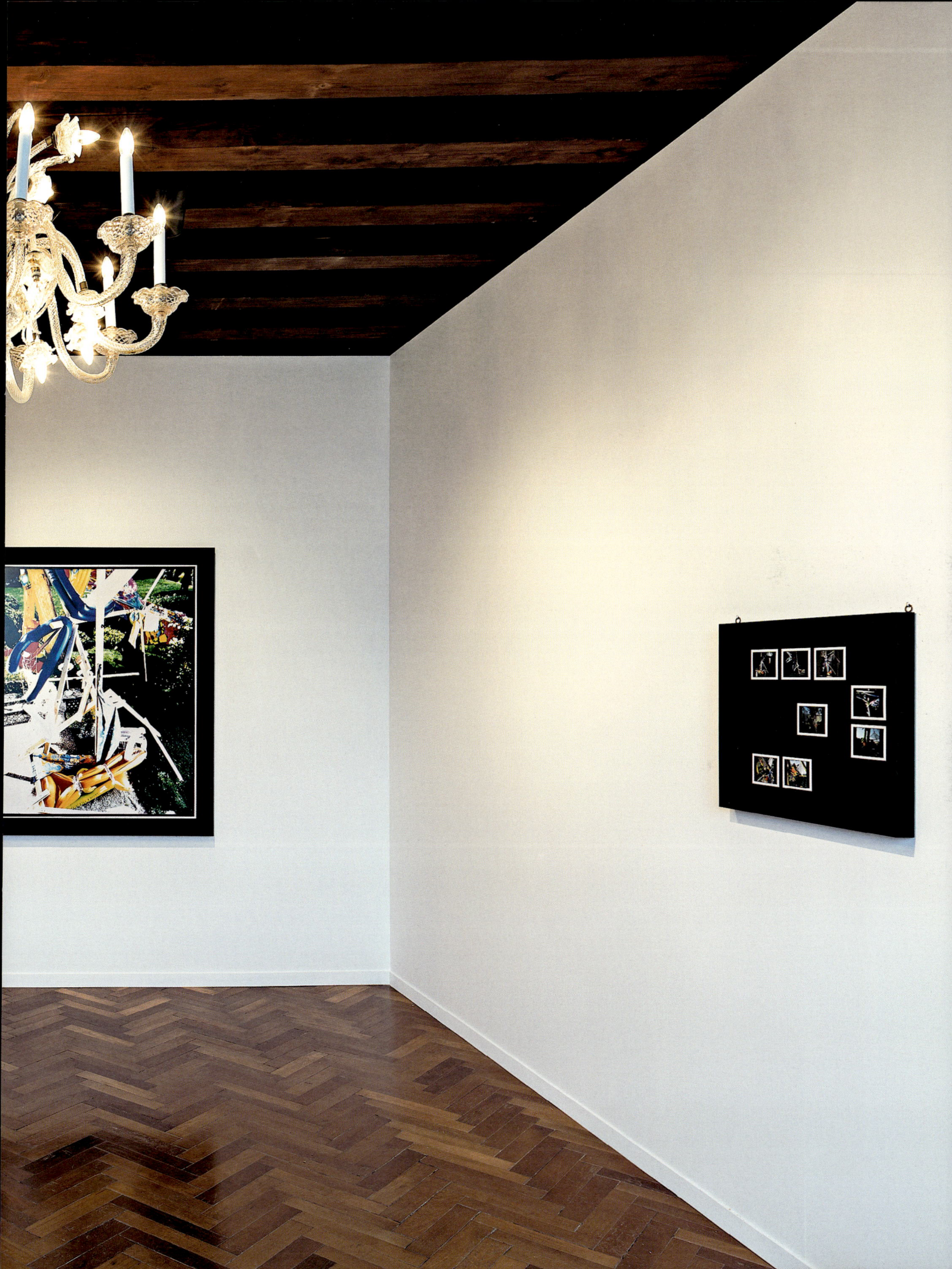

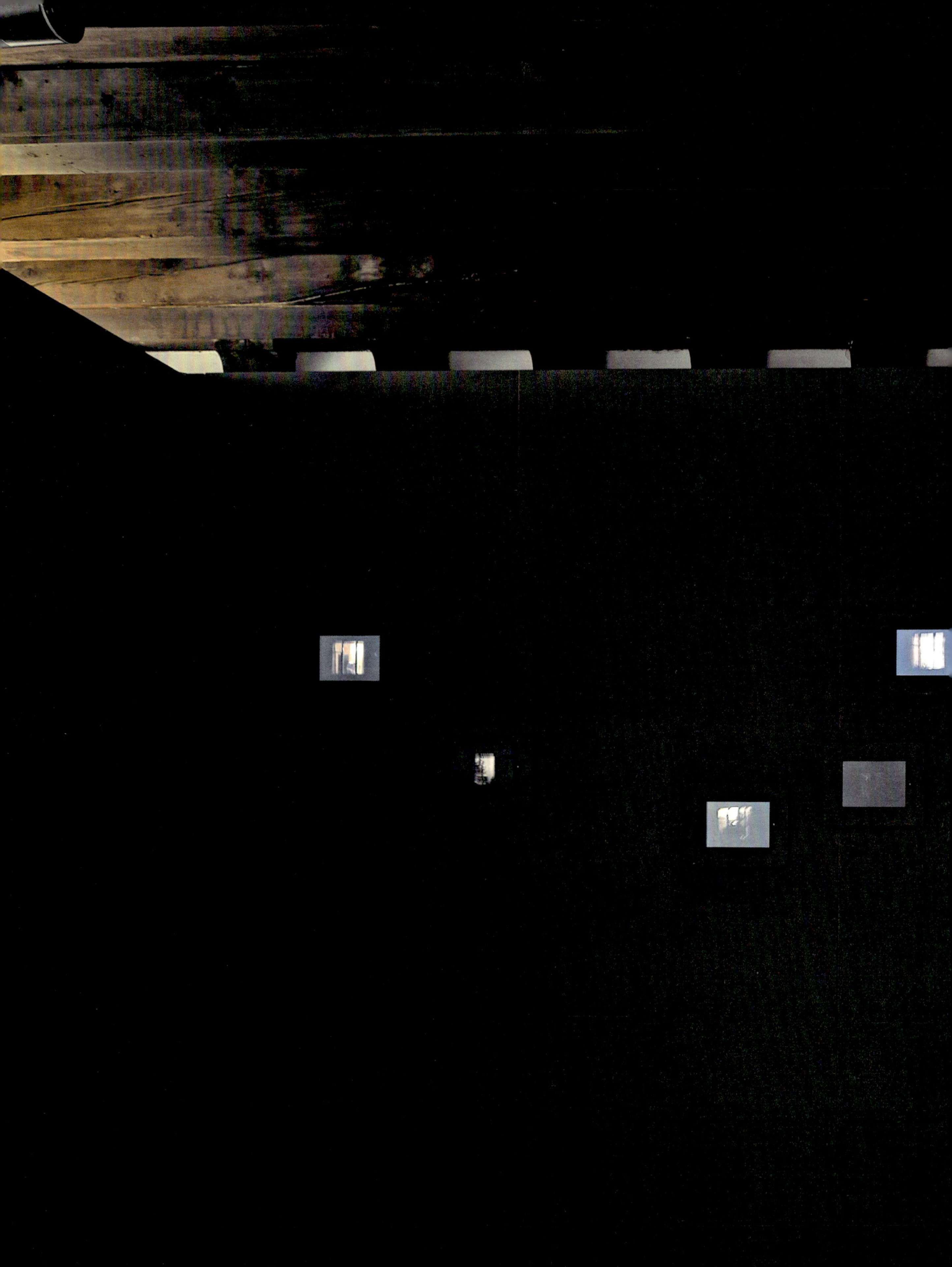

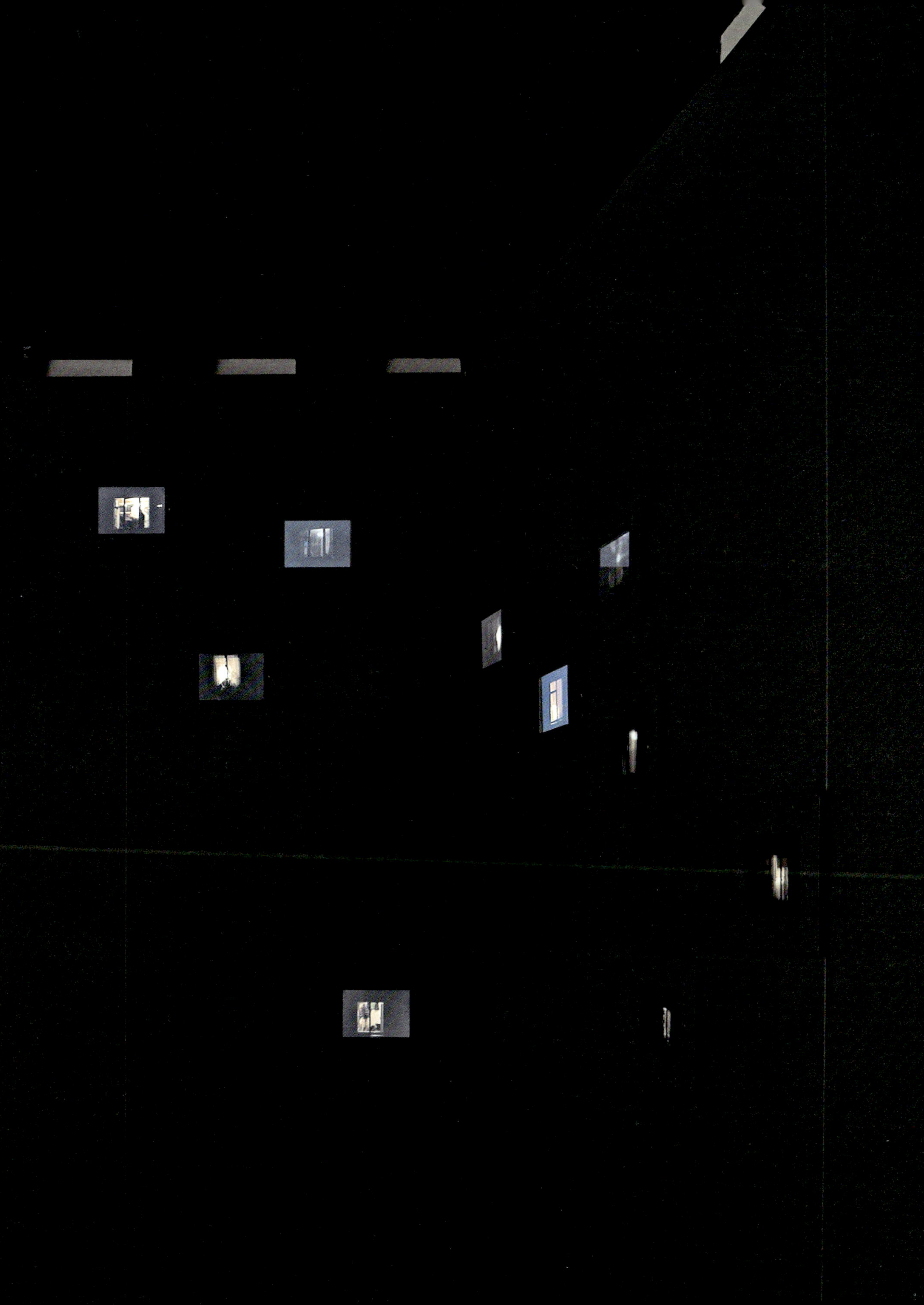

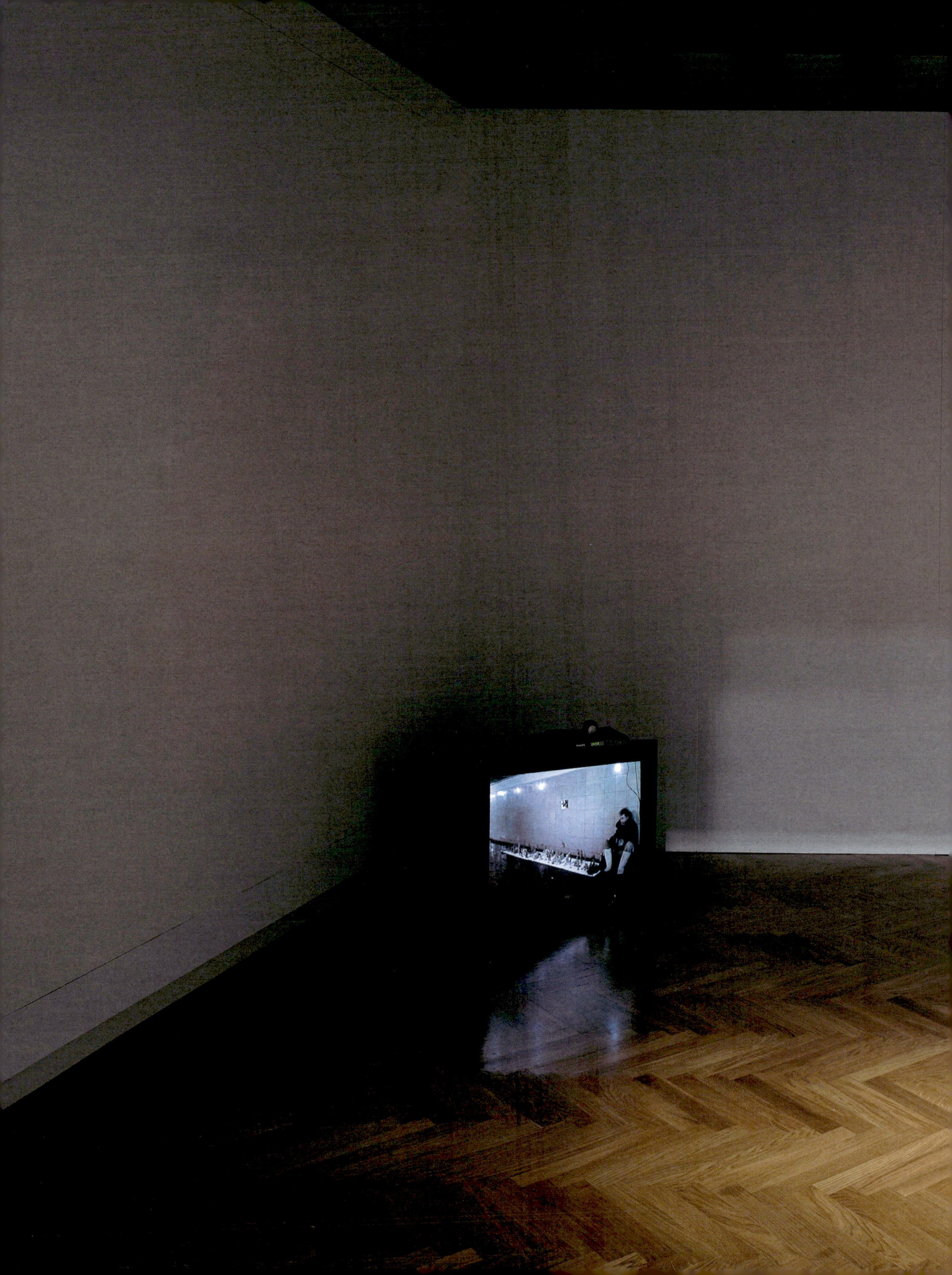

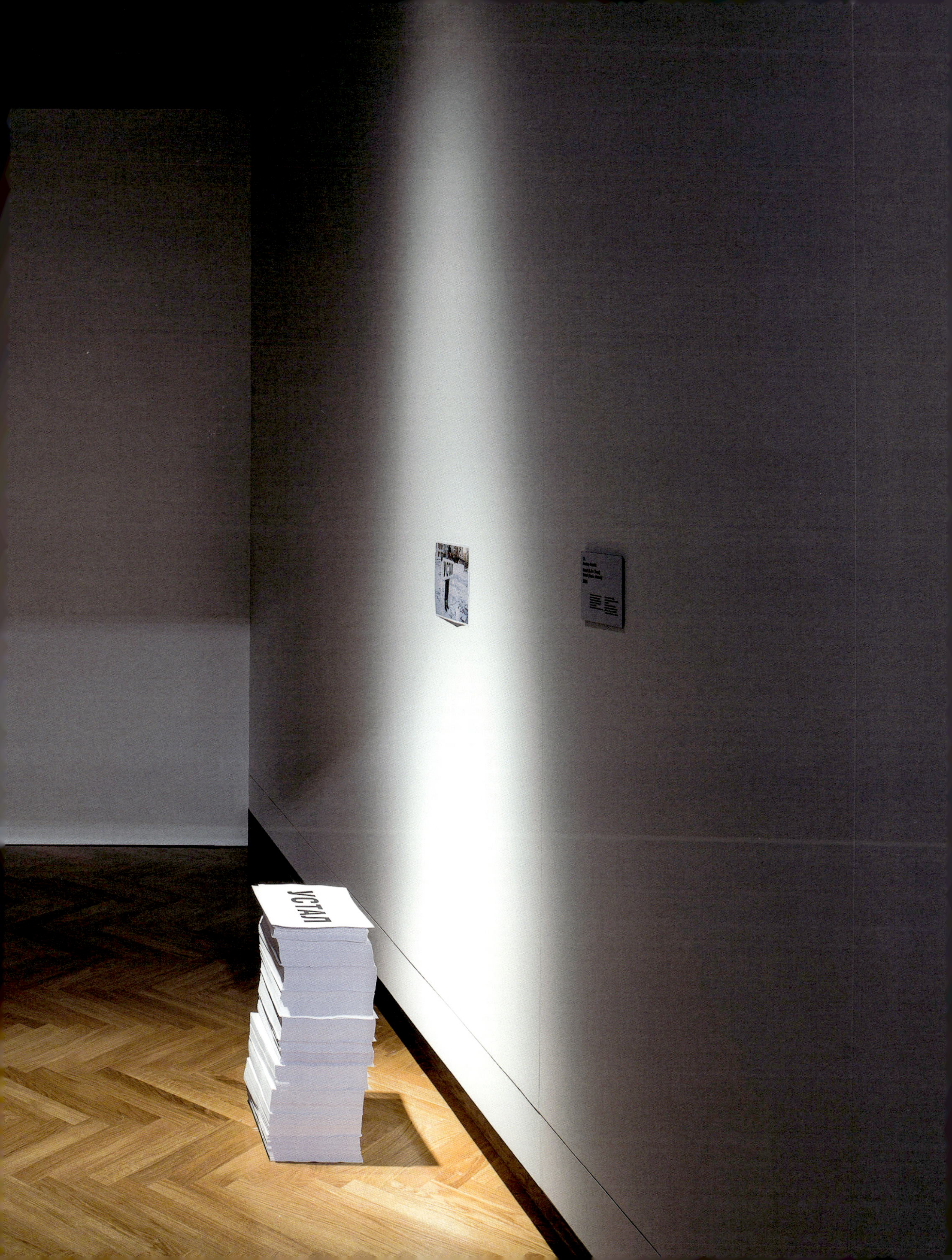

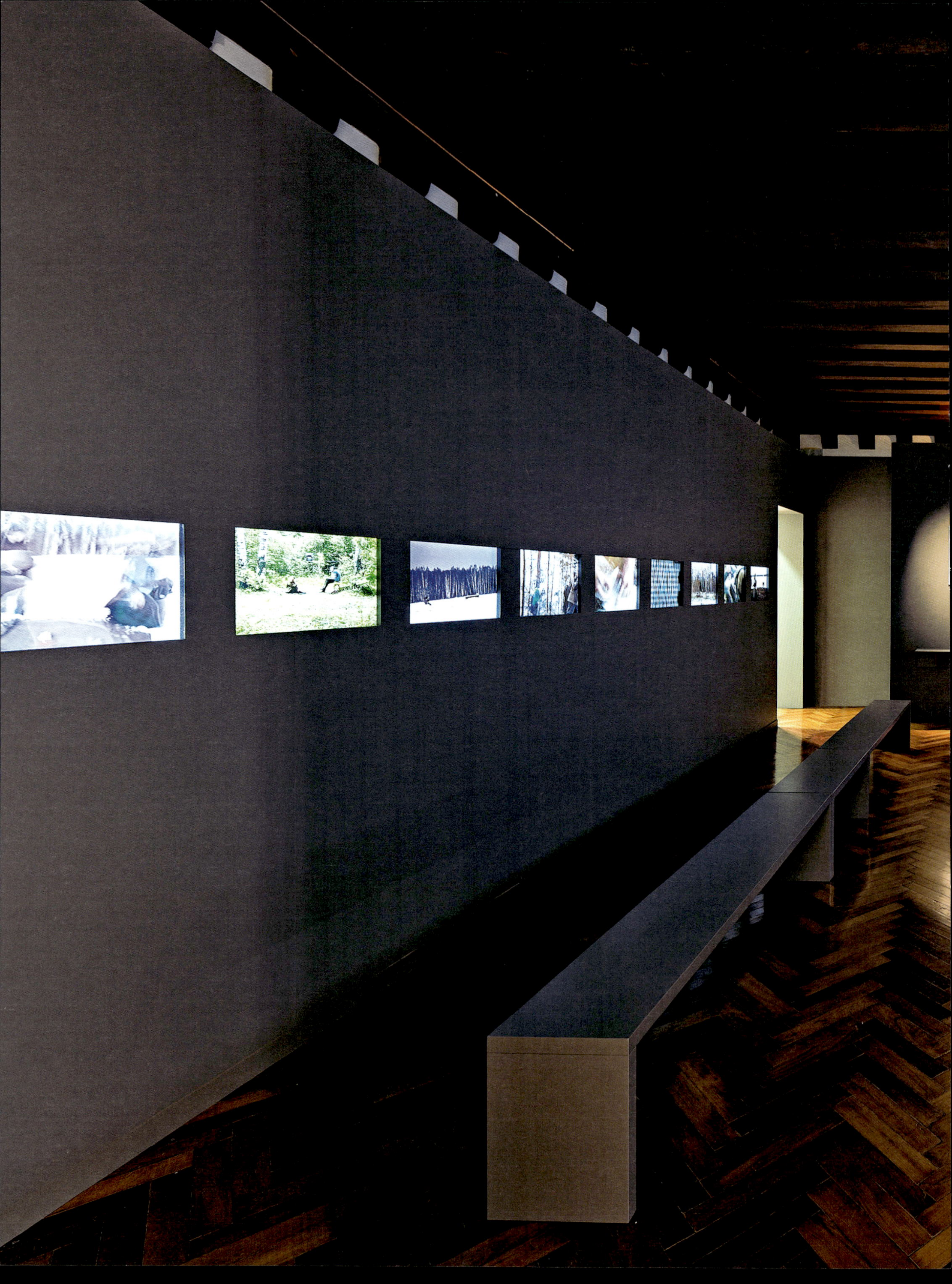

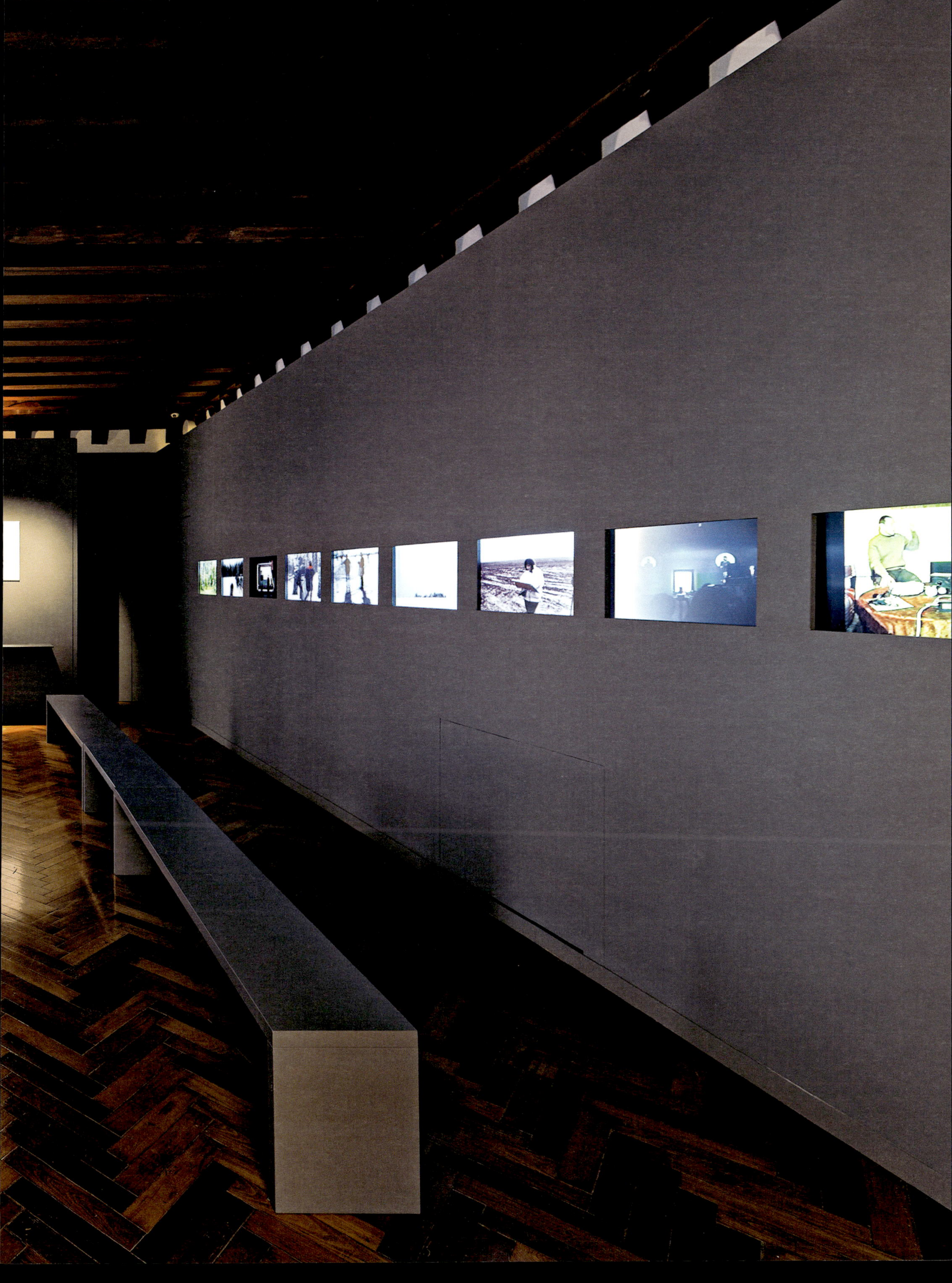

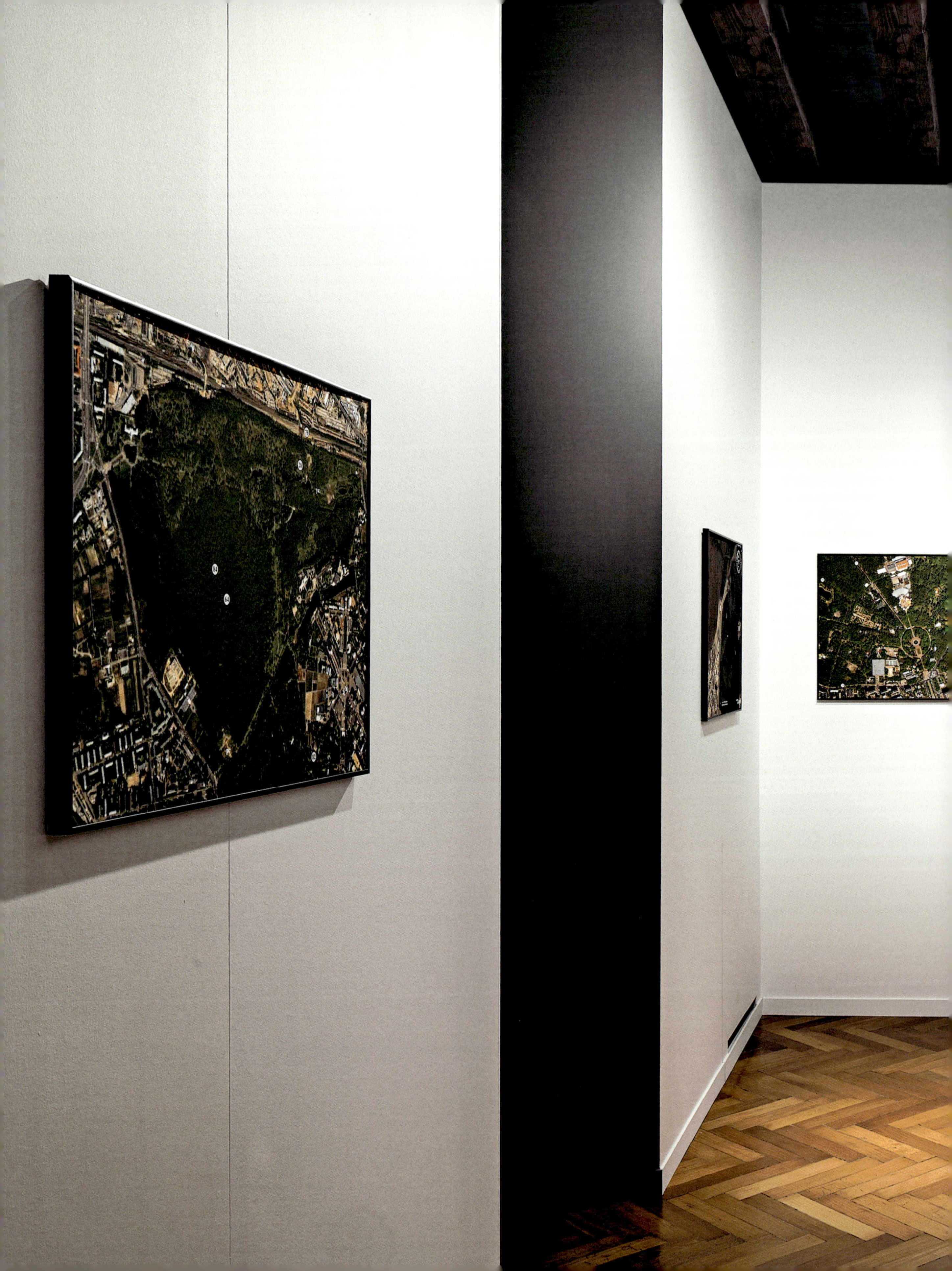

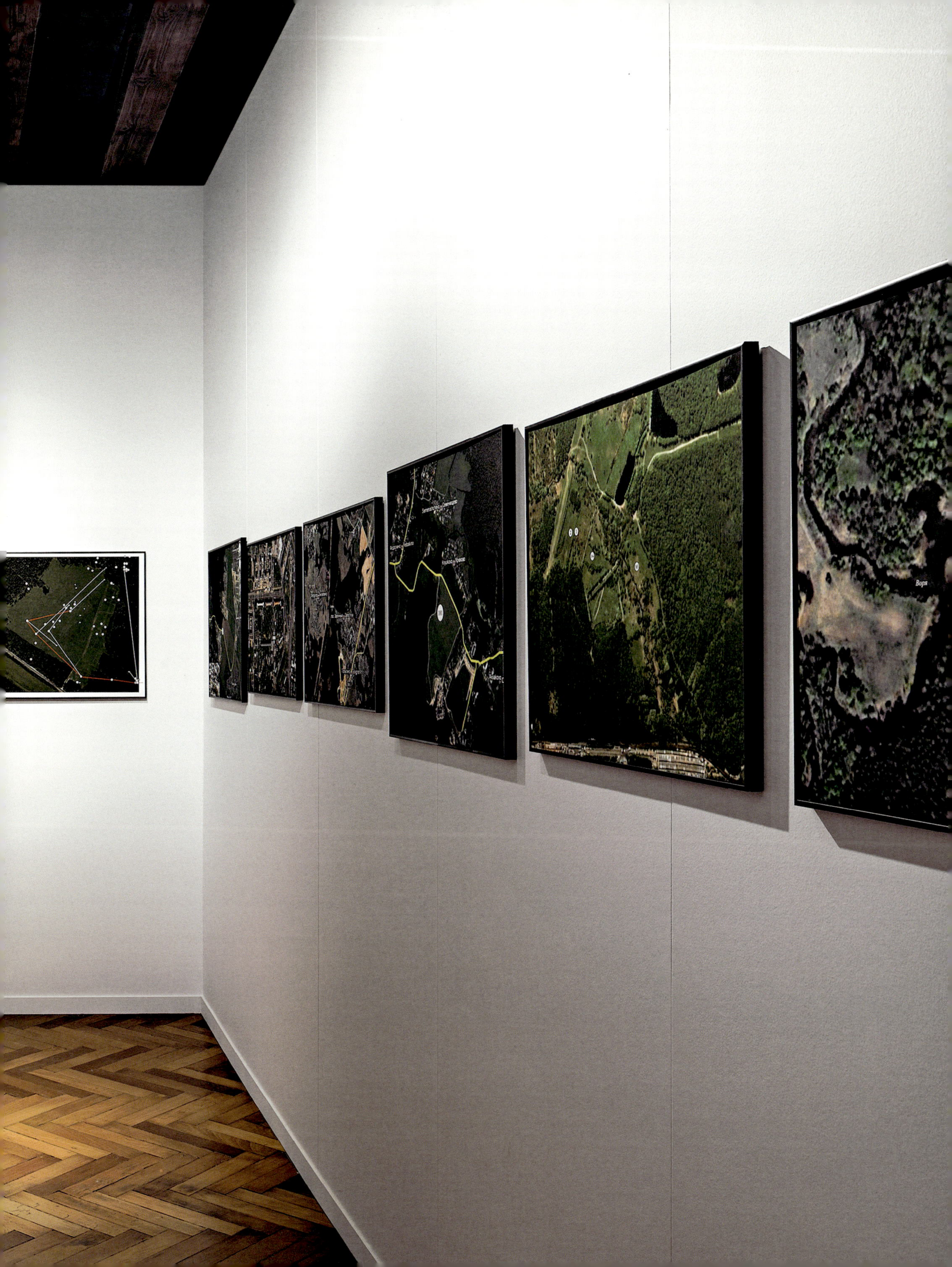

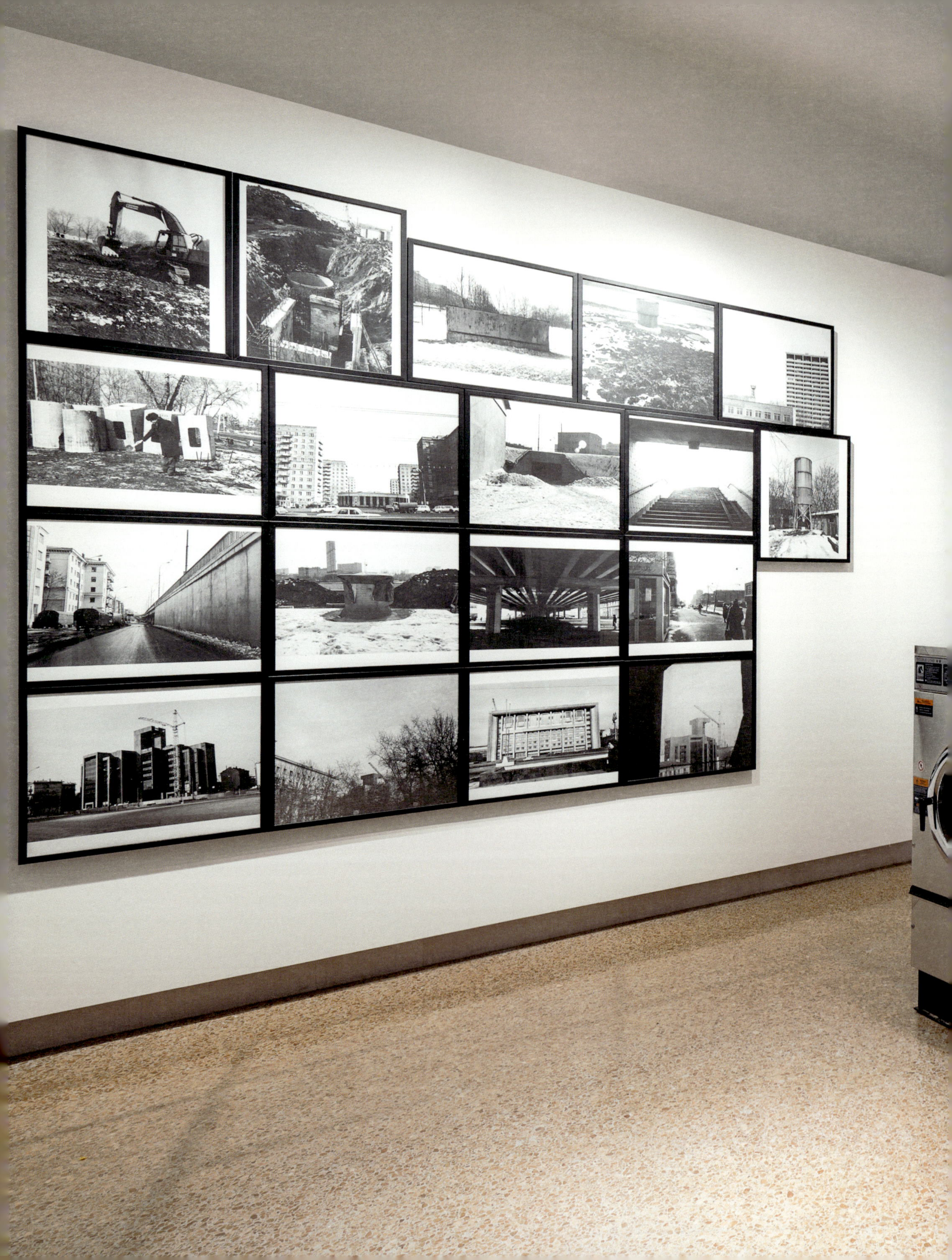

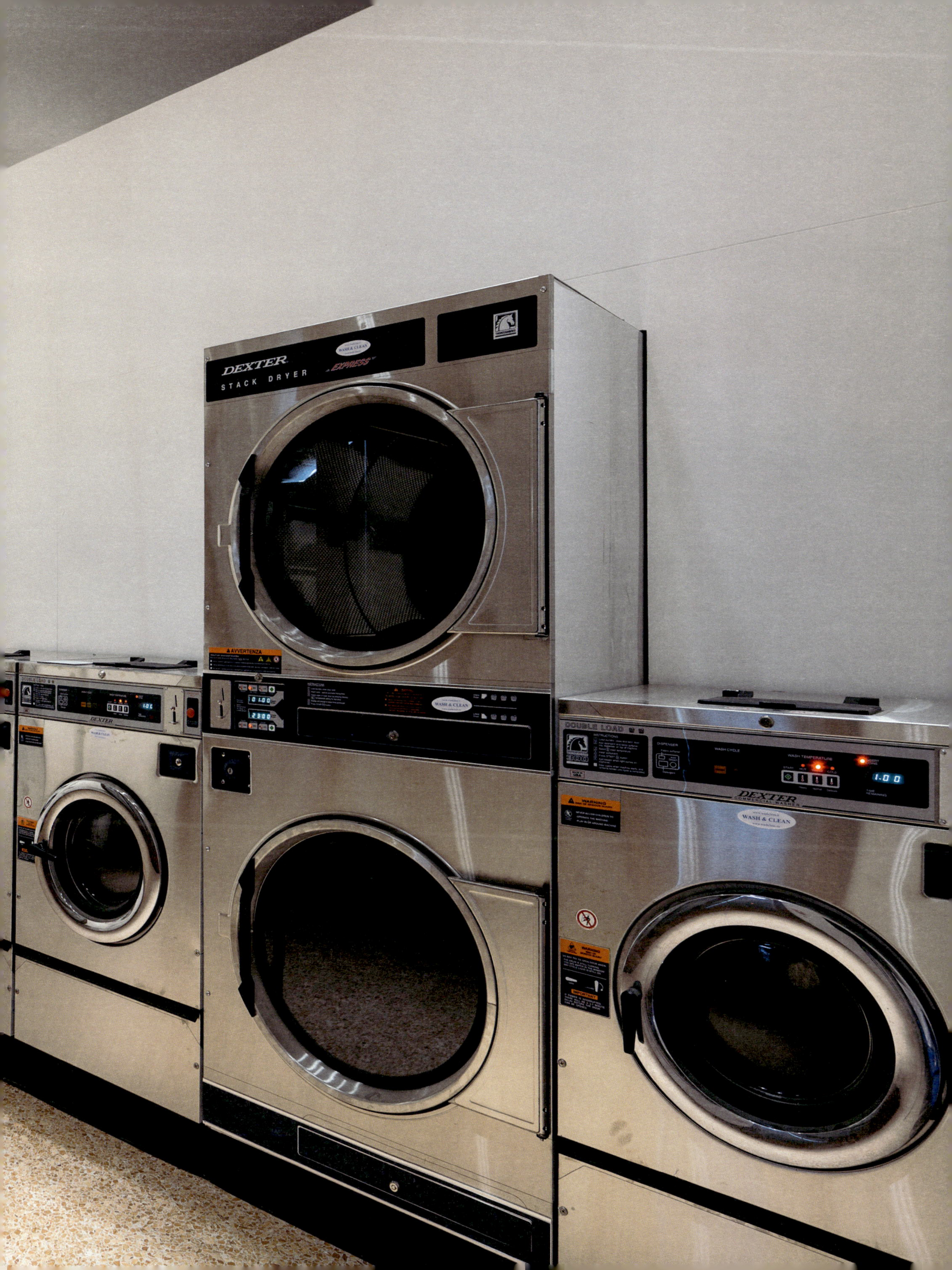
DEXTER
STACK DRYER
EXPRESS
WASH & CLEAN
DEXTER
DOUBLE LOAD
DEXTER
COMMERCIAL WASHER
WASH & CLEAN
AVVERTENZA
WARNING

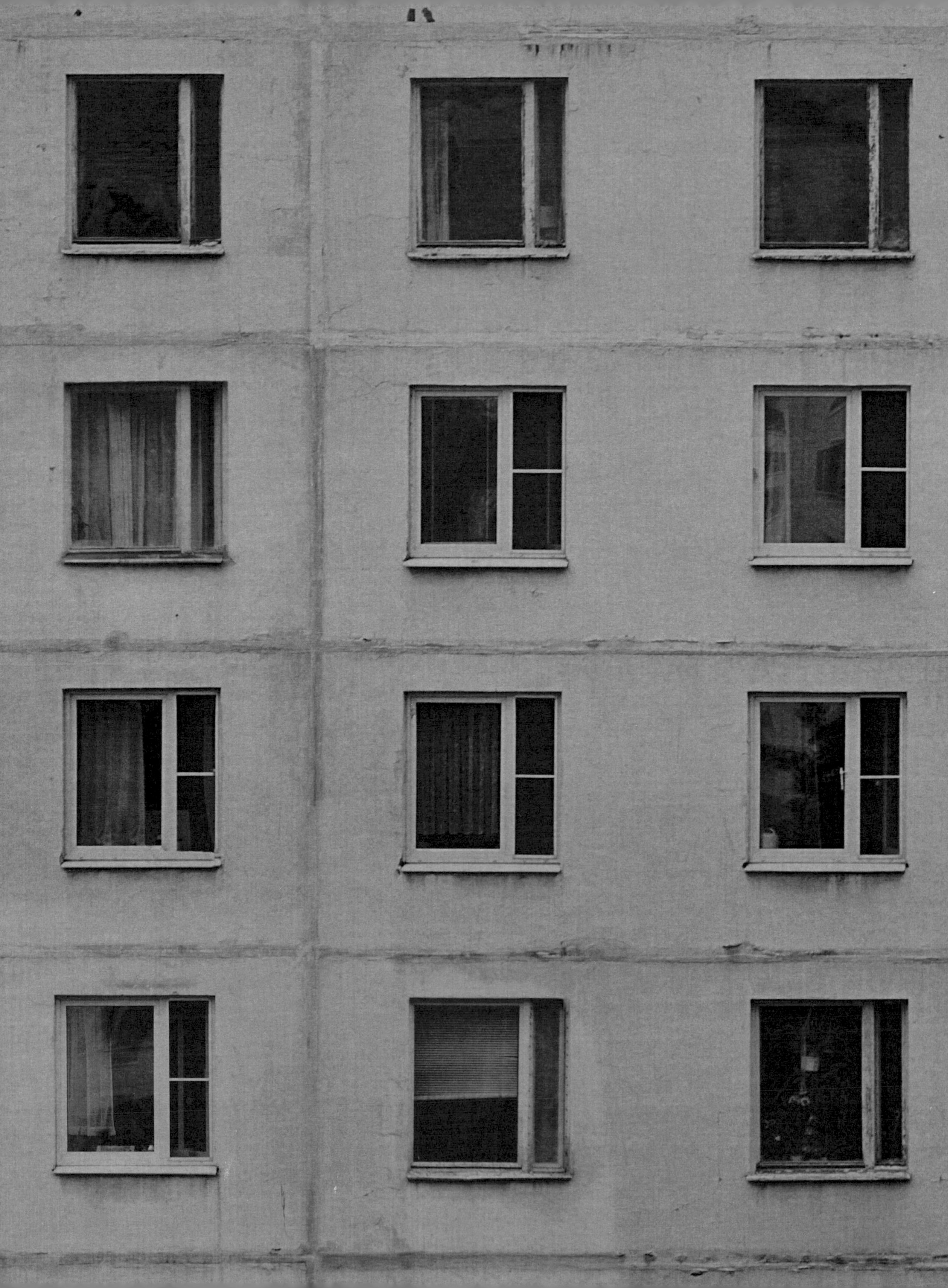

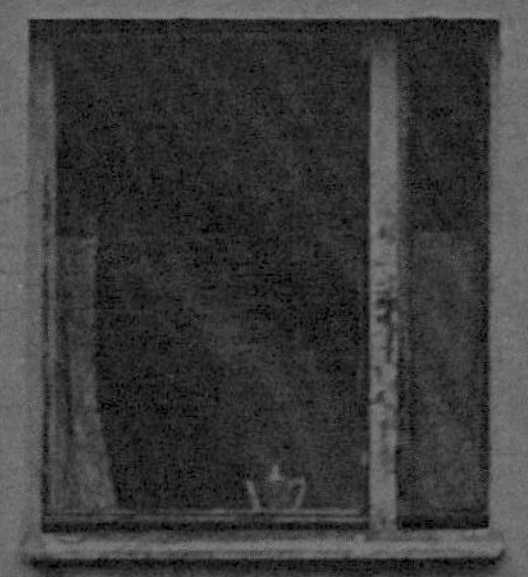

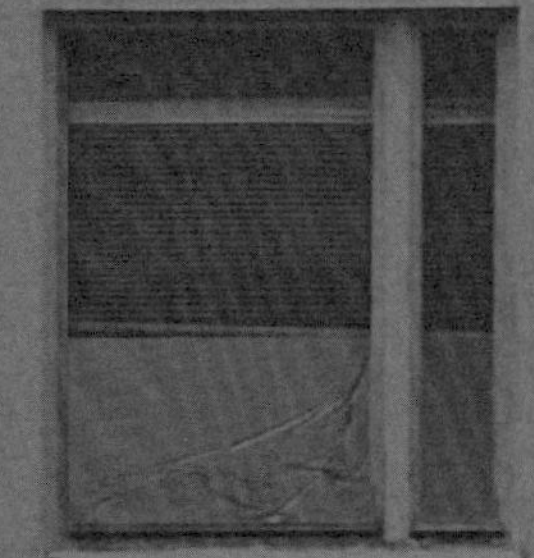

U R B A N   R E A D E R

This volume attempts to create a space of information and knowledge exchange
in which the contributions of different nature and registers intersect to create
an extensive urban reader.

It is a non-linear anthology merging from texts suggested by exhibition artists
and curators, translated or written *ad hoc*, as well as documents from newspapers, political manifestos referred to the particular context in which the art-
works appeared, or as comment of that latent cultural, social, political aspects
presumably useful to give back the idea of such complex transitional urban
space faced by the exhibition project.

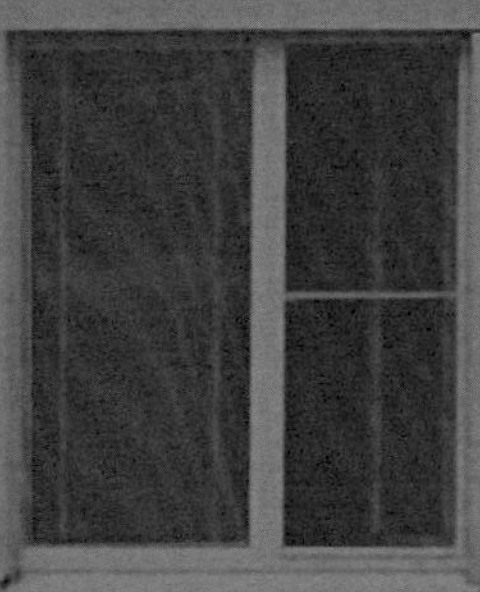

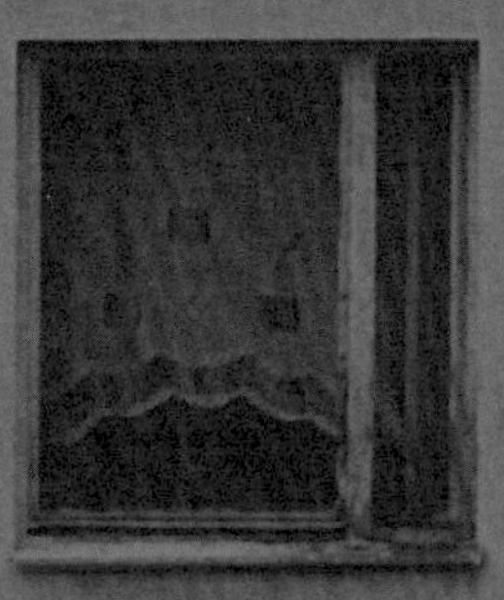

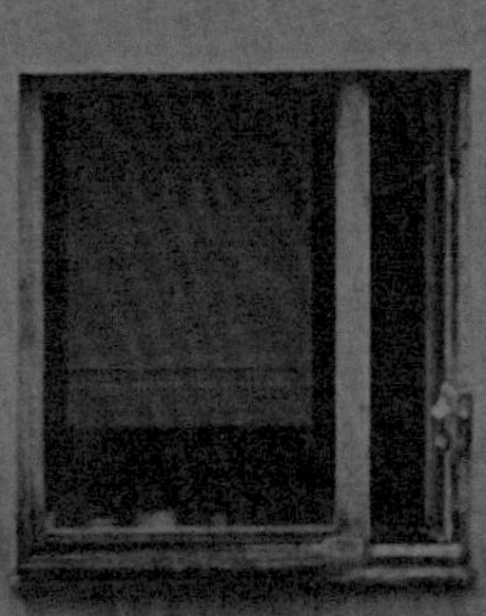

HOME OF THE FUTURE, 1962
ALEXANDER PEREMYSLOV

[...] Judging by the address, the issue concerned a new, experimental *microrayon*, the project of which in its time had evoked bitter and fundamental arguments. I also participated in them. But since work on the construction area, which extended into the forest near Moscow (this area now being within the city limits), had started to unfold, I had not been able to spend any time there. It was interest-

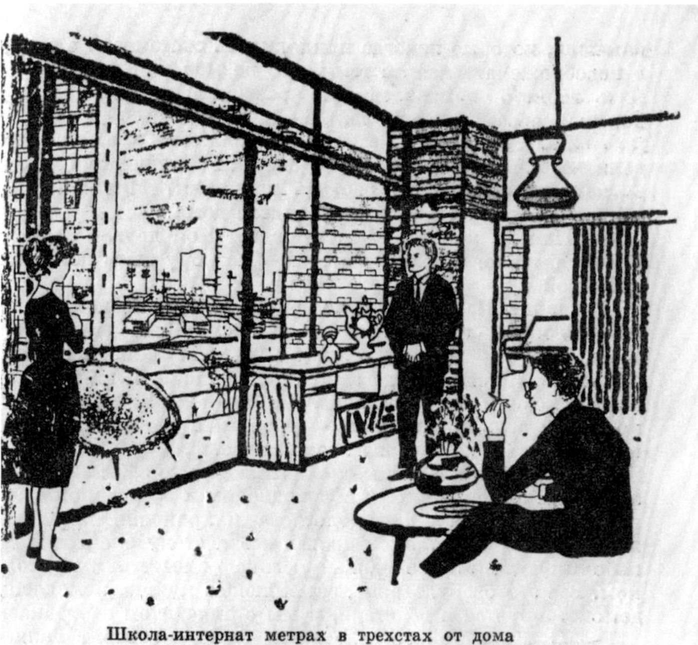

ing to see what kind of refinements had been put into the project, how it had been realized, what the daring inventiveness of the creator's quest had turned into...

Our bus rushed from the Vorontsovskaya metro station along a high-speed highway without intersections. The station. Far away, on a hill, the pavilions of International Exhibition are visible through the light smoke. From both signs, green hillocks approach the highway, or, more properly, the street. We find the side path that we need, which really should only be so referred to conditionally – it is a genuine street, and moreover a well-equipped one.

And so here we are already going along a hedge of thickly growing meadowsweet, currant, and yellow acacia bushes. Brightly blooming facades of buildings peek through the gaps between the slender trunks of pine, through the foliage of the poplars and birches.

The first impression is a surprisingly happy one. Nature is in harmony with the architecture – itself, as it were, a product thereof.

"It's beautiful!," I say.

My friend nods silently. His expression tells me that I haven't seen anything yet.

We turn into a wide alley leading into the heart of the *microrayon*. I recall the layout. This alley needs to have the form of a parabola into which the part and structures of the public center enter. And I was right: there's the stadium with small rostrums, and past it, a little bit to the right, the club building, with its enormous stained glass window and the glass roofing of the winter garden sparkling in the sun. Further on, past the swimming pool, is the semicircle of rows of an open theater. A few dozen more steps, and there ahead of us arise the hexagonal "honeycomb" of the greenhouse, the oval area of the park, and the rose garden.

Astonishingly beautiful vistas open up to the left. Here we have a corner of untouched forest, with knee-high grass, a natural vault of intertwined branches, an unbroken wall of hazel, the cool and half-light of thick shadow. And here are straight rows of just-planted linden trees, gazebos, flowerbeds, and fruit trees. Tall residential buildings arise one after another before us. One-story buildings of children's nurseries almost hidden in greenery.

From time to time, I compare these ever-changing images with the project. It is so much more impressive in reality than in the sketches, even well-drawn ones!

"We're going over there!" My companion takes me by the elbow and leads me over to the entrance to a building.

From the vestibule positioned in the first story of the public block, passing by the service department, staff cafeteria, laundry reception area, and row of automatic vending machines, we step into a hall. A high-speed elevator takes us to the eighth floor.

Each wing of the long corridor is about half devoted to spacious recreation facilities. This, the wide roof of the building, its overhangs wound about with vines, is also used for this.

A very tall man opens the apartment door. It's Gennady Pavlovich. Galina Sergeevna also comes out into the entryway. Five-year-old

Lidochka peeks out from behind the drapes. She's not in kindergarten on account of it being Sunday.

We're introduced to each other, and the hosts show us their new apartment. It has two relatively large rooms. The furnishings were thoroughly well thought-out and installed before they moved in. Convertible furniture was set up, with a movable partition between the rooms, lamps, and curtains, all with the stamp of good taste and high culture. We look into the bathroom, into the wall shelves, and nowhere does my professional criticalness find a chance to express itself.

erybody who had moved into the new building, in mind, and therefore their evaluation of an architect's project is in its way much more important than the opinions of professionals. Gennady and Galia had immediately been able to discern the main features of this project, which it had been necessary to defend in arguments with ill-wishers, with those who could not, or did not want to, understand the true purpose behind the development of our living complex. The opinion of people who have just moved in is very important – after all, they live here!

"We've been here only a month," Galia goes on,

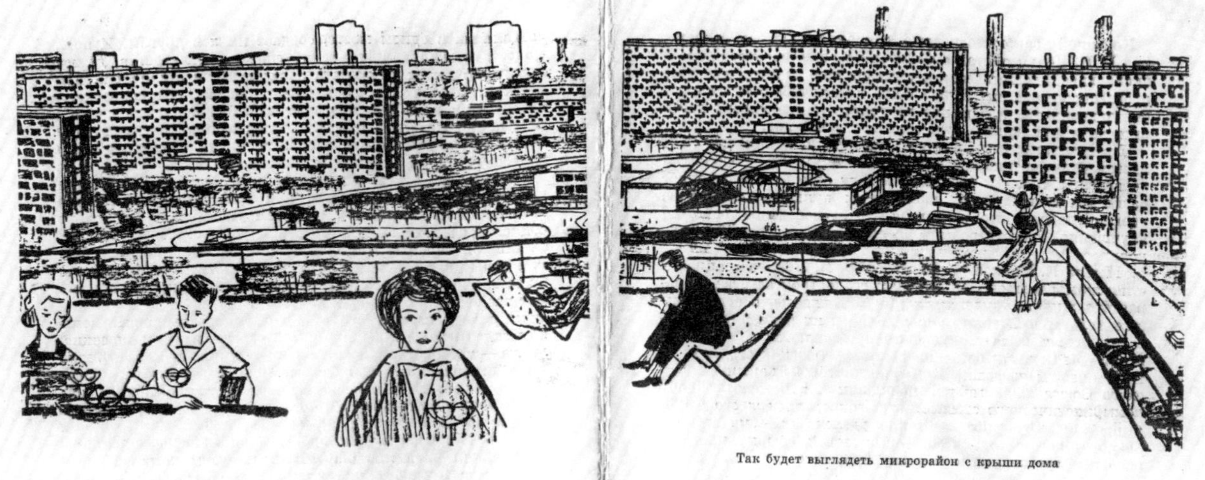

"We have a wonderful apartment," says Gennady with a smile. "And large as well. I'm really not joking. Galia also thinks so. Our apartment is not just two rooms, an entryway, and a bathroom; it's also a place for Lidochka in kindergarten, a regular table in the cafeteria lunch hall, and also..."

"All in all, a whole home," adds Galia. "We, the first group of residents, call it that. The whole *microrayon* is our home! Our older son, Andryusha – he's in fifth grade – he's also, if you can put it this way, always enrolled in boarding-school. And it's three or four hundred meters from here."

She leads us to the window and shows us a two-story building.

"They have a morning entertainment performance right now."

What the couple had said was not a surprise to me. My acquaintance with the project and the discussions revolving around it had left a rather clear stamp in my memory. Nevertheless, I listened to the story of these great people with much pleasure. What the architect had thought up was done with them, and ev-

"but we've seen all the advantages of the new system of raising children. And how did we start to bring up Andryushka? I had to leave the factory and stay at home for four years."

"I remember, I remember," my friend confirms. "When you went there, Galia would complain that she didn't want to be a housewife."

Gennady Pavlovich obviously didn't like these reminiscences.

"At that time," he says, "there wasn't much space in nurseries."

"You bet!," Galia clarifies: "I tried to hire a babysitter, and invited by aunt in from the country over winter, but pretty much I did everything myself. Gennady helped, of course, but it was hard for him since he was working and studying. Now I'm a student, and study in the evening."

Then the woman of the apartment remembered that she had forgotten to make us tea. We go to an integral compact machine for heating and storing food. There is an electric cooker built into the wall, a small sink, a refrigerator, and an extendable table. All this equipment replacing the kitchen was immediately shown in action, and we breakfasted with gusto.

"It was much easier with Lidochka," says Galia. "She went into the nurseries when she was six months old, although, it's true, one attached to the factory. And we had to go from job to job with her through the whole city, and while changing stations. Now we have children's facilities right nearby, which is better for the child. She doesn't cry anymore every morning when she has to leave mom at the entrance to the kindergarten. Just the opposite – she likes living as part of the group more."

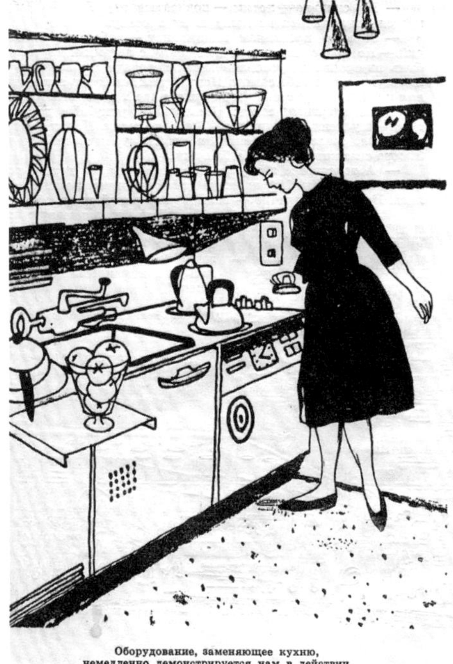

I inquired whether the prophylactic facility envisioned by the designer had come into being – to expose everybody going into the living complex or nursery to bactericidal lamps installed in the ceiling of the passageway. The couple confirms that they often bring their daughter to the rooms or spend time with her at various times of day through this route.

Contact with the boarding school is also constant. Andryushka discusses his lessons or the books he has read with his parents every day. "We see the children whenever we want," says Gennady.

"And as much as we want," Galia continues. "We can answer any question that they have."

"And we can take the initiative ourselves," adds Gennady. "But something else is very important in relating to children – to be internally ready to hand over to them everything that is best, what is in you. I remember how once I was pestering my father with some nonsense when he was busy with something, and he straightened me out, saying 'don't bother me! This isn't the time for you!' There have been problems between Alyusha and me. Then you feel bad about it and feel sorry for the child, but his feeling of being hurt doesn't go away that quickly. I judge myself..."

"That's all behind us now. We and the children are all completely happy. We haven't lost anything. This little," Galia makes a gesture with her hand indicating a miniscule amount. "We haven't stopped thinking of ourselves as one family. But how many wonderful new things have appeared in our lives!"

Deeply moved, I think, "Yes, this family can truly be envied, in the best sense of that word."

The telephone rings. Concluding the conversation, Gennady explains that the director of the building council has asked him if he will agree to work with tending the fruit trees during his shift tomorrow instead of cleaning up the public center as had previously been scheduled.

There it is! Every day, around two hundred people work on the territory – tending the trees and shrubbery, cleaning the roads, working in the greenhouses. This all gives the *microrayon* an elegant, attractive appearance and makes people's lives better. And each adult has only one shift a month.

"Now let's go around the whole territory," we decide, having barely finished our coffee.

Having consulted with her husband, Galia orders lunch on the telephone, which will be prepared for us in the cafeteria after our walk. Suddenly, I hear the name of my favorite food. "It's like in a health resort," I think.

We spent three hours walking around the *microrayon*, and there was no end to our discoveries. The new announced itself in things both great and small: in the miraculous details of daily life and in architecture, in the generous gifts of nature and in interactions between people.

More than anything else, I liked the boarding school, which was set apart in one corner of the territory. The classes and dormitories were spread out between eight two-story complexes connected by general school structures and glass walkways. A laboratory and manufacturing complex was located in the center. In front of it was a demonstration ground with an upright rocket ringed by a ramp. We saw children playing there.

"Look, Andryusha, it's your dad!," one of them shouted.

A boy who was tall for his age ran up to us. With the teacher's permission, he joined us, and we went along a broad alley into the public center.

Immediately beyond a little bridge over an artificial stream that passed through the whole park, we glimpsed an announcement board on which a message had just been affixed that two of the *microrayon*'s residents had just been awarded a prize for the creation of a new type of rose lily. Listening in the comments of people tarrying by the board, I was again convinced that the residents of the garden quarter were a friendly, tightly linked group capable of organizing their own daily lives and recreation.

After taking a look at the club complex – a viewing hall with 640 seats, a library, a swimming pool with a diving board, and, finally, an enormous winter garden that could be used as a foyer, or as a recreation hall, or as a reading or banquet hall – we returned to "our" group of residents, to its public area.

We had lunch in a spacious cafeteria filled with light. Everything here – the setting of the silverware and dishes, the high quality of the courses, and the varzious refinements of the process of self-service – bespoke great attention to the individual, to his health and time. I learned, by the way, that there are nine cafeterias in the *microrayon* – in each of the five original groups of residents (which also service the nurseries), in the eight-year boarding school, in the boarding school for older children, and in the homes for senior citizens. This takes the place of a minimum of three thousand individual kitchens and ensures nourishment for the population.

Sunday was coming to a close. When we left the rostrum of the little local stadium, having looked at the schedule of sporting events, it was already growing dark. The maple trees with their burgundy and olive-green foliage looked autumnal in the early evening, with the gleam of sundown sliding down their still sparse crowns. And for some reason the feeling was especially strong that I did not want to leave this place.

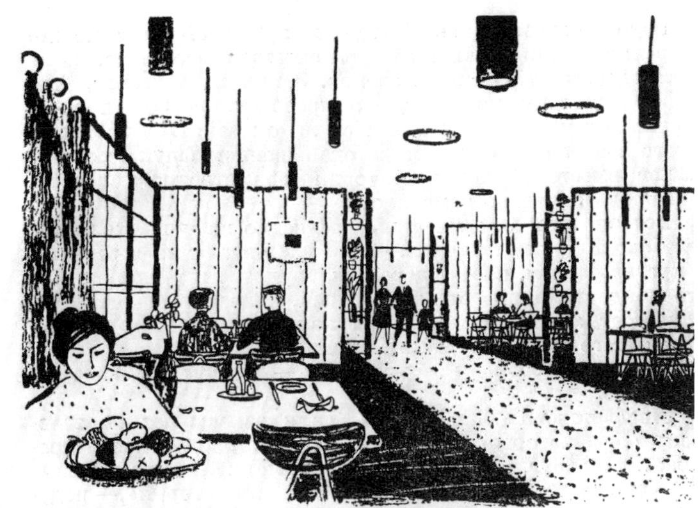

Alexander Peremyslov, extract from *Home of the Future*, Moscow, State Publishing House of Political Literature, 1962, pp. 8-17. Illustrated by Yury Sharonov

Contributed by Olga Chernysheva

ON THE EXTENSIVE INTRODUCTION OF INDUSTRIAL METHODS, IMPROVING THE QUALITY AND REDUCING THE COST OF CONSTRUCTION, 1954

NIKITA KHRUSHCHEV

Comrades!

It is a long time since we last had a National Conference of Builders and there is now great need for such a conference. It is my opinion that the present meeting will be to the great good not just of construction, but of all our work both in industry and in other sectors of our national economy. [...]

URGENT ISSUES CONCERNING

THE INDUSTRIALISATION OF CONSTRUCTION

[...] At the present time conditions exist for the extensive industrialisation of construction. What are these conditions? First and foremost, we now have a large pool of qualified workers and specialists. Our building organisations and construction-material-manufacturing industry employ many thousands of fine craftsmen and innovators in production. We have factories capable of supplying our builders with modern equipment that makes work easier and improves productivity. We have expanding manufacturing facilities that allow us to supply the construction industry with prefabricated reinforced-concrete struc- tures, parts, and construction materials. [...]

Extensive expansion of manufacture of prefabricated reinforced-concrete structures and parts will give enormous economic benefits. Our builders know that until recently there was debate over which of two paths we should take in construction – use of prefabricated structures or monolithic concrete. We shall not name names or reproach those workers who tried to direct our construction industry towards use of monolithic concrete. I believe these comrades now realise themselves that the position they adopted was wrong. Now, though, it's clear to everyone, it seems, that we must proceed along the more progressive path – the path of using prefabricated reinforced-concrete structures and parts. (Applause.) [...]

Use of pre-fabricated reinforced concrete will allow us to manufacture parts as is done in the plant-construction industry – will make it possible to switch to factory construction methods. (Applause.) [...]

Wall panels and ceiling/floor sections must be decorated on the factory floor. These products must arrive at the building site already finished, completely ready for installation. [...]

Concrete structures must be light, with no superfluous weight. [...] Brick, the main building material, has always been, and continues to be, used in cases where construction is mainly carried out by hand. In such cases great importance attaches to the weight of the material used in the walls, the weight of the brick. In our age – given the availability of concrete, electric motors, cranes, and other mechanisms – we have no excuse for continuing to employ the old methods of working. Everyone knows how much time and labour is need to make brick. [...] Instead of brick, wouldn't it be better to make concrete wall sections of a size that will be convenient for the lifting mechanisms at our disposal – i.e. weighing two, three, five tonnes? The advantages of using sections are high levels of productivity and high output. It's no accident that many other countries make extensive use of concrete, not brick, in construction. [...]

There can be no serious thought of industrialising construction if we are going to continue to increase the number of building organisations. Everyone surely realises that it is not in the power of small – and, consequently, weak – building organisations to employ industrial methods of working. We must set about decisively strengthening our building organisations. Without this there can be no question of industrialising construction.

Highly instructive in this respect is the reduction of numbers of building organisations in Moscow – where a single organisation, Glavmosstroy has been set up on the basis of the 56 Mossoviet building trusts and various ministries and departments. [...]

Our country is engaged in building industrial enterprises, residential buildings, schools, hospitals, and other structures on a large scale. This construction programme is of vital importance. We have an obligation to significantly speed up, improve the quality of, and reduce the cost of, construction. In order to do so, there is only one path – and that is the path of the most extensive industrialisation of construction.

[...] Given the scale on which we are building industrial enterprises, residential buildings, schools, hospitals, and cultural and services facilities, any delay in design work is unacceptable. Our entire country is covered in building sites. Every year the Soviet state allocates many billion rubles to construction. Literally each one of us is interested in construction work proceeding smoothly. It is unacceptable that building work often drags on as a result of the slowness of our design organisations and that sometimes design of even simple buildings lasts two years or longer.

The interests of industrialisation of construction dictate the necessity of reorganising how our design organisations work, of making production of standard designs and use of already existing standard designs the main element in their work. [...] Many employees of planning and design organisations underestimate the importance of standard design. [...]

They [architects] are all agreed that use of standard designs will significantly simplify and improve the quality of construction, but in practice many architects, engineers, and – in industrial construction – technologists too aspire to create only their own one-off designs.

Why does this happen? One of the reasons, evidently, is that there are flaws in the way we train our architects. Led on by the example of the great masters, many young architects hardly wait to cross the threshold of their architecture institutes or find their feet properly before wanting to design nothing but unique buildings and hurrying to erect a monument to themselves. [...]

We must select a small number of standard designs for residential buildings, schools, hospitals, kindergartens, children's nurseries, shops, and other buildings and structures and conduct our mass building programmes using only these designs over the course of, say, five years. At the end of which period we shall hold a discussion and, if no better designs turn up, continue in the same fashion for the next five years. What's wrong in this approach, comrades? [...]

If an architect wants to be in step with life, he must know and be able to employ not only architectural forms, ornaments, and various decorative elements, but also new progressive materials, reinforced-concrete structures and parts, and, above all, must be an expert in cost-saving in construction. And this is what comrade Mordvinov and many of his colleagues have been criticised for at the conference – for forgetting about the main thing, i.e. the cost of a square metre of floor area, when designing a building and for, in their fascination with unnecessary embellishment of facades, allowing a great number of superfluities.

The facades of residential buildings are sometimes hung with a multitude of all kinds of superfluous decoration that point to a lack of taste in the architects. Builders sometimes even have difficulty executing these decorations.

In this matter much influence has been exercised by the construction of high-rise buildings. In designing such buildings, architects have mainly been interested in creating a silhouette and have failed to take thought of what the construction and exploitation of these buildings would cost.

When a wall is given a complex contour simply for purposes of beautification, the consequence is unnecessary expenditure on the building's use as a result of large heat losses. [...]

We are not against beauty, but we are against superfluity. The facades of buildings should be of beautiful and attractive appearance, and this should be achieved as a result of the entire edifice having good proportions, well-proportioned window and door apertures, well-positioned balconies, correct use of the texture and colour of facing materials, and a proper presentation of wall parts and structures in buildings made from large sections and panels. [...]

IMPROVING QUALITY: THE MOST IMPORTANT TASK FACED BY OUR BUILDERS

Comrades, special attention should be paid to improving the quality of construction. We must build not merely quickly, but unfailingly well and sturdily, and we must value our reputation as builders. Buildings should be convenient for living in and convenient in exploitation. Badly built buildings have to be repaired after short periods of time, which means having to spend extra money. This applies to all types of construction.

First and foremost, I would like to talk about quality of construction in residential buildings. Are the walls and ceilings of our buildings well made? I think they are very well made. In our residential buildings, schools, hospitals, and other buildings the walls and ceilings are constructed in such a way that they will perform their functions for hundreds of years. There can be no doubt about this since we use reinforced concrete for construction. But it has to be said that the decoration of buildings is often done badly. What's more, many workers put up with clearly unconscientious work in decorating buildings. This has been said in full fairness by many comrades at the conference.

Recently comrades Bulganin and Mikoyan and myself had to visit many cities in the Far East, Siberia, and the Urals. [...] In the city of Sverdlovsk we lived in a hotel. This hotel was well and sturdily made. [...] And in this hotel we saw that the bathroom and toilet blocks were very badly built and that the quality of decorative work was poor. We asked for the hotel director and the city leaders and said to them: "Look how poor this work is!"

Evidently, there was a failure to require proper standards during construction.

Builders must be told about such failings – and there are many of them – and be told to drastically improve the quality of their work. Comrade Yudin, the Minister for the Construction-Materials Industry, and other workers in the construction-materials industry should not give themselves airs, but should learn from our friends in Czechoslovakia, who make fine construction materials and parts. (Applause.) They can also learn from the German Democratic Republic, where they produce fine facing tiles. It has to be said without beating about the bush that some comrades learn too little from others and, what is more to the point, don't even desire to learn. (Applause.) [...] Special attention should be paid to improving the quality of panels made of wood. [...] We must work constantly and insistently to improve the quality of decorating work. [...] In residential buildings the stairwells must likewise be well decorated. For decorating the external walls of buildings the best material is ceramic tiling. Ceramic facing is long-lasting, aesthetically pleasing, and does not change colour during use. [...]

The main thing is, it's vital that order should be kept: no construction should begin without an architectural design, without an estimate, or without detailed plans. (Applause.)

INCREASING THE PRODUCTIVITY OF LABOUR, CREATING A SUPPLY OF QUALIFIED BUILDERS

[...] It's well known that there is much room in the construction sector for improving productivity of labour and consequently for increasing salaries earned by workers. Such room is to be found in mechanisation of building work; correct use of the powerful equipment we have on our building sites; a switch to industrial methods of construction; improvement of workers' skills; better use of the advanced experience gained by innovators; and strengthening of production discipline. [...]

In order to raise the real wages earned by workers it is necessary to ensure a growth in labour productivity and a growth in the take-home pay earned by each worker.

There are many examples that provide convincing proof of the opportunities available for improving productivity of labour and increasing workers' wages. Here is one such example. I shall compare two schools of the many built in Moscow in 1954 – one in Tomkmakov pereulok and built out of brick; the other, in Kutuzovskaya sloboda, built from large blocks. Observe the difference in the amount of labour the two schools required. 7,360 man-days were spent on laying the brick walls and building cornices, ceilings and floors, staircases, and partition walls, while the same work in the building made from large blocks required 1,780 man-days – or only 24% of the number of man-days spent on the school made of brick. The average worker's pay for the above types of work at the school made from brick was 268 rubles per man-day, while in the case of the block-built school the respective figure was 1,432 rubles, i.e. 5.3 times more. If we consider all types of work done at the brick school, pay per man-day was 142 rubles, while for the second school it was 261 rubles, i.e. 1.8 times greater. As for use of cranes, during construction of the first school 314 machine-shifts were used; while for the second 164 – or 54% – were needed. This, comrades, is where there is room for growth in labour productivity and increases in pay! [...]

Comrades, I shall bring my speech to a close by expressing my confidence that builders, architects, engineers, workers in the construction-materials industry and in manufacture of machinery for construction and roads, and employees of design and research organisations will carry out with honour the tasks laid upon them by the Party and the Government; will improve still further the level, pace, and quality of construction in our country; will accelerate the bringing in of factories, mines, power stations, and manufactories; and will build residences, schools, and hospitals better and more beautifully. Goodbye until we meet again at the next conference of builders. I wish you continued success, comrades! (Wild, continuous applause. Everyone stands).

Excerpts from a speech at the National Conference of Builders, Architects, Workers in the Construction Materials and Manufacture of Construction and Roads Machinery Industries, and Employees of Design and Research and Development Organisations on December 7, 1954

X E N I A   S O R O K I N A
E X H I B I T S
V A L E R Y   S O R O K I N

Before us stands an imaginary exhibition from the work of my father, the artist Valery Sorokin, born in the USSR in 1952. This is a collection of projects to fill up public spaces he worked on from the end of the 70s until the mid-90s of the last century. The requests for the production of these works issued from the Union of Artists of the USSR, the organization that distributes state orders for landscaping and decorating public spaces. Despite the seeming success, the system of production relations often malfunctioned on account of competition between artists, insufficient funds, or various bureaucratic reasons. That is why a noticeable part of the projects have not been realized, just as many of the works have never before been displayed and were hidden from the eyes of the public.

Contributed by Xenia Sorokina

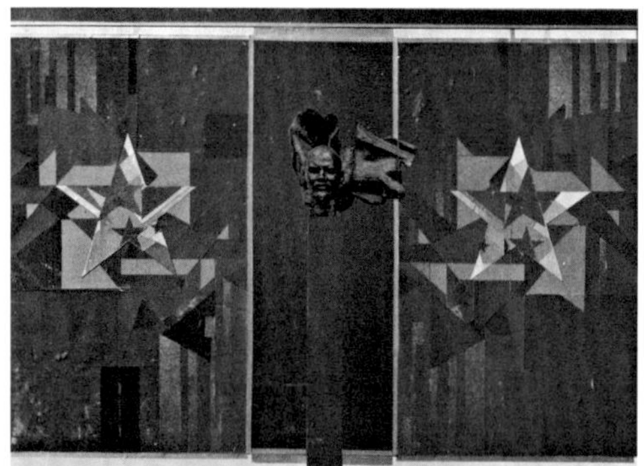

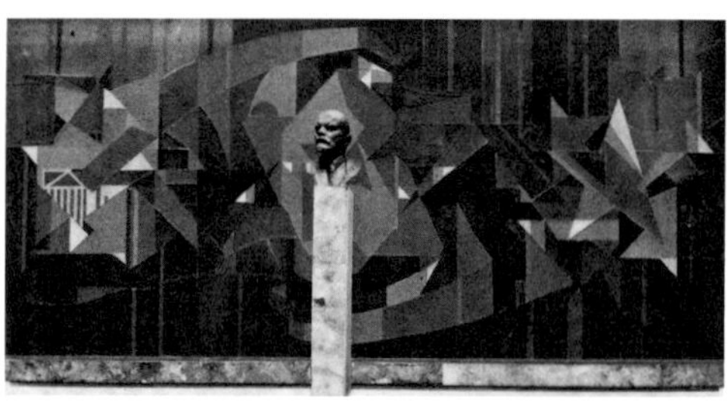

1987-1988
Collage, colored paper
Studies of a textile panel for the All-Union Exhibition of Young Artists in the Moscow Manege in 1978 were approved by the Arts Council, but were never realized.

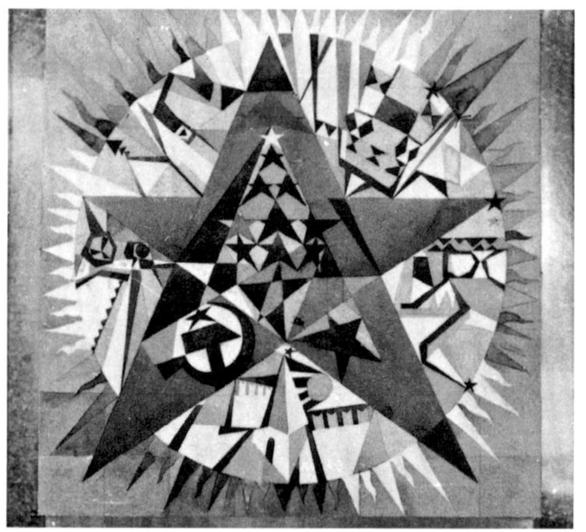

1985, Tapestry, hand woven
Hand woven tapestry project for the store Vremya
Study of a sculpture, gouache
Tapestry for the interior of the bookstore Vremya, beginning of 1980s, lost, paintings on the walls of the room were also not preserved.

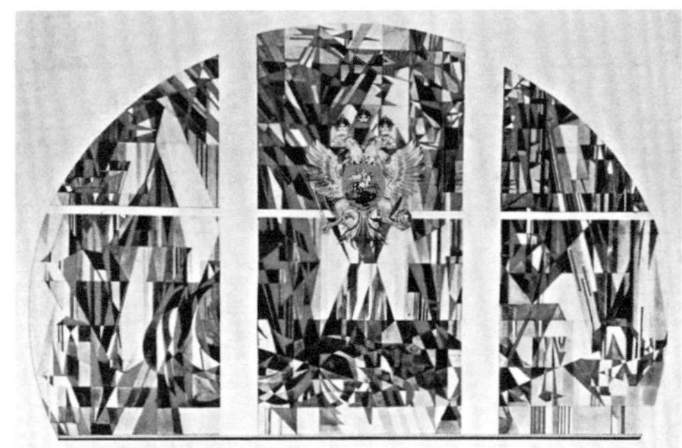

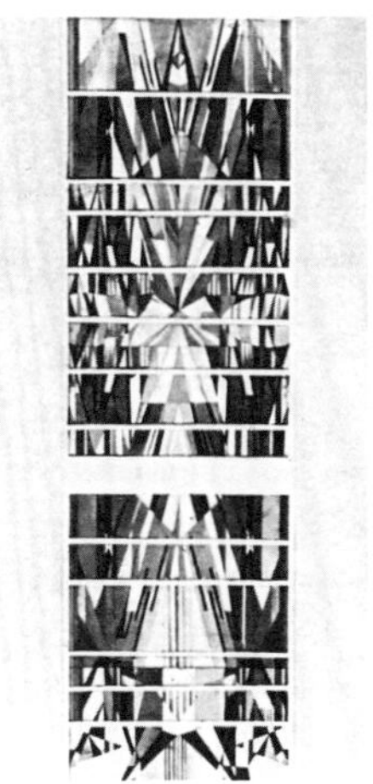

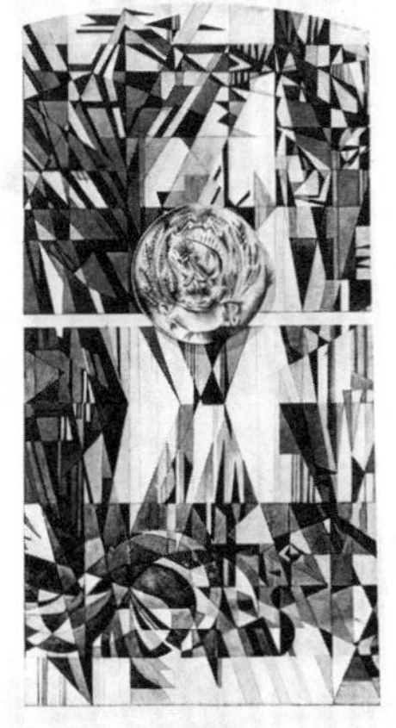

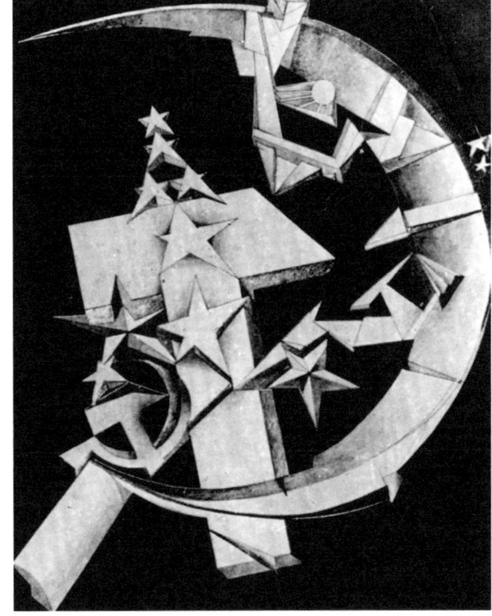

Hammer And Sickle. The Sixteen Soviet Republics, 1990-1991
Black and white photos of color sketches (paper, tempera)
The sketches were made before the fall of the USSR. The sixteen stars depicted in the sketch symbolize the republics comprising the Soviet Union.

1992-1993
Collage, paper, watercolor
Sketches of a stained-glass window for the Wedding Registration Office building in Astrakhan. The project was never realized; the work was given to another artist, who had proposed a smaller budget to produce the works. In an early black and white photo the emblem of Soviet Union was inscribed into the stained-glass window, in a later, color photo it was changed to the new, modern Russian emblem.

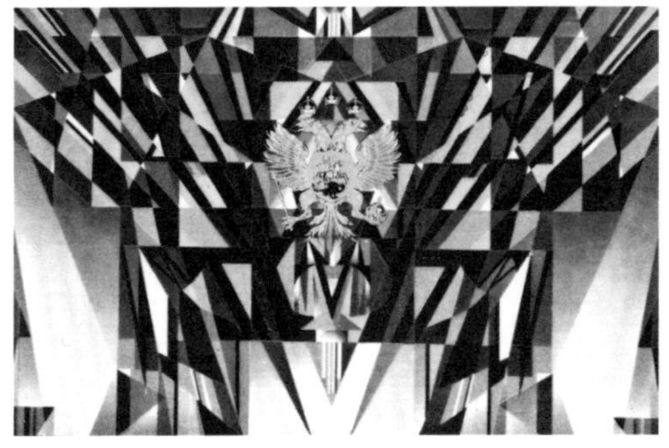

1986-1998
Fireworks
Paper, posters, collage
Initially the artist intended the work as a mosaic for the facade of the movie theater Yubileyniy in Astrakhan, but later he changed his mind. After twelve years he tried to offer the study, having changed it a bit, as a stained-glass window for an airport building in Astrakhan; however, his intention was never realized.

BELYAEVO 99 AND FOREVER, 1999

DMITRY ALEXANDROVICH PRIGOV

As a matter of fact, I don't have to say what Belyaevo is and where it's located. Even abroad I didn't run into any people who didn't know about it. They might not have known Tbilisi. Some might not know where, let's say, Latvia or Luxembourg are. But not Belyaevo. Only those who want somehow to stand out (or those with some unseemly aim) ask:

- Belyaevo? Where's that?

- Where, where? It's where it needs to be.

Sometimes, actually, this name is associated with a small patch between two exits from the famous metro of the same name. However, it's a remarkable place, attractive for its network of outstanding kiosks with amazing locally manufactured and imported goods. In the vicinity cozy cafes and restaurants with exotic names such as 'Zurbaran' and 'Cayman' are scattered about. One cannot ignore a huge complex of interactive and new anthropological installations and a European research center for virtual strategic developments there. In the morning crowds of people rush toward their headquarters and different ministry and agency offices.

But that's not the point.

The influence of Belyaevo is spread far beyond its limits, reaching into the south, for example, to remote settlements like Butovo. Belyaevo itself lies along the field lines of an invasion by an emanation of southern aeons into the north, which is given evidence by a foray of strong dry winds, which sometimes blow down everything in their path. Then rare small groups of people make their way along deep open air markets and hollows between breathing and crawling sand dunes. Coarse fabric protects them from sharp, whipping, bone cutting, diamond-like sand, which passes through and flies away and carries with it fine and residual dust of feeble organisms. Drifting past my seventh floor, they cast up their brown bleeding faces and with a glance inquire:

- How much longer?

- Be patient, you'll be there soon, - I reply to them. And they are patient. For a long time. A really long time.

However, then, at other times, on holidays, cheerful crowds drift past the same balcony on Volgin street. They pass by a tall dormitory for the Medical institute, the mysterious higher education police academy and the no less, but maybe even more mysterious Shemyakin Institute (not the painter Shemyakin but the real, famous Shemyakin). They pass by a luxurious shopping complex, located on the ground floor of the nine-story apartment complex #25, building 1. And then they see my balcony on the seventh floor of complex #25, building 2, where I am standing in a lightweight white silk shirt with an unbuttoned collar and greeting them. My wife is standing next to me in a white dress. The local wind tousles her fair hair and the hem of her dress. People shout, calling out greetings and slogans to Belyaevo's independence. I must say that for many years now entire delegations have been coming to me regularly, asking me to take the title of duke Belyaevsky - Bogorodsky with all the ensuing political and social ramifications, with the recognition of the full and indivisible sovereignty of our glorious land Belyaevo.

And believe me, it's really worth it.

At all times, significant, out of the ordinary and sometimes just outstanding people have lived here. Here they are, near and dear – Averintsev, before he moved to Vienna, Groys, before he moved to Cologne, Parshchikov, before he moved to the same Cologne, Erofeev, before he moved to Plyushchikha to be arm in arm with the central authorities. Popov also moved out. As well as Yankilevsky, he moved to Paris though. Both Rostropovich and Rushdie. But Kibirov and Sorokin still live here. Kabakov with Bulatov moved out, though. But Insaytbatallo and Staynlomato still live here. Shnitke, Pärt and Kancheli moved out, though. And people turn to me.

And there's nothing unusual in the fact that they turn to me. I am one of the pioneers of the latest settlement of these places, when there was no metro, no construction, and just our single white panel forlorn little house soared up. Grass swaying in the wind ran up to the very porch. I remember my wife resolved not to go out alone, even if she was running late for work, because of the cows, who closely came up to the front door and butted her with their layered horns. I would go out, drive them away, take my wife to the distant solitary bus and go for a walk with my son in abandoned apple and cherry orchards, blooming at the time with their first bright white outbursts. Back then we came across wild animal tracks and traces of ancient unmarred burials. And then a wild, almost primordial flame would blaze up along Kaluzhskoe highway. When I caught up with it, there were only ashes from the recently standing wooden houses, and the flame, buzzing and rejoicing, was moving deep into Moscow, destroying everything in its way. And now only a nauseating, sickening smell of burning came from the centre. And silence. Great terrible silence. From the top of Belyaevo for months we watched the city being slowly, as though reluctantly, built up and populated, and give itself anew the name Moscow. But it's not the point.

Delegations keep arriving and not backing down from their requests and wishes, already throw them directly in my face now:

- It's all because of your indecision!

- Just consider how much money, people's money, would have to be invested in building checkpoints and border equipment, in general passport creation and a census, in registration and eviction of foreigners. Just imagine the scale of such a humanitarian disaster! Why should ordinary people suffer? No, I won't take any harsh steps until tanks and assault weapons are brought to our borders. And they agree once again.

Why, repeated tragic events of past years are still on the minds of the older residents of Belyaevo, when the residents of Konkovo, having conceived of an inhuman ambition to stand level with the people of Belyaevo, completely lost it. The clashes began along the margins of Ostrovityanova and Profsoyuznaya streets. At first, it was committed, small groups of Konkovo residents disposed to the worst extremism. We worthily rebuffed them. Skirmishes broke out all along the perimeter of the south-west outskirts of Belyaevo. The people of Konkovo enlisted the help of people from Tyoply Stan and Bittsevskiy Park [former name of the Novoyasenevskaya metro station]. The outraged people of Yasenevo and Troparyovo, them-selves feeling threatened, rose up on our side. Soon, trying to resolve their longstanding baseless complaints the people of Kaluzhskaya and Vavilova joined the Konkovo's side. In turn the people of Leninsky Prospect and Universitet supported us. A little later the militia from Kuntsevo and consolidated detachment from Sadovo- and Triumphalno-Koltsevaya arrived. On their side stood the people from Varshavskoe and Kashirskoe Highways. At the approach of the squadrons of Sviblovo the wild and ferocious Kolomenskaya people were routed. The main battles reeled back to the Belyaevo rest area, to a gigantic lake. Soon all possible approaches were filled with crowds of endlessly embroiled people. The approaching people pressed down on the people in front of them and walked along their bodies, transforming them into a squelching homogenous slush as though a frightful possessing power was drawing them to an irresistible gravitational center. With stoic despair I observed as a powerful current flowed into the boiling waters of the lake and disappeared into them, while at last the rising waters, having enwrapped the city with a heavy, unwavering, smoothly gleaming (in my view) layer of water many meters long, did not cover the remaining people and did not gush forth into the city. From my seventh floor I followed the infrequent boats and sail boats, whose sails, having caught a southern wind, set out to the north. The island life of the rare survivors was by nature unsophisticated. They had to set up and establish everything anew. But that's how it was.

Much later on the border of the subdued Konkovo a merchandise market was built up. On the corner of Miklukho-Maklaya Street an alluring Mercedes auto center and the excellent store "Sedmoy Kontinent" were raised. There were a casino and hotel on Ostrovityanova Street. A nursing home comfortably stretched into a green rustling environment. In the farthest shady corner of the rest area a zoo was placed, where the oldest preserved rhinoceros, they say, one day looked into the eyes of the visiting Vladimir Ilyich and lived through the fascist invasion, which rolled into the very heart of Belyaevo. But Belyaevo held out. Now you can worthily evaluate my reserved and measured relationship to any kind of risky and ambiguous offers of authority and sovereignty.

Even so I didn't feel and don't feel any kind of

loss. Here beside me on the same central street of Belyaevo – Volgina Street – the Pushkin Russian Language Institute was set up, where students from all countries, associate professors, graduate students, and professors gather together, or rather, fly together like clouds – all together every foreigner who speaks Russian. They are all that I wish for, and they themselves want to be my guests. They visit me and fly back to their countries. There they occupy key positions at universities and research centers. Naturally, every day they carefully check all their steps against my expectations and advice. That is, they practically do as I wish. No project goes forward without my approval. No one can go to universities in America, Germany, France, England, Italy, Japan, etc. without my consent. It happens that the most famous Russian men of letters for years wait for my approval, actually reaching an unpleasant level of servility and obsequiousness. But what can you do – everyone wants to go. It's understandable. And I understand and forgive. And it doesn't only concern literature or arts there. My protégés fly out and occupy the most influential centers of geopolitical influence. So there's practically not a single significant world event that happens without my sanction and approval.

So think, why do I need peoples' squabbles? What do I need the excessive burdens and the regalia of an unattractive power for? I have only one concern – that the people of Belyaevo live and prosper.

M E T R O ,   1 9 7 9
M U K H O M O R   G R O U P

The invitations that had been sent out contained a schedule of the groups' travel plans around the Moscow subway. The travels lasted from 6 a.m. until 1 a.m., that is, from the moment of opening until the closing of the metro.

During the event members of the group "Mukhomor" met with people they had invited and kept travel journals.

The event's results:

Members of the group "Mukhomor" spent 19 hours in the metro without leaving and traveled through every metro station, making 43 stops. 15 meetings were recorded, 2 of which were by chance.

7:50 BELORUSSKAYA

Want to sleep and get the heck out of here. The thought of being here another 18 hours is oppressing. There are 3 (three) police officers at the station. They are walking around slowly and yawning from time to time. One of them is wearing glasses. We're taking photos and going to "Rechnoy Vokzal."

7:30-8:00 RECHNOY VOKZAL

There are almost no people. The few there are all have backpacks. Their faces are red, weather beaten. Along the way we had a little snack, since before leaving home we didn't have time for a proper breakfast. For the time being, we each partook of a sandwich and a cup (more exactly, a thermos top) of tea. Mood, thank God, is improving.

8:15 SOKOL

A very exotic place for photographs. We're climbing the stairs in the center of the hall like monkeys. Interesting: will anyone wake up so early to check our progress.

10:45 MEDVEDKOVO

We are all here at this station for the first time in our lives. We like it a lot. (That's a complete lie). We talked with the woman on duty at the station. A small misunderstanding. The topic exhausted itself immediately by the time we cleared up the misunderstanding. Let's not talk about it. Mood is up. Being here has become habit. Sitting in the train facing each other, we entertained ourselves: Kostya lowers his head – I raise mine, Kostya will raise his – I will lower mine. Semantic rhythm!

11:10 VDNKh

No one expected to see so many people. S. Mironenko and S. Gundlakh went to poop. We are continuing to study the press: the newspapers "Komsomolskaya Pravda" and "Sotsialisticheskaya Industria." Taking photos. Statistics: police officers – 5, patrols – 3.

11:10-12:00 Train from VDNKh to BELYAEVO

Traveling standing. A lot of people (bumping us!). Near the door a Vietnamese man is standing and reading a book in Vietnamese. We actually didn't poop, since we couldn't, and now we want to poop. V. Mironenko: "the pointlessness of what's going on is being sharply felt." Statistics: police officers – 2.

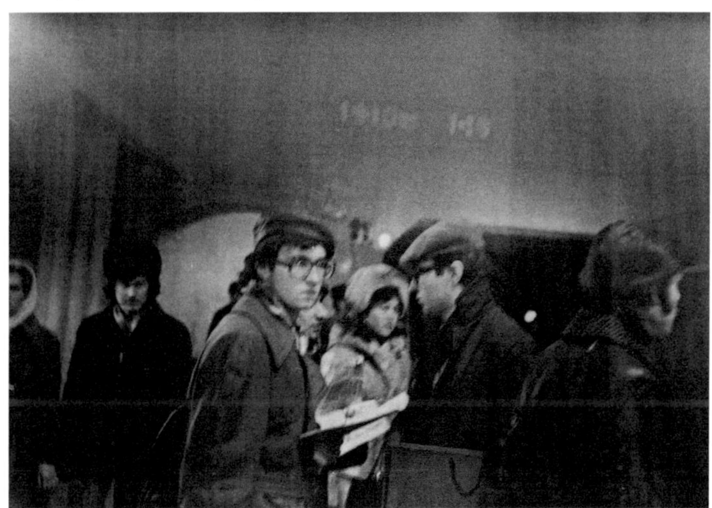

12:00 BELYAEVO

Belyaevo is empty. There, a cop passed by. Two officers and two ordinaries are walking by. I'm trying to read in English. I'm a Francophone. I'm feeling satisfactory.

12:20-12:40 LENINSKY PROSPECT

Statistics: police officers – 3. When I took a photo, a police officer walked up to me. (Conversation recorded exactly.)

Do you have permission?

What kind of permission?

To take photos in the metro!
What? It's really not allowed?
It's not allowed.
Well, but it's not written in the rules.
It's written.
In those hanging in the train cars?
No, in those near the station workers.
Sorry, I didn't know. I saw that foreigners were taking photos.
They're here as guests. They can take photos.
But aren't we at home here? Should we be able to? You can't at home.

waiting for his wife. The police officers took our passports, and checked whether we knew what our names were and where we lived.
You were just at Kutuzovskaya and took pictures of the men's and women's.
What kind of men's and women's?
Bathrooms.
Ah! Is that where the clock is? We're in a photo club. So here we are photographing.
We took a photo of a mirror since the train was reflected in it.
Excuse us, – They saluted and walked away.

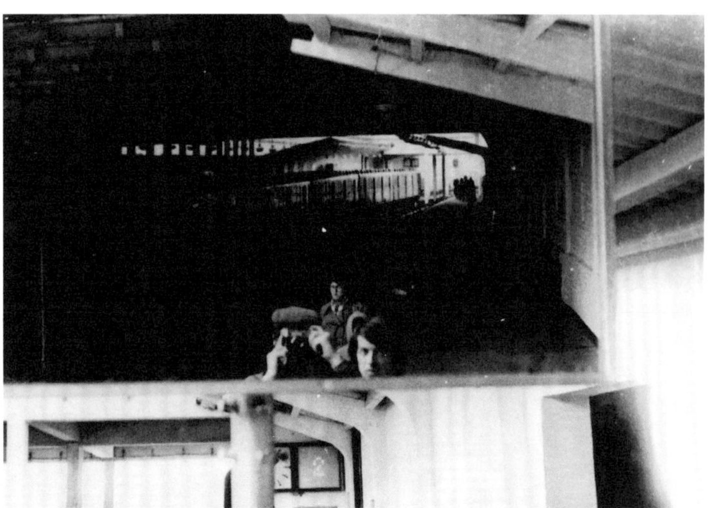

13:20 KUTUZOVSKAYA
Cold. Want to eat. It's snowing. Icicles are hanging from the ceiling of the station. We took photos. There are indeed significantly more police officers. Scary stuff. We're afraid they'll expose our film to light. Statistics: police officers – 4.

13:50 MOLODYOZHNAYA
Either we're being followed or we're starting to get persecution mania. In any case, a large number of police officers is constantly walking around us. There were 6 of them at "Molodyozhnaya." One of them sat down next to us in the train. 2 others were accompanying him, standing at the head and the tail of the train car. It's very much a shame that we have to be afraid. As if we're criminals or spies.

14:20 STUDENCHESKAYA
We stood still for 5 minutes. We were freezing. 5 police officers were walking around the platform. Three came up to us and requested our documents. Before that they asked us what we were doing there. Sven said that we were

14:40 BIBLIOTEKA LENINA
We met D. Vrubel. We didn't manage to photograph anything. There were 2 police officers. Vrubel went with us to Preobrazhenskaya Ploshchad.
Completely unexpectedly we met Vadim Shamatov, who Sven, Volodya, and Seryozha studied with in the same class. We're rejoicing in the warmth, remembering our school years. Picking apart our classmates. (Shamatov went to get wine). We hadn't seen Shamatov in four years.

15:10 PREOBRAZHENSKAYA PLOSHCHAD
Now police officers are traveling together with us in the train very often. Or we are simply noticing them frequently. Kostya is dozing off. We want to eat and smoke. There's not a single police officer at the station. We take photos at ease. Suddenly 2 men in metropolitan uniforms walk by, laughing at Vrubel's overcoat. They see that we're taking photos and say, "Perhaps we should ruin the film?" They laugh and leave.

15:25 KRASNOSELSKAYA
At Krasnoselskaya we ran into D. Machabeli. He was going to Sokolniki to drink beer. A. Monastirskiy arrived, bringing cookies with him. He and Machabeli rode with us until Komsomolskaya.

16:10 YUGO-ZAPADNAYA
4 cops. We arrived ahead of schedule. Reloaded film. The station is seemingly quiet and orderly. Kostya would have gladly smoked then, but he reeked of an onion (bulbous), which provoked our antipathy.

16:30-17:00 LENINSKIE GORY [Now Vorobyovy Gory]
Seryozha, Volodya, and Sven took a leak. Vru-

bel started messing with Kostya. A police officer walking by rebuked them. He said:
What are you horsing around for?
...?!
Cut that shit out now!
And he left.

17:30 ARBATSKAYA (ARBATSKO-POKROVSKAYA LINE)

5 police officers. The longest station of all. Natasha brought us some snacks. Sandwiches with rump steak, sprat pâte and two thermoses with tea. During our lunch 2 police officers stood opposite us and stared at us. A third one came up to them from time to time. We didn't expect that the police presence would get on our nerves so much. The worst thing was not the crowds, not the stupidity of what was going on, not everything else (hunger, desire to ease oneself, and to smoke) but being meticulously watched by police officers. We have the constant fear that they will come up to us and say... you weren't allowed to take any of those photos.

18:00 IZMAILOVSKAYA

It suddenly got dark. We were very surprised. Had a cigarette. We were freezing. Departing the station we made a mistake and went the wrong direction. Had to get off at Izmailovskiy park, get on another train, and go back.

18:30 SHCHELKOVSKAYA

Met Makarevich. He was smiling. We gave him some tea. Unexpectedly, another man came up to us, whom we didn't know but who, apparently, knew Makarevich. They signed our schedule.
The stranger said:
You have to do all this with humor.
We have to stretch the humor out over time, – we answered him.
Makarevich took our photo. Then we got on a train. Makarevich stood and looked at us until the doors closed and the train started. Then he waved.

19:00 PLOSHCHAD REVOLYUTSII

It was hard to photograph anything. Full of police officers. 6 of them. Somehow we artfully managed to take some photos. Now we're heading to Kakhovskaya.

19:40 KAKHOVSKAYA

Ilya Smirnov came. We took 20 kopecks from him. He said more people would come. 7:40 in the evening – the number makes me think of the Jews*. 7:43. A very young married couple, whom we didn't know very well, came. (Once we went over to their place at 12 a.m. and stayed there for about half an hour).
* 7:40 is the name of an Eastern European Jewish folk song.

20:00 AVTOZAVODSKAYA

Arrived. There were 2 police officers. We were about to take photos. Suddenly Kolya Kozlov arrived. He brought a painting by Chuikov wrapped in the newspaper "Literaturnaya Gazeta." We tried to peep into a slit but didn't see anything. Kolya went with us to Pushkinskaya station.

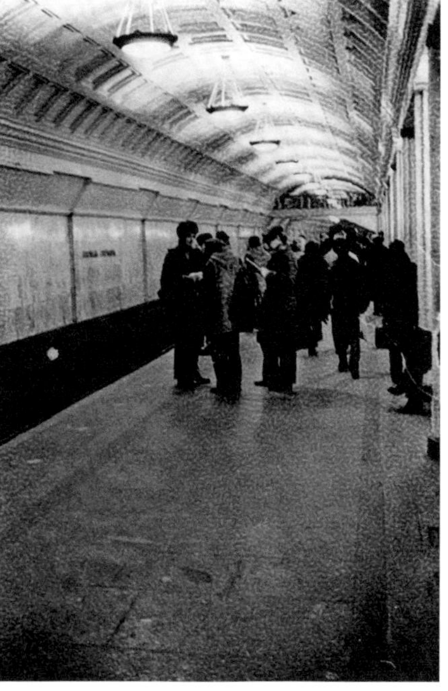

20:20 PUSHKINSKAYA

We had difficulties photographing again. Nonetheless we had already gotten the hang of taking photos under the noses of the police. We said goodbye to Kozlov and went to Planernaya.

21:00 PLANERNAYA

We didn't manage to take any photos at Planernaya – we ran out of film in both cameras.

21:20 OKTYABRSKOE POLE

Reloaded our cameras with the last of our film.

21:35 BEGOVAYA

No one came. Took several shots.

21:50 KRASNOPRESNENSKAYA

I'm taking photos. As soon as I put away the camera a cop passes by. Then I take photos again. The cop passes by again. Then I take photos again. The cop passes by again. And I always manage to hide the camera a fraction of a second before he shows up. He quickly and constantly walks around the whole station with some kind of preposterous periodicity. It's very comfortable and warm here.

Statistics – 3 police officers. No one came. We waited for 30 minutes. 3 police officers and a group of foreigners are walking around the station. Judging by the number of blondes, they're from Scandinavia. My organism is overwhelmed by a great feeling of orthodox TORPOR. Kostya is worn out. The torpor is accompanied by withdrawal. The passengers' faces show boredom. There's a cop standing in the train car again.

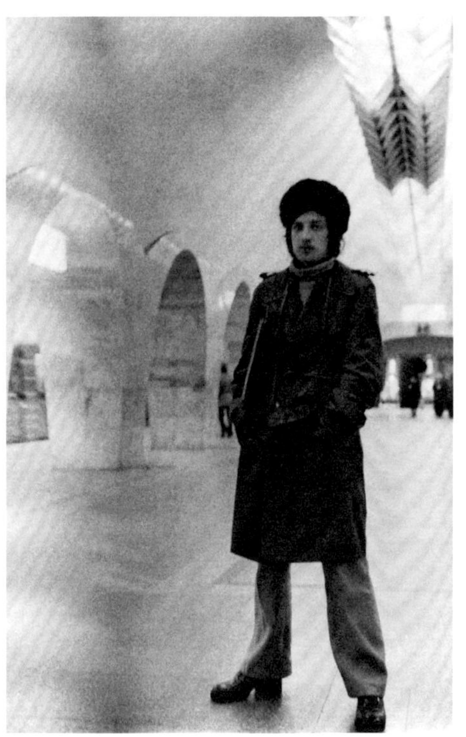

23:00 FILI
We didn't want to go. We were afraid of bumping into others again. We waited a very long time for the train. It's snowing. No one came. And we're freezing. Knowing that we've almost made it increases our tiredness. We're fairly fucking sick of all this. I think it only seems that way. And generally it's all coming to an end. It's a peculiar kind of high.

23:30 DOBRYNINSKAYA
We're sitting in the recesses. At times we lean out and take photos of each other. Complete mutual understanding. The arrival of a train is a rather poorly nourishing event (flashes of malnutrition!), mister wigmakers. A complete state of euphoria is approaching. A drunken man is walking around the station and yelling: "People! Hey, people!" Everyone keeps silent. Even the police officers haven't shown up.
[...] The time is 23:28. Dobryninskaya station. I'm sitting alone (SM) since Kostya was taken by a police officer because the former was sleeping on a bench with his face buried in his backpack. Sven and his brother went with them. Quote: "Let him get some fresh air." Another: "The metro is no place to rest and transport is a highly dangerous resource." They took another one of my neighbors sleeping on the bench. Mukhomor members have arrived and are swearing. It's better to wisely keep silent. [...] Kostya:
I was sleeping. I woke up because someone was shaking my shoulder. I thought it was one of the guys. I opened my eyes and saw a big cop in front of me and there was no one on the platform. He said: "Get up! Or do you want to go to a sobering-up center?" He took me by my white hands and led me to the exit. I say: "I'm not drunk..." and he: "look who's sprawled out here!" I would have been lost if Sven hadn't seen us and saved me.

23:50 KURSKAYA (circle line)
RECORD, 8 police officers.

00:00 PLOSHCHAD REVOLYUTSII
3 police officers left our train car. There's none at the station. We're standing, waiting for something. A group of young people are singing not quite a Tyrolean and not quite a Georgian song. About 30 seconds later they all leave to the transfer passage.

00:30 PLOSHCHAD NOGINA
Vanity of vanities! We're still alive! We should have finished with something amazing, as befitting the great Russian writers. But we're modest. Glory itself knocks on our door. AMEN. Life on the surface is much worse than in the depths.
Long live conceptualism! Hurray!!!! 19 hours underground!
For the first time – a world record! One can't live like that! BLAH

**Selected entries from the action diary.
From the collection of the Archive of
Contemporary Russian Art, Moscow**

KASHIRSKOE SHOSSE, 1983-1986
ANDREI MONASTYRSKI

[...]

19. Morning came at last, and Vera and Masha got up. We had breakfast, and I went out to buy groceries. Outside, my sense of being in an altered reality was even more acute. That silvery, luminous, otherworldly snow was coming down again. I was ill at ease and curious at the same time. I also felt inner forces of which I had previously been unaware, sensed the energy with which my body and things around me were charged. The newness and otherness of my environment gave all my feelings and perceptions a peculiar "after death" savor. Things seemed to be where they always were – buildings, trees, pedestrians, earth, sky, snow – but it was a different reality that wasn't like a dream or like normal, conventional reality. I remember thinking of it then as "angelic" reality.

The utter newness of my environment, the air, the whole reality constructed around me to the point of existential certainty, gave me a feeling of acute discomfort, of nakedness, even though, as I've already said, my body, in keeping with the new environment, felt more highly charged than usual – as if equipped with extra means of life support suited to the new environment. Sensing this "helmet" on me, I didn't feel in mortal danger, but was open to adventures and the unexpected – more on the level of images and sensations than events. I was fully aware that the reality I had come into was not that of an unknown planet, but the psycho-energetic reality of states of consciousness previously unknown to me.

Once in the store, I was relieved to get in line at the milk counter behind an elderly man who gave off an energy that was protective and positive for me. Outside the store, I had already identified him as an "angel" in my "angelic" reality. Subconsciously, I suppose, I hadn't forgotten that Satan himself is an archangel in the celestial hierarchy of Christian tradition. And I did feel the influence of negative currents. As I stood in line, I made a concentrated effort to ignore the unsavory youths standing in a small group by the window (in conventional reality, ordinary morning-after alcohol-

ics). They projected a guarded antagonism to me that was palpable. In energy terms, this was a group of demons, who made up, as would later become clear, a considerable part of the population of this "angelic" reality.

That morning, however, both in the store and outside, the prevailing feeling I had was an unusually pleasant sense of the crisp, sparkling purity of the air, the light and the whole atmosphere around me. It was as if the weather had suddenly acquired purely spiritual qualities of sympathy and benevolence, and the forecast for those qualities was exceptionally favorable.

20. I went home and put away the groceries. Everything was quiet. Neither Vera nor Masha suspected that inside myself I was as far from their psychic reality as if I had been on Mars.

Vera asked if I would take Masha to her grandmother's on Kirov Street and, while I was at it, take along a large drawing board after first sawing it in half. She had several students then and wanted to make the drawing board into easels.

I took the board to the kitchen, laid it on stools, drew a line down the middle with a ruler – and remembered that yesterday on Pushkin Square Anya had mentioned something about a line. She had said, without any connection to our conversation, that "there must be a line." Of course, I didn't know what she was talking about then. A week earlier, Father Alexei, hearing my confession at Zagorsk Monastery, had also spoken about a line. I well remember the mysterious phrase that ended our talk: "When you cross the line, you'll know!" What this line was and what I was supposed to know, I didn't understand. So it was natural that when I marked the board – located, as I was, in an "angelic" reality composed of naturalized symbols – I would associate this penciled line with the mystical lines of which they had spoken.

I began sawing the board with the feeling that I was sawing off my own fate. I was amazed by the precision and power with which I performed the task: I sawed through the wide, thick drawing board without pausing, really getting into the spirit (and noting, of course, the double meaning of that idiom). I sawed without tiring and made an ideally straight cut along the line. But when, at the very end, the board broke in two under its own weight, it cracked slightly, leaving flaws on one half. I set the two halves one against the other, with the flaws on the outside, and tied the boards together cross-wise, after which Masha and I got on our coats and went out. In addition to the boards, I was carrying a heavy mesh bag in my other hand.

21. We left the building, turned the corner onto Kondratyuk Street and passed between banks of snow piled high on either side of the walk. It wasn't long before a crying spell came over me again. I suddenly stopped and began to sob, tears running down my cheeks. I stood in the middle of the sidewalk, with people going around me, stood there in my winter hat with the earflaps hanging down, holding the boards in one hand and the bag in the other, and wept for what must have been five minutes. Masha was standing beside me and every so often, smiling and in a perfectly calm and unchildlike voice, said, "It's all right, don't cry." I think it was her unusual reaction to my tears (she was four at the time) that gradually brought me to my senses. Then, out of the blue, she said that "Mama" was coming. Judging by her strange, detached intonation – the mention of "Mama" was aloof and disinterested – it seemed unlikely that she meant Vera. It was presumably my mother who would come and comfort me or else some mystical mother-surrogate like the Holy Mother. I immediately stopped crying and asked her who she meant by "Mama." She didn't answer, but only smiled and said, "Good, let's go!" She rubbed her mitten over the flaws on the board, and we went on our way.

I had evidently been moved to tears by my sins, as if in expectation of immanent judgment over them. And these sins were embodied for me in the weight of what I was carrying – in the boards and bag. For some reason, the flaws on the one half struck me as especially grievous sins. One half of the sawn board represented my sins and the other half, my wife's sins. Her board had the flaws, which signified abortions (unfortunately, religious consciousness is extremely self-centered up to a certain stage). But my "burden of sin" also included the heavy bag. Curiously, as I describe all of this, some episodes are pleasant to write about, while others I find almost too tedious to relive. I've noticed that the pleasant-to-describe episodes are those where I think back to a state of unreflective madness. Essentially, these were blissful, all-consuming states of insanity – spells of genuine, natural madness imbued with the plenitude of faith, for which I still feel nostalgia (at least I did for some time after my "return").

22. In the full conviction that I was about to pay for my sins, I hung my head as I crossed the wide square in front of the Cosmos Movie Theater and entered the small park on the way to VDNKh Metro Station. Masha walked beside me, holding on to the bag and smiling the same solemn, concentrated smile. Halfway through the park, I had an important experience involving the "objectification" of sins. They were weighing on me more heavily and getting harder and harder to carry, especially the boards. I stopped and, without putting them down, began to pray. For some reason, it was important that I hold them till the last, until my grip loosened from the unbearable weight and the boards fell on the snow. This stubborn perseverance would seem strange at first glance. In a normal state, of course, I'd have just set them down in the snow while I rested. But it must have had something to do with the imperative given to the program of collective consciousness: "he that endures to the end will be saved." Of course, that phrase didn't figure at all in my consciousness; I was living it as psychodrama. It was simply important, no matter the reason, that I endure the lacerating pain from the rope tied around the heavy boards and hold on to the last, which is what I did. I remember feeling not only unbearable physical agony, but terror as well. Later, when the boards had slipped from my hands and I picked them up again, I was surprised to find that they hardly weighed anything at all. After that, I was unaware of their weight until the very end of the journey. When this hard-to-bear episode was over, I again wept tears of sorrow, though this time with a certain feeling of relief.

Again Masha said, "It's all right, don't cry," and we walked on. Near the rotunda of the metro station, she pulled me out of the way of a truck that was slowly backing up to a cigarette kiosk. I had seen that I was in the way, but was so absorbed in myself that I didn't think to step aside. From that moment on, I was essentially led around town by a four-year-old child – led firmly and with assurance – if anything, with even greater assurance, greater mechanical force, than I had felt from Anna on the way to the photo collection and back. I don't think it was Masha herself who was producing this impression of force; rather it was her grounding in the laws of conventional reality, its functionality. I, in my unstable angelic reality, was dangling down somewhere, like a toy dog on wheels being pulled along on a string by a four-year-old girl. I was absorbed in a nonfunctional "vision," not in doing and acting like the people around me. I acutely felt the incredible, inaccessible power of their reality – their bodies, actions and voices – and my own separation from them, my isolation. Although my appearance couldn't have inspired confidence, with head hung and tear-stained face, and though anyone could have seen that it wasn't I who was leading a child by the hand, but the child who was leading me, no one in the crowds around the metro, in the train or at the stations ever intervened or asked what was the matter.

I was so disoriented that I didn't know what station to get off at. We passed Kirov Station, and I must have come to for a moment and realized that we had missed our stop. We got off at Nogin Square and went through the underground passage to take the train back in the other direction. That passageway at Nogin Square remains in my memory as purely metaphorical, as a passage from one world to another: an angel child leading her father to the Other Side. As it happened, a greater than usual number of children were walking hand-in-hand with adults through that passage. It's interesting that each such "passage" (always metaphorized in its own way) was a passage to higher energy domains: I was passing ever upwards from one stratum to the next in the mental atmosphere of collective consciousness.

23. We left the metro at Turgenev Station. The air was permeated with luminous, glittering snow. As we came to the door in the Vkhutemas courtyard, we ran into Grandma (Vera's mother) on her way to the store. She gave me the keys to the apartment and took Masha with her. The elevator was out of order, so I started up the steps for the eighth floor with the heavy boards and bag. I remember stomping up the stairs with great relish, my feet thundering like an elephant's. I took the stairs easily in spite of the long climb and the weight I was carrying. I was also filled with a sense of mystical pleasure from this new "ascent"; that is to say, the climb was as metaphorized as my "passage" had been. At last alone, I felt extraordinarily powerful – a power to match my elephant stomp, though it might have been the other way round, and I was actually stomping from an excess of power, a kind of animal force. Gradually, as I climbed, the sound of my stomping took on a magical significance: I was either heralding my arrival to unseen forces or else scaring them away. Whatever it was, when I entered the dark apartment, which had several other occupants, I didn't try to make any less noise. On the contrary, I proceeded down the hallway with the terrible, sensuous clamor of the Archangel Gabriel come in power – and here I clearly meant to scare off unseen hostile forces in the wary, dimly lit communal hallway. But my monstrous din failed to rouse anyone, and I managed, without causing a scandal, to enter the room where Pyotr Michurin and Velimir Khlebnikov's sister Vera had once lived. I sat down on the couch opposite the window and began leafing through books on art.

Here too, the room, the view from the window and especially the all-pervading light, the books I was looking at – everything was different, tinged with the physical presence of eternity, ideality and grandeur. It was as if I had come into a lofty hermitage, climbed to a spiritual height from which everything shone in the light of divinity, purity and peace. At the same time, I felt alone – out of place, as it were. This "place out of place" that I found myself in seemed somewhere not far from those exalted places where our reality is designed and modeled, where the Forms reside, transform and arise, before passing through worlds to be embodied in the multitude of familiar everyday objects.

At this elevation, the existence of a Supreme Deity, a Creator, simply ceased to be a problem in the sheer certainty of his grace-filled presence, manifesting as peace and light. The least motion of mind in the direction of anything not here – whether God himself or something from the realm of everyday concerns – was submerged and dissolved in the rapturous fullness of being. This world of yet-to-be-embodied ideas, with its pervading atmosphere of the sufficiency of being "here and now," was somewhere close beside me. That world cast its reflection upon me, and yet I was on the outside. It was as if I – my consciousness – was the first stage of its embodiment, at one remove from that lofty world. Separated from it, I felt alone, but I was given to feel its presence, its reality. My consciousness was like a lens for One who is above and simultaneously within me, and that lens revealed – always with an only-just-created freshness – a child's dusty blue rubber ball lying on a carpet, a butterfly collection in a glass case under a piece of green velvet, peacock feathers in a vase, children's drawings many years old, potted houseplants, the walls, windows and roofs of old buildings in the neighborhood, the tiny figures of people below, high-rises in the distance, new buildings going up and on and on. Here, above the world, it seems, one can sit on a couch and be content with endless viewing, dispassionate observation, as if the world were no more than a quaint collection of polished tropical shells in a cardboard shoebox.

24. But then Masha and her grandmother came back, and I went home. Going down into the "world," I lost all sense of propriety and let my actions be guided entirely by my inner vision. After all those experiences "on high," I thought of angelic reality as a provisional, coordinating, intermediate reality between the programming reality of the Supreme Eidos and the conventional reality of physically manifested ideas conceived in the Eidos.
Before my first active "coordinating" act on Riga Square, I experienced several interesting perceptual distortions, only one of which, unfortunately, I can remember. Coming up on the escalator at Riga Station, about halfway to the top, I was again overcome by the feeling that I wasn't rising to the Earth's surface but to new "heavens." At first I closed my eyes and let myself bask in the feeling. But the impression grew so palpable in its certainty that even with eyes open I didn't lose the persistent – both inward and outward – metaphorical reality of "ascension." There were no visual hallucinations, no winged beings hovering about me, but the hallucinatory authenticity of the surrounding spiritual reality was compelling. As I rose on the escalator, I was simultaneously "rising" to a new energy level within my-

self. There was nothing in my consciousness then exterior to that impression, no place free of the illusion from which I could see it as illusion, and so the existential certainty of my "ascension" was absolute. This certainty gave me a strange double vision that split each event into two taking place in the same instant. Toward the top of the escalator, I again closed my eyes and suddenly had the feeling that either my legs or the escalator's steps were sinking below the level where I imagined the upper landing to be – the floor of the station's upper vestibule. I was fully convinced that if I didn't jump now or at least open my eyes, my legs would be cut off at the knees by the teeth into which the moving steps receded. I decided, however, to confront this fear and so, with eyes closed and legs held firmly together, I rode onto the marble floor like a boat onto a gently sloping shore. The sense of relief after all of this was incredible – so sure had I been that my legs were about to be cut off.

25. I emerged from the metro into a reality a little higher and brighter than the reality of the trip I had just taken underground. After my "escalator ascension," it was as if a filter in my head had been changed, making the glistening snow seem even brighter, space grander, and the inner essences of the passing people that inhabited this new reality more elevated and highly charged. The "all-seeing eye" or "third eye" scanned them for me only from angles that created a picture of the next "heavenly" level, so that the whole ensemble of new impressions and unfamiliar feelings that they stirred in me proceeded on an ascending scale of newness.
Leaving the metro, I set off for the bus stop, past the giant March snow piles and chunks of dirty, black ice that littered the ground. But since from above, in the air, it was very bright – light, silvery snow was still coming down – the snow piles and chunks of ice didn't obstruct the vista, and in everything there was still the festive spaciousness of a wider and more exalted world.
[...]

Fragment from the novel *Kashira Highway* (*Kashirskoe Shosse*), Moscow, 1983-1986 Translated by Carlton Copeland

TRIPS OUT OF TOWN, 1985
COLLECTIVE ACTIONS

33. The Russian World
Moscow region, Savyolovskaya railway line,
field near village Kyevy Gorki
17th of March, 1985
A. Monastyrski, S. Romashko, E. Elagina,
G. Kizewalter, I. Makarevich, MK
Viewers: I. Kabakov, V. Sorokin, I. Nakhova,
J. Backstein, N. Abalakova, A. Zhigalov,
E. Zhigalova, M. Chuikova, S. Anufriev,
E. Gorokhovsky, Nina, V. Naumets, V. Zakharov,
D. Prigov, A. Prigov, Yu. Leiderman,
S. Haensgen, I. and S. Kopystyansky, N. Alexeev

A group of viewers was met on a highway by S. Romashko, who offered the guests to proceed to the field along the path trod in deep snow. It is important to notice that S. Romashko followed the group in the rear. When the viewers approached the center of the designated field and stopped by the purple cloth with white canopy (in its center there was a tape recorder switched to play back), Romashko turned on the right, away front the trail, and began walking along the line of the forest towards the plywood rabbit standing on the forest's verge 70 meters away from the audience's position. The rabbit's contour (3 meters high) was established facing the field, its side facing the audience: from viewers' position it looked like a pole or a shield protruding from the snow.

While Romashko was trudging through deep snow towards the hare figure, escaping the audience's attention (as he was moving along the forest's line and avoiding the audience's line of sight), the viewers were listening to a record consisting of noise produced in the course of assembling and installing the hare figure (recorded two hours prior to the action). Besides that, in the course of Romashko's moving the viewers could observe Monastyrski's motionless figure, standing 70 meters away front the purple cloth, opposite to it and facing the audience. While standing in position opposite to the cloth and divided from the audience by snowy wild land (Monastyrski took his position before the audience's arrival by avoiding line, so there was no visible trace of his footprints on the snow), A. Monastyrski was evenly reeling white thread on the "Soft

handle" – a prefabricated object made of a thick cardboard circle with an outstretched handle; on one of its sides an image of a dialplate with hands was glued, while the other was formed by a red circle with silver five-bladed star in the center: on the disk's handle there were 200 meters of white thread spooled beforehand, so in the course of the action the thread was spooled front another reel over existing layer of thread. However the distance between AM and the viewers prevented the latter front seeing neither the "Soft handle" nor the process of spooling itself: the spooling was perceived as vaguely visible rocking motion of a formless object in AM's hands.

Some 6 or 7 minutes past the start of the movement S. Romashko reached his position and began gently rapping with his feet on lower part of the plywood hare, as if shaking snow off his boots. Gradually he applied more and more effort, so that the knocking sound arrested the audience's attention. For 3 or 4 minutes S. Romashko was increasing the power of kicking on the hare – first with the toes of his shoes, then with whole soles, and finally he kicked at full power, knocking the hare over. After smashing the hare, Romashko dragged it beyond the forest's verge and disappeared from sight.

As soon as Romashko disappeared in the forest with the hare, Monastyrski turned the "Soft handle" with the red circle facing the audience (its reverse side with hour-plate was indistinguishable against the background of Monastyrski's overcoat). Having finished reeling the rest of the thread – it took him 1-2 minutes – Monastyrski started moving towards the audience through the snowy plain. The snow was deep, and it took him no less than 7 minutes to reach the viewers' position. On approaching the purple cloth, Monastyrski removed the tape recorder from it and put the "Soft handle" red side up. Then he opened the white canopy, discovering under it nine white objects decorated with golden foil and wing-shaped golden furnishing. These objects were: 1. a glove 2. an enema 3. a walking-stick 4. a doll's head 5. a clothes brush 6. a rolling-pin 7. a toy ladder 8. a black bag with cardboard dripping pan inside 9. a folder titled "The Book of Nothingness" (see photo and article by AM "TZI TZI"). These objects were then put inside cardboard boxes with labels saying "CA The Golden Asp (then the object's name in brackets)" and given to those viewers who had pieces of cardboard (given to them beforehand) with appropriate objects' names. I. Kabakov received an individual tenth box labeled "CA The Golden Asp (the flask)" and was asked not to take out the flask (the box with the flask inside was buried in snow until given to IK).

After the distribution of objects the tape recorder with taped construction of the hare was switched off, and the viewers were prompted to make their way back to the highway.

After leaving the forest, the viewers found themselves on a snowy plain where a white hare, 3 meters high, stood facing them. He had a golden line across his belly, imitating the outline of his head. Under the line there was a label identical to those on cardboard boxes: "CA The Golden Asp (the golden asp)."

Having photographed with the objects near the rabbit, the latter was knocked down to the snow, and the viewers were prompted to put the boxes on him. Then Romashko and Monastyrski dragged the hare with boxes on it to the field some 10-15 meters away from the audience. AM took the flask out of the box (the flask was painted white and filled with black gasoline) and broke it with a stick; black gasoline poured over white objects and boxes. Then Romashko threw a lit match, gasoline ignited, boxes and objects burst into flames. At this moment a tape recorder was switched on (one of the action's organizers carried it on him), set to play back a recording of various railway announcements, such as "Train so-and-so arrives at platform number so-and-so at designated time" (the recording was made at Kursky railway terminal). When the objects on the hare stopped burning, AM and SR began throwing snow over them and soon buried the whole hare.

After shouldering a backpack with a tape recorder inside (the recorder was set to playing back pre-recorded by AM descriptional texts about "KD" in that particular case the action "Music inside and outside"), Panitkov headed towards the hangars on the opposite side of the field. Before proceeding to another section of his route he tossed the apple, approached it, picked up, then tossed again and again, thus approaching the location in front of the hangars where he was supposed to stop (anywhere according to his own will, but as closer to the hangars as possible). After reaching the selected point he replaced the tape in his recorder for a clear one and after setting the recorder to recording mode began looking through the notebook, at the same commenting its content to the recorder's microphone. The notebook consisted of a cover page on which Panitkov was to mark the title of the action described on the tape at the moment when he approached the location – it turned to be the description of the "The Gunshot" action. The cover page was followed by several photocopied A2 sheets from Lokeli Chandra's book *Esoteric iconography of Japanese mandalas* (India, 1971). On the last page there was a factographic form lobe tilled in with the action's timeline at different stages and signed by the participants.

Prior to looking through the notebook Panitkov was supposed to take the plastic apple to 3 pieces (as it was made of sections) and to scatter them, but in the course of action he did so after looking through the notebook.

After replacing again the tape with descriptional texts and switching the recorder to playback mode, he put the recorder into backpack, shouldered the backpack, took the notebook and returned to his initial position by the video camera. There the notebook was signed by all three participants, fastened at the right side with clamps (so that it couldn't be opened without unfastening the clamps) and handed over to Panitkov.

66. The Opening (to N. Panitkov)
Kiovogorskoe Field
7.3.1993
A. Monastyrski, S. Haensgen
After reaching a place "where no hangars can be seen" in a field (see "Means of a sequence" action). AM and SH handed over to Panitkov a black notebook and a big plastic apple.

73. On the Hill
17th March, 1990
Yaroslavskaya railway line, station Kalistovo
N. Panitkov, S. Haensgen, A. Monastyrski
Participating viewers: J. Bakstein, D. Ross, B. Boedanova, S. Blumberg
After climbing a high snowy hill steeply breaking to river Vorja with the rest of the ac-

tion's company, N. Panitkov installed around a tree a cardboard cylinder pasted with pictures from a north-Korean comic series, using rubber straps. At the same time S. Haensgen arranged on the snow (in storyline order) cardboard cards with similar images (70 pieces approx.). Then Panitkov cut the cylinder horizontally in the middle so that its upper part was lifted by rubber straps while the lower part fell down. Alter that the rest of the action's participants began dropping from the steep the cardboard cards set on snow by S. Haensgen.

Then Panitkov was prompted to go down the steep, collect all the accessible cards and set them in snow on the river's bank in storyline order, and he followed the instructions. In the course of the whole action Panitkov was equipped with a backpack that held a tape recorder set to playback. Its soundtrack consisted of descriptions of other KD actions. Panitkov also used another device to record his descriptions of found cards.

There were also two elements unexpected by the action's authors themselves. Both S. Haensgen and A. Monastyrski were surprised by the fact that the cardboard cylinder had been pasted with comic pictures by Panitkov, while Panitkov was unaware of the tape recorder in his backpack and the necessity to arrange the pictures found under the steep on riverbank. These elements of the action were not concerned during the preliminary discussion.

DMITRY PRIGOV, 1995

When Moscow was still a she-wolf
She ran through the forest beyond Moscow
It was only later she settled down
And became a first-class capital
Bringing forth children –
A large tribe of white-toothed Muscovites
Who alone were allowed to see
From a barely visible point in the heavens
The sudden flame fitfully bursting through
Growing, growing, swirling, dying
And taking everyone to its place in the sky
Moscow stands -- but there are no Muscovites

translated by Mark Coupar

Here is the Moscow that my life has known
Here's Leninskii prospekt, the Mausoleum
The Kremlin, Vnukovo, the Bolshoi and the Malyi
And at his post stands a Policeman
Here in the spring the parks and gardens bloom
Acacias, cherries, apples, lilac trees
Tulips, roses, hollyhocks, dahlias
Grass, field, meadows, forest and mountains
Above here is the sky and below is the earth
In the distance there are
Chinamen, Negroes, Yanks
Close by my heart is all the world, deprived of
                                        its rights
Around me all of Moscow grows and breathes
Growing out to Poland, out to Warsaw
To Prague, Paris and New York
And all around, to view it dispassionately
Everywhere is Moscow, everywhere are its peoples
Where there is no Moscow, there is simply a void

translated by Mark Coupar

It's better not to live in Moscow
Enough to know that it exists
Surrounded by its lofty walls
And by dreams remote and tall
And perspectives on the world around
Which soaring up affirm Its presence and confirm
Its presence and can form
Its presence in the waiting heart
And this is what it means to live in Moscow

translated by Robert Reid

Dmitry Prigov, *From Moscow and Muscovites*, from *Texts of Our Life*, Keele University, 1995, pp. 55-59

CREATION OF A TIME UNIT FOR THE DEAD ZONE, 2012
OBAMAINBERLIN

The "Dead Zone," since 2011, has been a territory on the German-Polish border between Frankfurt / Oder and Guben, where the art group OBAMAINBERLIN develop their own form of artistic practice. Their first exhibition at Kunstverein Rosenheim, the one founding their collaboration, was characterized by dialogical sculptures and installations, initiated by Nitschke taking hold of Zakharov's body of work. The Dead Zone results from a countermovement by Zakharov noting that, in Nitschke's work, he is interested above all in the decision to live in a region by the border that seems culturally emptied. The objective now is to further increase the seemingly unpromising surrender to this region, which is characterized by socialist industrial farming and by a settlement structure ruptured ever since the re-drawing of the border in 1945, and thus to also bring about a fundamental aspect of collaboration.

The Dead Zone, at the beginning of the project, was perceived first of all as a border area between Germany and Poland, between the West and the East, as a still perceptible transition between two hemispheres of some fundamentally different mentality and life. This transition exists as an emptiness, which brings about a questioning of where one spatially as well as culturally dwells.

The border area of the Dead Zone extends along the Or and Neiße rivers. The scenery characterized by those rivers is peaceful, static and sometimes enchantingly pleasant, in contrast to the agriculture that cleared the country with its giant fields.

The space where OBAMAINBERLIN go for their first excursion lacks any form of limitation and orientation, even if it extends along a border. The movement and artistic practice, not yet defined, at first had no restrictions in the Dead Zone that would allow localization and creating a reference for the activity within the space for self-questioning, in whatever way this activity would be formed. The first excursions in 2011 led to the establishment of a center, a unit of measure, a border and a map, that is, a model of the Zone.

This model shall be put into practice by the installation *Creation of a time unit* as a working hypothesis, delineation and systematic alternative to the framework "contemporary art," as a construction or mechanism in independent movement.

The first excursion on October the 30th, 2011 headed into the region without being limited in any way. The space visited was a still palpable vacuum between the West and East, which shows, for example, in the fact that the former German villages on the Polish side have barely been renovated. For decades the Polish, who were resettled here, originating from the border region with Russia, thought that these territories would eventually be restituted, and thus – not only because of their poverty – hardly altered their houses.

One task of the first excursion is to find a figure, a mask (of a scientist, a fool, a bureaucrat…), in order to bestow, under their framing ability, a point of view on the emptiness. The trip leads up to the square in front of the ruins of the Baroque castle in Zary (formerly Sorau). On the way, just before the entrance to the village Grodziszcze, Zakharov, in conversation, conceives a core motif of artistic practice in the "Dead Zone": its remoteness must be shown from the perspective of tender affection. In Zary in front of the empty windows of the castle facade Nitschke presents a gift to Zakharov, consisting of a lion mask and three angular boards torn out of card boxes with a part painted in black and white. When presenting the gift, from behind the lion mask, Nitschke describes the model of coexistence of artists outlined in the volume *Support* by Jan Verwoert. Here Verwoert draws on the image of St. Jerome and the Lion, who actually threaten each other's existences, but due to an unexpected reversal of their given relationship find a surprising form of peaceful coexistence. The present giving is interrupted by a young woman, who exhaustively inquires about the background of the mask, thus unknowingly becoming the addressee of the offering.

On November 6th, 2011 another excursion follows, where OBAMAINBERLIN are accompanied by a guest from Moscow. In mutual ignorance of the other having prepared an activity in the "Dead Zone," the first place headed for by Nitschke, who knows the area, is the remains of a bridge across the Oder river on the Polish side level with Fürstenberg. The bridge is unsecured and ends above the water at the edge of the last standing pillar. Here Nitschke stages a picnic with furniture brought along, goldenly aflame in the still warm evening sun of autumn. Accompanying the food, he describes a painting, the Embarkation for Cythera by Antoine Watteau, showing a group of young couples waiting for passage to the island of Cythera or having just returned. On the island they had been promised love without pain. The description is portrayed on a wooden box in the dimensions of the painting, on which the canvas is represented by a rectangle of plum jam. The description is spoken by Nitschke throught a vampire mask with extended canines and fake blood.

Subsequently, Zakharov measures the remains of the bridge with an old compass. It is adjusted according to a measurement so that the length can be measured in a unit developed specifically for the "Dead Zone." This unit is twice the body length of the director Orson Welles: 3.74 m. The illustration, with which Zakharov certifies the measurement, shows Orson Welles' portrait in a familiar picture, with a doubled hat.

From the two images or figures drawn from their own sanctioned cultural spheres, a real measurement is adopted and brought into the emptiness of the zone. The intersection of the imaginary axes of the body accurately transferred from the painting, whose subject is love, and of the measurement conducted by Zakharov, emanating from the body of a film director, constitute a zero, to which the next steps in the Dead Zone are related.

During subsequent research Zakharov encounters the so-called Antikythera mechanism, an ancient apparatus for the predictive calculation of solar and lunar altitudes and eclipses. This mechanism was retrieved in 1900 near the island of Antikythera, together with a comprehensive treasure trove of sculptures, from a ship wrecked there around 70 - 60 BC. A diagram of the mechanism, which is mainly composed of 13 cogs of varying size, is projected by Zakharov onto a map of the region, the center of the largest cog ending lying on the end of the bridge and the centers of the outer cogs on the town centers of Guben and Frankfurt / Oder. From the expansion of the diagram in relation to the map results a territory that now is limited by the figure of the diagram and then again is structured by the centers and peripheries of the interlocking spheres of the cogs. During following excursions the individual spheres – as a result of these actions performed there – are associated with particular themes and motifs. By reflecting on the relations between various places / spheres / actions that have come into being, the map becomes a machine, which in turn generates further possibilities of action.

CREATION OF A TIME UNIT FOR THE DEAD ZONE

Out of the art of setting a center and defining the area of the Dead Zone, a provisional hypothesis for a new project emerges: the first defining actions are based on some form of translation, where materials, symbolically as well as literally, are brought into the Dead Zone and are displayed there in a certain way. The allusions to Watteau's masterpiece or to the director Orson Welles themselves do not create an interpretation or a connection between the location and the introduced figures, but this relation becomes the motivation and background for an activity that flows into the emptiness and the openness of the Zone.

The absurdity of such an effort is confronted by structural thinking, a mental mechanism acting as the necessary counterbalance. The openness of the absurd can basically only result in perspective. Within one single action, an action that includes excursions as well, there is in each case a maze of relations which is defined in itself but which however does not exactly provide a sensible conclusion obtained through understanding.

The logic of the development of a unit being generated by Vadim Zakharov to concretize an experience of space and dimension that was shifted in the Dead Zone can be visualized in a series of reflections: the Zone derives from a double author; it is marked by a double hat. This author has no face: neither that of Vadim Zakharov, nor that of Niklas Nitschke. Thereby an iconic portrait that does not reflect certain authors or a cross-section view, but a third person, is put into the scene. All this is followed by the search for and selection of a familiar portrait of the director Orson Welles. His body

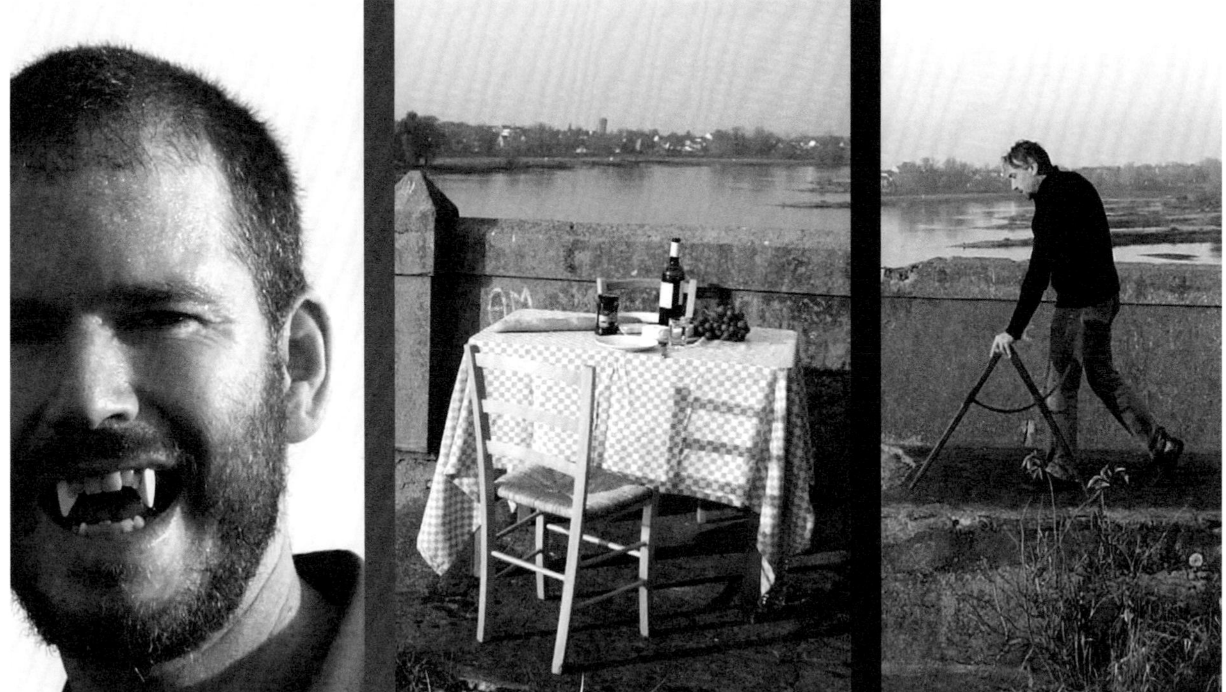

size, which also gets doubled, serves as the basis to derive the measuring system. For actualization and a realization the measurement has to be applied to any distance in the Dead Zone with a circle; the choice of the distance is derived from the dynamics of an excursion and a self-adjusting brush with the area.

The literalness of the measuring unit (which totals 3.74 m) is shown, and pictures documenting the action are put on display, a contraction of these events within the action that show they were indeed carried out on site. The painting by Wattenau, presented by Niklas Nitschke, is shown within the Zone, on the bridge, by means of a box which reproduces the dimensions and body of the painting. In both cases, the accuracy of the measurement is an indicator showing that nothing corresponds to the concreteness of this data in the Zone. The product is an experience of resolution which allows one to experience the Zone in a mode of an absolute dedication right where it is.

The creation of a measuring unit and defining of the space which marks the area of the artistic practice of OBAMAINBERLIN in the Dead Zone is followed by a project to create a specific time unit for the Zone.

They start by considering how the worldwide agreed time measurement, UTC (Coordinated Universal Time), which accompanies and integrates everyone, for example, through a Smartphone, can be excluded in the Dead Zone. An idea floats around to bury a clock someplace in the Zone in order to take the existing interval into consideration on one hand but to abandon it as an "object" and measuring unit of the Zone at the same time. They decide on using a cuckoo clock. Its clear cultural symbolic character accompanies the fact that, at least at times, its sound assimilates into the sound matrix of the area which includes the sound of the birds in the spring, the call of the cuckoos living here. The beating of the clock, in comparison to other types of clocks, has the characteristic of a call which acts as a challenge to the imagining of a clock. Its sounds come quietly from under the ground.

A personal time measurement (or concept) within the Zone is conceived based on a differentiation of several shifted times or clocks which are buried in the centers of the thirteen circles that constitute the map of the Zone and shall keep functioning there for the lifetime of their batteries. This allows us to expect that the structure of the Dead Zone, the scheme of the mechanism as a mental framework, on the one hand is anchored by the idea of the buried cuckoo clocks and their own activity in the real territory between Frankfurt / Oder and Guben, and on the other hand, is set into motion.

The idea of the temporally shifted striking of thirteen cuckoo clocks creates non-verifiable

Center (Bridge of Happiness and Death), 2011

Measurement and Map for the Dead Zone, 2011-2012

(the clocks distributed throughout the Zone cannot be observed) but still defined distances which correspond to spatial distances.

Through the act of the burial, the Dead Zone turns into plastic. The unity of the Zone on the official map is broken by the arrangement of the circles. The arrangement is vitalized by the constantly shifting rhythm of the clocks. This rhythm is reflected as a unity only in the imagination, it cannot be observed in reality.

The installation in the context of the exhibition *The Way of Enthusiasts* in the Casa dei Tre Oci in Venice introduces the project of the cuckoo clocks buried in the Dead Zone and initializes the plan of an autonomous time experience.

The installation presents thirteen different cuckoo clocks upon a row of black earth circles. The different diameters of the circles are prescribed by the arrangement of the Antikythera mechanism. The majority part of the clocks is shown in the central corridor of the Casa on the ground floor, all being placed in a row; three other clocks are exposed in other places within the building: in the stairwell, in a corridor, in the toilet. One of the clocks is lowered into the ground in the yard of the Casa as a representation of the planned burial of the clocks in the Dead Zone, along with a camera that transmits its picture to a monitor positioned next to the row of the clocks in the corridor.

On the day before the exhibit opening, at 2:00 pm, the cuckoo clocks at OBAMAINBERLIN will be put into use for the first time. The first clock tolls simultaneously with the tower bells of the churches in the surrounding area, all further clocks will be set in motion successively but as quickly as possible and they will also be set to two o'clock. The delay results from putting in the batteries, from setting the clock hand to the desired time, from awaiting the strike of the cuckoo. Proceeding this way down to the thirteenth clock, the delays will amount to 14 minutes and 59 seconds. This duration will be recorded as the time measuring unit for the Dead Zone.

At the exhibition in Venice, the successively striking clocks will generate a time slot where the same time will be proclaimed again and again. The simultaneously real and imaginary space of the Dead Zone will correspond to the rhythm of the changing temporal distances between the striking of the cuckoo clocks.

TOPOLOGIES OF TELEPRESENCE, 1930-2004

Walter Benjamin, extract from *Berlin childhood around 1900*, 1930s

At that time, the telephone still hung – an outcast settled carelessly be-tween the dirty-linen hamper and the gasometer – in a corner of the back hallway, where its ringing served to multiply the terrors of the Berlin house-hold. When, having mastered my senses with great effort, I arrived to quell the uproar after prolonged fumbling through the gloomy corridor, I tore off the two receivers, which were heavy as dumbbells, thrust my head between them, and was inexorably delivered over to the voice that now sounded. There was nothing to allay the violence with which it pierced me. Power-less, I suffered, seeing that it obliterated my consciousness of time, my firm resolve, my sense of duty. And just as the medium obeys the voice that takes possession of him from beyond the grave, I submitted to the first proposal that came my way through the telephone.

Jean Baudrillard, extract from *Ecstasy of Communication*, 1987

Private "telematics": each person sees himself at the controls of a hypothetical machine, isolated in a position of perfect and remote sovereignty, at an infinite distance from his universe of origin. Which is to say, in the exact position of an astronaut in his capsule, in a state of weightlessness that necessitates a perpetual orbital flight and a speed sufficient to keep him from crashing back to his planet of origin. This realization of a living satellite, in vivo in a quotidian space, corresponds to the satellitization of the real, or what I call the "hyperrealism of simulation": the elevation of the domestic universe to a spatial power, to a spatial metaphor, with the satellitization of the two-room-kitchen-and-bath put into orbit in the last lunar module. The very quotidian nature of the terrestrial habitat hypostasized in space means the end of metaphysics. The era of hyperreality now begins. What I mean is this: what was projected psychologically and mentally, what used to be lived out on earth as metaphor, as mental or metaphori-cal scene, is henceforth projected into reality, without any metaphor at all, into an absolute space which is also that of simulation.

Jean Baudrillard, extract from *Xerox and Infinity*, 1987

We lived once in a world where the realm of the imaginary was governed by the mirror, by dividing one into two, by theatre, by otherness and alienation. Today that realm is the realm of the screen, of interfaces and duplication, of contiguity and networks. All our machines are screens, and the interactivity of humans has been replaced by the interactivity of screens. Nothing inscribed on these screens is ever intended to be deciphered in any depth: rather, it is supposed to be explored instantaneously, in an abreaction immediate to meaning, a short-circuiting of the poles of representation.

Reading a screenful of information is quite a different thing from looking. It is a digital form of exploration in which the eye moves along an endless broken line. The relationship to the interlocutor in communication, like the relationship to knowledge in data-handling, is similar: tactile and exploratory. A computer-generated voice, even a voice over the telephone, is a tactile voice, neutral and functional. It is no longer in fact exactly a voice, any more than looking at a screen is exactly looking. The whole paradigm of the sensory has changed. The tactility here is not the organic sense of touch: it implies merely an epidermal contiguity of eye and image, the collapse of the aesthetic distance involved in looking. We draw ever closer to the surface of the screen; our gaze is, as it were, strewn across the image. We no longer have the spectator's distance from the stage – all theatrical conventions are gone. That we fall so easily into the screen's coma of the imagination is due to the fact that the screen presents a perpetual void that we are invited to fill.

Paul Virilio, extract from *A Landscape of Events*, 1991

If, a *contrario*, the two interlocutors communicate with each other through (real-time) interactive technologies, it is the absolute speed of radiation that will facilitate their *tête-a-tête*, their face-to-face encounter, and this happens no matter what intervals of space and time effectively separate them.

Here, the event *does not take place*, or, more precisely, *it takes place twice*, the topical aspect yielding to the teletopical aspect, the unity of time and place being split between the emission and reception of signals, here and there *at the same time*, thanks to the power of electromagnetic interactivity.

The problem of the *televisual horizon* of the ephemeral encounter, however, remains unresolved: indeed, if the transappearance of the appearance of co-present interlocutors is comparable, if not analogous, to that of the pedestrians or motorists evoked above, the *terminus* of their mutual perception differs. The horizon of the pedestrians who run into each other is the *end of the street*; the horizon of the motorists who pass each other going slowly is the *perspective of the avenue* - the vanishing point of the urban horizon demarcating the area of their effective encounter.

Friedrich A. Kittler and Matthew Griffin, extract from *The City is a Medium*, 1996

And this is reason enough to bring together the workings of the city with concepts from general information science. Reason enough, moreover, to decipher past media and the historical function of what we refer to as "man," as the play between commands, addresses, and data. ADDRESSES are data which allow other data to appear. In order to connect a computer's memory to the data bus, the address bus first must address a single unit of memory, and secondly the command bus must address the entire memory. Media are only as good and as fast as their distributors. When books were still antique endless rolls, you couldn't very well flip to a page or double-check a reference. Even in a handwritten medieval codex, the page numbers were not of much help, since varying copyists had, each to a different degree, distributed the text widely or narrowly with each individual copy. Gutenberg's printing press first made it possible that "this page here resembles thousands of others," meaning it can be found, using the table of contents or index, in every printed edition. Cities are no different. It was the police prefects of absolutism (such as La Reynie in Paris) who saw to it that the hand painted guild signs on the older houses conformed to the same standard and ultimately made them independent from the location of the house number. From the national postal service to the public telephone to the license plate on every registered vehicle, media are at work replacing people with their addresses. Stephan Daedalus, James Joyce's fictitious other, signed the front page of his geography book (of all books!):

Stephan Dedalus
Class of Elements
Clongowes Wood College
Sallins
County Kildare
Ireland Europe
The World
The Universe.

A bit more prosaic, but no less specific, are personal ads which include a telephone number and/or a regional specification based on the license plate. Whether or not someone picks up the telephone receiver is of secondary interest. There is a good reason for that, too. It sufficed, legally, in the nineteenth century when the registered letter from the authorities landed in the mailbox, even when it could be proven that the addressee was never at the given address. "The nymphs are departed... have left no addresses," wrote Eliot, granted about nymphs and their playmates? but even river deities themselves are addresses...

Because in the final analysis "to command" simply means "to address." This is true for the lowest level of digital computation devices, in the so called microcode, where the patent wars are the most vicious; and it also applies, as Althusser's analysis illustrates, to the lowest level of everyday city life: a citizen is anyone whom the cry? "Hey, you there!" of a police officer on the street causes to stop and turn around.

Jean Baudrillard, extract from *The City and Emptiness*, lecture at Moscow State University, 1997

When model cities are built, model functions are created, model artificial ensembles, and everything else changes, as it were, into leftovers, into dross, into useless inheritances of the past. When you build a freeway, a supermarket, a supercity, you automatically change everything that surrounds it into wasteland. In creating an autonomous network of high-speed, programmed traffic, you are at the same time changing the usual, traditional space of human interaction into a desert zone. This is precisely what happens with transport arteries alongside which abandoned territories form. This is precisely what will happen in the future as informational wastelands form alongside informational arteries, as a sort of informational fourth world arises – a sanctuary for all the castoffs, for all those who have renounced the means of mass information. An intellectual wasteland will be added to it, peopled by brains that have remained without work due to the maximal complexity of the informational networks themselves. They will people it in an immeasurable multitude, the descendents of those millions of unemployed who today have been exiled from the world of labor. Spaces, like people, will become out of work. Whole neighborhoods are being built of residential buildings and offices, but they are destined to remain forever empty due to economic crisis or speculation. They are leftover scrap, only leftover scrap and will always remain such; they are not traces of the past, not ruins constituting revered monuments of antiquity. These homes are monuments to the soulless entrepreneurial activity of man. Then one wants to ask how it is possible for civilization – which from the very beginning has produced itself, and calculatedly so, in the form of dross, has labored on its own useless construction, creating cities and metropolises that resemble enormous idle machines endlessly repeating themselves – to hate and despise itself; these phantoms are the result of investments of capital that have been brought to absurd sizes, just as have their ever-growing insufficiencies.

Peter Sloterdijk, extract from *Spheres*, 2004, vol. III, ch. 2

In distinction to previous unidirectional media (radio, television, newspapers, books), the telephone possesses a double ontological privilege: not only does it (mostly) transmit a call from real life, it also brings the person who was called, insofar as he also takes up the line in an (actually lived) simultaneity with the caller, to the same level of existence as the person who made the call from afar. Due to this effect of immediacy, it was appropriate to describe the telephone as a "bio-phone" – as nothing less than life can call. Someone on the line is always a far-away life that is made present, a voice with a message, perhaps even an invitation.

From daily newspaper *Voroshilovgradskaya Pravda*, 1992, January 9

September 23, 1989. Protvino scientific city near Moscow
A flying saucer appeared over the city at around 9 pm, when the resident L. went home.
On the crossroads from a road leading to a residential building that was under construction, two tall women (around two meters) in buddy-hugging silver costumes came toward her from around a pair of large boulders.
L. thought that they looked about 30 years old, with their light hair wound up in bunches, and on the top of their heads was a small cap with two small antennas. There was no fear, panic, or sense of bewilderment. L. confesses that she had the feeling that she had come across two old acquaintances. Suddenly, in a high-pitched voice, moving her lips, in normal Russian, albeit with what appeared to L. to be some difficulty, one of the women asked her to come along with them. L. went along with them quietly on the road for 80 to 100 meters, until she saw a small flying saucer on the roadside across from a transformer booth. There were no doors. The wall split open suddenly, and the women went in without stooping. The saucer was two meters in radius and about two and a half meters in height. The completely metal base was about a meter in height, with an illumination device with a diameter of 70 or 80 meters in the center and a transparent hood of unknown material. A control panel covered the entire perimeter of the saucer. Three seats were equally spaced from each other. L. saw a person sitting with his back to her in one of them. She concluded from his wide shoulders that he was a man. He did not speak or turn around during the entire experience.
"We're flying off," said one of the saucer's crew. L. was flustered and said in bewilderment that she had a lot to do today; she had to check her son's homework, make dinner...
"Look, I bought bread," she said, and – after a period of mutual silence – "would you like some?"

"We don't eat bread," they responded very kindly, in the same high-pitched voice. "You can try ours."
The woman handed L. a small piece of some something hard, which, after pondering for a moment, she swallowed. Its taste reminded her of white bread, but somewhat sweet.
"Good, now let's fly a little," said one of the women.
The saucer took off silently. In the illuminator, L. glimpsed Protvino quickly spinning and becoming smaller. They flew for ten minutes. L. stood for the entire time, holding firmly on to the back of one of the chairs. However, the flight was smooth and peaceful. Finally, the woman asked to be returned to the ground.
"Where do you live?," they asked her. "In one of the panel buildings on the edge of Protvino." "On what floor?" "The 14th." "Fine, we'll let you off on the balcony." L. had the presence of mind to refuse, saying, "what will my father and children say?" The saucer landed near a paid parking lot. "We'll meet again," they told L. "Alright, the next time that I have a little more time, we'll fly a little more," answered the brave woman, who exited the saucer and, not looking back, went home. You had no desire to look back at all.

Contributed by Stanislav Shuripa

PICARESQUES AND CYBERNETICS.
THE NEW BALANCE, 1982
MICHEL SERRES

The parasite is invited to the *table d'hôte*; in return, he must regale the other diners with his stories and his mirth. To be exact, he exchanges good talk for good food; he buys his dinner, paying for it in words. It is the oldest profession in the world. Traces of it are found in the oldest documents. There are a thousand known variations on this law of justice-rarely simple and often complicated-practiced in social, friendly, tribal, and familial everyday life, just like in the oldest comedy or the most recondite story. For example, the sponger pays in morals and the host gives, filled with guilt by this great yet imaginary duty. The moral is one discourse among many, some sort of specie that is legal tender. Each society allows a linguistic specie that can be exchanged advantageously for food. Influential and powerful groups are able to diffuse a forced lexicon in that way. Today it is economic, just as it was humanist not long ago, Voltairean before that, and religious a long time ago.

A vagrant, dying of hunger, found himself one evening at the kitchen window of a well-known restaurant. The aromas were delicious. He filled himself on them and that calmed his hunger pangs a bit. One of the scullions discovered the trick and, quickly coming outside, demanded money for what could be called the service rendered. The passer-by and the scullion were about to fight over their disagreement when a third person came by who offered to settle the matter. Give me a coin, he said. The wretch did so, frowning. He put the coin down on the sidewalk and with the heel of his shoe made it ring a bit. This noise, he said, giving his decision, is pay enough for the aroma of the tasty dishes. The roast is the thing eaten, and an aroma comes from it. The coin is the thing exchanged, and a sound comes from it. If the coin is worth the roast, then the sound of the coin is worth the aroma of the food. And he returned the coin to the passer-by. Justice is done.

An old tale that demonstrates a wise bit of knowledge. We are hollow and empty; we cannot fill ourselves with air and with sound.

We need something substantial to mend us. Two positions and two orders: substances and solids here, and there air and sound. According to this bit of wisdom, if there is to be an exchange, it must be of the same order. That is philosophy, the justice of the stomach. Solid for solid, substance for substance, and meal for coin of the realm; elsewhere, air for sound and vice versa. There are infrastructures – a serious matter – and there are superstructures where hot air is sold. The consistent and the diffuse. Every author and every language notes this division in its own way. And the heavy philosophers consecrate it.

The parasite invents something new. Since he does not eat like everyone else, he builds a new logic. He crosses the exchange, makes it into a diagonal. He does not barter; he exchanges money. He wants to give his voice for matter, (hot) air for solid, superstructure for infrastructure. People laugh, the parasite is expelled, he is made fun of, he is beaten, he cheats us; but he invents anew. This novelty must be analyzed. This sound, this aroma, passing for money or roast.

A paralytic was crawling about on hands and knees. Was it our athlete, wounded? A few steps away from a sumptuous repast, Tantalus, you can die of hunger if you are unable to move. He was collapsing in misery, rotting away in a black comer. One fine day, he saw a blind man who was bumping into a thousand obstacles and who thereby almost broke his neck. He could die by falling into a well if its lip were low and seemed to be a step and if his outstretched arms only touched the air. The paralytic calls him and offers to strike a bargain. The blind man will carry him and the cripple will be the guide. The two of them form one normal person.

An old tale that pushes the wise bit of knowledge out. You laughed at the parasite, but you do not laugh at the exchange of legs for eyes. Nevertheless: the blind man gives solidity, force, transportation, power that can be calculated in calories produced by such and such a food from a meal. In other words, energy on the normal scale. What does the cripple give in exchange in this new picture? He speaks, and that is that. He announces obstacles, he watches, he proposes a direction. Perched on the shoulders of a black force, he clarifies it and illuminates it. Soon we will have to say that he directs it, that he gives the force orders. After all, the contract he proposed to the blind man was a parasitic pact. For he pays in information, in energy on the microscopic level. He offers words for the force – yes, his voice, air, for a solid substance. Worse yet, he takes control and governs.

The parasite invents something new. He obtains energy and pays for it in information. He obtains the roast and pays for it with stories. Two ways of writing the new contract. He establishes an unjust pact; relative to the old type of balance, he builds a new one. He speaks in a logic considered irrational up to now, a new epistemology and a new theory of equilibrium. He makes the order of things as well as the states of things – solid and gas – into diagonals. He evaluates information. Even better: he discovers information in his voice and good words; he discovers the Spirit in the wind and the breath of air. He invents cybernetics. The blind man and the cripple are a crossed association of the material and the logicial, an exchange of the solid for a voice – that is the oldest story of the rudder [*gouvernail*]. And if the bolt of lightning governs the universe, here it is the look and the invitation to create a slant. The person who limps is the inclination. He is the difference, and he says so.

There are several fine balances in this. First of all, not all voices bear information; not all winds bear tidings. Not all smooth talkers are invited to dine: good *raconteurs* are distinguished from tiresome braggarts and from stubborn cavillers. The king of Prussia could choose; he preferred Voltaire, and the tsarina, Diderot. They would not have invited the ridiculous Jean-Francois Rameau. There is a market for good words, sometimes at a fixed price. Bad money often chases out the good. But this balance is evolved, sophisticated; it is useless at first.

Let us return to the paralytic, that is to say, to the governor. The one with energy, the producer of movement, can sometimes distinguish the useful message in the voices of the wind. Yet his blindness forbids him from ever regulating the message's usefulness. The cripple, perched atop his blind stare, could make him fall into a ditch. The blind man must trust the cripple. And the latter could be anyone. For the blind man cannot choose his mahout. Of course, he can distinguish messages from noise, but his lack of control allows him to be lied to. I shall warn you about all obstacles, and I shall lead you where you want to go. And so he goes quite like a sheep.

From that point on, anyone who wants to sit on the shoulders of an athlete does not want him to see well. He who likes to command can do so, but on one condition: the eyes of the producers, of the energetic and the strong, have to be poked out. Those who have energy necessarily cannot have information; thus, those with information can do without energy. Information is as precious as it is rare. Thus this rarity has to be provoked. The blind man and the paralytic already established these theorems and the new balance as well. They began with symbiosis, but that did not last very long. The parasite came back.

The balance of rarity functions perfectly in a space or an environment without information. Here the first signal that appears is worth all the money in the world, is worth life itself. The first bolt of lightning that inclines in chaos. The first olive branch in the beak of the dove on the flooded plains. Afterwards follows all the meaning. And history itself is derived from this spark. Begin with the black box, night, blindness. Thus you have to begin by removing all sources of information for the workers and producers. Horses are trained by putting blinders on them. Calves and chickens are placed in the dark, in school, as if they were simple, small men. You have to begin by dividing the work. The manual laborer has to be blind in relation to the paralyzed intellectual. The helmsman has no porthole; he hears his master's voice, he listens, he repeats, and he obeys. Just like the blind man a while back, who followed a voice. One furnishes energy; the other, information. One gives the force to work; the other, the directions. Matter and voice. Again this is an iniquitous exchange, but it works in history and not only in comedy. They must have found the parasitic diagonal very serious. They must have found the new balance intelligent. For the division surges up and makes a system very quickly: the intellectual producer is blind relative to the administrative paralytic and blinded by him, and so forth. This cybernetics gets more and more complicated, makes a chain, then a network. Yet it is founded on the theft of information, quite a simple thing. It is merely necessary to edit the laws and to withdraw knowledge from the greatest number. In the end, power is nothing else. It is measured on this balance. It is the relation and literally the balance beam between the loci in which information is stocked and those from which it is withdrawn. Who put out whose eyes? Where is knowledge located, and from what space is it absent? It is true enough that the division of manual and intellectual functions more or less matches the old relation of city and country, for example; this is what the rats show us.

This power, which could be called bureaucratic, seems to me to be stronger and stabler than that of force, which is never strong enough, or that of law, which is never just enough. It is based on knowledge, and worse yet, on information, on the signal, almost at the level of a reflex. Yet its genesis is paradoxical. That of strong powers is simple: it is a question of violence and death, warfare, muscles, and strategy. That of just powers is simple as well: it is a question of faith and of sacrifices, of martyrs and fanatics. Nothing out of the ordinary, nothing rare, nothing rare, nothing ridiculous. Here, the ancestor is a parasite. He is ridiculous, a joke. He claims to exchange his daring words for good food. But he is the only one we hear at the table. He is the only one we see on stage in Plautus. Him and his loud voice. Everyone laughs. By what miracle does everyone suddenly cry then? In the meanwhile, the master has lost the power to exclude him. He is there, well entrenched. Ruins the father, screws the mother, leads the children, runs the household. We can no longer do without him; he is our system itself: he commands, he has the power, his voice has become that of the master, he speaks so he is heard everywhere, no one else can talk. From the *table d'hôte* to the table of Orion – now he is on the shoulders, the master, Zeus-like. How could this have happened? How could the producers have suddenly been blinded? What hit them?

The producer plays the contents, the parasite, the position. The one who plays the position will always beat the one who plays the contents. The latter is simple and naive; the former is complex and mediatized. The parasite always beats the producer. The producer, always attentive to the game of the things themselves, supposes that the other does not cheat, since the things themselves are fine but loyal, as physicists say.

The one who plays the contents plays the object. He is an artisan; he is a scientist as well, but it is only the mastery of the world, subtle, wily, but not cheating. The one who plays the position plays the relations between subjects; thus, he masters men. And the master of men is the master of the masters of the world.

Some are of fire and some of location. Some whose word is of fire and some whose word is location. Those of location without fire are the masters-the cold ones. Those of fire without location bum madly, so strongly that around them, objects change as if in a furnace or near a forge. Flame of fire in the wind; the wind comes from where it will, blows where it will to stir up the fire. They are not the masters; they can be the slaves, but they are the beginnings. They are the noise of the world, the sounds of birth and of transformations.

To play the position or to play the location is to dominate the relation. It is to have a relation only with the relation itself. Never with the stations from which it comes, to which it goes, and by which it passes. Never to the things as such and, undoubtedly, never to subjects as such. Or rather, to those points as operators, as sources of relations. And that is the meaning of the prefix *para-* in the word *parasite*: it is on the side, next to, shifted; it is not on the thing, but on its relation. It has relations, as they say, and makes a system of them. It is always mediate and never immediate. It has a relation to the relation, a tie to the tie; it branches onto the canal.

There are those of sources and those of canals. The whole question of the system now is to analyze what a point, a being, and a station are. They are crossed by a network of relations; they are crossroads, interchanges, sorters. But is that not analysis itself: saying that this thing is at the intersection of several series. From then on, the thing is nothing else but a center of relations, crossroads or passages. It is nothing but a position or situation. And the parasite has won.

Michel Serres, extract from *Parasite*, Chicago, University of Chicago Press, 1982, pp. 34-39

Contributed by Urban Fauna Lab

FROM URBS REPRESSIVUM TO URBS PARANOICUM, 1994

VIKTOR MISIANO

Regularities which determined the life of the Soviet society and culture separated a town-urban sphere and an art-aesthetic sphere. A city with its productive effectiveness, ideological control and normal communicational processes was regarded as a space of power incarnate, whereas art embodied very intimate experience. The city was more a structure, a meaning of sociality than its scene, and it represented the territory of constant fear (Ilya Kabakov used this topic of urban fear in his installations and texts). Social space was repressive: pictures taken into the streets could provoke 'bulldozers' (as happened in 1974 in a Moscow suburb when the pictures exhibited at an alternative exhibition were smashed by the bulldozers). The social sphere could not become a place for art; it was regarded as a diseased zone or an enormous leper colony. Only the sphere of private existence had space for art, this zone was built within the urban space (the most vivid example of this was 'apt-art', when exhibitions took place in private apartments), or in the nature, outside the city limits (this was the program of 'Collective Actions', whose performances took place only in natural surroundings).

In those days urban enviroment served the logic of the ideological project. It was (or pretended to be) in permanent linear development, its dynamics aimed at constant perfection, communicational, functional and visual. That's why the main goal of this art was the creation of another, non-linear model of existence: the tradition of Moscow conceptualism created the poetics of non-communicative, non-functional and non-spectacular art. Art needed another spaceless dimension (in a famous installation by Kabakov a person flew into space with the help of a home-made catapult while on the table he left a model of the city; an object of horror and hatred). The horror is also based upon the discovery that it's a impossible to run away from urban sociality. The acceptance of social expectations, its ideological marks and the understanding of self-participation in urbanism have become moral revelation and purification. As a result of the ideological exorcism of Eric Bulatov, agitprop images were frozen into timelessness and dissolved, in a lighted spaceless sphere. Yet at the same time the escapist art reproduced the urban structure: Kabakov's installation or Andrei Monastirski's performances were still sometimes structured with the same stiffness as seen in the Moscow metro or on the 1st of May parades. The spaces of Eric Bulatov's pictures was constructed with the same impeccable logic as Stalin's Moscow reconstruction plan. But if the rhythm of the urban environment was characterized by the tiresome and monotonous, the rhythm of the aesthetic sphere was very dynamic and exiting. Within the context of the feeble leper colony real events took place only within the art sphere. Art was much more interesting that life itself. Nowadays the urban sphere is not structured by power and it in turn doesn't structure power. Nowadays we don't have a 'power' at all. Social life is not subordinated to the logic of the project, it is not attuned to linear development: it is situated in a permanent present. As a result the idea of escapism and the alternative project no longer make sense: there is no place to hide amongst the smoldering ruins. That is why nowadays the most valuable events do not happen in the museums or exhibition halls, which are degraded and dying and certainly not in the galleries, which don't really exist. New art is going onto the streets, it doesn't refer to the public, a category that collapsed together with the urban infrastructure, but to the crowd (groups such as 'These', 'Nezeziudic', 'Without Title'). Even the borders of the aesthetic and social have disappeared: people view coups as performances and bohemians sit in the Parliament. Power's collapse had the appearance of catastrophe giving birth to a precedent, returning the dimension of the event to society, giving elements of a big event to reality. All fragments of existing sociality are shaken up in the presence of the Big Event: each reproduces small catastrophes. The modularity of the event presumes an elimination of the aesthetic dimension: the essence of being becomes the representation of one's excesses. Reality lacking in monotony is shaken by paranoic rhythm.

Art fused with sociality divides its structure in the presence of the big Catastrophe: if its place is among the ruins of the urban sphere, then the most appropriate form becomes scandalous. (The first example here was that of Oleg Kulik who in April 1992 cut a pig in Regina Gallery and initiated an age of a scandal in art.) There is noting superficial in this action, it is the only chance to discover the essence of a 'crazy being'. The strategy of overcoming sociality or internal purification is no longer actual: if it's impossible to run society we can only overrun it. Only by producing something more valuable than the Big Event, it is possible to overcome the desire to produce such events. That's why the idea of the reduction of visual perception was unreal: catastrophes are always within the realm of sight. This was known even in Neron's time (what could be more richly visual than the live leopards of Anatoly Osmolovsky in the Regina gallery). The refusal of functionality also hasn't been real. In a time of infrastructural disintegration the main criteria of functionality becomes personal aggression and the effectiveness of its demonstration.

Here art is trying to catch privatizers, who privatize reality with the same enthusiasm as 'new Russians' privatize the tangible ('reality' is the main topic of the leading Moscow artists, from Dmitri Gutov to Anatoly Osmolovsky). The possibility of communication is yet another achievement of the post-catastrophic epoch: the event cannot exist if it is not obvious to the ordinary conscious. The main task of Alexander Brener, for instance, is to give a voice to the crowd: his irrational and brutal performances try to appropriate the uterine language of the street's many voice. The main idea behind the latest performance by Oleg Kulik is to capture a crowd's voice, by organizing his own electoral campaign in the streets of Moscow. Obviously, it's impossible to outdo the spectacle of the House of Parliament burning or to be more functional than the MMM share scandal, in which one part of the country was robbed and another part enriched. It's also impossible to be more explicitly communicative than in the electoral speeches of Zchrinovski. So, art has no chance to outrun reality. Real events happen in reality. Nowadays life is much more interesting than art.

From *Urbanaria project*, Ljubljana, 1994-1997

НАЗВАТЬ ПРЕЗИДЕНТА ПИ..РАСОМ СТОИТ 417 НОВЫХ РУБЛЕЙ

23 мая около 15 часов, группа называющая себя «Внеправительственная Контрольная Комиссия» (художники А.Осмоловский, А.Тер—Оганьян, литераторы Д.Пименов, Д.Модель, М.Демская) перекрыли улицу Большую Никитскую (бывшую Герцена) картонными коробками и всяческим хламом, привезенным на грузовике заранее. Акция была посвящена 30—летней годовщине студенческой «революции» в Париже в мае 1968 года. Над баррикадой были подняты лозунги 1968 года: «Запрещается запрещать!», «Будьте реалистами — требуйте невозможного!» и даже ругательства на французском. По заверению участников, акция собрала около двухсот студентов, интеллектуалов, художников и сочувствующих. Были оглашены требования: 1)1200 USD каждому участнику; 2) легализации наркотиков для каждого и т.д.

Понимая, что имеют дело с интеллигенцией, власти отозвали готовый к избиению ОМОН, и задействовали милицию толлько тогда, когда в 16.30 участники акции двинулись в сторону Кремля, неся транспаранты и скандируя: «Мы победили!». Тогда милиция перегородила путь и арестовала семерых организаторов акции. Поскольку были выходные дни (23 мая была суббота) и суды не работали, пятерым, двоих отпустили, пришлось досидеть в ментовских города (в 11—ом, 83—ем и 43—ем отделениях) до понедельника. В понедельник их судили в Краснопресненском суде и назначили административные штрафы от 200 до 500 рублей. В ходе судебного заседания А.Осмоловский назвал Президента РФ пи..расом, и был приговорен к штрафу в 417 рублей. НБП приветствует смелую и нестандартную акцию, хотя и не разделяет восторга перед парижскими студенческими волнениями мая 1968 года, считая их всего навсего бунтом избалованных маменькиных сынков французской буржуазии. Парижские студенты 68 года целый месяц мололи языками, даже не попытавшись взять власть. (Жирная свинья, Даниэль Кон—Бендит, член Европарламента, бывший «вождь» мая 1968 года, также не вызывает восторга. Скорее печальная биография ренегата). Однако НБП с интересом следит за развитием настроений в среде московского авангардного искусства и готова к сотрудничеству во всех формах.

Пресс—служба НБП

БАРРИКАДА НА БОЛЬШОЙ НИКИТСКОЙ

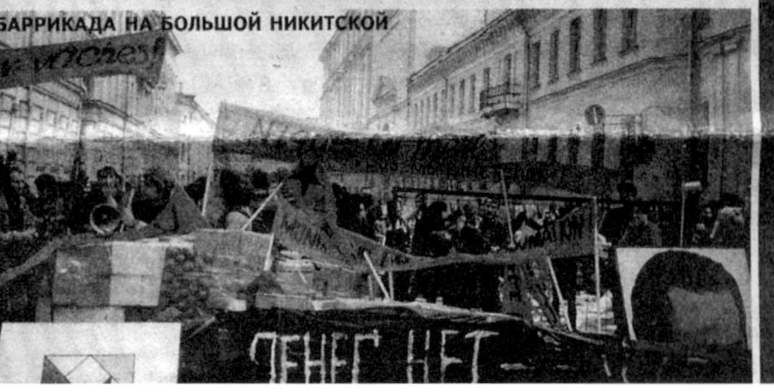

Calling the President a Faggot costs 417 New Rubles, from *Limonka* newspaper, 1998

On May 23 at around 3 in the afternoon, a group calling itself the Extragovernmental Control Commission (the artists A. Osmolovsky and A. Ter-Oganyan and the writers D. Pimenov, D. Model, and M. Demskaya) covered Bolshaya Nikitskaya street (formerly Gertsen street) with cardboard boxes and varieties of junk that had been carried by truck earlier. The event was dedicated to the 30th anniversary of the student "revolution" in Paris in May of 1968. The slogans of 1968 were raised over the barricade – "It is Forbidden to Forbid!" and "Be a Realist – Demand the Impossible!" – and even French obscenities. According to the participants, around two hundred students, intellectuals, artists, and fellow travelers showed up for the event. Demands were made: 1. US $ 1200 for every participant, 2. legalization of drugs from everyone, and others.

Knowing that they were dealing with the intelligentsia, the authorities refrained from having OMON beat anybody and sent in the police only when the demonstrators moved in the direction of the Kremlin at 4:30, carrying banners and chanting "We Have Won!" The police then blocked the way and arrested seven of the demonstration's organizers. As it was a weekend (the 23rd was a Saturday) and the courts were not working, they released two of them and stuck five in the city's police stations (in the 11th, 83rd, and 43rd departments) until Monday. On Monday, they were judged in the Krasnopresny Court and fined from 200 to 500 rubles. During the course of the trial, A. Osmolovsky called the President of the Russian Federation a faggot and was ordered to pay a fine of 417 rubles. The NBP welcomes this daring and unusual demonstration, although it does not share its infatuation with the Paris student uprisings of 1968, considering them to have been ultimately a revolt of spoiled mama's boys from the French bourgeoisie. The Paris students of '68 ran their mouths off for a whole month and did not even try to seize power. (The fat pig Daniel Cohn-Bendit, a member of the European Parliament and former "leader" of May 1968, does not evoke infatuation either, but more brings to mind the sad biography of a turncoat.) However, the NBP is watching with interest this development in the mood of Muscovite avant-garde art and is ready for cooperation in any form.

National Bolshevik Party press service.

Vladimir Tuchkov, *An Old Woman stole the Barricade*, from *Vechernyaya Moskva*, May 25, 1998

On Saturday, a group of artists and students, headed by a certain Anatoly Asmalovsky, blocked off Bolshaya Nikitskaya with barricades near the university that had been constructed from cardboard boxes and light building materials. Then, they began to scatter leaflets, chant curses against the bourgeoisie and corrupt authorities, and sang revolutionary songs. There was a great deal of noise. However, only four people were arrested by the police.

This demonstration, which was dedicated to the 30th anniversary of the Paris student revolution, had more of a theatrical than a commemorative character, which showed in its chants: "Freedom to Parrots!," "It is Forbidden to Forbid!," and "Long Live the Student Revolution!" Naturally, the government was by name called shit, thrice-cursed bourgeois and even worse. This demonstration could be understood if it had been born in the student milieu. But as the director was Mr. Asmalovsky, who does not live badly on this very same bourgeois money, an association automatically arises with Azef, Father Gabon, and other Russian provocateurs. In any case, some young French ladies who had gotten caught up in the crowd began singing the *Marseillaise* out of tune. However, soon they got bored with this comedy, and, checking a map of Moscow, went on to do more important things.

The situation developed for about an hour with no presence of the authorities. More precisely speaking, it did not develop, but gradually faded away, as shouting for a long time in solidarity with the miners is not only stupid, but can lead to mental derangement. Then, the rather surprised police leadership arrived. After extended negotiations and admonitions, a couple of dozen of men were brought in with body armor, truncheons, and firearms. Having closed ranks, they quickly understood that nothing very important was going on. An old woman came over from a construction site and announced that the barrier had been stolen from it. She quickly carried half of the barricade away to the building side with which she had been entrusted. Then television crews arrived. Mr. Asmalovsky read a prepared text into a pair of cameras about "we represent a terrifying force, we will sweep the corrupt government from the face of the Earth, we will build a kingdom of freedom." After that, they could depart.

The glorious victors moved on to Mokhovaya. However, four were rather rudely – with their arms twisted back – were shoved into police Volgas and carried off, probably, according to officials from Petrovka, to the police precinct on Granitaya street. Asmalovsky went up to the car himself, seemingly rather satisfied. The most terrible punishment for him would have been for the police to pay no attention to him.

БАБУШКА УПЁ

Владимир ТУЧКОВ

В субботу группа художников и студентов, предводительствуемая неким Анатолием Асмаловским, близ университета перегородила Большую Никитскую баррикадами, построенными из картонных коробок и легких строительных ограждений. После чего началось разбрасывание листовок, скандирование проклятий в адрес буржуев и продажных властей и революционные песнопения. Шуму было много. Однако в милицию забрали лишь четверых человек.

Данная акция, которая была посвящена 30-летию парижской студенческой революции, имела скорее не мемориальный, а опереточный характер, что сквозило в массовых речевках: «Свободу попугаям!», «Запретить запрещать!», «Да здравствует Великая Студенческая Революция!». Естественно, начальство поименно именовалось дерьмом, а треклятые буржуи и того хуже. Данную реакцию можно было бы понять, если бы она исходила из студенческой гущи. Но поскольку дирижером был г-н Асмаловский, неплохо существующий на эти самые буржуйские деньги, то невольно возникает ассоциация с Азефом, попом Гапоном и прочими отечественными провокаторами. При этом какие-то вовлеченные в массовку французские барышни нестройно запевали «Марсельезу». Впрочем, вскоре им эта комедия наскучила, и они, сверившись с картой Москвы, пошли заниматься более актуальными вещами.

Примерно час ситуация развивалась в отсутствии властей. Точнее не развивалась, а постепенно угасала, поскольку долго орать о солидарности с шахтерами — не только глупо, но и чревато устойчивым помутнением рассудка. Затем приехало недоумевающее милицейское начальство. После продолжительных переговоров и увещеваний привезли пару десятков бойцов в бронежилетах с дубинками и автоматами. Бойцы, встав в шеренгу, довольно скоро поняли, что большому делу тут не бывать. Пришла бабушка со стройки и заявила, что ограждения украли у нее. И быстренько уволокла на вверенный ей строительный объект половину баррикады. Потом подтянулись люди с TV. Г-н Асмаловский наговорил в пару камер заранее приготовленный текст о том, что «мы представляем страшную силу, мы сметем с лица земли продажную власть, мы построим царство свободы». После этого можно было и расходиться.

И торжествующие победители двинулись к Моховой. Однако четверо довольно грубо — с выкручиванием рук — были засунуты в милицейские «Волги» и увезены, как сообщили чины с Петровки, предположительно на Гранитную улицу, в отделение милиции. Асмаловский шел к машине сам, вполне довольный. Самым ужасным для него наказанием было бы отсутствие к его персоне милицейского внимания.

В заключение следует отметить, что широко разрекламированная акция была проведена на низком художественном уровне. И ее можно вполне отнести к жанру оперетты. Реальное действие продолжалось минут десять, после чего приглашенная публика стала скучать, не зная, чем себя занять. Да и г-н Асмаловский за это мелкое хулиганство (например, нарушение движения автотранспорта в течение 2 часов) больших лавров не пожнет. Сейчас, чтобы считаться подлинно актуальным художником, надо отсидеть в тюрьме как минимум полгода. Как это сделал г-н Бренер. А мазать лицо клюквенным соком, выдавая его за кровь, просто неприлично.

It should be noted in conclusion that the widely advertised demonstration was carried out at a low artistic level, something that can be attributed fully to its theatrical genre. The actual event lasted for ten minutes, after which the invited public began to get bored, not knowing what to do with themselves. And for his trivial mischief-making (for instance, disrupting vehicular transport for 2 hours), Mr. Asmalovsky will not reap a large windfall. Now, to be genuinely considered a great artist, you need to sit in prison for at last a year. That is what Mr. Brener did. But smearing yourself with cranberry sauce and making it out to be blood is merely vulgar.

IT'S ALL ABOUT PEOPLE, 2007
DAVID RIFF

Late last summer, before the schools in Russia reopened, a remarkable beer ad about post-Soviet space aired on Russian TV. Thirty seconds of feel-good Russian classic rock: an active bass and a prominent slide guitar wafted around a voice, always-already middle-aged, slightly flat after working a night shift. Four measure whole notes by the band: the staggered vocal names the brand. Krasny Vostok.

Where the sun rises / the east is red. A new day is dawning / over our land. // How can you resist. Cause' this land is not made of history's pages; it's not made through borders or territorial stages. Our land is made up of people and people are what make our land.

Obviously, the ad wants to mobilize the patriotism of its maturing target group, reminding it of forgotten values: hospitality, friendship, little evening get-togethers on the dacha. The Krasny Vostok commercial is supposedly all about people, but there are no people in the ad. In 2004, new legislation tried to curb the spread of beer as Russia's favorite soft drink. Among other restrictions, it introduced a ban of anything remotely alive in beer advertising, laying off all the cartoon characters, animals, and most importantly people: friendly, slightly crazy fat men, 19th century aristocrats, or teenage hipster heroes about to make it big. These roles have all been taken over by either the beer bottles themselves or their settings. The Krasny Vostok ad is no exception. It personifies (the) "people" as a golden spirit that floats out of the sunrise as a 3D animation: from close ups of fragrant grass, up over dewy meadows and out through the speckled trees, over pine-topped mountains and down a glittering river through a valley, across a suspension bridge into a city, where it reflects in the shop windows of a deserted 19th century Russian street, wafting through lace curtains into a cool, sparkling glass of amber beer standing solitary on a kitchen table. The beer commercial's potential inhabitants are kept out of public by the medium's laws.[1]

There is an overwhelming pressure to think of "post-Soviet space" in similarly abstract though far more foreboding terms, all of which present elaborations on a hegemonic notion of geopolitical Lebensraum of a "unified Russia." "Post-Soviet space" is somehow posited as a given that needs to be drained, reconfigured, and filled with something that always returns to the interior. The empty exterior is real estate and ad space: an inhabited ruin of "democratic socialism" about to turn into an unpopulated "sovereign democracy," a land of milk and honey (oil and gas) in which mayonnaise, beer, vodka, and money flow freely, unhindered by any human factor, sweeping away all edifices in their path to be replaced with billboards advertising a vast beer garden.

This brings us back to the real post-socialist city and how its social spaces are defined. When the weather gets warmer, circles of people hang out and drink beer in almost all backyards, parks, boulevards, squares, monuments, and the spaces around metro-stations with their 24-hour kiosks. You constantly hear somebody having fun, passing from one of these places to another. Social space is constructed by the order of consumption (beer, cigarettes, salted nuts, fast-food), in small groups, isolated from one another.

This obviously brings a potential for anomie (competing groups develop new affinities and repulsions) in liminal states of all-night open-air idling that the militia cannot prevent fully. Guitars and fistfights from May to September! The streets are the living room of the collective (Benjamin), and the collective is forever young. Lumpenproletariat, Neo-Nazi nationalists, consumer kids, Goths, headbangers, Lesbian punks, migrant workers, and even the occasional anarchist. Walking through Moscow or Petersburg in the summer, anyone with multitudinous political passions will wonder: what if more kids were not just drinking beer but talking politics? They have already captured public space. "Our universities?" Who knows? Maybe these kids are learning street-smarts on how to make representational space in the alienated intimacy of their encounters, finding something that makes them want to ride their bikes through the city in more tightly knit groups late at night when the traffic dies down? Can one politicize this new sociality? If the educators themselves must be educated (not to think in abstract terms of progressive nostalgia, but in concrete practices, something a text like this can only sketch out), what can we learn in the beer garden of common space, where the first impression of normal childhood is one of spatial awe?

Normal children in awe of space: Soviet town-planners suggested the common as a political potentiality, still empty, waiting to be filled. The conduits of post-Soviet cities themselves are certainly broad enough to suggest the sweep of politicized masses, and not only the flow of a collective subject, self-alienated in a pre-Marxian, young-Hegelian sense. Heterotopia in a vista onto space: radiating from a center that both sucks in and evacuates entire populations, Ultra-Haussmanized causeways and chtonic cathedrals suggest mass movements (not armies) so large that they displace clouds of dust heralding their advance overhead. The scale of this claim – much more than one sixth of the world – is unprecedented. It dwarves and subsumes real people in a very different way than the skyscraper canyons of Manhattan, or the starry sky in Grand Central Station.[2]

Normal children in awe of themselves: in the late summer of 2004, the workgroup Chto delat made a collective study of the Petersburg neighborhood of Narvskaya Zastava. It intended to probe the possibilities for militant investigation and political involvement in this space, and tested a variety of methods ranging from quite traditional sociological evidence-gathering to the psychogeographical technique of the Situationist dérive. I participated in this part of the project. Armed with cameras and logbooks, we set out to map the neighborhood's psycho-geographical zones and to document our impressions.[3]

Normal children everywhere: the social space of the dérive is a non-spectacular production site. But sometimes it looks like a spectacular stage set. The abandoned 19th century tenements to the north of the neighborhood on Shkapin Street served as romantic ruins for a really stupid German war movie that showed how human Hitler was. Here, we found a flower growing toward the sun, its secret heliotropism photographed by other people drifting and drinking beer on a Sunday stroll without theory.

Normal children, fixing fidelity on a historical point of departure: you arrive at Narvskaya Zastava on Stachek Square, dominated by the Narva Gate, a triumphal Palladian arch celebrating the Russian victory over Napoleon. It stands in the shadow of a house-sized fresco from the late 1960s that commemorates the site's central location in Russia's revolutionary history. It was here that the first shots were fired on a protest procession of striking workers, marching to present the Czar with a petition of demands on January 9th 1905. In November 1917, the square served as the place d'armes for the Bolshevik forces that stormed the Winter Palace. Now, another beer garden.

Normal children sucked into a historical vortex: Narvskaya Zastava's most famous section is defined by the constructivist buildings on and around the esplanade between Stachek Square and the Narva Gate to the north and Kirov Square to the south. In the mid-to-late 1920s, the area's working class population was "rewarded" for its revolutionary efforts with a model settlement for workers from nearby plants, including the famous Putilov (Kirov) Works. In the mid-1930s, however, the transformation of the neighborhood along constructivist-functionalist lines was abandoned. Its architectural endpoint is marked by the council building on Kirov Square, built in an increasingly domineering Stalinist style. The buildings on and around the esplanade express a collective industrial production cycle: house of culture, training center, collective homes, public baths, council building, municipal park, school (in the form of a hammer and sickle to commemorate the 10th anniversary of the October Revolution), public kitchen/messhall. A metro station was added in 1952, giving Stachek Square a triumphant dominant, and essentially destroying its function as an agora, making it into what the philosopher Mikhail Ryklin calls a "space of jubilation."[4] This breakup of the agora at the historical center of the neighborhood prepares the constructivist settlement for participation in a neo-capitalist consumer economy: the former factory-kitchen has housed a department store since the Soviet epoch. In the ground floor, there is a new theme restaurant with Russified dishes from "around the world," which are not exactly cheap either. But the theme restaurant retains a cafeteria look as a part of its décor, which imitates that of an IKEA restaurant.

Normal children on the run: in socialist architecture, the Euclidian Ultra-Haussmanized avenues represent more or less successful rationalizations of the industrial production cycle. Their communal flipside is the courtyard. Soviet architecture consistently tried to innovate residential courtyard architecture, doing battle against the tenement light shaft well as the epitome of alienation. So the worst inhuman *microrayon* apartment blocks contain generous green spaces with playgrounds, paths, and benches, open intimate spaces in which communal life is more than plausible. This terrain is ideal for drifting: having fled the broad streets and traffic, one moves from one courtyard to the next through intricate systems of arches, coming to rest in pockets of unexpected peace, as behind the 17 residential buildings on Traktornaya Street off Stachek Prospekt. Painted an unusual persian red, they open to the street with over-dimensioned half-arches, bringing in the sky with late summer cirrus clouds in a mad Leningrad sunset. In the 1920s, they served as communal worker's dormitories. Once these communes (ideally governed by neighborhood councils) fell apart through the state's repressive neglect, the living room of the collective was abandoned, overgrown, crisscrossed by footpaths, and covered with empty beer bottles and cigarette butts. But now, the old ladies who live in the buildings chase away the drinkers, lay gravel on footpaths, plant shrubbery, and install fountains, constituting their own Soviet Biedermeier version of imaginary-intimate community space. It's not just a personal project in vernacular garden architecture that installs the garden gnome of bad ontology. Instead, "it's all about people," a didactic projection of social space as it should be, with plenty of benches for the old ladies to gossip on, and a fancy playground for the kids. The communal bricollage of gardening pensioners somehow seems Kabakovian. It hearkens back to a time in which Soviet culture was already falling apart into a self-contradictory communitarian structure. As late modernist urban planning moved people out of communal housing to personalized panel block apartments in the satellite cities, the dialectics of urban alienation and communal intimacy underwent a decisive change. Communities took the place of the state, creating nooks and autonomous zones for informal exchange, colonizing parks and boulevards through moving bubbles of privacy. Paradoxically, it is the community of friends that appears as state socialism's gravedigger, as the collective enthusiasm of the Soviet sixties went sour and turned into a campfire repertoire of "songs about what really counts." But at the same time, communal reality continues the project of common space: until it is rendered productive by privatization, its underlying structure is still open, like the courtyard on Traktornaya Street. Even when the pensioners reclaim it, it can still serve as the site for an impromptu episode of knowledge production by a temporary workgroup of leftist artists and philosophers. So much is coded into its arches, until they become the trademark of a gated community.

Through the backyards of another constructivist settlement around the Red Triangle Rubber Factory where Dima Vilensky lived as a little kid, encountering old ladies who began to perform back at the camera, a kind of subalternity in the face of the spectacle's instrument, theatrically trying to throw a drunk off a bench. Frightened children from the Caucasus somewhere near a ramshackle squat, which Vilensky and Tsaplya later entered with a video camera to conduct interviews with admirable anti-fa anarchists. The long haul to the Baltic Railway Station, down the tracks past deserted institutional architecture from the 1970s. Instant coffee in a sad café. Across half-abandoned industrial zones, in search of immediate encounters. Halted production, overgrown with life. Where are the people, where are the workers? Alexei Penzin reports from the empty shop floor of the factory:

To judge by the discussions that followed, the participants were motivated by a nearly religious search for Contact, Encounter, or Event, for the imaginary meeting of the left-wing intellectual with the invisible specter of the Worker, ascending to the Golgotha of the stopped conveyor. But when we entered the abandoned factory's Cyclopean shop floor, instead of severe workers we found a multitude of colossal phalli (high-quality naturalistic graffiti, sprouting an interweave of 3-4 meters, climbing up the wall), whose exuberantly organic procreation rightfully animated this otherwise empty place of production. [...] But the promised Event never took place as a final point of assembly or coming together. Instead, there were constant displacements, transitions from one environment to another, as well as the realization of one's own position in relation to the position of the others – the impotence of changing anything here and now, in spite of the will that manifests itself in this strange, crypto-religious expectation of an Event, of Redemption... Impotence hangs over all of our confessions and exacerbates our in many ways exuberant stroll with an involuntary feeling of guilt.[5]

At this point, it became clear that our debates were not so much about the absence or betrayal of the proletariat, but centered on the collective non-action of drifting itself. Which collectivity constitutes itself in the process of the drift? What are this collectivity's limitations? And how can one break them? The group moves in its own space, obsessed with its own collective (leftist, neo-modernist, critical, radical, antagonistic) identity, unconsciously fetishizing its own collective autonomy and its friendship while insisting upon the use value of the inoperative activity itself, thus refraining from any genuinely political operation, other than the constitution of the micro-community that spends its free time together (while the fact that the same community produces commodities for the culture industry during business hours as a "start up venture" remains unmentioned). This is basically what I criticized after having a few drinks too many on the second day of the drift. After I said something about "irresponsible slumming through modernity's ruins," our discussion escalated into a shouting match. So I guess I hit a sensitive nerve.

Basically, I felt that our movement through urban space was carried forward by a speech bubble, which is why I was so critical. But then again, we had an excuse to insulate ourselves through chatter. The reason was on TV, in every café and restaurant, in every shop, on every face. On September 3rd 2004, the first day of our dérive: Beslan. The drama started on September 1st, the first day of school: flower rituals and children's songs. In the light of the tragedy, it seemed tasteless to enjoy the utopian boldness of a school in the form of a hammer and sickle.[6]

The geopolitical abstraction of "post-Soviet space" returned in full force when Putin made a speech on a broken TV in a cheap café with Soviet green minimal walls. He declared something that almost amounted to a state of exception, demanding national unity and new "power verticals." Talking Agamben all the way from the military-store on the canal, we reached Ekaterinhof park, where we parodied an American group-hug. Technopop blared across the empty band-stand. It was the last day of summer. Walking through the park, we eventually reached rusty joy rides: bumper cars and swings on fenced-off territory. There was even a booth with air rifles for target practice. Swings with wings: a bitter-sweet Soviet children's song called *Krylatie kacheli* was blaring over the loudspeakers. Most of the others left their stuff in my care on a bench in order to swing more freely, including Artiom Magun, who had been carrying around an elegant black umbrella. Community affects, back and forth. Lover reunited, adulterous embrace. The need for comfort didn't only come from the exceptional tragedy of murdered schoolchildren. Again, late Soviet antiquity was modernity's "normal childhood," a infantile-nostalgic version of the same Taylorized enthusiasm of movement when 20th century communism was still alive; to and fro, back and forth, flying, kissing. It's too bad that the footage in my camera was lost.

At some point, the joyride operators turned off the music and asked us to leave. We started talking about reduction and Alain Badiou. As we were crossing the bridge that separates park from city, Magun stopped in his tracks: "I've forgotten my umbrella." This made me feel very guilty. Leaving the others, Magun and I turned back.

We almost missed the swings: the gates of the little amusement park had already been padlocked. A guard-dog on a long leash was barking violently in order to protect her puppy. A heavyset young man was standing next to the guardhouse. We called to him through the fence. "Umbrella? Yeah. I saw an umbrella." Growing nervous – the umbrella might have been a bomb – Magun and I walked back to the bumper cars.

It was here that we ran into the other group, which was drifting in parallel. They embraced us euphorically, all chattering at once: "How was it? What did you see? Where are you going?" We couldn't answer them. We were looking for Magun's umbrella. Eventually, the militia-man who was guarding the playground unlocked the padlocks and let us out.

Post scriptum

Maybe it was this sense of communal impotence that prompted Chto delat to return to the historical center of Narva Square (this time in the smaller ensemble of Tsaplya, Nikolai Oleinikov, and Dmitry Vilensky), with a piece called *Angry Sandwich-People* (2005). The space of the present text is too small to provide any real contextualization of this piece. I only want to highlight one key difference. While the dérive in 2004 attempted to reflect social space through communal collectivity and the abandoning of production, this piece consciously explored the potentiality of social production site as an arena for political manifestation. Against the backdrop of the neo-modernist mural sandwich-people slowly gather, wearing a fragmented political poem on their chests.[7] Like real sandwichpeople, they belong to no definite class or age group, and have no predefined political identity: pensioners, activists, students, and children. Over the course of the slide show, they accumulate line by line, coming together and falling apart in varying constellations of singularity. This looks like a political manifestation but could actually be read as its opposite: a form of artistic advertising. But at the end of the slideshow, after the flow of images is over, one no longer sees bodies but hears their voices reading out their lines. This inner speech – a tragic chorus? – is tentative, threatening, satirical, and violent, full of potential violence, depleted pathos, and fragile hope. Suddenly, a definite negation is possible again.

[1] Both teaser and ad spot can be found as a Quicktime video at http://adme.ru/creativity/2006/07/27/7770.html.

[2] For more speculation on the difference between "Hegelian" and "Kantian" space, see David Riff/Sergei Sitar. *The Re-Discovery of Post-Soviet Space*, Chto delat No. 11: *(Im) possible Spaces*, Petersburg 2006.

[3] The entire project was documented more fully in Chto delat 7: *Drift. Narvskaya Zastava*, October 2004, http://www.chtodelat.org/index.php?option=com_content&task=category§ionid=17&id=131&Itemid=121.

[4] Cf. Mikhail Ryklin. *Hegel in the Spaces of Jubilation*, in *Third Text* 65, Vol. 17, Issue 4, December 2003.

[5] Alexei Penzin, *The Last Temptation of the Flaneur*, In: Chto Delat 7: *Drift. Narvskaya Zastava*, October 2004, http://www.chtodelat.org/index.php?option=com_content&task=view&id=170&Itemid=121.

[6] Cf. Alexander Skidan, *Derive Protocol*, Chto delat No. 7, *Drift. Narvskaya Zastava*, http://www.chtodelat.org/index.php?option=com_content&task=view&id=172&Itemid=121.

[7] Cf. Chto delat 11, *Why Brecht*, January 2006, http://www.chtodelat.org/index.php?option=com_content&task=view&id=226&Itemid=126. This issue of Chto delat was also conceived as a contribution to the first question of the dOCUMENTA (12).

From dOCUMENTA (12) Magazine, 2007

THE VOICE OF THOSE DEPRIVED OF VOICE, 2012

ILYA BUDRAYTSKIS

The events in Moscow of the last few days are becoming definitive for the future protest movement in Russia. As recently as half a year ago, no one would have believed that such an appearance of mass political demonstrations was possible, and even a few days ago no one could have imagined that people going out onto the streets would become an everyday practice independent of particular decisions or agreements. We had meekly waited for months for the results of negotiations with the mayor's office on the place where we would be allowed to gather at a strictly determined time, surrounded by metal grills and police cordons, closely listen to speakers coming one after another on the stage. The speakers waved their arms resolutely, repeated the same slogans, which were gradually becoming insufferable, and made impassioned calls to come the next event, which would be exactly the same. However, hidden behind these assertive invocations was uncertainty, a lack of understanding of what to do next. For its part, the government, which had become a little uncertain of what to do after the first demonstrations in December, had quickly come to its senses. It had gotten used to our readiness to play by their rules. They had succeeded in using our lack of social demands that are important for an enormous, but yet-passive, amount of people. They had succeeded, using the media and vulgar populist demagoguery, in opposing the participants in the demonstration to the rest of the country, which fears losing stability.

On March 4, using the sleaziest of methods, they managed to win the elections. But will this victory, a victory over the will and consciousness of simple people, long-term? It is already clear today that the current policy of the government will leave nothing of Putin's cheap promises. A new attack is beginning on standard of living and employment – entry into the WTO, an increase in fees and the retirement age, and de facto introduction of for-pay education (according to F3-83). Everything that we have become accustomed to consider characteristic features of the Putin regime is remaining in place – lawlessness on the side of the police, corruption that is off the scale, and lack of transparency of the enormous bureaucratic machine that sucks up budget revenue. Unfortunately, Putin's main resources are also still in place – the passivity of the majority, lack of trust in each other, fear of the authorities, inability to self-organize.

Here, on Chistoprudny Bulvar in Moscow, on the streets of Petersburg, Samara, and other cities, a new type of resistance in being born before our eyes. A movement of outraged people that can make decisions on its own, unyielding before the threats of the police, and, most importantly, showing the remaining millions of our yet-passive fellow citizens that this can be done and together we are in a position to change something. This is our main task.

When thousands of people created the Occupy Wall Street movement last fall in downtown New York, they raised the banner of "the 99%," those who are standing behind them, the very same common people who are tired of the 1% making their decisions for them. It is time for us to raise this banner, of the humiliated majority that has not yet lost its voice. We have come together here, on Chisty Prudy, in the hopes of hearing it.

From *#OccupyAbai* newspaper, 11 May 2012

ГОЛОС ЛИШЕННЫХ ГОЛОСА

Московские события последних дней становятся определяющими для будущего протестного движения в России.

Еще полгода назад никто не верил, что массовые политические демонстрации возможны, и еще несколько дней назад никто не мог бы представить, что этот выход на улицу станет ежедневной практикой, не зависящей от чьих-то решений и согласований. Несколько месяцев мы послушно ждали итогов переговоров с мэрией о месте, где нам дадут собраться, чтобы в строго определенное время, в окружении металлических рамок и полицейских кордонов внимательно слушать ораторов, сменяющих друг друга на сцене. Ораторы решительно махали руками, повторяли одни и те же постепенно надоедавшие лозунги и настойчиво призывали прийти на следующую, точно такую же акцию. Однако за этими наступательными призывами скрывалась неуверенность, непонимание — что делать дальше?

Со своей стороны, власти, немного растерявшиеся после первых декабрьских выступлений, быстро пришли в себя. Они привыкли к нашей готовности играть по их правилам. Им удалось использовать отсутствие у нас социальных требований, важных для огромного количества людей, пока сохраняющих пассивность. Им удалось, используя медиа и развязную популистскую демагогию, противопоставить участников митингов остальной стране, боящейся потери стабильности.

4 марта, пустив в ход самые грязные методы, им удалось одержать победу на выборах. Но будет ли это победа, победа над волей и сознанием простых людей, долговременной? Уже сейчас очевидно, что настоящая политика правительства совсем скоро не оставит камня на камне от дешевых обещаний Путина. Готовится новое наступление на уровень жизни и рабочие места — вступление в ВТО, повышение тарифов и пенсионного возраста, фактическое введение платного образования в школе (по ФЗ-83). Все, что мы привыкли считать родовыми чертами путинского режима, остается на местах — полицейский беспредел, зашкаливающая коррупция, непрозрачность огромной бюрократической машины, поглощающей бюджетные средства. Но сохраняется, к сожалению, и главный ресурс Путина — пассивность большинства, недоверие к друг другу, страх перед властью, неспособность к самоорганизации.

Здесь, на московском Чистопрудном бульваре, на улицах Петербурга, Самары и других городов на наших глазах рождается новый тип сопротивления. Движение возмущенных, способное принимать решения за себя, не сдаваться перед угрозами полиции, и главное — показать остальным, миллионам еще пассивных сограждан, что это возможно и вместе мы в состоянии что-то менять. Именно в этом — наша главная задача.

Когда прошлой осенью в центре Нью-Йорка тысячи людей создали движение «Оккупируй Уолл-стрит», они подняли знамя «99%», которые стоят за ними, такими же простыми людьми, уставшими от того, что 1% принимает за них решения. **Самое время и нам поднять это знамя — униженного большинства, которое пока лишено своего голоса. Мы собрались здесь, на Чистых прудах, в надежде его услышать.**

PROBLEM BOOK, 2012

IVAN BRAZHKIN. ALEXANDR BURLAKA. ANASTASIA RYABOVA. VLADISLAV SHAPOVALOV. MAXIM SPIVAKOV. TZUCHIEN THO. DMITRY VOROBYEV

1. Area of unseen luxury

Businessman X decides to show solidarity with the "Test Walk" [*] by strolling with his wife along the tree-lined walk around his house in the Zhukovka Hills community.

On the other side of the Moscow River, an activist equipped with a reel of cord, measuring tape and a protractor marks off a line segment between points M and N, from which two diametrically opposed trees (points A and B) can be seen on the walkway surrounding the house.

Segment MN and the angles it forms with the lines connecting its endpoints to points A and B:

$b = \text{MN} = 32.94\,\text{m}$
$a = \angle\text{AMN} = 88.33°$
$\beta = \angle\text{BMN} = 62.52°$
$\gamma = \angle\text{ANM} = 85.45°$
$\delta = \angle\text{BNM} = 111.98°$

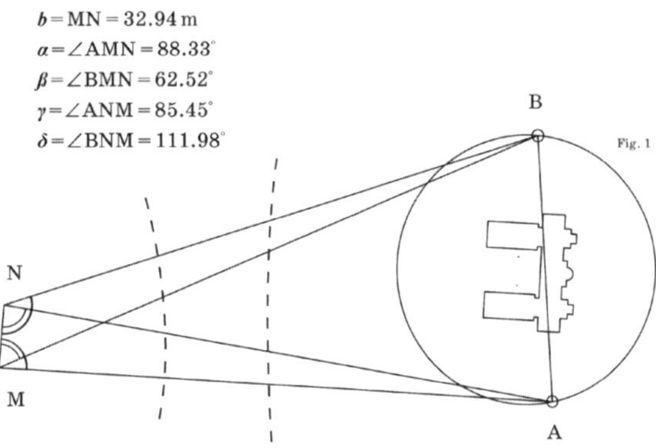

[*] In May 2012, large numbers of Russian citizens took "walks" in the streets of major cities to show their disagreement with the presidential election results. The walks were deliberately not announced as political events and were designed to test whether the authorities would disperse an unsanctioned procession that involved no slogans, amplifying equipment or speakers. Similar tactics had to be adopted due to the increasing practice of brutality by the authorities in charge of suppressing organized protests. The authorities did not interfere.

Problem:
How long will the solidarity walk take, assuming that the community is protected by a security service and that the businessman and his wife have an average strolling speed of 2.196 km/hour?

Answer:
The solidarity walk will take 12 minutes.

2. Molecular cuisine

December. A ventilation duct leading to the surface from a sushi bar in an underground shopping center emits saturated vapor at a temperature of +40° C. A hungry homeless person warms himself by the grating. When breathing normally, he inhales 0.35 liters of vapor into his lungs in a single breath (0.50 liters) and exhales 50 ml of water per hour.

Problem:
How long will it take for one portion of miso soup (350 g) to be absorbed into his lungs if respiratory rate is 14 breaths per minute, relative humidity = 100% and the vapor's moisture content $A = 51\,\text{g/m}^3$? How much moisture will he lose through breathing in this same period of time?

Answer:
One portion of miso soup will be absorbed into the homeless person's lungs in 23.34 hours. During this time, he will lose 1.167 liters of moisture through breathing.

3. An activist's dream

The number of protesters is constantly rising. On November 7,
40,000 people show up on Red Square to demonstrate against
government abuses. In May, a crowd of 80,000 fills Red Square.
On July 14, there are 120,000 demonstrators, exceeding the
square's capacity by several thousand. The walls of the buildings
surrounding Red Square are gradually pushed back by the sheer
political power of these human masses ...

Red Square, bordered by the Historical Museum, GUM,
St. Basil's Cathedral and the Lenin Mausoleum, is a rectangular
area with sides measuring: a = 85 m, b = 4a = 340 m. Crowd density
at demonstrations averages three demonstrators per square meter.

Problem:
How many meters do the buildings bordering Red Square have to
be moved in order to accommodate 120,000 demonstrators?

Answer:
The Kremlin walls, Mausoleum and GUM have to be moved back 7.5 m.
The Historical Museum and St. Basil's have to be moved back 30 m.

---

4. Useful area of a stadium

Ninth-grader Pete runs three laps around the school stadium in
3.4 minutes at an average speed of 17.654 km/hour. The length of
the stadium is 3.5 times its radius.

Problem:
How many 22-storey office buildings with floor space of 26,400 m²
each will fit inside the stadium?

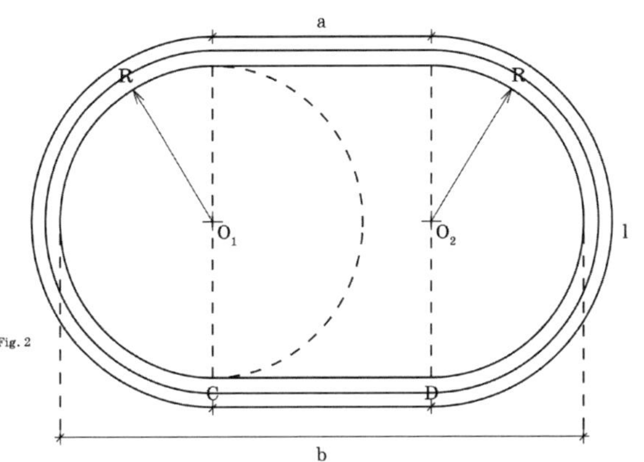

Answer:
The school stadium will hold 6.63 office buildings.

---

5. Stop capitalism! Pressurized slogans.

The political slogan "Stop capitalism!" contains fourteen letters,
one space and one exclamation point. It takes about one second to
write a single letter or exclamation point 30 cm × 35 cm in size.
The entire slogan (35 cm × 5 m on average) takes around thirty
seconds. A 400-ml can of aerosol paint is used up in 496.1 seconds.
One such can costs 180 rubles.

Problem:
How many "Stop capitalism!" slogans can be made using one 400-ml can? How much does each anti-capitalism slogan cost?

Answer:
1. 16.5 slogans will fit inside a single 400-ml can.
2. Each anti-capitalism slogan costs 10.90 rubles.

---

6. Hired demonstrators

With the surge in mass political activity in Russia, the services of hired demonstrators are becoming increasingly popular. Organizers of political movements often use the services of the message board massovki.ru [crowds of extras] to recruit manpower. According to the information posted on the site, the average pay for a hired demonstrator is 500 rubles per event.

The working conditions of these hired laborers are often deplorable, including irregular hours as well as workplaces and sanitary conditions that fail to meet even minimal standards. Their compensation may be held up or not paid at all, and they have no social benefits.

Let's say that Citizen N works regularly as a hired activist. Knowing the heavy demands of his profession, he decides to organize a demonstration of one thousand of his colleagues in support of workers' rights for hired demonstrators. Citizen N must pay the standard fee to each demonstrator.

Problem:
How many demonstrations must Citizen N work in order to save enough money to pay these hired demonstrators, taking into account the fact that brigade leaders (one brigade leader per twenty flag-wavers) are paid ten times more than rank-and-file demonstrators (a2) and that party functionaries (one spin-doctor per 5 brigade-leaders) are paid ten times more than brigade leaders (a3).

Answer:
Citizen N must work 2,500 demonstrations in order to pay a thousand colleagues to attend his demonstration in support of workers' rights for hired demonstrators.

---

7. Mattresses block rivers, but open new ways!

The not-too-distant future. Moscow has been taken over by police forces. Near the Kremlin, the Moscow and Yauza rivers are teeming with protesters. People are using inflatable mattresses to form floating camps. Navigation is completely blocked, and barges and tourist boats are unable to pass. The city has thus found new channels of protest.

The surface area of the Yauza and Moscow rivers inside the Garden Ring is 76.7 ha. Protesters are equipped with four types of mattresses. There is an equal number of each type of flotation device.

Mattress sizes:
1. children's mattress with pillow, 157 × 88 cm, large enough for two adults and four children
2. floating mattress, 189 × 76 cm, gray with headrest, large enough for two adults and two children

3. floating mattress, 183 × 69 cm, with colorful headrest,
large enough for two adults and two children
4. Intex Supreme 66724 air mattress, 191 × 137 cm, large enough
for three adults and six children

Problem:
How many air mattresses of each type will be required to block all
Moscow rivers and canals inside the Garden Ring? How many people should there be on flotation devices in order to block the city's
waterways inside the Garden Ring?

Answer:
1. 116,920 air mattresses will be required to block all Moscow rivers and canals inside the Garden Ring. 2. There should be 613,830 people (263,070 adults and 350,760 children) on flotation devices in order to block the city's waterways inside the Garden Ring.

---

8. Cobblestone as a Weapon of the Proletariat[*]

Sergey Sobyanin, in his first two months after taking office as mayor
of Moscow in late 2010, replaced 400,000 m² of asphalt sidewalk in
the capital's central district with standard concrete paving stones,
190 × 90 × 50 mm in size. The cost per square meter was 3,700
rubles[**]. In clashes with riot police during the March of Millions[***]

[*] *Cobblestone as a Weapon of the Proletariat*
is a well-known work by Soviet sculptor
Ivan Shadr, modeled in plaster in 1927 and
cast in bronze in 1947. The plaster cast is
stored in the Tretyakov Gallery. In 1967 a
bronze copy was erected in the Park of the
December Uprising in Moscow's Presnensky
District. The figure depicted is a generalized
representation of an early-twentieth-century proletarian fighting for revolutionary
ideals and freedom.

[**] The rate of the Russian ruble against the
euro when these problems were being prepared was 39.65 rubles.

[***] On May 6, 2012, following the presidential
inauguration, citizens marched to protest
the start of yet another Putin presidency.
According to the organizers, around 70,000
people took part in the march, and some
2,000 activists were detained as a result
of clashes with police. When this text was
being prepared, 16 people had been charged
with rioting.

---

in May, protesters used pieces of asphalt paving as weapons, since
Bolotnaya Square and the surrounding area, where the events of
May 6 unfolded, had unfortunately not been paved with the easier-
to-handle stones.

Problem:
How much would it have cost city authorities to arm
70,000 marchers (as estimated by the event's organizers) with one
standard-size paving stone each for one well-aimed throw?

Answer:
It would have cost city authorities 4,128,900 rubles to arm 70,000 demonstrators.

---

9. Reduction factor

According to police statistics, 300 people showed up at the March
25 demonstration for honest elections in front of Mariinsky
Palace in St. Petersburg. According to human rights activists,
350 demonstrators were arrested. After the arrests had been
made, at least 500 demonstrators remained on the square.

Problem:
How many people took part in the May 4 solitary picket against the
law prohibiting "homosexual propaganda," assuming the reduction factor used by the Department of Internal Affairs?

Answer:
0.353 person took part in the solitary picket against the law prohibiting homosexual propaganda.

THE LUZHKOV ERA. ARCHITECTURE IN A PERIOD OF TRANSITION, 2012

DARIA PARAMONOVA

More than 20 years have passed since the collapse of the USSR. At first glance, today's society has little in common with that of the early 1990s. However, strictly speaking we are only a continuation of it. My personal connection with the 1990s, as a part of my own past, accords rather poorly with the opinion of colleagues and experts regarding Moscow architecture from that period. This architecture has often been openly criticized, especially after the departure of former mayor Yury Luzhkov. Experts in preservation and architecture critics are of the same opinion: "mediocre design," "the physical framework won't last more than 50 years," "there's a lack of subjects worth preserving." The general opinion boils down to the architecture in the Post-Soviet space being too much of a compromise. Too many external circumstances – social, political, economic – have affected this architecture for it to be considered a proper artistic phenomenon on its own. In other words, the legacy of the period is doomed to perish, according to most observers.

It doesn't seem too difficult to prove that Post-Soviet architecture has no artistic value. True, it doesn't spark with originality, nor does it solve any social problems. Furthermore, it's often built of low-quality, non-durable materials. But perhaps architecture of a new period should be judged according to different criteria than those we traditionally use to judge historical architectural heritage?

After the collapse of the USSR, the ideological vacuum, which replaced the extinct socialist values of "labor, justice, equality," began to be quickly filled with the new values of "profit, property, democracy." At the same time a need emerged to build, almost from scratch, a consumerist world, a thing so despised during the Soviet era. Society rushed to praise the world of comfortable capitalism.

During a short period of time – only 20 years – in Moscow, as well as in Russia, two distinct cultures have emerged and managed to replaced each other – "revolutionary" before the 2000 and "stabilization" until now. However, one unaltered phenomenon persisted in the city during this time – mayor Yury Luzhkov. I use his name to designate this period in the development of Moscow architecture. Yury Luzhkov was appointed mayor in 1992. He was a controversial but nevertheless striking figure. He belongs to the first generation of media politicians, celebrity-politicians, politician-businessmen, and populist politicians. His image was created around symbols which were simple and clear to people – a cap, honey, a broom. His income, his personal life, his opinions were discussed in the press and by the public even after his dismissal. Luzhkov's personal involvement in architectural decisions made him a founder of the new architectural style. "Luzhkov style," as his critics called it, was synonymous with kitsch, tastelessness, and a bluntly commercial architecture reminiscent of a stylized decoration.

The first step in my work to discover the effects of the Luzhkov era was a mechanical gathering of data. That is, a kind of a catalogue of seemingly questionable achievements. However, in the process of the work many buildings tended to be arranged into groups with criteria different from those of architectural classifications. I arranged objects by the newly created criteria based on social and political events of the 1990s and the 2000s. Certainly, architectural criticism of the period has created some notions to describe the emerging styles, among them so called Moscow eclecticism (defined personally by the mayor), or Luzhkov style. However, it seems to me that these notions neither include nor implicate nor describe the complexity and contradictory character of the emerging architectural phenomena. Therefore I have created my own alternative classification.

UNIQUE

Unique objects were designed to be singular and were subjected to the personal taste of the client, architect, or authorities. The goal of uniqueness was primary. Unique objects didn't have city-planning or social objectives, they interacted with the city through the enthusiastic or negative reaction of the spectator. They cannot be judged the same way as architecture of past epochs – aesthetically, from the viewpoint of proportions of elements, tectonics, and general harmony. The aim of the Unique objects was not the creation of harmonious compositions, but a manifestation of a society built of individuals. The objects were created from different elements like collages in order to be special, singular, and to speak as loudly as possible about their authors and/or their clients.

The distinctive feature of Unique objects is form surpassing and determining an architectural ideology. They embody a style created by their context with a speed unusual for architecture. Thus they are constantly in danger under threat of going out of fashion. This is not a matter of decades, as in previous periods – unique object might become irrelevant immediately after construction is completed, when the façade is revealed.

Within this phenomenon, a number of stylistic tendencies can be singled out. These tendencies were shaped by a rapid shift of accents and the manifestation of one's individuality as a fashion – these aspects became particularly relevant in different periods of time. I have marked out six such tendencies:

Play – exaggerated architectural irony, exercises in bright colors and interpretations of forms – "uplifting" motifs, boldness, enthusiasm, fearlessness in the face of the new.

"Contemporary" (necessarily in quotation marks) – creation of a modern look by the use of new external finishing materials (blue mirror glass) and simple geometric forms – construction of a "world of victorious capitalism" as soon as today, surpassing of gradual development, realization of a "leap" in development.

Sculpture – dynamic use of abstract expression forms, form for form's sake – abstraction, isolated thinking, construction of isolated mini-worlds, conflicting with or refusing to accept reality. Self-containing objects.

Context – follows existing context and strives to be unique at the same time. This leads to the creation of a new context, new environment – a split personality, modesty, a manifestation of stability, maturity, civilization.

Neo – (as in neoclassicism) – using and adapting historical styles, sometimes in a quite thorough and detailed manner, sometimes with the author's interpretation – conservatism, eternal values.

"Metabolism" (also in quotation marks) – so called "creative reconstruction," when a building is given a second life with the addition of large, dominating volumes, created in a modernist style, overhanging, devouring, most often seizing the original building from the top – crossing the present with the past, rebuilding the past.

PHOENIX

There are few Phoenix objects – you can count them on your fingers. However, they are entrusted with great responsibility. They were created for the "rectification of ideological errors" of past years and as an attempt to address "pre-Soviet" historical epochs. These tendencies are embodied in the architecture through the idea of recreation.

Recreated buildings would become an instrument for forging new values, a new history, a new collective memory. The utopian approach of restoring historical justice would be applied in downtown Moscow. However, the cultural utopia would in fact be merged by a commercial one. The "commercial functionalism" – as I call it, is a new function of the city space to be a source of profit – invariably went hand in hand with any city-building or architectural activity. It radically transformed the idea of recreation. The rebuilt Cathedral of Christ the Savior became the symbol of the mutated idea of recreation. The project was re-designed and "improved" in the process of construction – as a result, a multifunctional complex emerged in the stylobate of the building, ensuring the "rentability" of the construction.

In the late 2000s Phoenix objects underwent another transformation. The vocabulary of Moscow architects and those interested in the issue was enriched by a new important phrase – "resolution of the commission." The commission decides whether to execute or to pardon. A new formula appeared – "demolition with subsequent recreation." This is the most significant manifestation of the Phoenix phenomenon – from then on, buildings have literally been resurrected immediately after the demolition. One of the most striking cases of such accelerated reconstruction was the demolition and recreation of Voentorg, as well as hotel Moskva. This is the apogee of the penetration of two key notions of the Luzhkov era – recreation and "commercial functionalism." The last generation of Phoenix objects from the late 2000s had a certain mystic quality. During this generation, what had never existed was "recreated." In a certain sense the last, fourth phase unmasks the idea of recreation itself. Embodying the need to address Russian history, the first phase was a response to real demand, modern requirements were added during the second phase, and the third phase imitated the well-grounded procedure. When all the elements mentioned above were combined, the fourth phase became truly absurd. In 2007, the Tsaritsino complex was restored in a form in which it had never existed before. The last Phoenix object of the Luzhkov era was the recreated Kolomensky palace. Transferred to another location, turned by 90 degrees, forged of monolithic material, and paneled with wood, it was opened on 4 September 2010. On 28 September Luzhkov was dismissed.

MASSIVES. MUTANTS

Modern panel blocks I call simply Massives in my classification, from the Russian phrase "Residential Massives" (Zhilye Massivy). Being the most effective way to get a return on investments, new neighborhoods weren't designed to create residential areas. This is why residential massives in the Post-Soviet society became simply massives. Massives of square meters.

In the last 20 years, privatization has become the most important thing phenomenon in the life of Muscovites. The introduction of private property in the early 1990s drastically changed the way city-dwellers interacted with their places of residence. The ownership of a space filled with air, limited by walls, floors, and ceilings, at a certain height became material evidence of changes in life. But most importantly, this space could be put on the market. Monetization of flats and the growing demand for comfortable living, induced by new values, led to a construction boom and the emergence of the most stable currency of the subsequent decades – square meters. The crossing of the *microrayon* model with the emerging market economy resulted in an architectural mutant. The principles of planning, which were developed in the Soviet era, ideally suited the ideology of the future communist state – that of universal equality. In the new period these principles moved into a new, in fact, nonviable model, accompanied by a complex of external improvements that only camouflaged it. Everything that couldn't return an investment vanished from planning schemes. Standard components demanded visual diversity. Enviromental quality wasn't considered at all, since it didn't affect the cost of flats, due to lack of alternatives. Soviet residential areas were created according to the principles of zoning and accessibility to key public objects. They were ideologically oriented towards creating a comfortable environment for life and leisure of the worker, tired after hard working day in the factory. Massives, on the contrary, were built around a visual, flexible, expressive planning solution and the multiplication of square meters, which raised in proportion the cost of flats, as if emphasizing the importance of new values – the seeming freedom of choice, a mark of the free society, in accordance with the income of the seemingly free citizen. Ideally fit for the ideology of the Soviet state, the Massives perfectly suited the ideology of the newborn capitalism in the Post-Soviet era.

IDENTIFIERS

Social stratification on the basis of income inequality brought to life new kinds of real estate. In the early 1990s new terminology appeared, including "elite," "social," and "business class" housing. Various social groups demanded different approaches to the external and planning solutions of residential houses. This led to individual housing projects, as opposed to the standard, serial nature of the Massives. Unlike Unique objects, buildings in this group lack a client, i.e. one for whom the house is built. More precisely, there is a client, but it is more of a generalized character suggested either by the intuition of the architect or market research. The accuracy of a hit with a desired image ensures the success and the realization of a project. Later the evolution of this individualistic line in the architecture of the last two decades would lead to a situation when the style and image of an architectural object in general would have to fit with the group of familiar stories with which the client identifies herself himself. A "market of urban stereotypes" emerged. Identifiers are special markers of a kind which help the city-dweller to discover which consumption group he belongs to in the emerging market space.

Identifiers include stylistic tendencies which emphasize the importance of local images. The particular qualities of these images reveal their origin. Therefore, the transformation of the images is the transformation of consumers themselves. One of the first popular images was the Legend/Fairytale – using the elements of a castle/palace – pinnacles, forged decorations, the crossing of something very private (an image of a castle, a country estate) with a high-rise building. The result is a "gigantic multiple-apartment cottage." Various references to Stalinist architecture are also popular – elements of classic architecture in arbitrary order, natural stone, bricks, camel and brown colors, bay windows, and rotundas. An imitation of belonging to the intellectual elite. A true star of this style, a symbol of the omnipotence of investors, and an apogee of anonymity is the Triumph Palace – a building claiming the name of the "eighth Moscow high-rise." This new Moscow high-rise doesn't have an architect author; an unpronounceable abbreviation is behind the "highest residential building in Europe."

FUNGUS

A phenomenon that I call "Fungus" is a radical manifestation of the "commercial functionalism." Fungus includes various mostly temporary constructions in the service of commodity-money relations of city-dwellers. This is a response, embodied in space, to the fact that city space can generate profit. Mostly due to the lack of any regulation or external interference during a rather long period of time, the nature of Fungus resembles very much the nature of a living organism adapting to the characteristics of its environment. Fungus "grows" in any part of the city where the conditions exist – or more precisely, where its growth is not controlled. Fungus typology is vast. It includes monofunctional commercial objects, such as all kinds of city advertisement, kiosks, shopping centers and markets, i.e. meta-objects with commerce as their sole function. One of the important aspects of the Fungus kingdom is its anonymity – these objects don't have authors, Fungus is very often illegal and grows uncontrollably, despite its large size. Its distribution in the city space follows certain natural patterns. Fungus settles in sites where there are high concentrations of people. It favors closed spaces hidden from external light, for example, pedestrian subways, tunnels, and colonnades. Another peculiar quality of Fungus is its "family" mode of existence – one object immediately attracts others; they form a spawn – mycelium. Fungus is difficult to eradicate, one object attracts others, hence its tendency to form concentrated sprawls. Fungus tends to have a parasitic mode of living. Fungus can be classified according to the type of parasitic behavior: symbiotic–may have mutually beneficial or antagonistic relations, i.e. defend or destroy its "host"; type of distribution – surface-based: advertisements, signs favoring old buildings, construction fences and façades of modernist buildings; individuals – free-standing singular Fungi. The smallest individuals are kiosks, the biggest are shopping malls and markets. Fungus is characterized by the following appearance traits – a wealth of bright typographic compositions, simplified design, lightweight and mobile materials – plastics, aluminum, and cardboard. Fungus has a fragile structure that emphasizes its function – it is easily moved, transported, and changes its location and purpose.

"The role of Fungus in the city and human economy can not be overstated." Fungus exists in all types of city environments. These are both the objects serving the city-dwellers' firsthand needs and the objects of infrastructure crucial for the prosperity of individual businesses. In other words, Fungus is a stakeholder in mutually beneficial ecosystems which form the nature of a city. On the other hand, however, Fungus can cause severe harm. When capturing a certain territory, Fungus can inflict harm upon the external characteristics of the objects or the environment, and can even be the cause of death of some city territories. While it exists, Fungus has often been subjected to different kinds of regulation, but it still remains an important representative of the city ecosystem. The distribution of Fungus radically changed the external characteristics of city space, its fabric, and the behavioral models of its citizens.

Liquid city. The legacy of the period of transformation has a fragile structure. The process of transformation itself cannot be captured. Moscow architecture after the collapse of the USSR emerged in a moment of transition from one society to another. It has a gene of eternal liquidity. Most of this architecture is not designed "for centuries to come." Its fluid essence presupposes the possibility of constant cyclical changes of fashions, tastes, and tendencies.

The determination of the value of a certain object according to existing canons leaves out "inferior" architecture. Buildings created with contemporary materials will hardly remain after 50 years to become objects of architectural heritage. A textual record is a way of describing,what may perish in five years. In a certain sense it is a way of preservation in itself.

Contemporary architecture of Moscow hasn't invented its own style and hasn't created any masterpieces in the usual sense. Nevertheless, it has recorded, reflected, and emphasized the most important events of a period of transformation.

Excerpt from an essay written as part of the educational program at the research studio *Preservation*, Strelka Institute of Media, Architecture and Design

VOLGA PSYCOGEOGRAPHY, 2012
LABORATORY GROUP, SAMARA

The participants in the conversation are members of the Laboratory artistic group based in Samara: Vladimir Logutov, Ilya Samorukov, Konstantin Zatsepin, Aleksandr Lashmankin

1. AN ENCOUNTER WITH URBAN SPACE AND THE PRACTICE OF DISORIENTATION

Vladimir Logutov: What is the usual experience of an urban environment? Every person has internal psychogeographic "maps" that they "carry around with themselves." We do not experience our own "encounter" with space in a familiar environment. A person has a visual scheme of space and he passes through it, relying on certain, provisionally speaking, landmarks. He travels on the bus without seeing it. A person really encounters space only after he has become estranged from it. When you go somewhere for a year, and then come back and again encounter this space, you truly see it. While in the case of dérive, an encounter with space occurs, and therefore processes of disorientation begin to function. With their help, a psychological effect is produced in which you suddenly for no apparent reason see this space, as it were, anew, for the first time. For me, the main thing in dérive is encountering a new point of space each time. It's interesting that this always occurs through certain "doors." That is, there exists a sort of "entrance" into this state, a mechanism of displacement, the role of which can be played, for example, by a sign. Let's say that I'm walking down the street in some particular way and suddenly I decide to do it differently, to break my existing habit. And now that I'm doing something different, there's a shift in which a certain encounter takes place. I can sit on the ground, lie down, look at the surrounding world from beneath, for instance, from a height of twenty centimeters off the ground. In this way I see space completely differently.

Aleksandr Lashmankin: Things become unaccustomed and you begin to distinguish details that were earlier hidden. A strange feeling arises that you have moved into some other reality. A city is not only a space, but also the particular rhythmic system of the city. If we change our rhythm of motion, our perception of reality also changes; our subjectivity changes.

V.L.: A person has a particular psychogeographic map that he can adjust. It's like finishing off a picture; you can touch it off, but without creating it, without reaching out to it, but really seeing it. To see this new picture of reality, you need to instill particular habits in yourself. You create your own space, your own city.

A.L.: By the way, a city can be disclosed not only as an architectural reality, but also as a human reality. You remember how we unexpectedly found an ashberry tree on the street that hadn't been cut down, but surrounded by the wall of a house that had been specially curved so as to not hinder the tree from growing. Architecture had adapted to nature so as not to kill it. Someone could have killed this tree, but instead he was ready to spend time and effort to save it.

Konstantin Zatsepin: It seems to me that the most unique case of dérive is connected with falling – for various reasons – out of one's accustomed social dimensions. It is an incomparable "trip" to come home at seven in the morning. Traditionally, this time, which is maximally far away from any strolling around, is extremely socially organized. Streams of people travel about on their strictly defined working routes. You can meet only either doormen or the most hardcore urban marginals, the homeless. There are a lot of them in fact, a lot more than it usually seems to us, because we don't seem them in our everyday lives. But there they are, walking along beside you, and at that moment it seems like the whole city consists only of them and you have fallen into their reality, into a whole world peoples with characters. It has its own semiotic system, its own structure of codes, of recognition. These people reckon with each other without thinking of us. And we don't think of them. We are indistinguishable "white noise" to each other. They live as if in nature, in a forest. For them, the city is devoid of urban signs.

A.L.: Yes, the city looks completely different to different social groups. Therefore, alternative groups can observe it from one side, as a completed visual picture.

2. STALKING IN A RAREFIED ENVIRONMENT

V.L.: In the local context of Samara, the most visually interesting object that there is is the Volga. A colossal boundary between two banks, two worlds.

K.Z.: The dominant feature of the landscape here is horizontality. In Samara, wherever you are, the feeling of being in a flatland never leaves you. You don't recognize yourself in the stone jungle. There is no boundary between the urban and the nonurban. From above, the geographical contours of Samara distantly resemble Manhattan. However, their landscapes are simply opposite. There what is important is that contrast between the verticality of the buildings and the flatness of the water. Here, everything is flat. Even the mountains on the other bank are low and create a perfectly even horizon. The Samaran model of vision is a sort of generalized Mark Rothko, that is, the perception of the landscape "in stripes": the river, small mountains, the sky...

Ilya Samorukov: The geographical space of Samara is not only flat, but completely rarefied. All this Volga wideness is an important dissipating factor for perception.

K.Z.: Yes, the Volga emptiness, especially palpable in the winter.

A.L.: The very act of contemplating the river space acts on the psyche in a relaxing way. The effect has been described: when the gaze is not hindered by anything on which is could focus, the brain "discharges." We are beings that fill in 85% of what they see in a picture. This is a physiological fact: when we see an open space undisturbed by any verticality, or cerebral cortex starts to relax. Because the work that needs to be done to "fill in" such a space is minimal. It discharges, freeing the brain from unnecessary work on producing reality.

K.Z.: And consciousness passes from external objects, turning inward. It focuses on itself.

A.L.: While someone in an urban milieu needs to meditate for a long time to achieve this state of mind, here it's enough to just look at the Volga for five minutes to receive the same "purifying" effect.

K.Z.: By the way, various types of horizontality can be distinguished. For instance, Kazakhs on the steppes are one thing. The view of the steppe is clearly a different type of "relaxation" than we have with water.

A.L.: Water, in contrast to the steppe, is a barrier that cannot be crossed.

V.L.: It can only be passed over. Moreover, water is a dynamic environment, in distinction from the steppe, which is static.

K.Z.: And that's why the subject located on the steppe thinks of motion on it as something natural. While we understand about the river that it's necessary to exert effort, embark on an adventure.

I.S.: Our neosituationist dérive is one such "adventure," fully bound up with our local context.

V.L.: A sort of "stalking."

I.S.: I remember our "hikes" together with contemporary visionaries who had come to Samara at different times. We always go along the Volga, no matter who has come. And while we're walking, we start to become aware of our distinctiveness. There's something symptomatic about this. People from the capital feel a genuine shock when they come into contact with real nature. For them, its spooky to be in the middle of a river, on the ice, right after they've been sitting in a restaurant. Our spatial experience is different. The practices of entering into nature are internally closer to us. They are inherent to us from the beginning, like, for example, ethnicity. While wandering around with people from other cities, a completely different conscious understanding was operating in us of the naturalness of interacting with open natural landscapes.

3. NATURE AS A WORK

K.Z.: In our local space, there are other symbolic points of attraction. For example, the enormous abandoned quarry that supplied the limestone for the city constructions.

V.L.: That quarry is an important instance of antiurban space. The whole from which the body of the modern city came. A "track" on the body of nature.

A.L.: Yes, a lacuna that formed after they took the body out of it that makes up the urban structure.

V.L.: To put it in another way, it is nature, from out of the body of which they removed what later became the city. We have interpreted this place as a closed-off space, a "gallery" of sorts, where an open type of work can be created. Here, we are creating a particular object, adding, as it were, to its aesthetic "body."

K.Z.: Moreover, this body is absorbing not only a material side, but also the context of possible utterances, meanings, symbols that can be thought up around the object. In this way, its symbolic body can grow endlessly, "being filled in," coming back here again.

V.L.: In this case, the artistic technique is time itself, its flowing.

I.S.: For example, tires on a tree. A tree growing through one tire can be an accident.

V.L.: But not two.

I.S.: That is, there need to be some "border width" that shows the nonaccidental nature of this idea.

A.L.: Yes, we come later on, add some points, finish the picture. Moreover, it can develop on its own, "adding to itself." Later two tires will hang there, almost torn into pieces by the mighty tree. If we keep going there ten years, a new, completely formed environment may arise.

V.L.: In principle, this is an open work that can never be completely brought to an end. This idea of a slow, open work is also absolutely antiurban.

K.Z.: I would not divide the natural from the urban so sharply. In the end, not only is the urban a result of nature, but nature is the result of human activity.

K.L.: Sure, we have in essence never even seen the Volga; we've seen only Saratov's water reservoir. We always forget that it is not simply a river, but a chain of reservoirs. It is not the Volga, but in many ways an artificial object.

I.S.: In general, isn't contemporary nature something that man has created? The idea of a dichotomy between culture and nature has not worked for a long time. We have not seen a single wild tree for a long time; all the trees are cultivated.

K.L.: The idea of nature in general arises as something initially human. When there were no people, there was no nature. Even untouched natural objects like national parks have remained in this form only thanks to human activity.

K.Z.: Our local specificity may consist in this – a blurring away of any dichotomy or difference: between the natural and the urban, the artistic and the extra-artistic? The appearance of any oppositions in our situation inescapably entails their becoming problematic, put into doubt.

TONY SMITH, 1966

[...] It was a dark night and there were no lights or shoulder markers, lines, railings or anything at all except the dark pavement moving through the landscape of the flats, rimmed by hills in the distance, but punctuated by stacks, towers, fumes and colored lights. This drive was a revealing experience. The road and much of the landscape was artificial, and yet it couldn't be called a work of art. On the other hand, it did something for me that art has never done. At first I didn't know what it was, but its effect was to liberate me from many of the views I had about art. It seemed that there was a reality there which had not had any expression in art. The experience on the road was something mapped out but not socially recognized. I thought to myself, it ought to be clear that's the end of art.

**From *Talking with Tony Smith*,
by Samuel J. Wagstaff Jr., *Artforum*,
December 1966**

Contributed by Alexandra Sukhareva

SOVIET ARCHITECTURE OF THE FIRST FIVE-YEAR PLAN, 1980
VIGDARIA KHAZANOVA

[...]

Nikolay Kuzmin was occupied with the spatial organization of the environment that man lives in. The author's method boiled down to the rigid partitioning of man's life outside of manufacturing into a series, as they said at that time, of needs, processes, and functions. 1) relaxation-sleep, 2) relaxation requiring quiet and isolation, 3) relaxation connected with movement and noise, 4) individual work (mental) requiring quiet and isolation, 5) collective work, 6) child-rearing, 7) nourishment, 8) public service [...] Out of all the components of the daily process architecturally the most uninteresting for the author turned out to be the forcedly passive part, like sleep, which requires isolated quarters. Kuzmin resolutely wrote: "In a commune home workers sleep in a bedroom but live in a cultural center."[1] Waking up at 6 in the morning to a radio alarm, communards could tidy their rooms in five minutes and start their exercises. Families in the usual meaning of the word do not exist. Children live independently, occasionally interacting with their parents. But Kuzmin specifically defined even the word "parents" – like "husband" and "wife" previously, as the former "family framework." They differ from other members of the commune only in their ability to use a "double sleeping cabin."

[1] Nikolay Kuzmin, *Problems of the Scientific Organization of Everyday Life.*

Vigdaria Khazanova, from *Soviet Architecture of the First Five-Year Plan*, Moscow, Nauka, 1980

Contributed by Alexandra Paperno

IDA, LAURA, MARISA: IN A MUSEUM TO WASH SHEETS AND BLANKETS, 2012

FABIO BOCCATO

On the island of Giudecca an exhibit by the Russian artist Arseniy Zhilyaev attracts locals and tourists: It's a free laundromat. A day spent among laundromat visitors.

Venice. "It will be taken away on the 25th of November," the rumor was spread around Giudecca that brought women rushing here. On entering the laundromat one can clearly feel a nervous excitement, especially among the people waiting in line. The laundromat is open every day except Tuesdays and Sundays. Business hours are from 10 am to 2 pm. "It's only open 5 days a week and for 4 hours a day – it's not enough!" *signora* Laura, who lives nearby, almost yells. And so she is already standing in line here at 9:30 am in the cold wind. Behind her in line are three more people. The *signora* is using two of the four washing machines. A blanket, dark colored clothes, bedding. A young Spanish girl reproaches her: "There are a lot of us here, and we all need to wash things." *Signora* Laura raises her voice: "I already waited two hours the other day but then I had to leave. There's a line and today it's my turn. I need all morning to wash everything." They're both yelling, but the *signora* comes out on top. "On the other hand, after she's done we can have the same right to the machines," whispered the girl when the *signora* had left. "As it is, we'll all patiently wait our turn."

Zhilyaev's laundromat has been quite successful. No one calls it by that name in Giudecca but none the less "the owner" is Russian. His name is Arseniy Zhilyaev. In fact, the laundromat is a work of art, and the people who come here, including *signora* Laura, are his collaborators even though they don't realize it. The laundromat has a name. It's called, with a little bit of sarcasm, "Forthcoming Dawn." The public laundromat is indeed located inside the building Casa dei Tre Oci, in which *The Way of Enthusiasts* exhibition is taking place, organized by the Moscow V-A-C foundation, a project with a collateral program of the Architecture Biennale. Only the laundromat closes at 2 pm, while the exhibition itself is open until 6 pm. Entry is free. The washing machines and two dryers are in a room on the first floor to the right of the staircase. Installing a laundry facility in an exhibit in a palazzo directly across from St Mark's Basilica is truly a unique experience. But at the same time it's a quite ordinary situation for the hundreds of people who use the laundromat – from the people who live close by to the tourists from the neighboring hotels.

Moreover, the laundromat is free. One needs only to ask for detergent, a token for the washer, and another for the dryer. Of course, there are those who take one token, and there are those who take more (like, for example, *signora* Laura, who explains that it's better to wash everything twice). A young man working at the exhibition hall watches to ensure that visitors don't use their own detergent and clog up the machines like they had done earlier. "On average we give out about 80 tokens a day," says Ilaria from the Civita Tre Venezie, which together with the Fondazione Froma manages the Casa dei Tre Oci project. And she adds, "This artwork has transformed into a real public place. Entire blocks of people come here." In response to the visitors' argument Ilaria laughs, "Well perhaps, they raise their voices a bit sometimes, but everyone's great. They stand in line, help each other, explain everything to newcomers." Someone arrives with a pillow, someone with a large plastic bag, even someone with a suitcase. Anna Maria, a woman in a jumpsuit with a wool headband, asks a young American whether he can help her fold up her sheets, and in the end becomes interested in knowing whether he ever wants to get married. Another girl here has a date with a hairdresser, and she's asking what she should do – style her hair or get a new haircut. Some curious people come up to take a look at the exhibit. The soviet laundromat replaced a real, pay laundromat that a few months ago was still not far from here. It appears that it closed due to protests from the people living above it. "We actually really need it. What will we do without it?" says *signora* Marisa, sorrowfully shaking her head.

Fabio Boccato, *Ida, Laura, Marisa: In a museum to wash sheets and blankets***, from** *Corriere del Veneto***, November 19, 2012**

Contributed by Arseny Zhilyaev

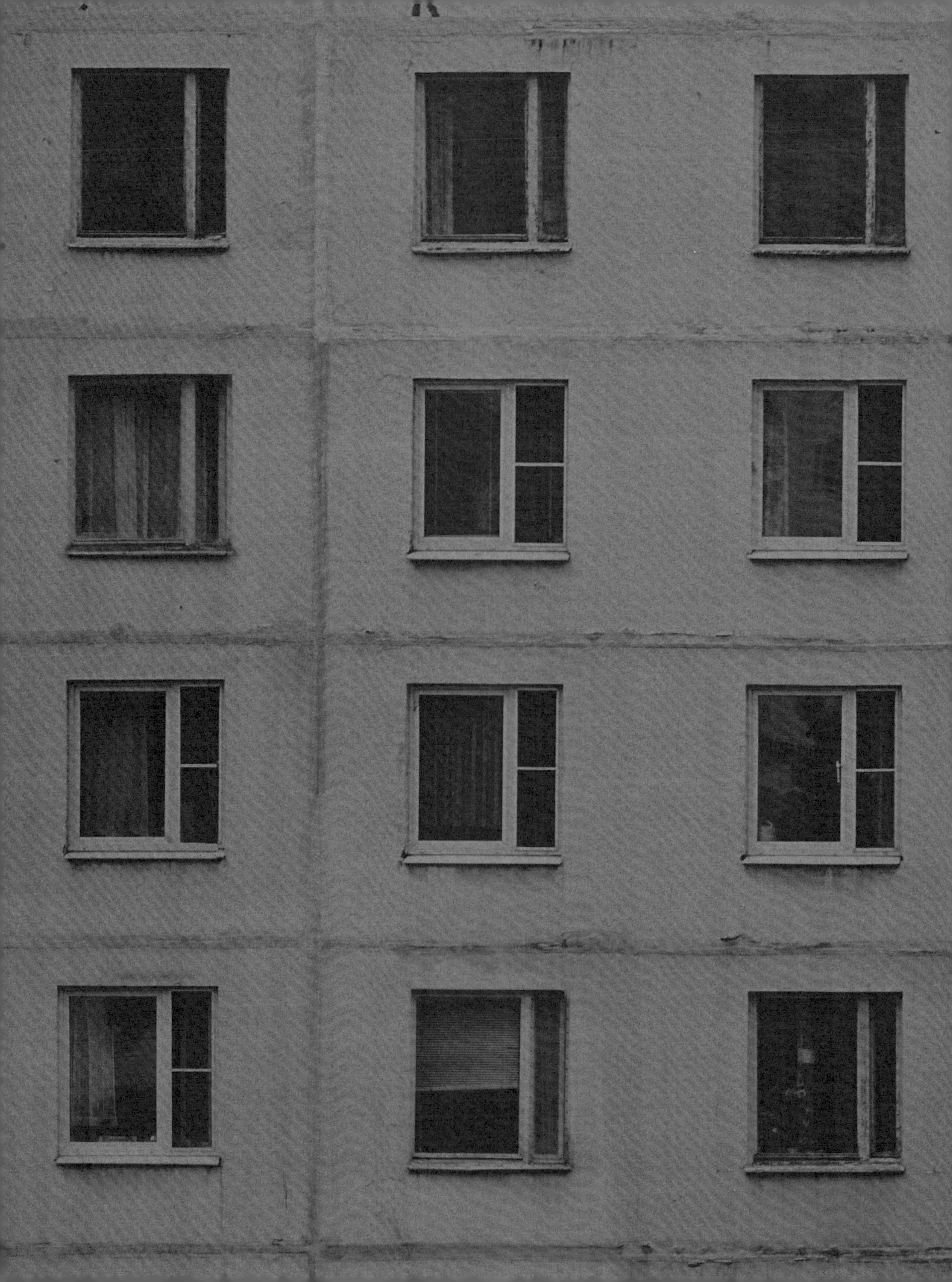

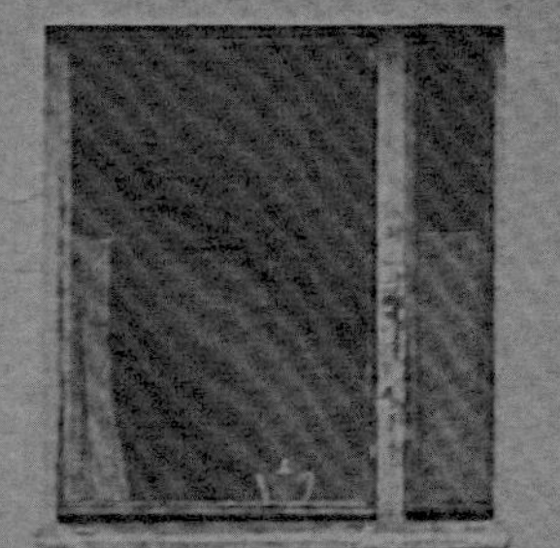
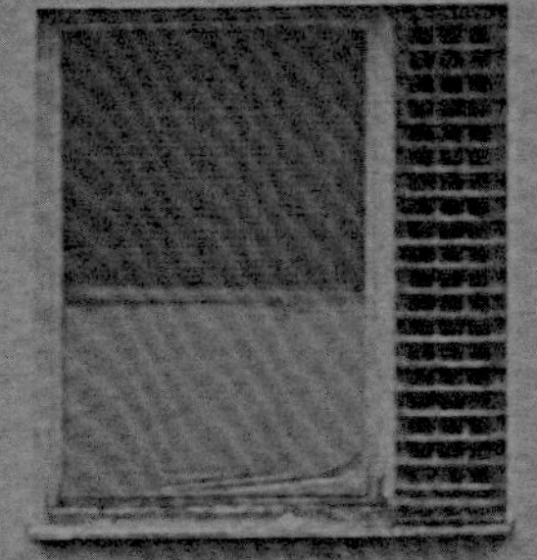
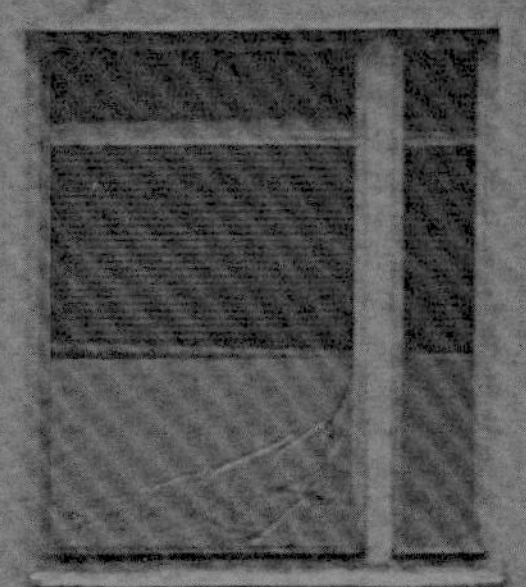

BIOGRAPHIES

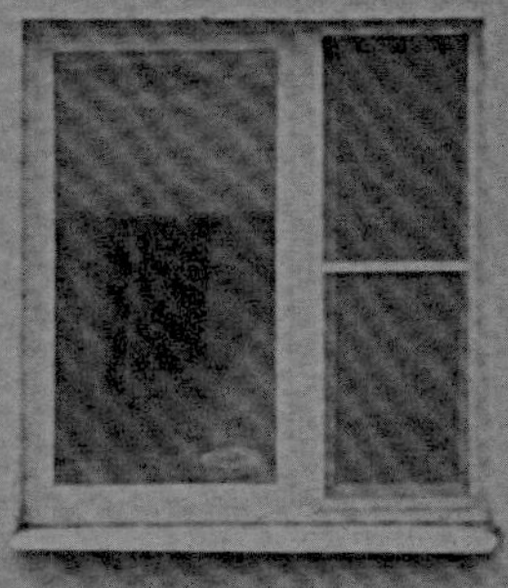
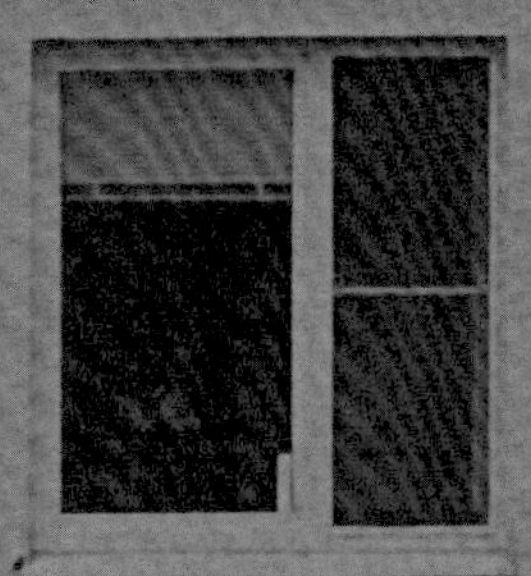
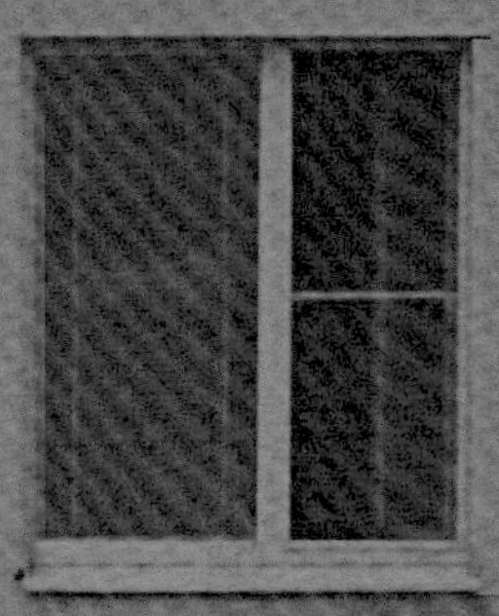

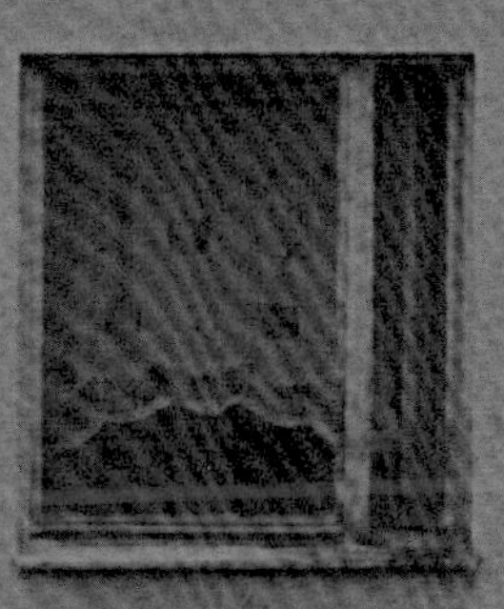

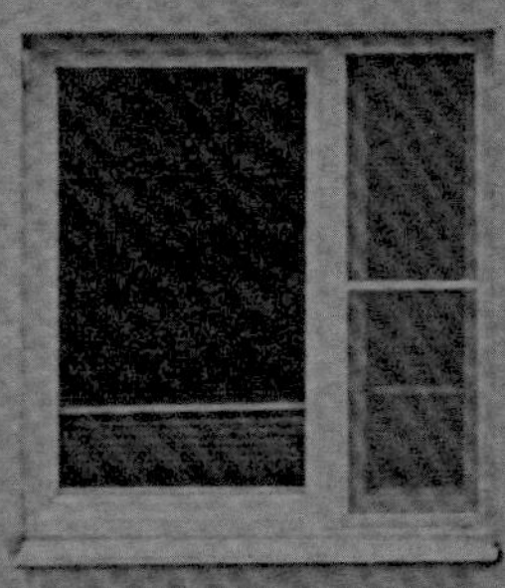
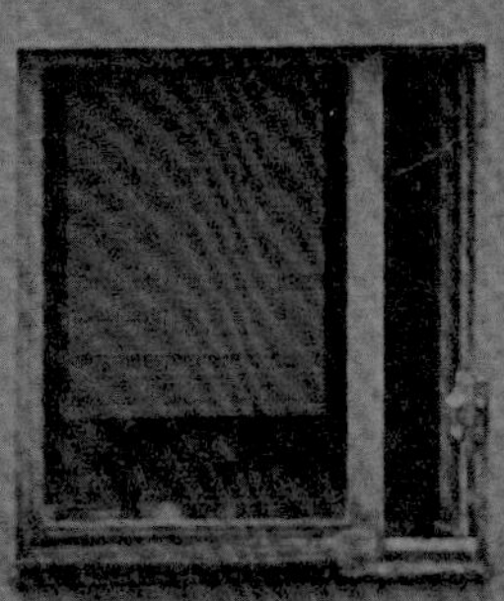
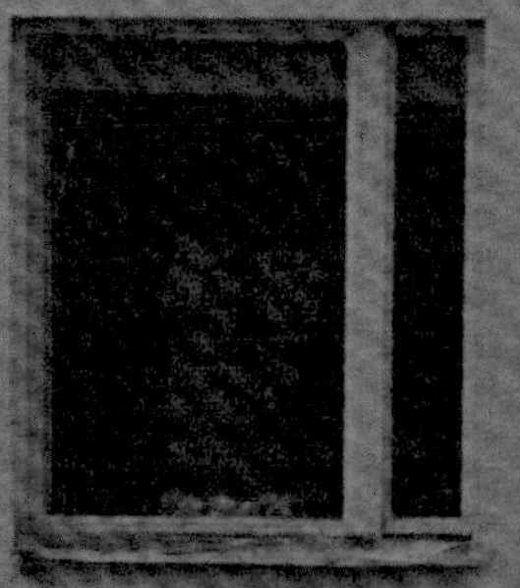

THE ARTISTS

IVAN BRAZHKIN

Born in 1985 in Rostov-on-Don,
lives and works in Moscow

Ivan Brazhkin started as a poet and musician. He has been participating in exhibition projects in Russia and abroad since 2002. He took part in numerous actions of Radek Community (2002-2004), collaborated with various leftist political organizations. Works with different media, from video and installation to graphics and sculpture. His work critiques the period of capitalism's normalization, when new market values cultivating individualism and consumption were superimposed on the old ways of life. Within his latest group shows are *Monuments and documents*, Tretyakov State Gallery, Moscow, 2012; *Angry Birds*, Warsaw Museum of Modern Art, 2012; *The False Calculations Presidium*, Museum of Business and Philanthropy, Moscow, 2011; *Impossible Community*, Moscow Museum of Modern Art, 2011; *Art against nazism*, Moscow metro, 2011; *ON/OFF*, special project for the 4th Moscow Biennale of Contemporary Art, 2011.

ALEXANDR BURLAKA

Born in 1982 in Kiev,
lives and works in Kiev

Graduated from the Kiev National University of Construction and Architecture. Architect and member of the art groups "Gruppa Predmetiv," "Melnychuk-Burlaka" and of the interdisciplinary curatorial association *Hudrada.*

Whithin his selected exhibitions: *Ukrainian news* (together with I. Melnychuk), Centre for Contemporary Art Ujazdowski Castle, Warsaw, 2013; *In charge of the edition*, Visual Culture Research Center, Kiev, 2012; *Search. Other spaces* (together with I. Melnychuk), Foundation Center for Contemporary Art, Kiev, 2013; *City Porn* (together with I. Melnychuk), Visual Culture Research Center, Kiev, 2011; The First Ural Industrial Biennial (together with N. Kadan), Ekaterinburg, 2010; *"IF"* (together with N. Kadan), PERMM, Perm, 2010. He took part in the Ukrainian-Polish special project *Double Game*, part of the Arsenal 2012 (Warsaw), Kiev, 2010.

OLGA CHERNYSHEVA

Born in 1962 in Moscow,
lives and works in Moscow

She studied at the Moscow Cinema Academy and Rijksakademie Van Beeldende Kunsten in Amsterdam. Olga Chernysheva captures everyday life in post-communist Russia in her photographs, videos, paintings, drawings and object-based works. She observes sceptically and ironically uncovering the humour and contradictions that underpin Russian society as it goes through a long period of upheaval. Her works lyrically investigate the fabric of individuality and self-sufficiency, and meditate upon the role of the artist in a time of flux.

Her solo exhibitions include *Pro-portions*, The State Russian Museum, Saint Petersburg, 1995; *Second Life*, 49th Venice Biennale, Russian Pavilion, 2001; *Emerging Figures*, White Space Gallery, London, 2005; *Isle of Sparks*, Foxy Production, New York, 2007; *Adventure Istiklal*, Istanbul Biennial, Yapi Kredi Kazim Taskent Art Gallery, Istanbul, 2009; *Olga Chernysheva*, Calvert 22, London, 2010; *In the Middle of Things*, BAK, Utrecht, 2011; *Clippings*, Galerie Volker Diehl, Berlin, 2011.

COLLECTIVE ACTIONS GROUP (CA)

From 1976 in Moscow

The group was founded in 1976. Now, nearly 35 years later, most of the CA original members: Andrei Monastyrski, Nikolai Panitkov, Igor Makarevich, Elena Elagina, Sergei Romashko, Sabine Hansgen continue to work together (Nikita Alexeev left the group in 1983 and Georgy Kizewalter in 1989). The group staged 125 performances which have been documented in the ten-volume (volume 11 is a work-in-progress) *Trips Out of Town* anthology. As early as 1977, only a year alter the group was formed, *Flash Art*, at the time a leading international art magazine, published a major article about CA with a photograph of one of their performances on the cover. The same year documentation of CA's actions was exhibited at the Venice Biennale. The group's actions attracted *creme de la creme* of the flourishing Moscow avantgarde scene which at the time was really on the world level. Ilya Kabakov, Oleg Vasiliev, Eric Bulatov, Ivan Chuikov, Vsevolod Nekra-

sov, Boris Groys, Lev Rubinstein, Dmitry Alexandrovich Prigov, Alexander Rabinovich, Alexei Liubimov, Leonid Sokov, Francisco Infante, Eduard Gorokhovsky, Joseph Backstein, Mukhomor and Medical Hermeneutics art groups and many other artists, poets, musicians and critics were all there – as viewers as well as participants and therefore co-creators.

ALEXEY DUSHKIN

Born in 1964 in Moscow,
lives and works in Moscow

Alexey Dushkin is an artist and designer. He was born in Moscow in a family of famous Soviet architects and artists. Studied at Moscow Architectural Institute (MARKHI). He is the member of Russian Designer Union. Dushkin is a participant and winner of major international exhibitions and festivals including ARCH MOSCOW (2010, 2012), International Festival of Architecture & Interior Design (2011, 2010, 2004), Moscow Biennale of Contemporary Art (2009), ART MOSCOW (2009). He has collaborated in a number group exhibitions such as *Living Space* (together with Alexandra Paperno), Paperworks gallery, Moscow, 2010; *For Fair Elections* (together with Natalia Vitsina), Paperworks gallery, Moscow, 2012.

ALEXANDRA GALKINA

Born in 1982 in Moscow,
lives and works in Moscow

After studying at the school of contemporary art of Avdei Ter-Oganyan in Moscow in 1997-1998, Galkina became a member of the Radek Community until 2005. In her practice, Galkina observes and highlights discreet elements found within Russian urban environment. She aims to draw attention to the extent in which urban living promotes or restricts civil-rights, personal liberties, and independent decision-making processes.

Her solo exhibitions include *Painted-Over Graffiti, Stencils*, Tretyakov State Gallery, Moscow, 2003-2004; *Untitled*, Vitrina Gallery, ARTStrelka Cultural centre, Moscow, 2005; *You're under arrest* (in collaboration with David Ter-Oganyan), Basmanny District Internal Affairs Department, Moscow,

2006; *Peep Show*, Cheryomushki Apartment Gallery, Moscow, 2009.

Actively participates in exhibitions in Russia and abroad: *Na kurort!*, Baden-Baden, 2004; *Collective Creativity*, Kunsthalle Fridericianum, Kassel, 2005; *Accomplices*, Tretyakov State Gallery, Moscow, 2005; *Modus R: Russian Formalism Today*, Newton Building, Miami, 2006; *Progressive Nostalgia*, Centro per l'arte Contemporanea Luigi Pecci, Prato, 2007; *The Young. Aggressive*, Musashino Art University Museum & Library, Tokyo, 2008; *Modernikon. Contemporary Art from Russia*, Fondazione Sandretto Re Rebaudengo, Turin, 2010; *Angry Birds*, Warsaw Museum of Modern Art, 2011; *ON/OFF*, special project for the 4th Moscow Biennale of Contemporary Art, 2011.

KIRILL GLUSCHENKO

Born in 1983 in Kaliningrad,
lives and works in Moscow

Studied at Moscow Institute of the Problems of Contemporary Art and Valand School of Fine Arts, Gotheborg, Sweden. He participated in several exhibitions, among which are *Curated by Vest*, Greta Insam Gallery, Vienna, 2011; *Interiority*, Proekt Fabrika, Moscow; *From the Realm of the Practical Knowledge*, special project for the 4th Moscow Biennale of Contemporary Art, 2011; *Junk*, Moscow Museum of Modern Art, 2009; *Art After the End of History*, Central House of Artist, Moscow; *Kafka 575*, National Center of Contemporary Art (NCCA), Kaliningrad.

Kirill Gluschenko works mainly with book production and photography. His latest projects are created as the books published by Gluschenkoizdat, the artist's imaginary publishing house that sends the artists to the small towns of the former Soviet country and creates the book about it. Through the portraits of the cities he observes the mythologization of the Soviet Union reality.

GNEZDO GROUP

(GENNADY DONSKOY, MIKHAIL ROSHAL, VIKTOR SKERSIS)

From 1975 to 1979 in Moscow

Gennady Donskoy, Mikhail Roshal and Victor Skersis were 18 years old in 1975 when they established the group "Gnezdo" (The Nest). They attended Vitaly Komar and Alexander Melamid's class at the art school in Moscow and for five years produced valuable works prefiguring many types of street actions and performances of the Russian art scene of the next three decades. In 1975 they made their first intervention at the House of Culture of the Exhibition of National Economic Achievements (VDNKh) that signed the beginning of their collaboration. The group broke up in 1979.

MARIA KAPRANOVA

Born in 1988 in Krasnogorsk,
lives and works in Moscow

Studied the Theory and History of Culture in Russian State University for the Humanities. Currently studying at the Moscow School of New Cinema. She works as a film editor with various kinds of video production, documentary, feature films, music videos.

ANDREY KUZKIN

Born in Moscow in 1979,
lives and works in Moscow

Andrey Kuzkin graduated in 2001 as a graphic designer from the Moscow State University of Printing Arts. In 2006 he became a member of the Moscow Union of Artists. He has since then participated in numerous group and solo exhibitions.

These include *Andrey Kuzkin. First Personal Exhibition. Everything I Wanted To Say, But Found Myself Unable To*, Art-Strelka Gallery, Moscow, 2009; *Identity Crisis*, Open Gallery, Moscow, 2009; *The Space of Silence*, Red Banner Factory, Saint Petersburg, 2009; *America: between Europe and Asia*, Shiryaevo Biennale, Shiryaevo village, Russia, 2009; *Modernikon. Contemporary Art from Russia*, Fondazione Sandretto Re Rebaudengo, Turin, 2010; the 6th Berlin Biennale for Contemporary Art in 2010.

VLADIMIR LOGUTOV

Born in Samara in 1980,
lives and works in Samara

Studied Fine Arts at Samara Teachers' Training University (2002-2006) followed by the scholarship for art studies at Stuttgarter kunstverein, Stuttgart, Germany (2005).

Logutov is primarily a video artist, he often combines film and computer editing to highlight the concepts of accidental and spontaneity amidst the routine. He also work in painting, installations and sculptures. Organized and curated several exhibitions and festivals of contemporary art. He participated in the numerous international art projects such as *The Unseen*, Fourth Guangzhou Triennial, Guangdong Museum of Art, 2012; *Modernikon. Contemporary Art from Russia*, Fondazione Sandretto Re Rebaudengo, Turin, 2010 and Casa dei Tre Oci, Venice, 2011; Moscow Biennale of Contemporary Art (2007 and 2009); *MODUS R*, Art Basel Miami Beach, 2006; *Urban formalism*, Moscow Museum of Modern Art, 2007.

ANDREI MONASTYRSKI

Born in 1949 in Pechenga,
lives and works in Moscow

Since 1975 the practice of Monastyrski oscillates between installation, action objects, writings and performances; one of the leaders of Collective Actions (CA) group (1976-2010); author of *Trip Out of Town* anthology by CA group; originator of *Moscow Archive of New Art* anthology (1986-1990); originator of *Glossary of the terms of Moscow Conceptualist School* (1999). He participated in group exhibitions of Appartment Art (1982) and Club of Avant-garde (KLAVA) in Moscow as well as in many other exhibitions in Russia and abroad.

Monastyrski represented Russia at the 54th Venice Biennale. His solo shows include *Andrei Monastyrski*, V-A-C Foundation, Moscow Museum of Modern Art, 2011; *Earthworks*, Stella Art Gallery, Moscow, 2005, *70s and other works*, Navicula Artis, St. Petersburg, 2000; *Gosagroprom*, Obscuri viri, Moscow, 1998, *Branch*, XL Gallery, Moscow, 1996.

MUKHOMOR GROUP

(SVEN GUNDLAH, KONSTATIN ZVEZDOCHETOV, VLADIMIR AND SERGEY MIRONENKO, ALEKSEY KAMENSKY)

From 1978 to 1984 in Moscow

Mukhomor was a conceptual and performance group with a substantial presence in the Moscow underground art scene. The strategy of the group was directed at deciphering the banalities and imprints that have been established in social consciousness. For six years they created a large number of paintings and drawings, and a wide range of texts and actions. A significant number of literary and artistic works, represented by the legacy of the Mukhomor, have individual authorship. However, in accordance with the principles of the group, all the paintings, drawings, manifestos, poetries, short stories and sketches should be labeled with the "muhomor" logo.

The group broke up in 1984 after its work was officially forbidden, with three of its members being drafted into the army.

NIKLAS NITSCHKE

born in 1970 in Biel,
lives and works in Brandenburg

After first solo exhibitions in Munich and New York (2000-2001) he concentrates on collaborations, with HORTEN (B. Ruzicska, A. Hopf), Michael Hofstetter, among others. Selected exhibitions and projects: *Bizepteur* (with Michael Hofstetter), Gallery RuzicskaWeiss, Düsseldorf, 2009; *Walking in different directions*, KIT, Düsseldorf, 2008; *The Others*, Marienkirche, Frankfurt (Oder), 2007; *odds and ends*, Gallery RuzicskaWeiss, Düsseldorf, 2007; *JACK:JACK* (with Gregor Russ), Gallery Nusser&Baumgart, München, 2007; *Poussin* (with Athina Ioannou), Gallery Ruzicska Weiss, Düsseldorf, 2005; *glue*, Berlin (2004); *Silent Companion*, Berlin, 2003.

OBAMAINBERLIN

(VADIM ZAKHAROV, NIKLAS NITSCHKE)
From 2009

OBAMAINBERLIN is a collaboration between Vadim Zakharov, a Russian artist and Niklas Nitschke, a German artist and professor. Their exhibition history includes *OBAMAINBERLIN*, Neuer Berliner Kunstverein, Berlin, 2013; *OBAMAINBERLIN*, Kunstverein Rosenheim, Rosenheim, 2011.

ANATOLY OSMOLOVSKY

Born in 1969 in Moscow,
lives and works in Moscow

Anatoly Osmolovsky began his career as a writer, and was a member of the literary group "Vertep" before 1989. Between 1990-92, he was the leader of the E.T.I (Expropriation of Art Territories) movement, and participated in a series of street performances, including *E.T.I-TEXT, Silent Parade, Forefinger*, and others. In 1995, Osmolovsky founded *Radek* magazine, which sought to create a space for radical politics, and to develop paths for intellectual resistance and anarchist tactics for decision-making. In 1998 he organized the "Non Governmental Control Commission" group, and "Vote against everyone! Now" movement. Osmolovsky's move into sculpture over the last decade is manifested in a series of major works that mark his shift towards investigating the vexed legacy of both Russian icons and the early-twentieth century *avant-garde*.

Actively participated in exhibitions in Russia and abroad: 25th Biennale de San Paulo, 2002; *Utopia Station*, 50th Venice Biennale of Contemporary Art, 2003; Dokumenta XII, Kassel, 2007; *Ostalgia*, New Museum, New York 2011; *Modernikon. Contemporary Art from Russia*, 54th Venice Biennale of Contemporary Art, 2011.

Selected personal exhibitions include *The Day of Knowledge, Leopards are Burstling Into the Temple...* Regina Gallery, Moscow, 1991-1992; *Situative Action fur PDS*, Kunstlerhaus Bethanien, Berlin, 1996; *The Way Political Positions Turn into Form*, Stella Art Gallery, Moscow, 2004. Founder of educational program and editor-in-chief of eponymous art magazine *Base*.

YURI PALMIN

Born in 1966 in Moscow,
lives and works in Moscow

Yuri Palmin is an architectural photographer. Commissioned by leading Russian architects and professional media both locally and worldwide. Worked on assignments from McAdam Architects, Antonio Citterio & Partners, McAslan & Partners, Skuratov Architects, Tchobann Voss, Alexander Brodsky, Nikolay Lyzlov and others. Works appear in *AD Magazine, Vogue, World Architecture* (UK), *RIBA Journal* (UK), *Icon Magazine* (UK & US), *Domus* (Italy), *Abitare* (Italy), *Mark Magazine* (NL), *EXIT* (ES), *Project Russia* magazine and others.

Collaborated for the projects with Russian artists Alyona Kirtzova, Vladislav Efimov, Alexander Brodsky. Selected exhibitions include *Zurich + Moscow*, Moscow, Zurich, 1991; solo exhibition at The Schusev State Museum of Architecture, 2001; *Berlinwallpaper*, with Vladislav Efimov, Krasnoyarsk, 2004; *The Wooden Age*, Moscow, 2009; *EVENTO*, Bordeaux, 2009; *Architect Leonid Pavlov*, Moscow, 2010. Participated in Venice Biennale of Architecture with Alexander Brodsky (2009), Venice Biennale of Architecture (Russian pavilion), 2010.

ALEXANDRA PAPERNO

Born in 1978 in Moscow,
lives and works in Moscow

Studied art in New York at the Cooper Union for the Advancement of Science and Art, where she received her degree in fine arts in 2000. In 2004 her first solo exhibition was held at the National Centre for Contemporary Arts (NCCA), Moscow. Since then Paperno has presented many solo projects such as *Popular Astronomy* at the Moscow Museum of Modern Art in 2009 and *Walls* at The Schusev State Museum of Architecture, Moscow in 2012, and has participated in numerous exhibitions, including Prague Biennale of Contemporary Art, Moscow International Forum of Art Initiatives, Moscow Biennale of Contemporary Art.

ALEXANDER POVZNER

Born in 1976 in Moscow,
lives and works in Moscow

Povzner is working in the ready-made tradition. But he slightly distorts the ready-made nature of things with which he works, deforms the context of use of the objects and places them in the situations that evolve their potential formalism.

Studied sculpture at Surikov Moscow State Art Institute (1997-1999) and Moscow Institute of the Problems of Contemporary Art (2008). His solo exhibitions include *Brutto*, XL gallery, Moscow, 2012; *I have been here!*, Open gallery, Moscow, 2012; *Works*, Proekt Fabrika, Moscow, 2011. Among the group shows are the 4th Moscow Biennale of Contemporary Art, 2011; *contra mater*, Stroganov Art School, Moscow, 2011; *From the Realm of the Practical Knowledge*, special project for the 4th Moscow Biennale of Contemporary Art, Moscow, 2011; *Phantom monuments*, Garage Centre for Contemporary Culture, Moscow, 2011; *Interpolare*, Ve.Sch, Wien, 2010; *Genius Loci*, Moscow, 2007.

DMITRY PRIGOV

Lived and worked from 1940 to 2007 in Moscow

Dmitry Prigov was a writer, poet and one of the most eclectic artists of the Moscow Conceptual School. Trained as a sculptor at the Stroganov Art Institute in Moscow, he began writing poetry in the 1950s, then worked as a municipal architect and created sculptures for parks. In 1972, he and

Boris Orlov rented a studio, which became a meeting place for artists and poets of the underground. In 1982, together with Viktor Erofeyev and Vladimir Sorokin, they formed the EPS group, whose cultural mission was in deconstructing various forms of Soviet ideology by including taboo contexts. On the eve of Perestroika, he did a street action by posting up a series of his poems, *Forewarnings*, to the street walls. For that action he was hospitalized in a mental institution and released only after the intervention of famous cultural figures. There was never a single official exhibition of Dmitry Prigov in the USSR but many of them took place later like *D.A. Prigov, Citizens! Please mind yourself! Works on paper, Installations, books, readings, performance and opera*, 1940-2007, Moscow Museum of Modern Art, 2008 or *Dmitry Prigov: Dmitry Prigov*, Università Ca' Foscari, Collateral event of the 54th Venice Biennale, Venice.

ANASTASIA RYABOVA

Born in 1985 in Moscow,
lives and works in Moscow

Anastasia Ryabova is an artist who combines a lot of networking with individual projects: artistsprivatecollections.org, supostat.org, megazine.biz go along the curatorial and printing initiatives. Ryabova uses all of these projects to rethink institutional conventions and test the status quo.

She actively participated in projects in Russia and abroad: *In Charge of the Edition*, Visual Culture Research Center, Kiev, 2012; GALERIE ARTPOINT, KulturKontakt, Vienna, 2012; *Connected by art*, Schwerin State Museum, Germany, 2012; *Whatever that is?*, Kalmar konstmuseum, Kalmar, Sweden, 2012; *Monuments and documents*, Tretyakov State Gallery, Moscow, 2012; *Toasting the Revolution*, Family Business gallery, New York, 2012; *The False Calculations Presidium*, Museum of Business and Philanthropy, Moscow, 2011; *Media Impact. International Festival of Activist Art*, special project for 4th Moscow Biennale of Contemporary Art, Moscow, 2011; *Phantom monuments*, Garage Centre for Contemporary Culture, Moscow, 2011; *Modernikon. Contemporary Art from Russia*, Fondazione Sandretto Re Rebaudengo, Turin, 2010; *Russian lettrism*, Central House of Artists, Moscow, 2008.

In 2011 she was awarded Kandinsky Prize for *Artists' Private Collections* project, and Soratnik Prize.

SERGEY SAPOZHNIKOV

Born in 1984 in Rostov-on-Don,
lives and works in Rostov-on-Don and Moscow

Sergey Sapozhnikov is a photographer and artist based in the south of Russia, where he has worked a great deal, experimenting with filming artificial structures integrated into the half-natural, half-urban environment of the city outskirts. The chaos of his installations is a reference to the potential of liberation from the structure of organized space and codified behavior. He is persistent in his research of the potential of color in photography, and hand printing technology.

He participated in many exhibitions in Russia and abroad: *Dreams of reason*, Torun, Centre of Contemporary Art, Warsaw, 2013; *Toasting to the Revolution*, Family Business Gallery, New York, 2012; *Géneration P.*, Grand Résérvoir de l'hôpital de Bicêtre, Le Kremlin-Bicêtre, Paris, 2012; *Angry Birds*, Warsaw Museum of Modern Art, 2012; *Once upon a Present*, SC Gallery, Zagreb, 2012; *ON/OFF*, special project for the 4th Moscow Biennale of Contemporary Art, 2011; *Modernikon. Contemporary Art from Russia*, Fondazione Sandretto Re Rebaudengo, Turin, 2010; *Sense and Sensibility*, ARTPLAY, Moscow; *History of Russian VideoArt*, Volume 3, MAMMA, Moscow, 2010; *Workers and Philosophers*, Moscow School of Management Skolkovo, 2010; *Art After the End of History*, Central House of Artist, Moscow, 2009.

VLADISLAV SHAPOVALOV

Born in 1981, in Rostov-on-Don,
lives and works in Moscow

Vladislav Shapovalov, an artist, has been a member of Radek Community (1999-2008), a participant in the School of Contemporary Art of Avdei Ter-Oganyan (1997-1998) as well as of the first edition of seminars by Anatoly Osmolovsky. As a member of Radek Community he participated in many of its projects, exhibitions and actions e.g. *Theoretical airborne operation* (Art-Klyazma Festival, Moscow, 2002) and *Hunger strike without any demands* (Zverev Center for Contemporary Art, Moscow, 2003). He was a publisher and editor of weekly DIY bulletin *HandRadek* (1999), contributor of *Radek* magazine. Shapovalov participated as an artist, organizer and supporter in exhibitions and activities which took place in artists-run space France gallery (Moscow, 2001-2006) and in the exhibition *The False Calculations Presidium* (2012).

STANISLAV SHURIPA

Born in 1971 in Yuzhno-Sakhalinsk,
lives and works in Moscow

He is an artist, writer and curator. His artistic practice includes installation, painting, photography and sculpture. Through various media Shuripa addresses relationships between the experience of social space and systems of its description such as representations of knowledge, computer simulations, languages of abstract art, corporate design and architecture.

Among group shows are *Decorating The Beautiful*, Tretyakov State Gallery, Moscow, 2012; *People and The City*, CCA Winzavod, Moscow, 2011; *Modernikon. Contemporary Art from Russia*, Fondazione Sandretto Re Rebaudengo, Turin, 2010; *Lessons of History*, Palais de Tokyo, Paris, 2010; *Gradual Change!*, Nordin Gallery, Stockholm, 2010, *Emergenze Creative* 2009, Museum of Modern Art, Ravenna, 2009; *Two Formulas for an Imperial Monument*, Museum of Art, Gothenburg, 2009.

Recent curated shows are *Rituals of Resistance*, Proekt Fabrika, Moscow, 2013; *Seems Something is Missing Here*, CCA Winzavod, Moscow, 2012; *Counterillusions*, House of Culture of the Factory ZIL, Moscow, 2012. Shuripa lectures at Moscow Institute of the Problems of Contemporary Art since 2007, he writes for *Dialog Iskusstv* magazine (Moscow), *Base* magazine (Moscow) and *Moscow Art Magazine* (Moscow) in which he is also a member of Editorial board.

XENIA SOROKINA

Born in 1986 in Astrakhan,
lives and works in Moscow

Studied painting in Art College, theater directing and stage design in Moscow Art Theatre School and The Russian University of Theatre Arts (GITIS), as well as at the Institute of Contemporary Art, Moscow in 2011. In her artistic practices Sorokina combines different media as video, drawings and performance to research the connection between her personal story and modernity as aftermath of historical and cultural. She is an active participant of group projects, among which are *Something was missing there*, Winzavod art centre, Moscow, 2012; *Sanatorium of Arts*, Tretyakov State Gallery, Moscow; *Intimate Capital*, collateral program of 2nd Moscow International Biennale for Young Art, 2010; *New Formalism*, Museum of Urban Sculpture, St. Petersburg, 2010; *Unbearable Freedom of Creativity*, VDNKh, Moscow; *Cloud Harp*, LABORATORIA Art&Science Space, Moscow, 2009; Apartment exhibitions *Art to home, Freedom, Equality and Brotherhood* and others.

MAXIM SPIVAKOV
Born in 1984 in Moscow,
lives and works in Moscow

Maxim Spivakov is an artist and a designer who graduated from the Moscow State University of Printing Arts (2008). As an artist he participated in several exhibitions including *The False Calculations Presidium*, Moscow, 2012; the 3rd Moscow International Biennale for Young Art, 2012; *In charge of the Edition*, Kiev, 2012 and the upcoming Bergen Assembly *Monday Begins on Saturday*, 2013. As a designer he conceived a temporary pavilion for the Garage Centre for Contemporary Culture, Moscow, 2012.

ALEXANDRA SUKHAREVA
Born in 1983 in Moscow,
lives and works in Moscow

She has been studying in Moscow and Gothenburg. Among her recent projects are *From the Realm of the Practical Knowledge*, a special project for the 4th Moscow Biennale of Contemporary Art, Moscow, 2011 and solo exhibition *Eurauraga*, Proekt Fabrika, Moscow, 2011; in 2012 she took a part in dOCUMENTA (13), Kassel. In 2010 she moved from Moscow to the region of Dubna – small town for a nuclear research, where in her local studio produced most of the recent works. Such as based on toxic substances *Doxa* (2012) created for windows of the House of Culture of the Factory ZIL (Moscow) before its reconstruction in 2012, and *The core of the day* (2012) for the exhibition *Things, Words and Consequences*, Moscow Museum of Modern Art, 2012. One of the main interests of her work lies between a history of perception, resources of poetry understood at large and capacity of indescribable to stay indifferent to descriptions.

SUPOSTAT
From 2011 in Moscow

Is a platform for collaboration of artists, architects, sociologists and professionals from other fields. It conceptualises the conditions of its own existence and it creates temporary working groups dedicated to the artistic explorations of problematics relevant for the current cultural situation as a whole and to its particular manifestations. Since 2011 it initiated the research exhibition *Production of spectator*, One Work gallery, Samara, 2001 accompanied by a series of conversations published on the website supostat.org concerning the topic of public and spectatorship in contemporary culture, opening an online complain forum for submission of unbiased critical responses that might otherwise never be voiced about 4th Moscow Biennale of Contemporary Art. In 2011 published a newspaper called *Common Ground* concerning problems of common, social and public, supported the online art-career simulator *Talent Calculator*.

SZ GROUP
(VICTOR SKERSIS, VADIM ZAKHAROV)
From 1980 to 1984 in Moscow

The group was founded in 1980, the artists elaborated the ideas of Moscow conceptualism and investigated the topics related to the very nature of the functioning of art and culture. There are two periods of SZ activity: 1980-1984 and through out 1990. In 1980s they developed the themes of functioning, simulations in culture, phantoms, symbiosis and collaboration.
SZ practices included performances, painting, graphics, texts and "amateurish music." In 1982 there was the first personal exhibition of the group at the APTART gallery. In 1990 they reunified for one project that was based on 'The Brothers Karamazov' by Fedor Dostoevski.

DAVID TER-OGANYAN
Born 1981 in Rostov-on-Don,
lives and works in Moscow

David Ter-Oganyan was a key member of the radical Radek Community (1998-2008). In his computer drawings and paintings, he fuses sub-cultural gestures and avant-garde references in a post-activist art of narrative minitiatures. Ter-Oganyan has had solo exhibitions *Shadows*, XL Gallery,

Moscow, 2004 and *Black Geometry*, Guelman Gallery, Moscow, 2009.
He has taken part in various group shows in Russia and abroad; *Angry Birds*, Warsaw Museum of Modern Art, 2012; *Ostalgia*, New Museum, New York, 2011; *Drawing Spaces*, Impronte Contemporary Art, Milan, 2010; *Get Connected*, Künstlerhaus Wien, Vienna, 2009; *Progressive Nostalgia*, Centro per l'Arte Contemporanea Luigi Pecci, Prato, 2007. Ter-Oganyan has participated in the 10th International Istanbul Biennial, 2007 and in the 1st Moscow Biennale of Contemporary Art, 2005. In 2011 he was awarded the Henkel Art Award.

TZUCHIEN THO
Born in 1980 in Kota Kinabalu,
lives and works in Paris

Tzuchien Tho is an Associated Researcher at the Centre Internationale d'Etude de la Philosophie Contemporaine in Paris where he runs a seminar on the intersections of the formal sciences (mathematics and logic) and 20th century French philosophy and of the Berlin-Brandenburgische Akademie der Wissenschaften where he works on a project on the mathematical roots of Leibniz's dynamics.
In January 2011, he defended a thesis in philosophy under the direction of O. Bradley Bassler (University of Georgia): *Leibniz's Laboratory of concepts: the status and structure of infinitesimals as metaphysical laboratory*. In 2009 he has been researcher in resident at the Jan Van Eyck Academy in Maastricht where he has animated with Pietro Bianchi and Giuseppe Bianco a monthly seminar on the concept of materialism and reflexivity. He recently edited and translated together with Giuseppe Bianco Badiou and the Philosophers: *Interrogating 1960s French Philosophy* published by Bloomsbury Academic in 2013.

URBAN FAUNA LAB
(ALEXEY BULDAKOV, ANASTASIA POTEMKINA, EKATERINA ZAVIALOVA)
From 2011 in Moscow

UFL is a platform for the study of parasitic and symbiotic relationships and associated mutual adaptation in urban environments at the intersection of architecture, biology, philosophy, contemporary art. These types of relationship can be attributed to the expansion of the parasitic species on gentrified areas, or localization of wild life in the city parks.

The laboratory was founded in 2011 by the artists Alexey Buldakov, Anastasia Potemkina and Dmitry Potemkin. Architects Ekaterina Zavialova and Dmitry Orlov were also involved in the research and installation of UFL projects at different stages. They were shown at *Urban Fauna Zoo*, Art Squat Forum, special project for the 4th Moscow Biennale of Contemporary Art, 2011; *The False Calculations Presidium*, Moscow, 2012.

The group is elaborating now *The Park of Urban Fauna* as a long term research project, an area of the urban environment, specifically adjusted to be inhabited by urban animals and providing conditions for their observation and scientific research. It will operate as the scientific, architectural and artistic research site.

DMITRY VOROBYEV

Born in 1974 in Leningrad

Based is a sociologist based in St. Petersburg and Pskov. Graduated from St. Petersburg State University (1997) and European University at St. Petersburg (2005). Since 1998 he has been working at the Center for Independent Social Research (CISR), St. Petersburg. Vorobyev has taken part in over ten art projects and his primary interests include political sociology and urban studies, he made research for the Institute of Environmental Architecture and Planning of Technical University of Berlin in 2003-2004. He is an author of several publications.

VADIM ZAKHAROV

Born in 1959 in Dushanbe,
lives and works in Berlin

Is an artist, a critic, an archivist of Moscow art, a curator, a publisher, based in Moscow and Berlin. He was awarded the Innovation Prize, (2006) and the Kandinsky Prize (2009). Zakharov will represent Russia at the Venice Biennale in 2013. Project and realisation of the Theodor W. Adorno Monument, Theodor W. Adorno Platz, Frankfurt am Main (2003). His solo exhibitions include *Ideological Defile*, National Centre of Contemporary Art (NCCA), Nizhny Novgorod, 2013; *No distance*, GMG Gallery, Moscow, 2008-2009; *Vadim Zakharov. 25 years on one page*, Tretyakov State Gallery, Moscow, 2006; *Mouse hunting* (with Andrei Monastyrski), Stella Art Gallery, Moscow, 2004; *Last Point of the Editor Pastor Zond*, Gallery Hohenthal&Bergen, Berlin, 1998; *The last stroll through the elysian fields*, Kölnischer Kunstverein, 1995.

ARSENIY ZHILYAEV

Born 1984 in Voronezh,
lives and works in Moscow

Arseniy Zhilyaev is an artist, writer and political activist. Zhilyaev's artistic practice poses questions about the political and social legitimisation of art. He studied at the Institute of Contemporary Art in Moscow, 2006-2007, before completing an MA at Valand School of Fine Arts, Gothenburg in 2010. He was the winner of the Soratnik award in 2010 and was nominated for the Innovation Prize, 2009.

His recent exhibitions include *Museum of Proletarian Culture*, Tretyakov State Gallery, Moscow, 2012, *Pedagogical Poem* (together with Ilya Budraytskis), Presnya Historical Museum, Moscow, 2012; *Radio October*, Proekt Fabrika, Moscow, 2010; *Rational egoism*, Regina Gallery, Moscow, 2010 and the following group exhibitions: *Modernikon. Contemporary Art from Russia*, Fondazione Sandretto Re Rebaudengo, Turin, 2010; *History Lesson*, Palais de Tokyo, Paris, 2010, *Russian Utopias*, Garage Art Centre, Moscow, 2010; and *Open Doors Day*, Moscow Museum of Modern Art, Moscow, 2010.

CONTRIBUTORS

ILYA BUDRAYTSKIS

Born in 1981 in Moscow,
lives and works in Moscow

Historian, political activist, based in Moscow. He is a post-graduate student in the Institute for the World History, Russian Academy of Science.

Ilya Budraytskis has collaborated with the artists David Ter-Oganyan and Alexandra Galkina in art projects since 2005. As a member of the "Learning film group" he participated in the 4th Moscow Biennale of Contemporary Art, 2011 and numerous international exhibitions. In 2012 he co-curated *Pedagogical Poem*, an interdisciplinary educational and artistic project at Presnya Historical Museum, Moscow.

From 1997 he is intensively engaged in the political activism: in 2001-2004 as an organizer of the Russian contingents on mobilizations against G8, European and World Social Forums; from 2011 he has been an activist and spokesperson for Russian Socialist Movement (RSD); in 2003-2006 worked for the Institute for Globalization Studies.

Co-editor of the book *Post-Post-Soviet? Art, Politics and Society in Russia at the Turn of the Decade* (Chicago University press, 2013); member of the editorial board of *Moscow Art Magazine*, regular contributor to the number of political and cultural newspapers and magazines.

VIKTOR MISIANO

Born in 1958 in Moscow,
lives and works in Moscow
and in Ceglie Messapica

Viktor Misiano was a curator of contemporary art at the Pushkin National Museum of Fine Arts, Moscow (1980-90) and the director of the Center for Contemporary Art (CAC), Moscow (1992-97). In his freelance practice Misiano was on the curatorial team for *Manifesta 1*, Rotterdam (1996) and curated the Russian section of the 3rd Istanbul Biennial (1992), the 46th and 50th Venice Biennale (1995, 2003), the 1st Valencia Bienal, Spain (2001), the 25th and 26th São Paulo Bienal (2002, 2004), the Central Asia Pavilion at the 51st Venice Biennale (2005), and *Progressive Nostalgia: Art from the Former USSR*, Centro per l'arte contemporanea, Prato (Italy); the Benaki Museum, Athens; KUMU, Tallinn, and KIASMA, Helsinki. His latest exhibition project is *Impossible Community* realized 2011 in Moscow Museum for Modern Art and awarded with National "Innovation" prize as the "Best exhibition of the year." In 1993 he was a founder of the *Moscow Art Magazine* and has been its editor-inchief ever since and in 2003 he was a founder of the *Manifesta Journal: Journal of Contemporary Curatorship* (Amsterdam-Ljubljana) and since then has also been an editor there. From October 2010 he is a Chairman of the International Foundation Manifesta. He has been awarded an honorary doctorate from the Helsinki University for Art and Design.

DAVID RIFF

Born in 1975 in London,
lives and works in Moscow and Berlin

David Riff is a writer, translator, artist, and curator based in Moscow and Berlin. He has written widely on the history and present of contemporary art in Russia as an art critic, and also has translated broadly, his most recent project a forcoming volume of the Soviet aesthetic philosopher Mikhail Lifshitz. He is a member of the workgroup Chto delat/What is to be done? and has also been involved in other artistic collaborations such as the Learning Film group or the Karl Marx School of the English Language. Recent curatorial contributions have included the international exhibition *The Potosi Principle* (as curatorial correspondent), the Ural Industrial Biennial (with Cosmin Costinas and Ekaterina Degot), and Auditorium Moscow, a discussion platform and exhibition (with Ekaterina Degot and Joanna Mytkowska). He is currently co-curating *Monday Begins on Saturday*, the first edition of Bergen Assembly, a new triennial of contemporary art in Norway. Riff teaches at the Rodchenko Moscow School of Photography and Multimedia.

C U R A T O R S

KATERINA CHUCHALINA

Born in 1978 in Astrakhan,
lives and works in Moscow

Katerina Chuchalina is a contemporary art curator, currently works as a curator and program director at V-A-C Foundation, a non-profit institution committed to the production of contemporary Russian art. She is a contributing curator to *Andrei Monastyrski* exhibition (Moscow Museum of Modern Art, 2010) and numerous exhibition of Russian artists in Moscow and London. She wrote for several exhibition catalogues including *The world belongs to you* show, Palazzo Grassi, Venice, 2011. Her previous experiences include curatorial assistance at *Modernikon. Contemporary Art from Russia*, Fondazione Sandretto Re Rebaudengo, Turin, 2010; *Ostalgia*, New Museum, New York, 2011, collaborations with the Moscow-based Laboratoria Art&Science Space, and the London-based White Space Gallery. She studied Linguistics at the Astrakhan University, Cultural Studies in Moscow, History of Arts and Project Management in City University in London.

SILVIA FRANCESCHINI

Born in 1985 in Milano,
lives and works in Milano

Silvia Franceschini is a researcher of contemporary art and design based between Milan and Moscow, where she works as an independent curator and writer. She is a member of the curatorial board of Viafarini DOCVA / Documentation Center for Visual Art (Milan) where co-curates ANOMALI, an articulate research and exhibition program focused on the present of Italy. She is currently conducting together with Valerio Borgonuovo and in collaboration with the Centre Pompidou a research project on GLOBAL TOOLS, a counter-school of architecture, art and design founded in Italy and held from 1973 to 1975. Her previous experiences include curatorial assistance for the Venice Biennale of Architecture 2010; Centre Pompidou - Design Department (2008) and Musée Galliera - Photography Department (2007) in Paris. She is a contributor for different art and design magazines as *Afterall*, *Domus*, *Abitare*. She studied at the Design Faculty of the Politecnico di Milano and at the Strelka - Institute for Media, Architecture and Design in Moscow where she conducted a research about the institutionalisation of the contemporary art system in Russia after 1989.

DARIA PARAMONOVA

Born in 1980 in Moscow,
lives and works in Moscow

Daria Paramonova is an architect, a researcher and a teacher. She lives in Moscow and followed by her graduation from Moscow Architectural Institute (MARKHI) on 2005, Daria started to work as an architect with Alexander Brodsky, who is famous as an architect as well as contemporary artist. She also had taught as a teaching assistant at the Department of Civic Architecture in MARKHI. In the academic year of 2010/2011, she was a student of Institute of Media, Architecture and Design Strelka, where she researched the issue of ageing of Moscow's architecture of the Luzhkov era. She is now writing a book based on the research project. Today Daria works simultaneously at two places: as a Director and architect of Bureau Alexander Brodsky and as a supervisor of one research studio at the Strelka Institute.

KUBA SNOPEK

Born in 1985 in Wroclav,
lives and works in Moscow

Works for Strelka Institute of Media, Architecture and Design (Moscow), from which he graduated in 2011. He is involved in urban planning projects in Russia, he is also teaching – at Strelka Institute and MGIMO University, Moscow. Before he came to Strelka, Snopek worked in architectural offices in Poland, Spain and Denmark. Working for Bjarke Ingels group (2009-2010), he participated in two theoretical urban planning projects for the 2010 Venice Biennale.

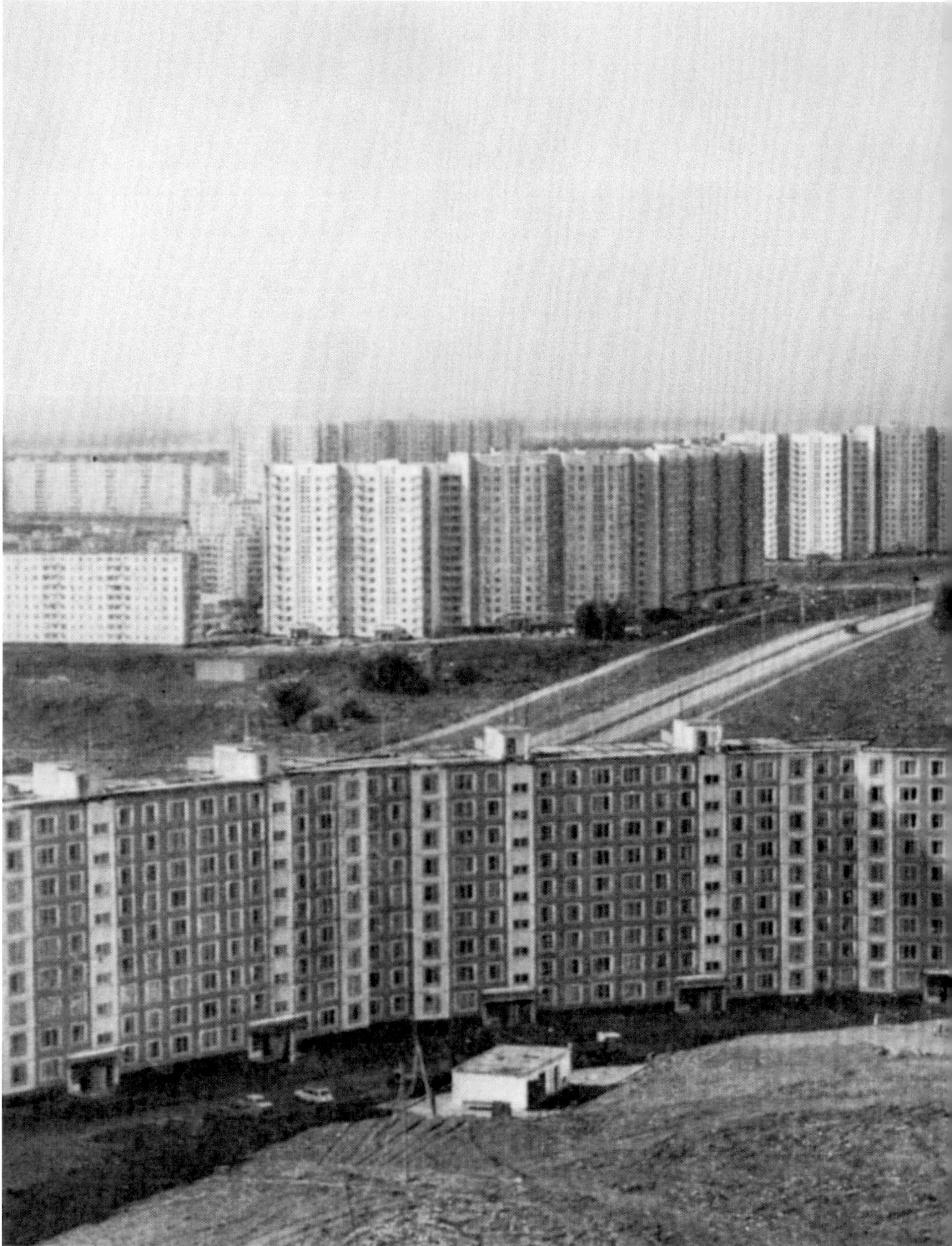

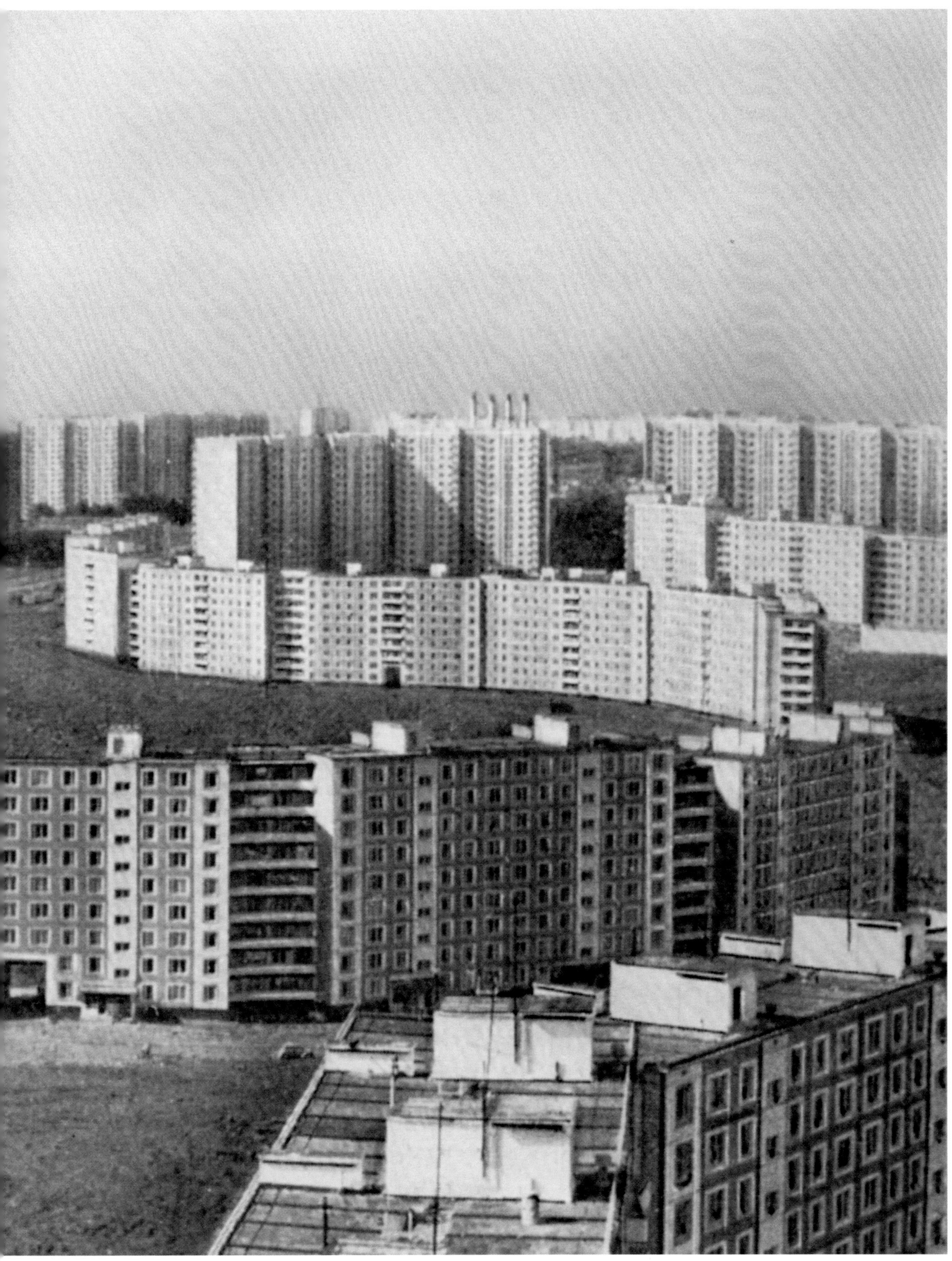

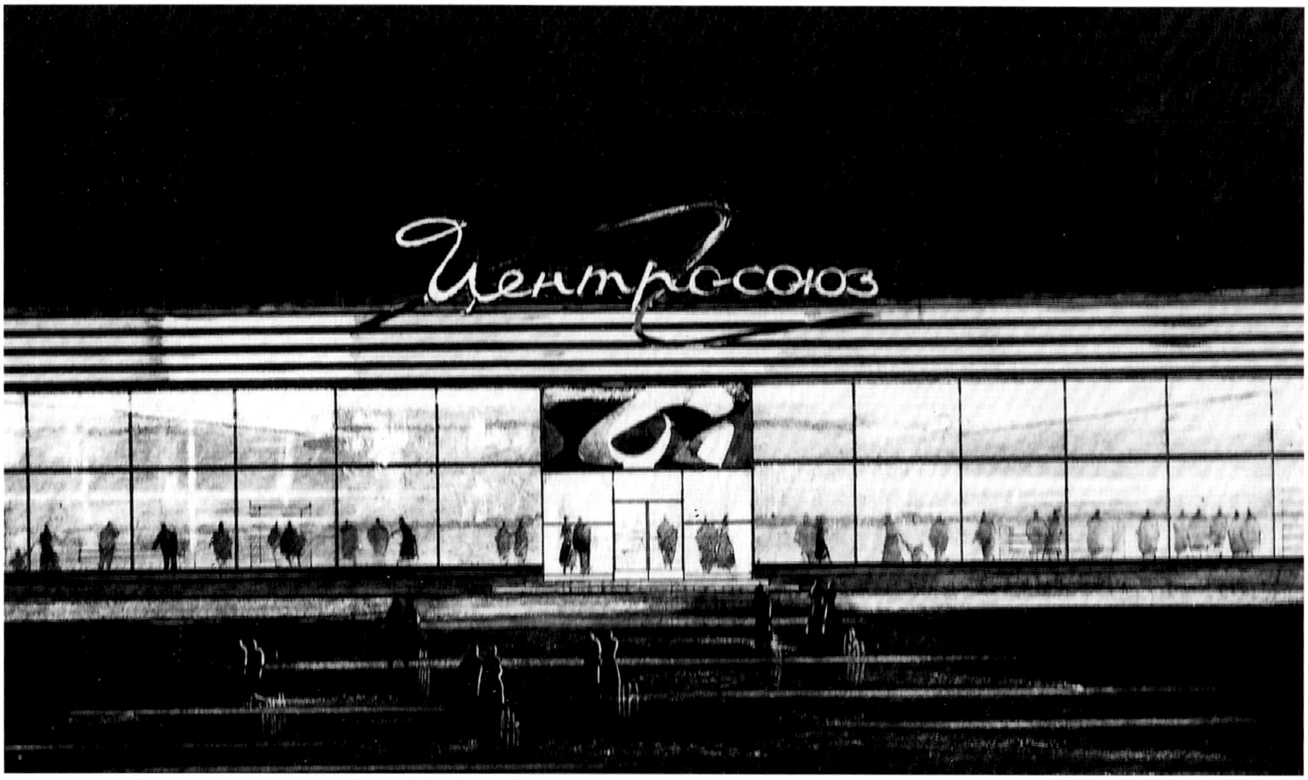

Киев ЗНИИЭП

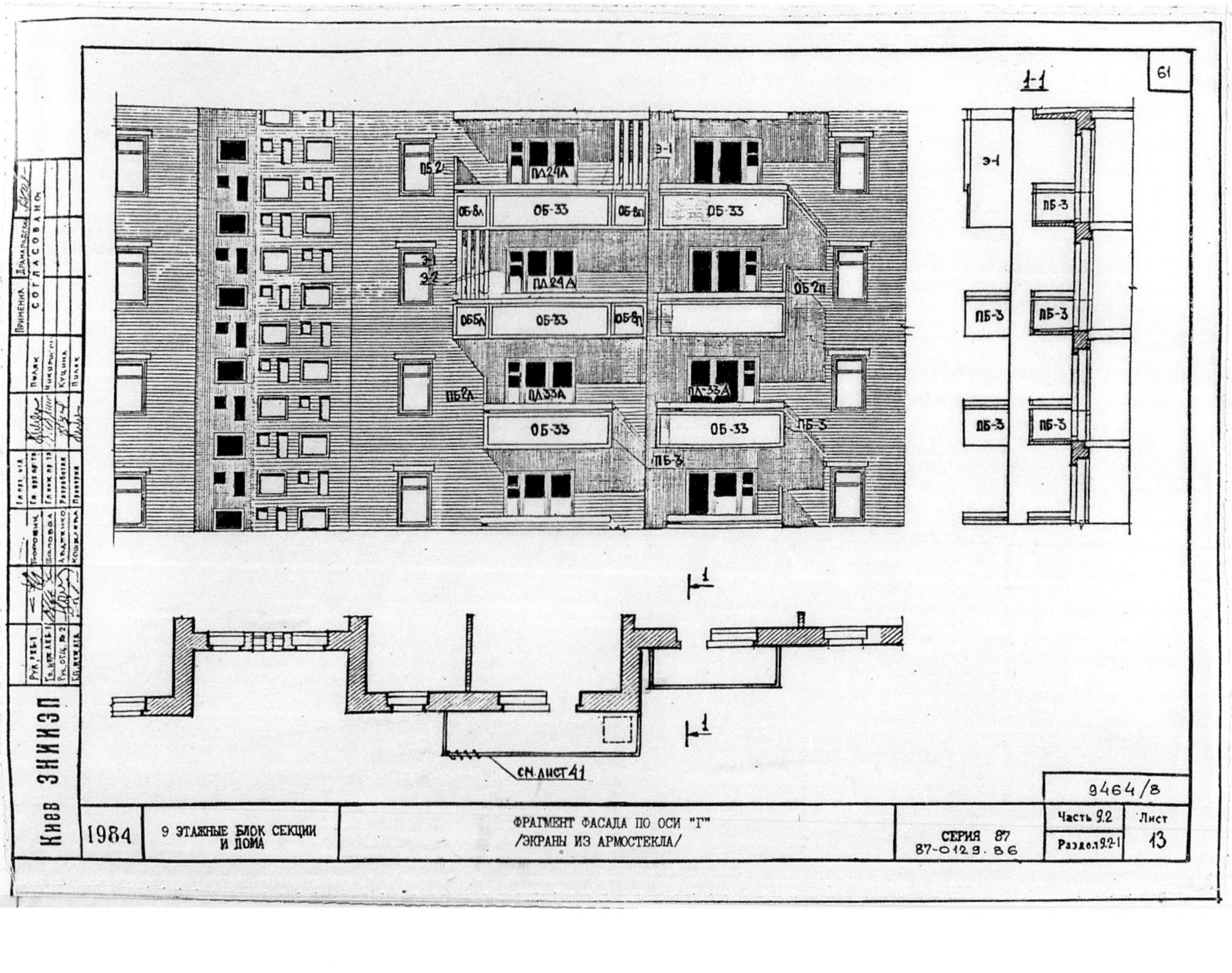

1984

9 ЭТАЖНЫЕ БЛОК СЕКЦИИ И ДОМА

ФРАГМЕНТ ФАСАДА ПО ОСИ "Г" /ЭКРАНЫ ИЗ АРМОСТЕКЛА/

СЕРИЯ 87
87-012 9. 86

9464/8

Часть 9.2

Раздел 9.2-1

Лист 13

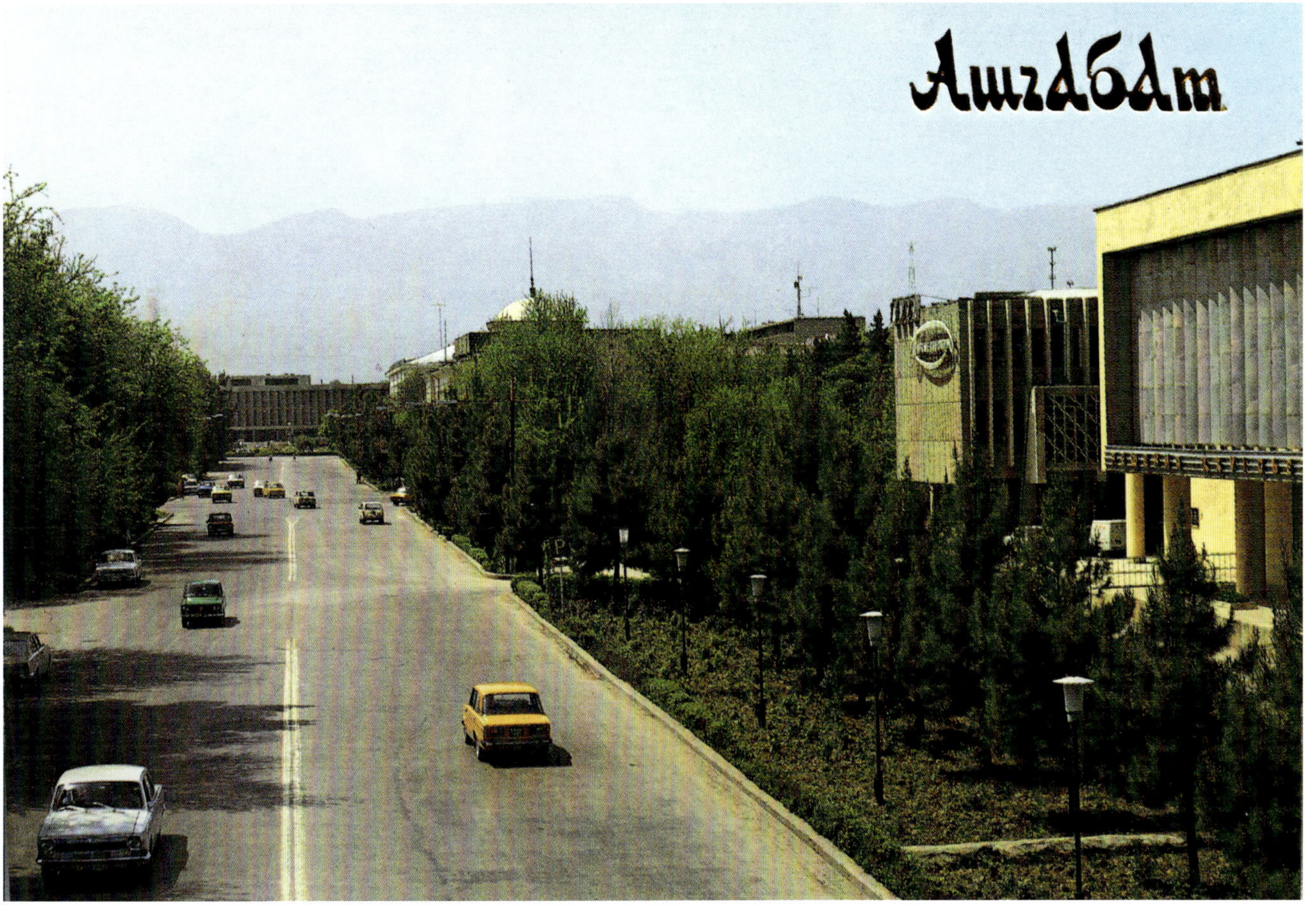

Ашгабат

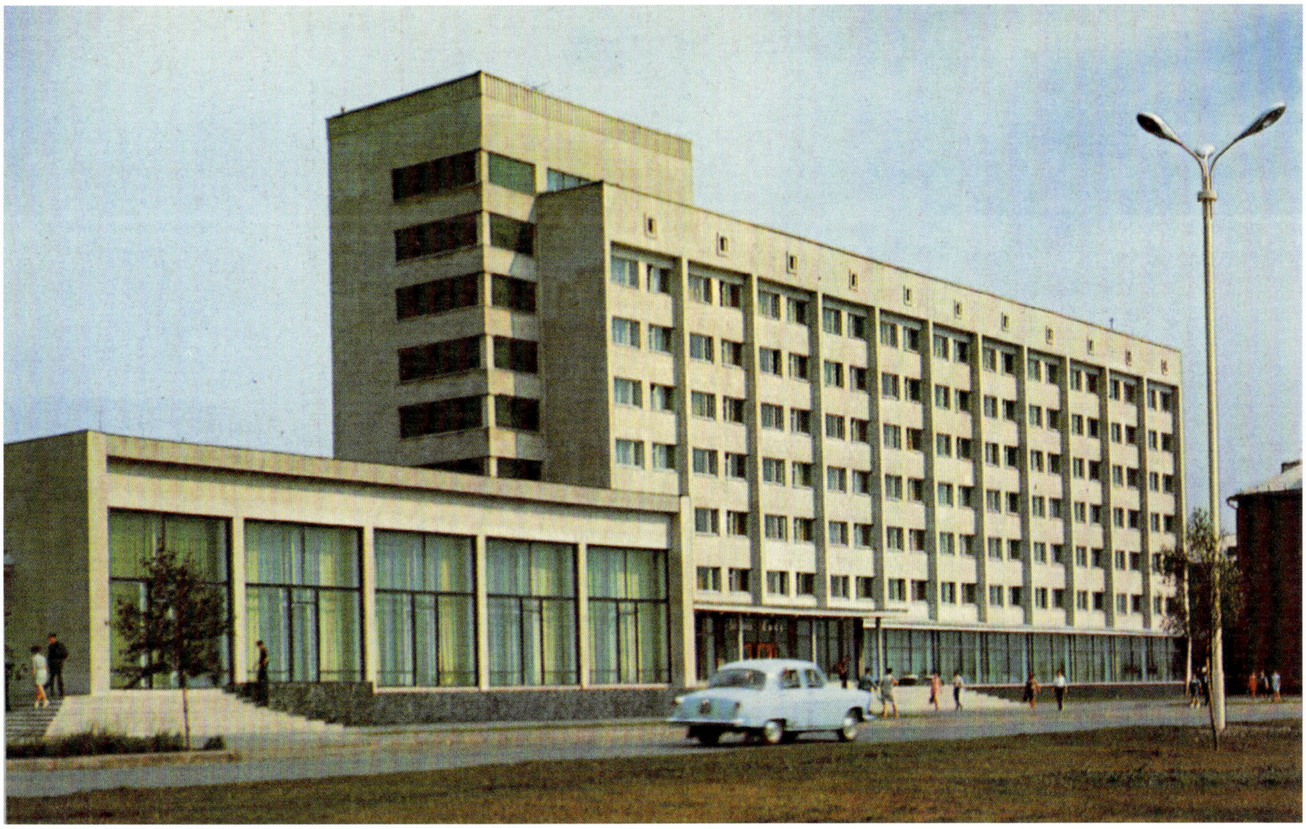

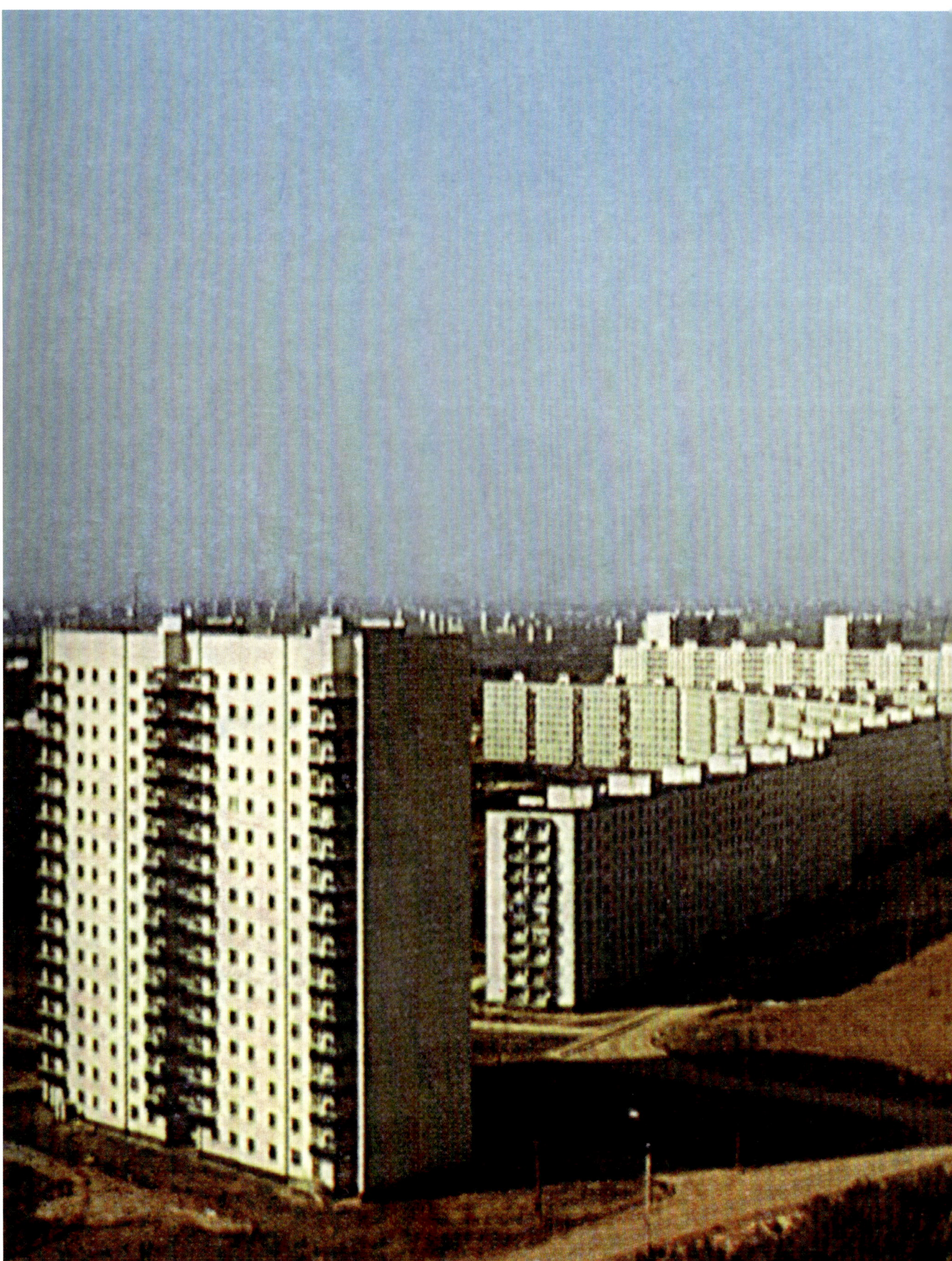

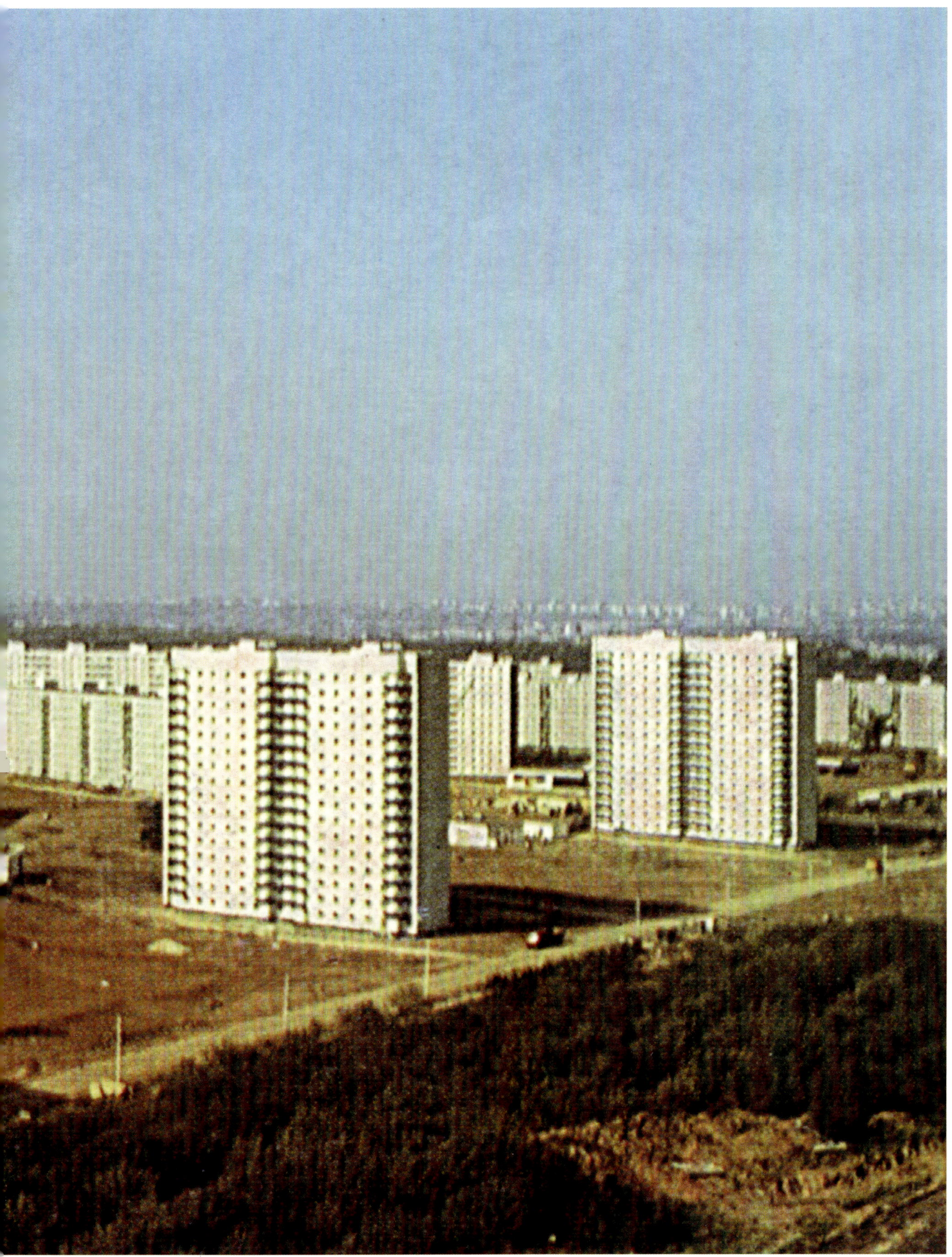

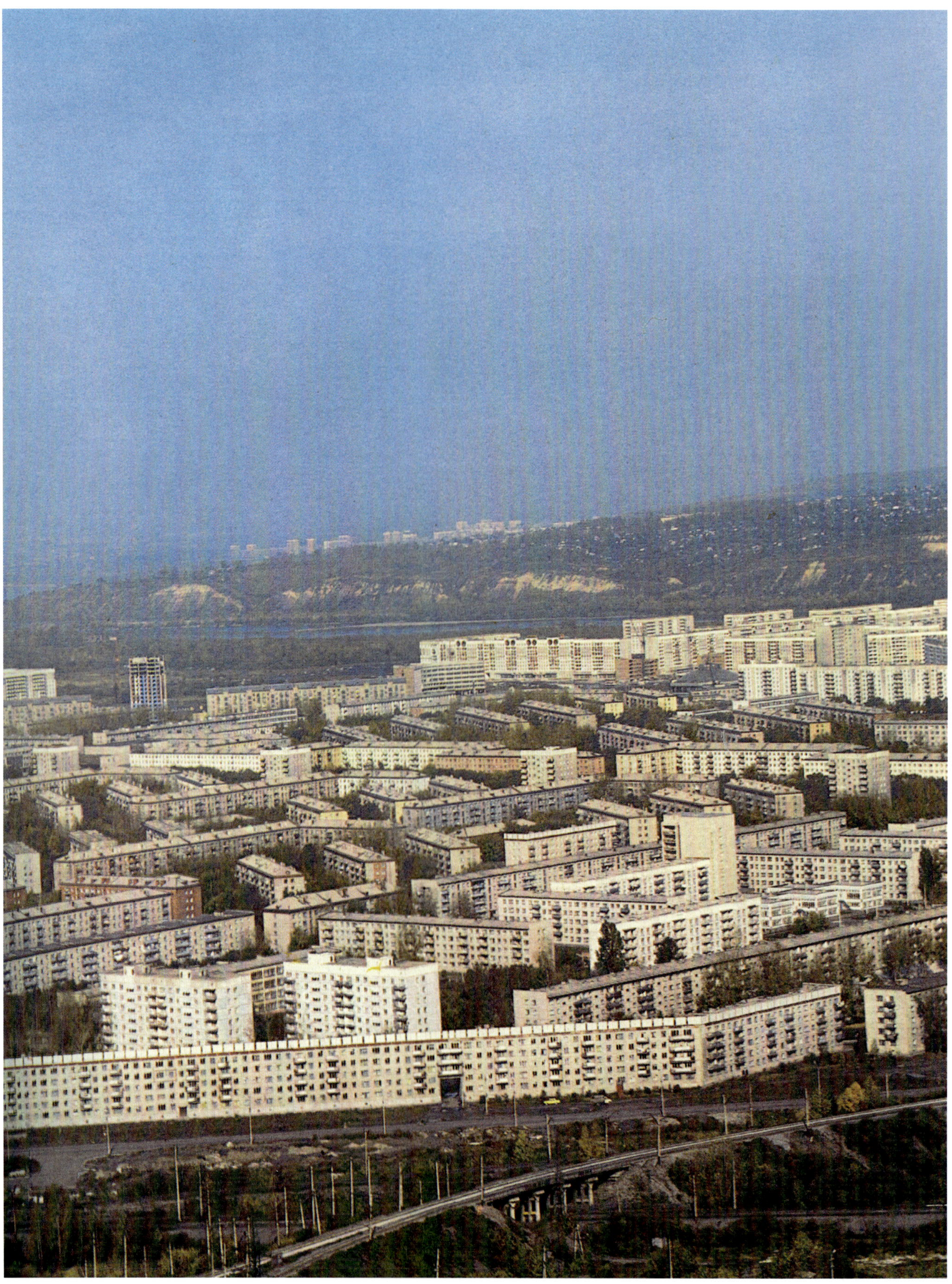